FIGHTING IRISH
Legends, Lists and Lore

Karen Croake Heisler

www.SportsPublishingLLC.com

Unless otherwise noted, all photos were provided by Notre Dame Sports Information and the Notre Dame Archives.

Sports Publishing L.L.C. has made every reasonable effort to identify and contact any photographer whose photo appears in this book. If any oversights were made, please contact Sports Publishing L.L.C. and corrections will be made in future editions.

Publishers: Peter L. Bannon and Joseph J. Bannon Sr.
Senior managing editor: Susan M. Moyer
Acquisitions editor: Mike Pearson
Developmental editor: Travis W. Moran
Editorial assistant: Aaron E. Geiger
Art director: K. Jeffrey Higgerson
Dust jacket design: Joseph T. Brumleve
Interior layout: Joseph T. Brumleve and Kenneth O'Brien
Photo editor: Erin Linden-Levy

Sports Publishing L.L.C.
804 North Neil Street
Champaign, IL 61820
Phone: 1-877-424-2665
Fax: 217-363-2073
SportsPublishingLLC.com

Printed in Canada

Library of Congress Cataloging-in-Publication Data

Heisler, Karen Croake.
Fighting Irish : legends, list, and lore / Karen Croake Heisler.
    p. cm.
    ISBN-13: 978-1-58261-752-7 (hard cover : alk. paper)
    ISBN-10: 1-58261-752-X (hard cover : alk. paper)
 1. Notre Dame Fighting Irish (Football team)--History. 2. University of Notre Dame--Football--History.   I. Title.
GV958.N6H45 2006
796.332'630977289--dc22
                                            2006023874

Contents

Acknowledgments

Writing a book is an arduous task—whatever the subject. No author can truly complete the task on his or her own. And properly thanking those who offer guidance, support, suggestions, and help is an even tougher assignment. Where do you begin?

My heartfelt thanks go, first and foremost, to the sports information staff at the University of Notre Dame. Having been lucky enough to work in three of the most respected sports information offices in the country and for a trio of the "pillars of the profession," I know how hard those folks work to make life easier for writers, commentators, analysts, columnists, coaches, administrators, and the general public. They worked 24-7 long before it became a cliché, and in today's world of instant media, their jobs have gotten even more demanding. Yet, they handle each request with patience and respect. John Heisler, Bernie Cafarelli, Tim Connor, Pete LaFleur, Chris Masters, Bo Rottenborn, Alan Wasielewski, Sean Carroll, Susan McGonigal, and Carol Copley made my job easier because they do theirs so well.

I owe a debt of gratitude to sports information student assistant Michael Scholl for his invaluable help and dedication in scouring the files for pictures.

At Sports Publishing, Travis Moran deserves a gold medal and Mike Pearson a blue ribbon for convincing me that I could do this.

Sports rule our house and have for a very long time. Although I grew up in a day when my high school did not have a girls' basketball team (my kids still don't believe me), sports provided a bond between my father and me and gave me the courage to pursue a career a bit out of the ordinary. Working in sports for a brief time provided me lifelong friendships with some of the most wonderful, witty, loyal, and caring people you could ever meet. And now, as the parent of two sons, sports have allowed me to share their dreams, their hopes, their accomplishments, and their failures. Sports have brought us together and helped teach some of life's most important lessons—dedication, teamwork, integrity, fair play, and compassion.

This book is meant to stir those memories in all of us—of people and events that taught us something about life and helped us celebrate a common bond, whether we won or lost.

Foreword

When I was a kid growing up in Bloomfield, New Jersey, I knew all about Notre Dame. My father, Frank, was the starting quarterback on Frank Leahy's unbeaten team in 1948 (a 14-14 tie in the last game of the season at USC kept the Irish from their third straight national title), and he was a member of Notre Dame's national championship teams in '46 and '47. My five brothers and a sister who attended Saint Mary's, could sing the fight song on cue. We had heard all the stories about Leahy, and my dad's teammates—George Connor, Johnny Lujack, Bill Fischer, Ziggy Czarobski, Leon Hart, Terry Brennan—so many of them legends in Notre Dame's storied football past.

Although I was a huge Irish football fan, basketball was my favorite sport, and Austin Carr was one of my boyhood heroes. When I had the opportunity to come to Notre Dame on a basketball scholarship and carve out my own place in Irish history, I took it. I didn't know who was prouder—my father, "Uncle Bert" (aka Angelo Bertelli)—the 1943 Heisman Trophy winner and my father's best friend—or me.

My four years at Notre Dame were incredibly successful, both on and off the court. I still take great pride in the fact that our 1978 team made it to the Final Four, but I can't help but admit some disappointment that we, the Irish, have yet to return. There's a tremendous basketball history at Notre Dame, and the program sometimes is overlooked simply because it has yet to win a national title. When I played at Notre Dame, we beat four No. 1 teams, and were ranked in the top 10 for 58 of the 64 regular-season weeks from 1977-81. Our class, which included Tracy Jackson, Gilbert Salinas, Orlando Woolridge, and Stan Wilcox, won 92 games and lost just 26. If we had won an NCAA championship, we'd be talked about in the same breath as the great teams of Duke and North Carolina.

My time at Notre Dame was well spent, and I have great memories of the place as well as the people who helped shaped my professional and personal life. I made lifelong friends there—too many to mention—and will be forever grateful for having had the privilege and honor to represent the University as a student-athlete. When I came back two years ago as part of the All-Century basketball team, I was overwhelmed by the reception I received. It was a thrill to share the spirit of Notre Dame with my family, just as my dad had done with my brothers and me.

Football and basketball obviously draw the most attention at Notre Dame, but the student-athletes in all the other sports work just as hard and play such a big part in making the campus a special place. During my four years at the University, I attended many other sporting events on campus. (I even threw the javelin for the track team one meet.) This book honors all the student-athletes who wore a Notre Dame uniform since intercollegiate athletics became such an integral part of life there. It will bring back memories for Irish fans of every sport, while allowing us to remember how special it is to be a part of Notre Dame's history.

— **Kelly Tripucka, Class of 1981**

Introduction

Sports have played an integral part of student life at the University of Notre Dame since its earliest days as a frontier school in northwest Indiana. The first leaders recognized the value of student participation in athletics as a way to build character, stay physically fit, and engage in social activities.

In its early years as an all-male Catholic institution, Notre Dame enrolled students from first grade through college. Nearly all of the students participated in a variety of recreational sports. During the bitter and snowy winters, students skated across the frozen lakes of St. Mary's and St. Joseph's. They swam in those same lakes during the hot and humid summer days. Whenever weather cooperated, students bicycled across the small campus. Faculty members taught students the European team sports of cricket and soccer. In addition, the increased popularity of baseball throughout the United States had led to daily pick-up games on the Notre Dame campus. Despite the variety of activities offered, Notre Dame's intercollegiate athletic program, one of the most illustrious in the United States, debuted in lackluster fashion on a damp and chilly Wednesday afternoon in November 1887.

On this particular afternoon, several players from the University of Michigan football team traveled by train to South Bend to "teach" their Notre Dame counterparts how to play the game. After a two-hour tour of campus, the players changed into their uniforms. A group of cassock-clad priests watched from the sidelines as the teams played one "inning" of football. Michigan claimed an 8-0 victory, but its grateful host treated the team to lunch before sending the students back to Ann Arbor. Even though there hadn't been any pep rallies, television cameras, hordes of sportswriters, or ticket scalpers on that cold and wet fall day, the University of Notre Dame, whose faculty and administrators had long recognized the value of sports and competition, took its first step toward athletic notoriety.

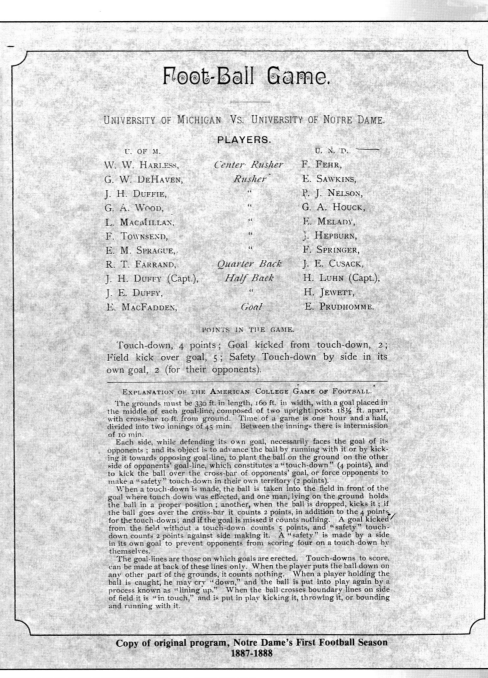

NOTRE DAME'S FIRST FOOTBALL PROGRAM.

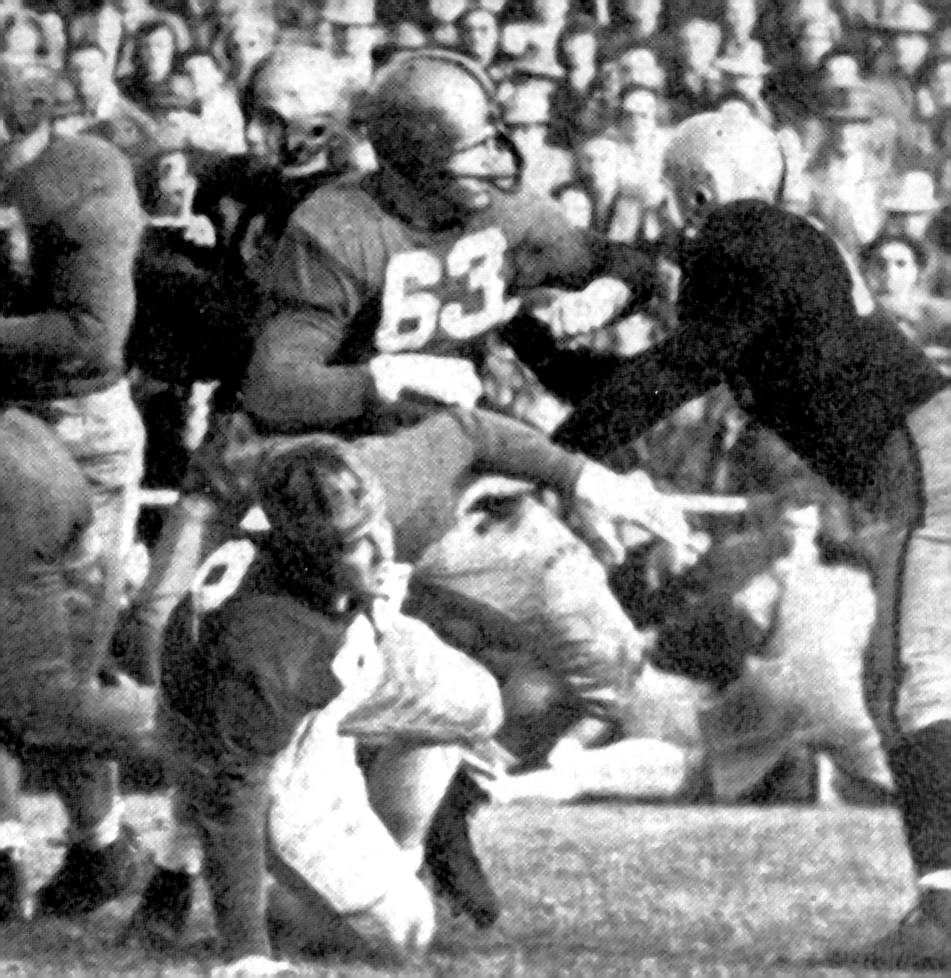

Irish Moment

After receiving a "lesson" in the game from the University of Michigan in the fall, Notre Dame invited its old friends from Ann Arbor back for two more scrimmages during the spring. Although the boys from South Bend lost both contests, they did score their first touchdown. Notre Dame student Harry Jewett is credited with the touchdown; however, the referee had waved off an earlier score by Frank Springer. According to historical accounts of the games, sparring with the referees had marred the competition. The result was that Notre Dame was no longer a gracious host, and Michigan was no longer the eager football teacher. What had begun as a friendly competition ended in a fierce rivalry—an atmosphere that still prevails between the two schools in just about every sport.

ABOVE:
ADRIAN "CAP" ANSON.

BELOW:
1889 BASEBALL TEAM.

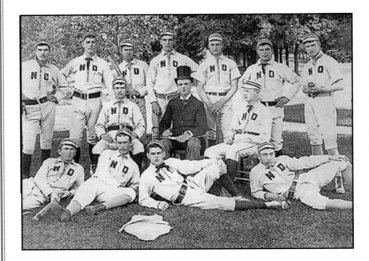

Irish Legend

Major League Baseball Hall of Famer Adrian Constantine "Cap" Anson, one of the greatest players of the 19th century, honed his skills while playing in an intra-school baseball league with his brother Sturgis at the University of Notre Dame in the mid-1860s.

Anson, born in 1852, was the first white child born in Marshalltown, Iowa, a pioneer town settled by his father. Baseball soon became Anson's passion, and he played year round; in the winter, he practiced in his father's barn. Longing to play on his town's top team with his father and brother, Anson worked hard on all aspects of his game, but his devotion affected his studies negatively. In addition, he was often fighting with his classmates. In hopes of taming Anson's wild spirit, his father sent him to the University of Notre Dame in 1866, a time when the school accepted students as young as 14. He played second base on the intra-school team "The Juanitas." Sturgis, Anson's brother, was the squad's star centerfielder.

After two years, Anson returned home, and three years later, he began playing for Rockford. He signed with the Philadelphia Athletics in 1875. The following year, he started a long career with the Chicago "White Stockings" (now the Cubs) of the National League. Anson played at the major league level for 27 years, serving as a player/coach for 15 of those seasons. He was the first player to reach 3,000 hits, and he still holds the National League record for most seasons with a batting average of .300 or higher (18). As a manager, Anson was the first to rotate pitchers and instituted base-stealing as part of his offensive strategy. He demanded a commitment to conditioning and fitness from his players and is credited with creating "spring training."

Anson's baseball career ended as manager of the "Chicago Colts" when his players refused to play for him because of his demanding demeanor. The Chicago newspapers then renamed the team the Chicago "Orphans," claiming that the squad had lost its "father."

After leaving baseball, the colorful and controversial Anson starred in a Broadway play and vaudeville shows. He also traveled the world, introducing the game of baseball to several countries.

Although his positive contributions to baseball are numerous, Anson also is remembered as an avowed racist who led the campaign to keep African-American players out of Major League Baseball.

Irish Lore

Although football had been on campus informally since the late 1860s, every true Irish fan knows Notre Dame played its first "official" football game against the University of Michigan on November 23, 1887. Two teams, the Reds and the Blues, had occasionally knocked heads even though administrators, faculty members, priests, and parents debated football's merit as a sport. An official cheer, "Rah, Rah, Rah … Nostra Domina," emerged in 1879.

Two former Notre Dame students, George DeHaven and W. Harless, discovered that their "new" school, the University of Michigan, had become impressively proficient at the game. They contacted Brother Paul, who arranged athletic activities at Notre Dame, and offered to schedule a "teaching" session with the Champions of the West, who were on their way to Chicago for games.

Following the *Rugby Rules of Football*, the teams intermingled for a demonstration game before regrouping with their official squads for a "real" contest. The following week, students formed a rugby football association and sponsored two campus teams, or as they were then called, "elevens."

LEFT:
1887 FOOTBALL TEAM.

Time Capsule

- On November 1892, Grover Cleveland was re-elected during the presidential election, becoming the first chief executive to win two non-consecutive terms of office.

- To celebrate the 400th anniversary of the October landing of Christopher Columbus, students in public schools across the United States recited the "Pledge of Allegiance" in unison.

- On May 5, 1893, the crash of the New York Stock Exchange triggered the panic of 1893 and an economic depression.

- Sir Frederick Arthur donated the Stanley Cup, which would be awarded annually to the best professional hockey team.

- During the 1892-93 school year, the Notre Dame theatre presented three student plays: *The Recognition* by faculty member Reverend Auguste Lemonnier, *William Tell* and *Louis XI*.

ABOVE:
1892 VARSITY BASEBALL TEAM.

Irish Moment

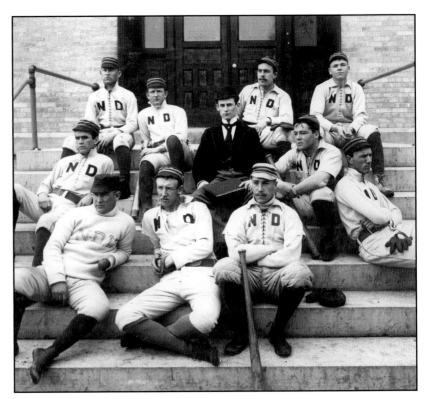

In 1892, football returned to the Notre Dame campus after a two-year absence. Still without a coach, Captain Pat Coady, whose two brothers had played quarterback in 1888 and 1889, recruited several students to take up the sport. Notre Dame won its first game of a season, a 56-0 lopsided victory over South Bend High School. Ed Brown scored five touchdowns. About a month later, in late November, Notre Dame encountered a much tougher opponent, Hillsdale College from Michigan. After falling behind 6-4 in the first half, Notre Dame rallied for a 10-10 tie.

Although Notre Dame had been playing off-campus competition in baseball since 1888, the University finally made baseball a varsity sport in 1892. Once again, the University of Michigan served as Notre Dame's inaugural collegiate opponent. Notre Dame handed the visitors from Ann Arbor a 6-4 loss that day. Ironically, baseball was the most popular sport on campus through the first decade of the 20th century. Although there were less than 200 students at Notre Dame at the time, the University's varsity baseball team was regarded as one of the best in the country.

Irish Legend

Dezera "Zeke" Cartier earned his place in Notre Dame athletic history by dropkicking its first field goal in a 9-0 victory at Northwestern in 1889. He also was credited with a 25-yard run in that game.

But Cartier also distinguished himself as a second baseman on the Notre Dame baseball team in its inaugural varsity season in 1892.

A native of Ludington, Michigan, Cartier was one of the first Notre Dame athletes to letter in more than one sport.

Irish Lore

Don't bother looking for Willie McGill's name in the Notre Dame Baseball Media Guide, but the right-handed pitcher should probably get credit for the team's first varsity victory.

Baseball had been a popular sport at Notre Dame and a team from campus had regularly played squads from South Bend, nearby Goshen and Muskegon, and the Commercial League of Chicago. Once the Notre Dame nine played the Pioneer Cadets of Philadelphia, a team made up of members of a delegation from St. Michael's Parish, who had come to campus to attend the annual convention of the Catholic Total Abstinence Union.

In April 1892, Notre Dame made the move to intercollegiate baseball and had scheduled its only home game of the inaugural season against the University of Michigan, a baseball power that had not yet lost a contest.

Afraid of being embarrassed, the Notre Dame team "secured the services" of McGill, a former student at the University, for the day. He allowed only three hits, and Notre Dame won its first game, 6-4.

Irish Moment

Notre Dame began to take football seriously in 1893. Although still without a coach, Notre Dame scheduled five games for the season, including a year-ending contest with the University of Chicago, a football power at the time.

In the first game against Kalamazoo, Notre Dame scored 34 points and held the team from 60 miles north scoreless for an impressive victory. Another Michigan school, Albion College, proved a much tougher foe, but Notre Dame escaped with an 8-6 win. The next two games were played in late November snowstorms, but inclement weather did not stop Notre Dame from staking a 28-0 shutout of De LaSalle and a 22-10 decision over the Hillsdale College "Dales."

Notre Dame made its first appearance in a New Year's Day game in 1894 against the University of Chicago. The University of Chicago team had played many of the established Eastern schools that participated in football and was much more experienced than the group from Notre Dame.

The University of Chicago won its home game against Notre Dame, 8-0, but football took hold on the South Bend campus that season, and life, as Notre Dame students knew it, would never be the same.

The Notre Dame baseball team, which did not play in 1893, returned to the diamond in the spring of 1894, beating Albion but losing to Purdue and Minnesota.

ABOVE:
FRED SCHILLO.

RIGHT:
1893 FOOTBALL TEAM.

Irish Legend

Fred Schillo gave new meaning to the term "five-year plan."

A Chicago native, Schillo played five years for Notre Dame—not particularly unusual for players in those early days of unregulated intercollegiate competition.

He began his college career in 1892 as a left tackle and returned to that position in 1893. During that season he ran for 89 yards in an 8-6 win over Albion and scored a touchdown against De LaSalle. He moved to the backup right tackle position in 1894.

Schillo then took a year off from the sport, but he came back in 1896 as the starting left tackle. During his fifth and final season, 1897, he started at right tackle.

Notre Dame compiled a 16-6-3 record with Schillo in the lineup.

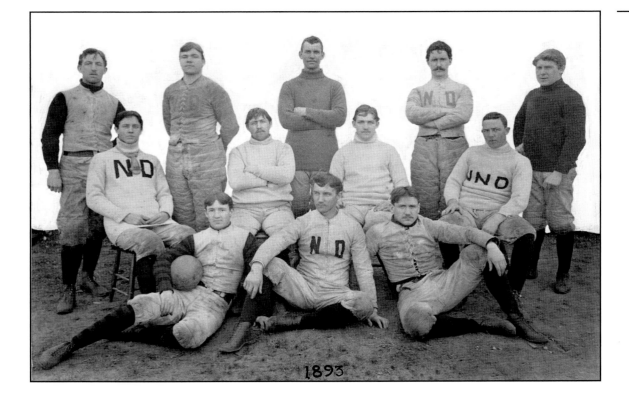

1893

LEFT:
1893 FOOTBALL STARTERS.

Irish Lore

During the mid-1890s, Notre Dame awarded an average of 30 bachelor's degrees a year.

Although the curriculum was expanded, student enrollment was still less than 700, and many students wanted to get through college quickly so they could go out into the world and get a job. Most students majored in "commercial course," an early-day business curriculum.

As more residence halls arose on campus, athletic rivalries developed between students, whose loyalties to their dormitory mates were fierce. Intramural teams participated in all sorts of sports, from basketball to rowing, from baseball to billiards. Each hall had its own recreation room, and students routinely gathered for "smokers."

1894-95

ABOVE: 1894 FOOTBALL TEAM.

Irish Moment

Notre Dame hired its first part-time football coach in 1894.

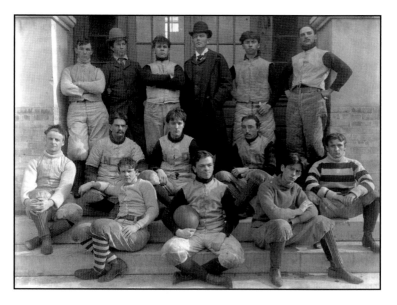

James L. Morison, who had once played tackle at the University of Michigan, convinced his players that conditioning and speed would lead them to victory; Morison guided Notre Dame to a 3-1-1 record. Wins came over Hillsdale, 14-0; Wabash, 30-0; and Rush Medical, 18-6. That game featured an appearance by a student band, led by Professor Newton Preston. Notre Dame played Albion to a 6-6 tie in the second game of the season and lost 19-12 in a season-ending rematch—a game that was called because of darkness.

Morison, however, left campus after the season to take the head coaching job at Hillsdale College.

In baseball, Notre Dame dropped its first two games to Michigan and Rush Medical but ended the short season with a three-game winning streak, beating Illinois, Wisconsin, and Purdue.

Irish Legend

In 1894, the December 17th edition of *The Notre Dame Scholastic* described right guard Daniel V. Casey as an "invaluable acquisition to the eleven this year." Standing just shy of six feet, Casey apparently was particularly good at his assignment—knocking the opponent's center off his feet.

What *The Scholastic* did not mention was that Casey, a member of the Class of '95, is listed on the weekly magazine's masthead. In that December 17 publication, Casey contributed an essay on Christmas that ran on the first page. And, on page 232, there is a poem entitled "To My Football Suit" by D.V.C.

The poem follows:

Farewells I've spoken
And fond ties broken,
But, by this token,
O canvas mine

My best endeavor
Is vain to sever,
I find, for ever,
This bond of thine!

Oft have I worn thee,
Long would I mourn thee
If fate had torn thee
And me apart,
Though stains deface thee
They do but grace thee,
Naught can replace thee
In my fond heart.

Thy seams are ragged,
Thy edges jagged,
Thy knees all bagg'ed
Thy rents, a score;
But though art dearer,
Thy beauties clearer,
My love sincerer,
Than e'er before.

Thou'rt rather muddy,
A trifle bloody,
Thou'rt quite a study,
In gray and red;
But gold can't buy thee,
Or ragman eye thee,
Or soap come nigh thee,
'Till love is dead.

Casey's sentiments are most likely shared by athletes of all sports.
Casey also wrote his graduating class poem, "Hope and Life."

Irish Lore

June 1895 marked Notre Dame's first annual "reunion" event. Former students were invited back to campus to renew old friendships, visit with former teachers and administrators, marvel at new campus facilities, and celebrate their affection for their alma mater. Festivities included picnics, lectures, dinners, and sporting events.

Now, over 110 years later, the annual Notre Dame Reunion weekend in June, sponsored by the Notre Dame Alumni Association, carries on the valuable tradition established in 1895.

Irish Moment

In his first and only year as the Notre Dame football coach, H.G. Hadden almost did it all.

Hadden, who often inserted himself as a replacement for starting center Rosy Rosenthal, led Notre Dame to lopsided wins in its first two games of the season, outscoring its opponents, 38-2.

But the third time out in 1895, Notre Dame played the Indianapolis Artillery on a snow-covered field in South Bend. In that game, Hadden played left tackle, returned kickoffs, recovered a fumble, and carried the ball four times. Despite his efforts, Notre Dame suffered its only loss of the season, 18-0. Some Notre Dame fans thought their team lost because the brother of the referee played for Indianapolis.

In Hadden's fourth and last game as player/coach, Notre Dame beat the Chicago Physicians and Surgeons, 32-0. Bob Brown and Lucian Wheeler rushed for more than 150 and 116 yards, respectively, marking the first time two Notre Dame players broke the 100-yard rushing mark in the same game.

ABOVE:
1895 BASEBALL TEAM.

RIGHT:
1895 FOOTBALL TEAM.

Irish Legend

Jack Mullen, a 5-9, 155-pound tight end from Iona, Minnesota, played six (yes, six) seasons of football for Notre Dame and served as captain in three of those years.

Students often came and went during that era, and there was no NCAA or similar governing body to oversee athletic competition. So, Mullen joined the team in 1895 and started each of the next five seasons. During his career, Notre Dame went 24-11-3.

A fierce competitor, Mullen scored several touchdowns in his unusually long stint with the Notre Dame football team. His longest was a 90-yard run in 1896 against the

South Bend Commercial Athletic Club. That same year he reportedly walked off the field with several teammates to protest a bad call in a 4-0 loss to Chicago Physicians and Surgeons.

During his last season, 1899, Mullen decided to let several of his teammates serve as game captains throughout the year. He must have sensed that it was finally time to get a real job.

Irish Lore

As interest in college football and baseball grew, many Notre Dame students lamented the fact that they did not have an official cheer or rallying cry. Witty students often "reworked" the official cheers of their opponents from Michigan and Purdue, but Notre Dame wanted something to call its own.

The Scholastic submitted three proposals in its June 1 edition. They were:

LEFT:
CREW OF THE 1895 SILVER JUBILEE.

N.D.-Hurrah! D.U. –Hurrah!
The Gold-Hurrah! The Blue-Hurrah!
Houp-a-rah, hoo, rah-hoo, rah-hoo!
Notre Dame, Ray Hurrah! N.D.U.

Or

Notre Dame, Notre Dame, Rah-Hurrah!
Notre Dame, Notre Dame, Rah-Hurrah!
Rah-Hurrah, Gold! Rah-Hurrah, Blue!
Notre Dame, Rah-Hurrah! N.D.U.

Or

N.D., Notre Dame, Rah-Hurrah!
N.D., Notre Dame, Rah-Hurrah!
Rah-Hurrah, Gold! Rah-Hurrah, Blue!
Rah-Hurrah! Notre Dame, N.D.U.

There is no mention of the "winning cheer" in subsequent editions of the magazine.

1896-97

The Early Years

Time Capsule

- In November of 1896, William McKinley defeated William Jennings Bryan in the U.S. presidential election.

- Harrisburg, Pennsylvania, was destroyed by fire.

- After hearing news accounts of his death, Mark Twain told the *New York Journal*, "The report of my death was an exaggeration."

- Baltimore won its third consecutive National League pennant with a 90-36 record.

- Notre Dame students presented five plays on campus— *Penmark Abbey*, *Corsican Brothers*, *Ticket of Leave Man*, *Her 1st Appearance*, and *One Way to Make a Fortune*.

ABOVE:
1896 FOOTBALL TEAM.

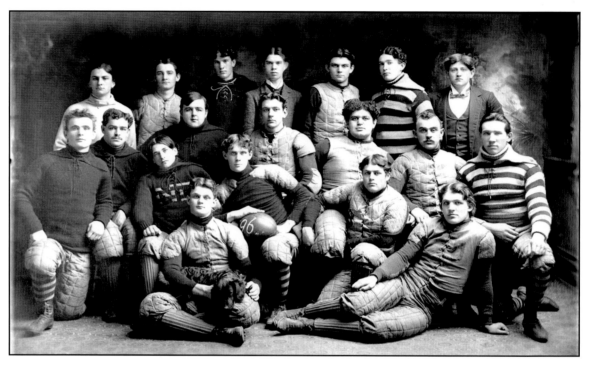

Irish Moment

Notre Dame amended its Athletic Constitution in 1897 to address several concerns of its president, Reverend Andrew Morrissey.

Students were not allowed to play on any team for longer than six years—four as an undergraduate and two as a graduate student.

Athletes now had to be "bona fide" students, taking a full course of studies. Players who had been paid for their athletic services would now be suspended from their teams.

Students needed to maintain a grade of 75 in all classes, or they would not be allowed to compete.

During its first forays into the world of college football, Notre Dame often met resistance when trying to schedule matches against other colleges in the Midwest. Father Morrissey felt Notre Dame would be best served by developing a strong intramural program—rather than playing sports on the intercollegiate level. However, Morrissey also realized that participating in intercollegiate sports, despite the financial burden, helped bring students to Notre Dame.

Irish Legend

Frank Hering took over as Notre Dame's first full-time football coach in 1896. Hering, who had actually played against the Irish in 1893 and 1894 as the quarterback for the University of Chicago, also served as captain and quarterback. Eligibility rules were virtually nonexistent in those days.

One of the toughest parts of Hering's job was convincing Notre Dame students to play. Football was not a glamour sport, and many felt it wasn't worth the effort.

Although he also taught English and studied law at Notre Dame, his primary responsibility was football. He expanded the schedule and added Purdue and Michigan State to the slate. During his three years on campus, Notre Dame compiled a 12-5-1 record.

Hering also served as coach of Notre Dame's first varsity basketball team in 1898. He is probably best remembered for his campaign to create a national holiday for mothers. In February 1904, Hering gave a speech entitled, "Our Mothers and Their Importance in Our Lives," before the national convention of the Fraternal Order of Eagles in Indianapolis and began a mission across America to honor mothers everywhere. Ten years later, Congress granted Hering his wish by declaring the third Sunday in May as "Mother's Day."

Irish Lore

In 1896, seven prestigious universities in the Midwest had created the Western Conference to establish standards and guidelines for intercollegiate athletics. Now known as the Big Ten, the conference initially included the University of Illinois, the University of Chicago, the University of Michigan, the University of Minnesota, Northwestern University, Purdue University, and the University of Wisconsin.

Notre Dame applied for membership but was rejected, marking the beginning of the University's longstanding status as a football independent.

He harbored no bitterness toward the University for its actions. In a letter written from his ship, he told his former classmates, "I often think of Notre Dame. I can picture her daily, and in my reminisces of her, a tear is often brushed away … I shall always hold Notre Dame near and dear to me."

On February 15, 1898, Shillington died when his battleship, the *USS Maine*, sunk after exploding in Havana Harbor off the coast of Cuba. That event triggered the start of the Spanish-American War.

A mounted shell, taken from the sunken ship, honors Shillington's memory. First erected in front of Brownson Hall, Shillington's former dormitory, it was later moved to the Joyce Center.

Ironically, Notre Dame's first official victory in basketball came just one day after Shillington's death.

LEFT:
1897 FOOTBALL TEAM.

Irish Lore

Hard as it is to believe, most historical accounts note that the citizens of South Bend often rooted for the opposing team during Notre Dame sporting events in the early years. "Town and gown" relations where not always amicable, and many "townies" felt no allegiance to the Notre Dame teams.

The relationship began to warm in the late 1890s as attendance at collegiate athletic events grew. South Bend residents realized that Notre Dame's athletic teams could bring business, profit, and goodwill to their community. The University as well as the athletes welcomed their newfound support.

RIGHT:
J. FRED POWERS.

Irish Moment

Track and field enjoyed resurgence in popularity during the spring of 1899. The varsity team won several dual meets, including a trouncing of intrastate rival Purdue. In that contest, Notre Dame took first place in all 10 events and eight of the second-place finishes.

Just before the turn of the century, track meets featured a variety of events, including the 100-yard dash, the 120-yard hurdles, the one-mile bicycle race, the one-mile walk, the high jump, the shot put, and the broad jump. Captain J. Fred Powers, often called the best athlete in the West, routinely won many field events, including the shot put, the pole vault, the running broad jump, and the discus. In one meet alone, he accounted for 21 of Notre Dame's points.

Track, which undoubtedly received a boost from the new facilities on campus, also re-emerged as an inter-hall sport. Dormitories now sponsored teams in track and field as they did in baseball, basketball, and tennis.

Irish Legend

J. Fred Powers served as captain and coach of the Notre Dame basketball team in its second season of varsity play, 1899. Notre Dame won the two games it played, a 19-6 victory over South Bend C.A.C. and a 21-11 decision against Rush Medical.

Also, a two-time monogram winner in track, Powers earned two basketball letters as a center. He was the team's leading scorer in 1898—averaging six points a game. No one bothered to keep records the next year.

But Powers was an even bigger star for the Notre Dame track team: a proficient performer in nearly every field event, he usually accumulated the majority of the track team's points, and led Notre Dame to a pair of consecutive state championships.

In two seasons of basketball, Powers led Notre Dame to a 3-2 record, including three straight wins after losing its first two varsity games. Most would have thought the game of basketball had a bright future on the South Bend campus.

But for a variety of reasons, basketball then took an eight-year absence as a varsity sport. It did not help that the Fieldhouse, the home of the football, basketball, baseball, and track teams, burned down in 1900. When the building reopened a year later, basketball did not return. It would be 1908 before Notre Dame would field another team on the hardwood.

LEFT:
1898 FOOTBALL TEAM.

Irish Lore

Rev. Andrew Morrissey, C.S.C., who served as Notre Dame's president from 1893-1914, once remarked, "Athletics … to be sure is subordinate to morals and the attainment of the mind, but its functions are positive."

Under his watch, Notre Dame erected a new gym on campus in 1898. The facility was 200 feet long by 100 feet wide and was 25 feet high. The building featured a dirt floor, but also contained lockers, showers, and an "apparatus room." The gym was spacious and open, unobstructed by pillars, so baseball, track, and football could practice inside during the winter.

The gymnasium was dedicated during a track meet on March 3, 1899, featuring Notre Dame, the University of Chicago, and the University of Illinois.

Students were devastated nearly a year and a half later, when the gym burned to the ground in a November 9, 1900, fire.

1899-1900

Time Capsule

- The Battle of Tirad Pass was fought in the Philippine-American War on December 2, 1899.

- Explosions of blasting powder killed 200 in a Scofield, Utah, coal mine.

- President William McKinley placed Alaska under military rule.

- In January 1900, the American League of Professional Baseball Clubs organized in Philadelphia with eight founding teams.

- After a trip to Europe, Notre Dame president Andrew Morrissey expanded the curriculum, offering economics and more history classes as well as making plans to add a school of architecture.

ABOVE::
1899 BASEBALL TEAM.

Irish Moment

Notre Dame football took another step toward the big time in the fall of 1899 as it played a 10-game schedule. The season started in September, instead of October, with the season finale in late November.

Coach Frank Hering left the team midway through the season, and assistant coach James McWeeney took over the coaching reins. Notre Dame posted impressive shutout victories over Michigan State, Lake Forest, Indiana, Northwestern, and Rush Medical, but lost to

teams considered among the best in college football at the time—the University of Chicago and Michigan. Notre Dame also struggled to a 10-10 tie with Purdue. Although Notre Dame finished at 6-3-1, the team still had not defeated a recognized football power.

Ironically, the biggest crowd of the season turned out for the season finale against the Chicago Physicians and Surgeons. Over 2,000 fans watched Notre Dame drop a 5-0 decision at home.

Notre Dame, although somewhat disappointed in its win-loss record, tried to convince its fans that the team should be crowned state champion. Indiana, which had lost to Notre Dame, and Purdue, which had tied Notre Dame, both lost games to in-state opponents, while Notre Dame did not. That may seem a weak argument to most football experts, but to Notre Dame students the logic made perfect sense.

Irish Legend

April 21 was Norwood Gibson's lucky day—twice.

The 5-10, 180-pound right-hander and second baseman pitched two no-hitters for the Notre Dame baseball team, and both occurred on April 21 against Michigan.

Gibson first accomplished the feat in 1897 in a seven-inning stint during the season-opener against the Wolverines. Notre Dame finished that season 4-2, its first with a coach, Frank Hering.

Three years later, on April 21, 1900, Gibson tossed another no-hitter in the first game of the season against Michigan. He pitched six shutout innings as Notre Dame won, 8-0.

The 1900 schedule, which featured 17 games, was much more ambitious than previous campaigns. Notre Dame won all but two of those contests.

A native of Peoria, Illinois, Gibson compiled a 20-9 win-loss record during his four years at Notre Dame. He then spent four seasons (1903-06) as a pitcher for the Boston Red Sox.

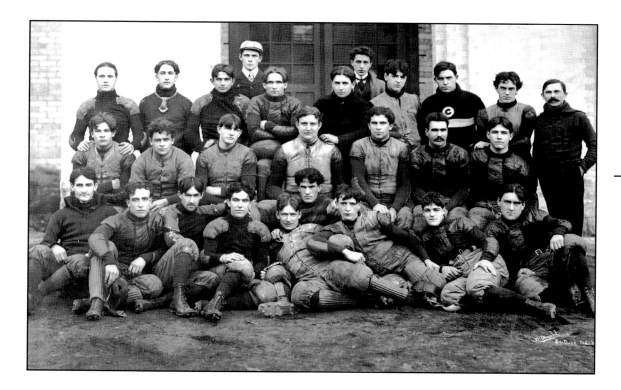

LEFT:
1899 FOOTBALL TEAM.

Irish Lore

Notre Dame students, particularly those who participated in collegiate or intramural athletics, began debating the consequences of using tobacco after an article appeared in *Popular Science.*

A professor from Yale had compared weight gain, height, "chest girth," and lung capacity among students who smoked and those who didn't. The study recommended that athletes could improve their performances by not smoking.

The *Notre Dame Scholastic* said that tobacco was "the source of evil in its use" and urged all students, not just athletes, to avoid the temptation.

Irish Moment

Notre Dame's track team faced a bleak outlook for the 1901 spring season. The University's gymnasium, where the track team trained, had burned to the ground the previous fall. And its former captain and star, J. Fred Powers, chose to no longer participate in athletics. But Notre Dame proved the track prognosticators wrong with a stellar season that produced numerous records.

During an indoor meet with the University of Chicago and the University of Illinois, Captain P.J. Corcoran and teammate Douglas Staples, a freshman, both broke the world record in heats for the 220-yard dash. Corcoran actually broke Staples' briefly held mark in the final event with a time of 23.5. Corcoran did not lose one race during the season.

Notre Dame's track team won all but one meet that year, often doubling the number of points of its competitors. It dominated the annual Western Intercollegiate Meet in Chicago, winning by 72 points, despite not entering a participant in the mile run or the bicycle races. Notre Dame athletes took first place in nine of 12 events.

Half-miler Billy Uffendall eclipsed the Western Intercollegiate and Indiana state marks in his event during 1901.

Notre Dame's 1901 track team dominated its region with spectacular individual efforts throughout the year.

RIGHT:
RED SALMON.

Irish Legend

Louis "Red" Salmon, Notre Dame's first All-American, led Notre Dame to a 28-6-4 record during his four seasons as one of the best halfbacks in the "West."

He earned his first varsity letter as a freshman in 1900 and was renowned for his "line bucking." As a sophomore he began to demonstrate his uncanny scoring and punting ability. During his senior year (1903), Notre Dame won eight games and tied one. Salmon scored 15 touchdowns and kicked 30 extra points for a total of 105 points (touchdowns were worth only five points in 1903). He averaged 11.7 points a game that year, while Notre Dame's defense allowed only 10 points all season.

As captain his junior and senior years, Salmon scored 36 touchdowns in his Notre Dame career, a record that stood for

over 80 years. Tailback Allen Pinkett finally surpassed that mark with 53 career touch-downs in 1985. Pinkett also broke Salmon's long-standing season point total (105 points) by scoring 110 in 1983. Pinkett, however, had the advantage of six points per touchdown.

Salmon, listed as 5-10, 175 pounds, also could boot the ball better than most of his peers. A 70-yard punt was a routine kick to Salmon.

Despite Salmon's success on the field, most sportswriters, including those who were his classmates, couldn't spell his name correctly until his senior year. Prior to that, he is referred to as "Sammon."

After graduation, Salmon stayed on campus for another year to coach the football team when the man hired for the job failed to arrive in South Bend. Notre Dame went 5-3 under his guidance in 1904.

Salmon also played right field for the Notre Dame baseball team as a senior.

Irish Lore

In the early 1900s, students at Notre Dame took classes in elocution and oratory. Students were drilled in parliamentary law and taught the principles of argument. Sophomores, juniors, and seniors were then required to participate in a weekly debate and presentation.

Competitions were held throughout the year, and the top "survivors" represented Notre Dame at the Intercollegiate Competition in Indianapolis. In 1901, Notre Dame won the state title.

1901-02

Time Capsule

- Vice President Theodore Roosevelt assumed the presidency on September 14, 1901, following the death of William McKinley.

- Cuba gained independence from the United States on May 20, 1901.

- The first movie theatre, Electric Theatre, opened in Los Angeles.

- The American yacht *Columbia* defeated the Irish yacht *Shamrock* in the America's Cup race.

- The Notre Dame Natatorium was refurbished to provide more swimming opportunities for students and faculty. The indoor pool was used for classes as well as recreational swims.

Irish Moment

Notre Dame football had come a long way in a few short years. The schedule had expanded to 10 games a year. The competition had gotten a bit tougher as Notre Dame annually played some of the best teams in the "West," including Purdue, Indiana, and Northwestern. And while those in the know were starting to notice Notre Dame, the program had not yet compiled an impressive enough record to warrant much attention.

That started to change in 1901 with its most successful campaign to date.

In the season opener, Notre Dame tied the South Bend Athletic Club, a last-minute stand in for Milwaukee Medical, 0-0. Nineteen-year-old captain Al Fortin, who had been playing for Notre Dame for four years, blocked a field goal attempt to preserve the standoff. After a 6-0 win over Ohio Medical, Notre Dame dropped a 2-0 decision to Northwestern when a bad snap on a punt helped the team from Evanston score a safety.

Notre Dame then reeled off seven straight impressive victories, including wins over Purdue and Indiana to secure the state championship. During the 1901 season, Notre Dame recorded six shutouts and allowed only three touchdowns. Football notoriety was not exactly around the corner, but this team moved Notre Dame one step closer to the national stage.

ABOVE:
AL FORTIN.

RIGHT:
1901 BASEBALL TEAM.

Irish Legend

Ed Ruehlbach, a pitcher from Vermont, played for the Notre Dame baseball team from 1901-1904. He started his career in the outfield and was a proficient hitter, often ranking among the squad's leading hitters. He was noted for his speed on the base paths and in the outfield as well as his control on the mound.

But most of his success, and later claim to fame, occurred on the mound. As a member of

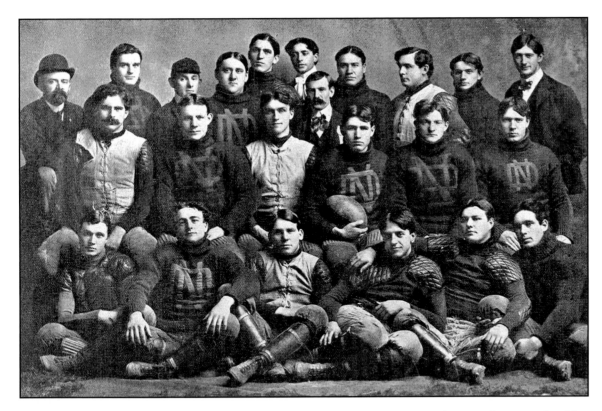

the Chicago Cubs, Ruehlbach became the first major league pitcher to throw a double-header shutout against the Brooklyn Dodgers on September 26, 1908.

Ruehlbach played for the Cubs from 1905-1913. He also spent two seasons with the Brooklyn Robins and a year with the Newark Pepper. The 6-1, 190-pound right-hander finished his career in 1916 with the Pittsburgh Pirates and Boston Braves.

Irish Lore

During the 1902 baseball season, Notre Dame played a five-game series against the Chicago White Sox. Although Notre Dame tied one game and lost four others, the professional team claimed only one decisive victory. The first game ended in an 8-8 tie after 12 innings. The White Sox won the next four games by scores of 16-14, 11-3, 8-5, and 7-6.

The Chicago players were

feted at a dormitory smoker in Brownson Hall. The students had provided cigars to the members of the White Sox as a gift. Veteran Chicago shortstop George Davis told his hosts, "Gentlemen, my only regret is that I cannot stay here two months longer."

1902-03

- The Senate ratified the Hay-Herron Treaty, which granted the United States the right to build the Panama Canal.

- In October, the United Mine Workers ended a five-month strike.

- The "Teddy Bear" was introduced to Americans in February 1903.

- Maurice Garin won the inaugural Tour de France in July 1903.

- The University purchased San Jose Park, a "summer resort" located 60 miles north of South Bend and five miles outside of Lawton, Michigan, to use for students who could not return home during the school's hiatus.

Irish Moment

Notre Dame's baseball team and its fans had high hopes for the 1903 season. More students than ever showed an interest in competing, and there were spirited battles for the 15 places on the squad. Many experts predicted that the Gold and Blue would finish as the best team in the "West."

Although Notre Dame won 17 games—the most victories in one season since the sport began—and lost only five, many on campus considered the season a huge disappointment.

Nearly every defeat came at the hands of an opponent Notre Dame should have beaten quite handily. All five losses were by less than three runs. One fan attributed the unexpected defeats to "just bad luck."

Notre Dame still easily claimed the state championship by beating intra-state rivals Indiana and Purdue twice during the season. William Higgins and "Nig" Ruehlbach shared the pitching duties, while Lawrence Antoine was Notre Dame's top threat at the plate.

Irish Legend

The most prestigious award bestowed on student-athletes at the University of Notre Dame honors the memory of former outfielder Byron Kanaley, who played in 1903 and 1904.

When Kanaley tried out for the 1903 baseball team, most of his peers didn't think he had a chance. More than 60 players attended the sessions, and Kanaley had a reputation as a poet and an orator, not an athlete. Surely his baseball skills could not match his academic prowess.

An outstanding scholar, he often contributed essays and poems to the _Notre Dame Scholastic,_ a weekly student publication, and he excelled as an orator on the debate team. As a senior, he led Notre Dame to its fourth consecutive debate title. His team argued that states should not have the right to tax personal property.

But the Weedsport, New York, native loved baseball and impressed coaches with his hitting and fielding during practices. As a junior, he made the team and played a major role in its success as a leftfielder. Kanaley was a two-time monogram winner for the baseball squad. After graduation, he became a successful banker in Chicago and served as a lay trustee of the University from 1915 until his death in 1960.

To this day, the male and female senior monogram winners who are considered exemplary as students and leaders receive the Byron Kanaley Award.

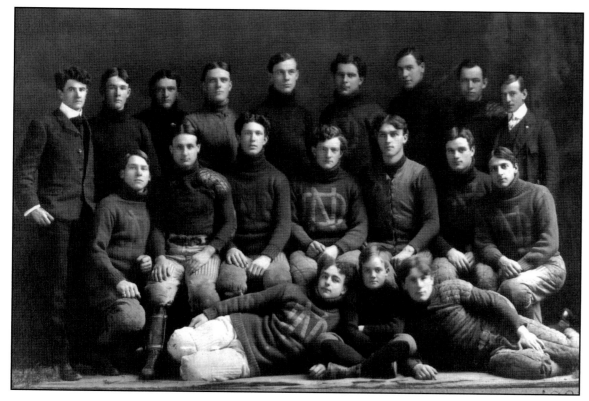

Irish Lore

During the summer of 1903, several Notre Dame students spent the summer at San Jose Lake in southwestern Michigan. It was not unusual for students whose families lived great distances from Notre Dame to not make the trip home for the school recess. Travel was often difficult and expensive. The University provided a summer haven where students could take classes, work, and enjoy the recreational benefits of a lake community.

H.J. McGlew, who served as the assistant manager of athletics at Notre Dame, and J.P. O'Reilly, the sporting editor of *The Scholastic,* organized a Fourth of July athletic competition that drew 2,000 visitors from the nearby Michigan towns of Marcellus, Decatur, Paw Paw, Schoolcraft, Burr Oak, Kalamazoo, and Blue Ridge.

Notre Dame students, as well as competitors from the surrounding areas, competed in the high jump, pole vault, shot put, dashes, and broad jump. There were also weight lifting events and a basketball game. Although the college boys proved victorious in every event, the students and community members celebrated the holiday at the end of the day with an elaborate musical program.

1903-04

Time Capsule

- The Great Baltimore Fire destroyed 1,500 buildings in 30 hours.

- The first tunnel beneath the Hudson River was completed.

- On December 17, 1903, Orville Wright became the first to successfully fly an aircraft with a petrol engine at Kitty Hawk, North Carolina.

- Pitcher Cy Young of the Boston Americans threw the first perfect game in the modern era against the Philadelphia Athletics at the Huntington Avenue Grounds on May 5, 1904.

- Notre Dame students received demerits through a detailed code of conduct. Breaking silence in study hall accounted for 25 demerits, while students caught smoking received 150 demerits. Once a student accumulated 150 demerits, his parents were notified by letter. Three hundred demerits were cause for expulsion.

Irish Moment

Notre Dame's incredible success during the 1903 football season revived the lively debate of whether the University deserved consideration among the "Western" powers.

The football team won eight games and tied one, outscoring its opponents by a whopping 291-0. The only "blemish" on the impressive record was a 0-0 standoff against Northwestern in a November 14th game played at Chicago's South Side Park, an American League baseball stadium. Halfback Frank "Happy" Lonergan scored on a 45-yard touchdown run, but the play was called back after Notre Dame captain and coach Louis "Red" Salmon was penalized for illegal use of the hands on a block.

Salmon became Notre Dame's first All-American, earning a spot on Walter Camp's third team. Camp, considered the greatest football expert at the time, said Salmon would have been a clear choice for higher honors if Notre Dame played in the Western Conference. Strength of schedule mattered even back then.

Although Notre Dame was not a member of the "Big Nine," the 1903 football season put others on notice that the University was serious about the sport and had every intention of succeeding.

ABOVE:
1903 BASEBALL TEAM.

RIGHT:
1903 TRACK TEAM.

Irish Legend

Henry "Fuzzy" McGlew might have been one of the most versatile athletes during the early days of Notre Dame football.

Once called the best quarterback in the state of Indiana by an opposing coach, McGlew was the team's signal caller in 1901, leading Notre Dame to an 8-1-1 record. He returned as quarterback in 1902, and Notre Dame finished 6-2-1. His best performance that

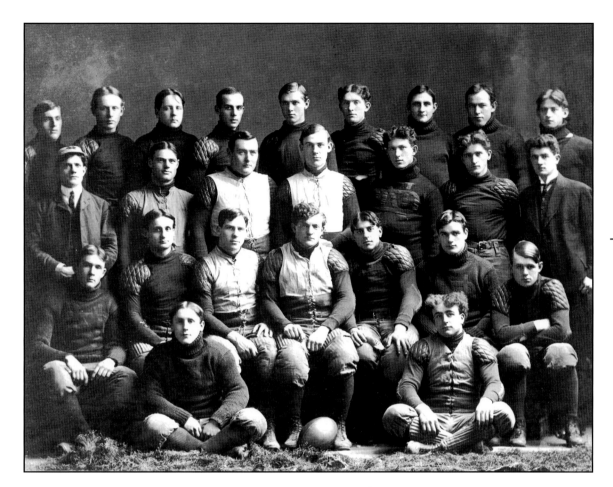

LEFT:
1903 FOOTBALL TEAM.

year came in a lopsided win over the American Medical College when he rushed three times for 80, 65, and 40 yards and scored a touchdown.

During Notre Dame's 8-0-1 season of 1903, McGlew moved to left end, often paving the way for teammate Louis "Red" Salmon to the end zone. A standout on defense as well, McGlew helped Notre Dame shutout its opponents for the entire year.

A native of Chelsea, Massachusetts, McGlew never once fumbled the football for Notre Dame and earned a reputation as a play-maker. As a student, he also served as the assistant manager for athletics and worked on scheduling and organizing events.

Irish Lore

An article in the October 31, 1903 edition of *The Scholastic* admonished students for their lack of manners, particularly in the dining hall.

"We are all conscious of our duty to perfect our intellectual faculties, but we sometimes lose sight of the necessity of developing the social man," wrote the anonymous author.

Students were chided for their tardiness as well as their greediness and selfishness at the table. Other complaints included students' inability to use knives properly, taking food from the dining hall, talking boisterously, using toothpicks at the table, and being rude to the waiters.

ABOVE:
1904 FOOTBALL TEAM.

Irish Moment

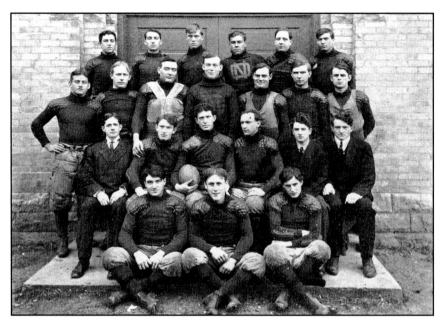

After its stellar season of 1903, Notre Dame football fans expected more of the same in 1904. The team had lost most its "stars" from that undefeated season, but the biggest standout of all, player-coach Louis "Red" Salmon, had stayed on campus after graduation to coach his alma mater.

Plagued by injuries, the team struggled through a disappointing 5-3 season. Perhaps the most noteworthy event of the year was Notre Dame's extended road trip to play the University of Kansas in Lawrence. The team had routinely traveled to Ohio, Illinois, Michigan, and Wisconsin for games, but the trip to the Great Plains state marked the first time Notre Dame had ventured that many miles for an athletic competition.

Although the teams seemed evenly matched at the beginning of the game, Kansas eventually won 24-5. However, the team made a stop at the World's Fair in St. Louis on the trip back to South Bend, giving the players a chance to have a little fun after their long trip west.

Irish Legend

William Draper ranked as one of the best all-around track performers during his four years on the Notre Dame varsity track team.

Although he also lettered three times in football, Draper earned most of his acclaim on the track. He competed in the dashes, the high and low hurdles, the running high jump, the running broad jump, the shot put, and the discus. At one time, he equaled the world record in the 50-yard dash with a time of :05.25. He also owned a variety of school records in almost every event he entered.

He also entered (and won) at several track meets throughout the country as an independent, even though he was always referred to as "Draper of Notre Dame."

As a senior, he won the state championship in the discus but was bothered by a sprained ankle in the running events.

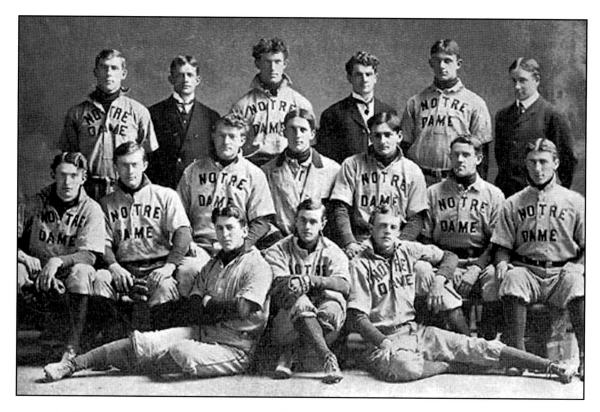

LEFT:
1904 BASEBALL TEAM.

A fullback and punter on the football team, Draper was a native of Chicago. After graduation, he continued to help "train" others on the Notre Dame track team. During the 1906-07 season, he served as the University's athletics manager.

Irish Lore

In an effort to keep pace with its opponents from the Western Conference, the Notre Dame football team began using a "charging machine" during practice.

Developed by a coach at Northwestern, the apparatus helped teach linemen how to charge fast and low as a unit.

Perhaps part of the cost of the equipment was off set by the income generated from the sale of football season tickets to students at $2 apiece. Student fans were affectionately referred to as "the rooters."

1905-06

Time Capsule

- Congress passed the Meat Inspection Act and the Pure Food and Drug Act.

- On April 18, 1905, an earthquake along the San Andreas Fault destroyed much of San Francisco, killing at least 3,000 people and leaving another 300,000 homeless.

- Albert Einstein submitted his doctoral dissertation, "On the Motion of Small Particles."

- The New York Giants' Christy Mathewson threw 27 consecutive scoreless innings to lead his team to the 1905 World Series title over Philadelphia.

- William Arnett, a former slave in Kentucky before the Civil War, was hired to build a replica of the log chapel on the Notre Dame campus. The original, constructed by Father Sorin and his missionaries, had burned down in 1856.

ABOVE:
FRANK SCANLAN.

Irish Moment

The spring of 1906 marked the beginning of one of the most successful eras in Notre Dame baseball. Over the next three seasons, Notre Dame compiled a 61-8 record, losing five games in 1906, two by one run in 1907 and just one in 1908.

Notre Dame recaptured the state championship it had lost the year before by winning eight of nine games against in-state opponents in 1906. It repeated that feat in both 1907 and 1908.

Baseball played its games on Cartier Field and attracted a significant fan base for its home games.

Catcher "Johnnie" Murray led the 1906 team in hitting with a .365 batting average as a sophomore. He also boasted the best fielding percentage on the team and was assessed only one error the entire season.

As good as the 1906 squad was, the next two Notre Dame baseball teams would be even better. The 1908 squad outscored its opponents 185-33, while pitchers Frank "Dreams" Scanlan and Jean Dubac combined for an impressive 32-5 mark over three seasons.

Irish Legend

Notre Dame's exploits on the field of competition often inspired students to recount the glories in song and poems. Wesley J. Donahue, a student editor of *The Scholastic*, paid tribute to the 1906 baseball team with his poem, "Champions of the State."

He wrote:

I sing a song of the Gold and Blue,
Of the team that fought and won,
Of heroes tried and heroes true
Who bowed in defeat to none.
The champions of the State, boys,
The champions of the State;
O heroes true to the Gold and Blue
Are the champions of the State.

The years may come and the years may go,
But they shall not dim the fame
Of the men who brought the pennant back to dear old Notre Dame.
The champions of the State, boys;
The champions of the State;
O heroes true to the Gold and Blue
Are the champions of the State.
Then give three cheers, three heartfelt cheers
 For the team of the Blue and Gold;
O'er N.D.U. let the pennant wave
As it did in the days of old.
The champions of the State, boys,
The champions of the State;
O heroes true to the Gold and Blue
Are the champions of the State.

Irish Lore

Although football was growing in popularity, more and more critics were expressing concern about the safety of the sport. In 1905, 18 players were killed and almost 150 seriously injured nationwide during games.

Most the injuries occurred because of "the wedge." Offensive players often arranged themselves like bowling pins around the ball carrier and pushed forward. The defense attacked "the wedge" by having a defender "sacrifice" himself in front of the lead blocker. The ball carrier was often tossed over the huge pile to gain yardage.

A November 25, 1905, article in *The Scholastic* contended that the majority of the injuries had happened during high school or small college games. There were fewer injuries in games between collegiate powerhouses because those players were well conditioned and trained. *The Scholastic* also blamed "obnoxious" bullies for "ungentlemanly playing" and suggested the sport employ certified referees who could toss the hooligans from a game when they got out of hand.

Calling football a "strenuous and merry game," *The Scholastic* advocated keeping the sport safe but physical. By 1910, the wedge, the flying block, and flying tackled were outlawed.

LEFT:
JEAN DUBAC.

RIGHT:
1906 BASEBALL TEAM.

Irish Moment

Losses have always been painful for Notre Dame football fans, and students have never been satisfied with just a winning record. Championships, titles, and big victories are expected.

After a 5-3 record in 1904 and a 5-4 mark in 1905, Notre Dame wanted to right the football ship. Thomas Barry brought his impressive coaching credentials to South Bend from Brown. A member of Walter Camp's All-American team in 1902, Barry was athletic, bright, and fair minded. He had also coached at Bowdoin and attended Harvard

Law School. Plus, he had played minor league baseball for Buffalo and Montreal.

Shortly after arriving on campus, Barry placed a notice in *The Scholastic*.

It read:

"Wanted: Men between the ages of 15 and 30 to report to Coach Barry today, and every day at 3 o'clock. Each man will be presented with a football suit, free of charge, and all that is expected of the recipient is that he appear on the field in said suit."

Football rules had changed in 1906. The forward pass was now legal, but Notre Dame used it sparingly, preferring to pound out its touchdowns on the ground. Barry's system seemed to work—at least through the first five games. Notre Dame shut out Franklin, Hillsdale, the Chicago Physicians and Surgeons, Michigan State, and Purdue.

Notre Dame's hopes for an undefeated season were dashed when the Blue and Gold traveled to Indianapolis for a game against Indiana for the state championship. Indiana kept the Notre Dame offense at bay and earned a 12-0 victory.

Two weeks later, Notre Dame downed Beloit, 29-0, for its sixth victory and shutout of the 1906 season.

Irish Legend

Forest Smithson, who captained the Notre Dame track squad in 1907, twice broke the world record in the 40-yard low hurdles, but his mark received no recognition because his timers were Notre Dame officials.

A versatile athlete, Smithson also equaled the world record in the high hurdles. This performance counted because it occurred in a conference championship meet.

Smithson also competed in the 100 and 220-yard dashes as well as the shot put and discus for Notre Dame.

Irish Lore

No one knows for sure just who coined the nickname "Fighting Irish" for Notre Dame's athletic teams.

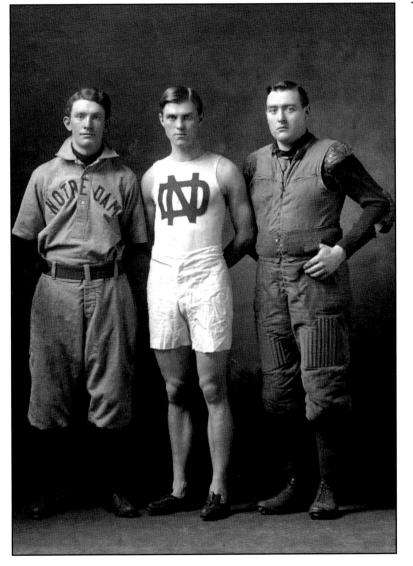

An article in a 1904 *Milwaukee Sentinel* referred to Notre Dame's football lineup as a group of "Fighting Irishmen," but few seemed to notice or take issue with the reference.

Purdue University's student newspaper, *The Exponent*, noted in a 1907 preseason baseball column that "the Irish (Notre Dame) will be our most serious opponents for championship honors and should give other western teams a run for their money."

In a 1909 football game against Michigan, Notre Dame fullback Pete Vaughan reportedly scolded his teammates for not upholding their heritage. The widely accepted version of the tale is that Vaughan told them, "You're all Irish and you're not fighting."

But the nickname didn't stick until sportswriter Francis Wallace, a Notre Dame graduate, used the term regularly in his columns for the *New York Daily News* in the 1920s.

1907-08

Irish Moment

Notre Dame fielded a varsity basketball team for the first time in eight seasons. Although several dormitories sponsored teams that often played local teams from the area over the years, the University had not sanctioned a basketball squad until coach Bertram Maris orchestrated its return to intercollegiate competition.

During the 1907 Christmas break, several Notre Dame students formed a team that played eight games against several top college and independent teams in the Midwest. That group, which billed itself as the All-Collegiate Basket Ball Team, won five of its contests and later comprised the nucleus of the revived varsity program.

In its first game of the season, Notre Dame downed the South Bend Athletic Club, 66-2. The next opponent, Kalamazoo College, lost 78-8 as Notre Dame racked up its largest margin of victory in history—a record that still stands today. Freshman forward Justin Moloney scored a game-high 34 points, a single-game scoring mark that lasted 45 years.

The basketball team finished its season at 12-4. Two of its losses came at the hands of Wabash College, which fielded the best team in Indiana that year.

Irish Legend

Ray Scanlan served as captain of the Notre Dame basketball team for two years and also earned two monograms as a catcher on the University's baseball team.

Ironically Scanlan's greatest honor on the basketball court did not come until 1957 when he was named to the Helms Athletic Foundation's 10-man All-American team.

Irish Lore

Notre Dame's student body has always been a rather athletic lot, even in its early days. Many able-bodied young men did not try out for football, and *The Scholastic* urged those sideline athletes to uphold the honor of their school by putting on the pads.

The Scholastic wrote:

"It's up to you, Mr. College Man, to make your team a winner or loser this year. Get out and try. Football like college does not make the man, but brings out what's in him. If you think you have it in you come out; if you think you haven't, let some one else prove it other than yourself. The team needs you, and you, if you are to be a Notre Dame man, need the team."

LEFT:
BERT MARIS.

1908-09

RIGHT:
HARRY "RED" MILLER.

Irish Moment

After not playing a varsity schedule for eight seasons, the Notre Dame basketball team tried to make up for lost games in its first two years back.

Finishing 12-4 in 1907-08, the 1908-09 team scheduled 40—yes, 40—games between December 2 and February 27. Seventeen of those contests were played during a 20-day span from December 17 through January 5. Notre Dame played on Christmas Eve, Christmas Day, and the day after Christmas as well as New Year's Eve and two games on New Year's Day.

There was no athletic director at the University to regulate scheduling so Coach Bertram Maris and student manager Fay Wood concocted the barnstorming scheme. Notre Dame won 26 of its first 28 games, including a school record stretch of 22 in a row. That streak was snapped on February 10, 1909, by the Buffalo Germans, the top professional team of the era.

Notre Dame ended the year with an impressive 33-7 mark. Only the University of Chicago (12-0) and Kansas (26-3) boasted fewer losses than Notre Dame that year.

However, the top-heavy schedule evoked charges of professionalism, and Notre Dame significantly scaled back its next season to just 14 games.

Irish Legend

The Notre Dame football team finished the 1908 season with an 8-1 record, outscoring its opponents, 326-20. Six of the victories were shutouts, and the only loss was a 12-6 setback at Michigan. Captain Harry "Red" Miller played a huge role in Notre Dame's success that year.

A 6-0, 176-pound halfback from Defiance, Ohio, Miller was the first of five brothers to play football at Notre Dame. A four-year starter, he was named all-state and third-team All-American as a senior in 1909 when he led Notre Dame to a 7-0-1 mark. During that season, Notre Dame defeated Michigan, 11-3, in South Bend, and the Wolverines coach Fielding H. Yost remarked after the game that "it was certainly a treat and took some of the sting of defeat away to watch that red-headed Irishman shake 'em off."

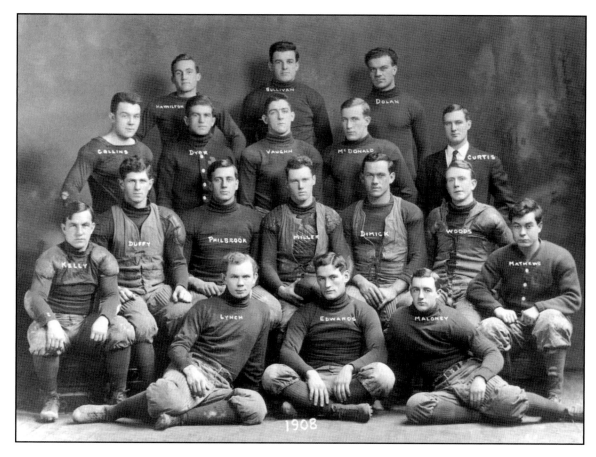

Miller's brother Don, who played for Notre Dame from 1922-24, later became one of the Four Horsemen, while Red's son Creighton led the Irish to the national championship in 1943 and was eventually inducted into the College Football Hall of Fame.

Irish Lore

Generally regarded as one of the best and certainly most recognizable college fight songs, the "Notre Dame Victory March" was first performed in the Rotunda of the Administration Building on Easter 1909 as part of the Notre Dame Band's traditional holiday concert.

The song was written in the early 1900s by two brothers—Michael and John Shea. Both were Notre Dame graduates. Michael, who graduated in 1905, wrote the music, while John, who earned degrees in 1906 and 1908, provided the words. Copyrighted in 1908, a piano version of the song was published that same year.

The "Notre Dame Victory March" was played publicly in the winter of 1908 when Michael, who later became a priest, played it on the organ of the Second Congregational Church in Holyoke, Massachusetts.

The Sheas later presented the song to the University and it first appeared under its copyright in 1928.

Ironically, the song was not played at a Notre Dame sporting event until 1919.

Irish Moment

1909-1910 was a terrific year for Notre Dame athletics.

The football team was generally considered the champion of the "West," after compiling a 7-0-1 record with wins over Michigan State, Michigan, and Wabash.

In his first year as coach, Frank Longman moved Notre Dame one step closer to the top of the football ladder. Alumni and students were so thrilled with the team's success that they presented each player with a personally engraved watch fob designed as a miniature football in solid 14-karat gold. Longman was given a silver loving cup with an inscription that read, "In Grateful Appreciation of Services Rendered in winning the Western Championship in Football, 1909."

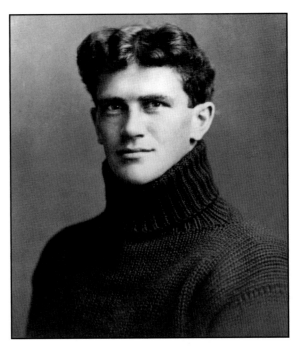

Although the basketball team faced a pared down schedule in 1909-10, coach Bertram Maris led Notre Dame to a 10-4 record and the state championship. In the final game of the season, Notre Dame avenged an earlier loss to Wabash with a 28-19 victory. The win kept the state championship banner flying in the Notre Dame Fieldhouse for another year.

Time Capsule

- On May 11, 1909, Congress established Glacier National Park in Montana.

- A hurricane killed 350 people in Louisiana and Mississippi on September 10, 1909.

- On September 9, 1909, Comet Halley was first recorded on a photographic plate.

- African-American boxer Jack Johnson knocked out white boxer James J. Jeffries in a heavyweight boxing match on July 4, 1910, sparking race riots across the United States.

- The University of Notre Dame now enrolled over 1,000 students and awarded doctorate degrees.

ABOVE:
FRANK LONGMAN.

RIGHT:
PETE VAUGHAN.

Irish Legend

Pete Vaughan, a 6-0, 195-pound fullback, played for Notre Dame in 1908 and 1909. Many think Vaughan deserves the credit for the nickname of his alma mater's athletic teams.

During the 1909 Michigan game, he supposedly called out his teammates for not playing a very physical game against the Wolverines. At least half of the players on the 1909 roster boasted last names of Irish decent—Kelly, Duffy, Dolan, Brennan, Maloney, and Ryan. He accused his teammates of not "fighting like Irishmen." Whatever he said must have worked because Notre Dame came back and beat Michigan, 11-3, in Ann Arbor before a crowd of 5,000 that included the most famous football "critic" at the time, Walter Camp.

Vaughan also made history that day when, after scoring a Notre Dame touchdown, he knocked down a goal post by running into it with either his head or shoulder. After the play he couldn't remember much of anything.

Penciled in as a starter for the Notre Dame basketball team, he missed the entire season after injuring his leg in football.

Irish Lore

Thanks to its impressive 7-0-1 record, the 1909 Notre Dame football team was considered by many to be the "Champion of the West." Notre Dame ran up 236 points while only allowing its opponents 14. The one stain on a perfect season was a 0-0 tie at Marquette in the last game of the year.

Sportswriters throughout the Midwest heaped praise on Notre Dame, and many let their imaginations flourish when dreaming of a matchup between Notre Dame and Yale, the perennial champion of the "East."

Walter Eckersall wrote in *The Chicago Tribune,* "Notre Dame easily defeated Wabash in a manner so decisive that it goes a long way in demonstrating the strength of the Catholics this year."

The Cincinnati Times-Star declared, "But when it comes to the championship of the whole West, there can be no gainsaying the claims that Notre Dame up there in Indiana is It with a capital 'I.'"

The Indianapolis News went so far as to make the bold statement that Notre Dame might even beat Yale if the two ever met on the gridiron.

"Notre Dame can not be denied," said the newspaper, "and although the football supremacy of the East has generally been conceded, it looks as if the West has this year developed one eleven that is capable of holding its own with the champion of the East."

1910-11

- On May 15, 1911, the United States Supreme Court declared Standard Oil an "unreasonable" monopoly under the Sherman Antitrust Act and ordered the company to be dissolved.

- A fire at the Triangle Shirtwaist Factory in New York City on March 25 left 145 workers dead.

- The Wright Brothers delivered commercial freight via an airplane on November 11, 1910, flying from Dayton to Columbus, Ohio.

- Ray Harroun drove the Marmon "Wasp" to victory in the first Indianapolis 500 on May 30, 1911.

- Knute Rockne left his job at the Chicago post office and enrolled at the University of Notre Dame to pursue an education.

Irish Moment

By earning the "Champion of the West" crown in 1909, Notre Dame's football team gained a few fans as well as a couple of enemies.

As Notre Dame grew into a football powerhouse, many of the more established schools refused to add the University to their schedules. An anonymous source supposedly told one Notre Dame official, "It is no glory to beat you, and it is a disgrace to be beaten by you."

Even its most traditional rivals turned their backs on Notre Dame.

The University of Michigan cancelled its November 5 contest against Notre Dame in South Bend just one week before the game, claiming that two of Notre Dame's tackles, Ralph Dimmick and George Philbrook, were ineligible. Both had been students at Whitman College in 1907-08.

Although eligibility rules were often hazy in those days, managers of opposing teams usually exchanged rosters prior to the start of the season, allowing coaches to question whether a certain player was legit. Notre Dame claimed that Michigan had indeed certified the eligibility of both Dimmick and Philbrook almost a year in advance. But Michigan's athletic director denied he had ever agreed to such an arrangement and called the three-year football contract null and void.

Notre Dame and its fans were obviously disappointed, especially since the football team had handed the Wolverines an unexpected loss the previous year in Ann Arbor. Even *The Washington Post* weighed in on the growing controversy. One sportswriter wrote, "There is no reason why the word of a man like the vice president of Notre Dame should be doubted..."

Michigan's hometown press also questioned the decision. *The Detroit News* asserted that "the Wolverines did more damage to themselves than to the Catholics."

Michigan, Notre Dame's first football opponent, had played a team from South Bend nine times since that initial contest in 1887, winning the first eight games between the two schools. But after canceling the 1910 get-together, Michigan would not play Notre Dame in football again until 1942.

However, the football season was not a total loss. Notre Dame finished 4-1-1 and notched its 100th win in the sport by beating Ohio Northern, 47-0, on November 19.

Irish Legend

Outfielder Fred "Cy" Williams led the Notre Dame baseball team to a 55-13 mark during the 1910, 1911, and 1912 seasons. He also participated in track and football at the University. But the Wadena, Indiana, native became an even bigger star in the National League after graduating from Notre Dame with an architecture degree in 1912.

Williams, the first major leaguer to hit 200 career home runs, won the National League batting title four times in his 18-year professional career.

After signing a contract with the Chicago Cubs after graduation, Williams emerged

as one of the era's most prolific hitters. Six times he hit for over a .300 batting average, including a high of .345 in 1926. Managers so feared his prowess at the plate that some used what became known as the "Williams shift," moving all three outfielders to right field since he rarely pulled the ball left.

Williams also liked to hit for power. In 1923, he tied Babe Ruth for the home run crown with 41. During his career he hit 12 inside the park home runs and seven grand slams.

The Cubs traded him to the Philadelphia Phillies after the 1917 season, and Williams played there until his retirement following the 1930 campaign. He had a different manager in each of his first 14 seasons.

After his baseball career ended, Williams put his Notre Dame education to good use. He left his imprint on the Three Lakes and Clearwater Lake, Wisconsin, area by becoming as prolific an architect as he was a hitter.

Irish Lore

Knute Rockne would eventually become perhaps the most famous football coach in history. But during the 1910-11 school year, Rockne was a little known freshman on the South Bend campus.

After being frustrated with his lack of success on the football field, Rockne tried out for the track team and became its most consistent performer in the pole vault. In his first meet for Notre Dame, he vaulted 10'6". He cleared 12 feet later that year.

Despite winning the event many times throughout the track season, Rockne didn't become a household name on campus. In fact, *The Scholastic* routinely referred to him as "Rochne" throughout its chronicles of the 1911 track campaign. His name was misspelled in every article until the 1912 season.

Time Capsule

- New Mexico joined the union as the 47th state on January 6, 1912, and Arizona followed as the 48th state on February 14.

- A 11/11/11 cold snap blanketed the Midwest, setting record highs and lows in many cities on the same day.

- The RMS *Titanic* sank on its maiden voyage after hitting an iceberg on April 14, 1912. More than 1,500 people died.

- Fenway Park opened its doors to Boston Red Sox fans on April 20, 1912.

- Over 10 percent of Notre Dame's student population held citizenship in a Latin American country.

ABOVE:
GUS DORAIS.

RIGHT:
1912 FOOTBALL TEAM.

Irish Moment

Students could not complain or whine about Notre Dame's athletic fortunes in 1911-12.

Under the guidance of first-year coach John Marks, the football team outscored its opponents 222-9 on the way to a 6-0-2 record. Notre Dame gave up a fluke touchdown to Ohio Northern in the first game and would not allow another score until Wabash managed a field goal in a late November game. Two scoreless ties against Pittsburgh and Marquette, third in a row for the two Catholic schools, kept Notre Dame from claiming a perfect season.

The game of football was changing, and Notre Dame adapted its style of play to keep pace. This year's squad featured speed and a balanced scoring attack. Quarterback Gus Dorais perfected his passing game, and his two favorite targets were Charlie Crowley and Knute Rockne.

Once football season ended, students turned their sights toward basketball. The team responded by posting an impressive 16-2 mark, its best record to date. Although Notre Dame had beaten Wabash, Rose Poly, and Earlham, the University was forced to share the state crown with Purdue.

Notre Dame's baseball team carried the momentum through the baseball season, winning 19 of 24 games.

The biggest disappointment of the year was the failure of the senior class to provide an organized cheerleading squad to lead the student "rooters."

Irish Legend

Alfred "Dutch" Bergman became Notre Dame's first four-sport athlete after earning 13 monograms in football (1910, 1911, 1913 and 1914), basketball (1914-15), baseball (1914-15), and track (1911, 1912, 1914, 1915).

As a right halfback in football, Bergman used his speed to become a powerful threat in the open field. In track he competed primarily in the sprints. He played shortstop and outfield and also pitched for the baseball team. In basketball, Bergman was the first guard off the bench.

Notre Dame football annals list Bergman as 5-9, 160 pounds, but the baseball records list him as 5-7, 155 pounds. The truth probably lies somewhere in between. But no matter his true height and weight, Bergman was quick, fast, and agile.

A native of Peru, Indiana, Bergman set a Notre Dame record when he returned a kickoff for 105 yards against Loyola. Yet, surprisingly enough, he did not score. At that time, football fields were 110 yards long. Bergman took off from his own goal line but was tackled on the Loyola 5. Notre Dame won, 80-0, that day.

Bergman's two brothers also attended Notre Dame, Art lettered in three sports, while Joe earned monograms in football and baseball. Ironically, all three shared the nickname "Dutch."

Irish Lore

A pair of Notre Dame track stars was chosen to compete in the 1912 Olympics in Stockholm as members of the U.S. Olympic team.

George Philbrook, who captained the 1911 Notre Dame team, won three events at the Western tryouts in Chicago. He was scheduled to compete in the shot put, javelin, and discus, as well as the pentathlon and decathlon.

Forrest Fletcher, the captain of the 1912 team, took first in the standing broad jump at the Western tryouts and was to compete in that event as well as the high jump in Stockholm.

However, American Jim Thorpe emerged as the legend of the 1912 Olympics, winning both the pentathlon and decathlon and laying claim to the title of world's greatest athlete.

Another Notre Dame student, Harry Hebner, represented the United States in the 100-meter backstroke in swimming. A year later he won the world championship in that event.

Although swimming was not made a varsity sport until 1958, Notre Dame students have been required to pass a swim test to complete their physical education requirement at the University for years.

ABOVE:
DORAIS TO ROCKNE.

RIGHT:
CAPTAIN KNUTE ROCKNE (1913).

Irish Moment

Notre Dame put together its first undefeated, untied season in 1912 by pulverizing just about every opponent on the seven-game schedule. Traditional opponents Michigan, Michigan State, Purdue and Indiana were missing from the slate, but Notre Dame crushed the seven teams brave enough to take on the emerging Western power.

Notre Dame scored 116 points in the opener against St. Viator and followed that with games of 74, 39, and 41 points. The only close contest was a 3-0 squeaker over Pitt on the road in early November.

Although Notre Dame had played Marquette to two scoreless ties and a 5-5 deadlock in the previous three seasons, Coach John Marks' squad shut out the Milwaukee school 69-0 in the season finale. In that game fullback Ray Eichenlaub scored four touchdowns.

The 1912 team was small but fast—just the way Marks designed. Under his tutelage, quarterback Gus Dorais and end Knute Rockne perfected their lethal passing combination.

Nearly every member of the 1912 team was scheduled to return the following season. Notre Dame football followers sensed the University was on the doorstep to greatness and nationwide notoriety. Enthusiasm and expectations were high. The December 7 issue of *The Scholastic* wrote, "The brighter day that we have been looking for is about to dawn, we feel sure, and Notre Dame will soon come into her own."

Irish Legend

Knute Rockne does not own the best winning percentage among Notre Dame football coaches.

That honor belongs to John "Jack" Marks, who never lost a game in two seasons as head football coach. A graduate of Dartmouth, Marks brought his Eastern football knowledge to campus and introduced modern football to Notre Dame. He created an offensive juggernaut as his teams outscored their opponents 611 to 36 over a two-year period. He inserted speed into the mix of brain and brawn. Considered a great football "mind" by many in the game, Marks should get credit for creating the passing combination of quarterback Gus Dorais and end Knute Rockne.

In 1911, Marks led Notre Dame to a 6-0-2 record.

LEFT:
1913 FOOTBALL TEAM.

His team gave up just one touchdown in the first game of the season. The following year, Notre Dame allowed four TDs but put together an amazing 7-0 mark, finally beating arch nemesis Marquette, 69-0, at Comiskey Park in Chicago on the last day of the season.

Marks left after that 1912 season. Notre Dame had hired Jesse Harper, who had played for Amos Alonzo Stagg at the University of Chicago and had coached at Wabash College, to serve as head coach of all four Notre Dame varsity teams—football, basketball, baseball, and track.

Irish Lore

Ralph "Rusty" Lathrop, a 6-foot-2, 185-pound right-hander from Fenimore, Wisconsin, came oh-so-close to pitching a no-hitter for Notre Dame on April 26 against Arkansas.

He did not yield a hit through eight and two-thirds innings that day. But Lathrop got lazy when his pitching foe came to the plate for what would have been the final out. The Arkansas pitcher was not about to let his rival get the better of him. He reached out and hit a fastball that dropped just past the infield dirt to reach base safely.

Lathrop's no-hitter was gone, but Notre Dame won easily 11-0. Lathrop struck out 15 Arkansas batters, while walking just four.

FAR LEFT:
KNUTE ROCKNE.

LEFT:
RALPH LATHROP.

1913-14

The 1910s

Time Capsule

- On January 5, 1914, Ford Motor Company promised workers an eight-hour workday and a minimum wage of $5 per day.

- President Woodrow Wilson made Mother's Day a national holiday on May 14, a concept first advocated by former Notre Dame football coach Frank Hering.

- After the U.S. and Panama signed the Panama Canal Treaty on August 5, 1914, the Central American waterway opened to traffic on August 15.

- Detroit's Ty Cobb won his eighth straight American League batting crown, hitting .368 in 1914. His streak would be snapped after the 1915 season, but Cobb would win three more batting titles for a career total of 12.

- For the first time in its history, the University of Notre Dame made a profit—however slight—on intercollegiate athletics.

ABOVE:
1914 DOME.

RIGHT:
1914 FOOTBALL TEAM.

Irish Moment

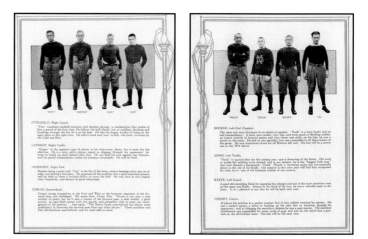

Every Irish football fan worth his Blue and Gold knows that the 1913 season propelled Notre Dame—and Knute Rockne—into the national spotlight.

New coach Jesse Harper had inherited a talented team of veterans from the undefeated campaign of the previous year. Fans and sportswriters were predicting and expecting more of the same, even though the schedule included a road trip against one of the most powerful teams in the East—Army.

Before the season started, West Point was desperately in need of an opponent. Yale had cancelled its game with Army, leaving a hole in the Cadets' schedule. A student manager wrote to almost every school he could think of, asking if its football team would be interested in playing. Harper, who also served as Notre Dame's athletic director, answered, "Yes." But, the businessman in him also demanded a $1,000 guarantee to help pay the team's expenses.

Army knew that Notre Dame was good—at least in the Midwest. Still, most football

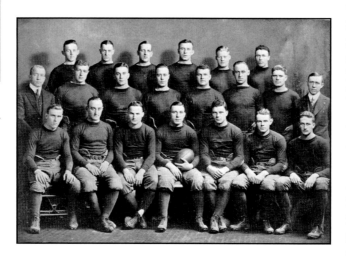

observers felt the Cadets were still far superior in athletic ability and football savvy. Plus, they all had shoes. Notre Dame took 18 players East on an all-day train trip. Only 14 had cleats.

But every player brought his "game," as well as his desire, fortitude, and drive.

Notre Dame decided to surprise Army by using its passing game—frequently. Until this game, most football experts thought the pass should only be used in desperation—or when there's little chance of error. But on this day, quarterback Gus Dorais completed 14 of 17 passes for 243 yards and two touchdowns—totals unheard of in 1913.

Rockne was Dorais' favorite target and hit the senior end for long gains of 35 and 40 yards and one score. Rockne also helped out on defense, flipping an Army back near the Notre Dame two-yard line and sacking the Cadet quarterback on the next play to set up an interception by Dorais that he ran back for a touchdown.

Notre Dame's offense also mixed in the run, which befuddled the Army defense even more. Would these guys run? Would they pass? Army certainly didn't know. Even future World War II generals Dwight Eisenhower and Omar Bradley, both members of the 1913 Army team, couldn't figure out how to stop Notre Dame.

When Dorais wasn't throwing, he was handing off to fullback Ray Eichenlaub, who rushed for a pair of touchdowns.

Notre Dame shocked the collegiate football world with its 35-13 victory that day. Plus, the University gained recognition and acceptance. Other teams wanted to play Notre Dame, and fans were willing to pay to see this new-fangled offense. Football at Notre Dame was in the black.

Irish Legend

Quarterback Charles "Gus" Dorais became Notre Dame's first consensus All-American in 1913 after leading his team to a stunning 35-13 upset of perennial Eastern football power Army.

Most Irish fans know the story of Dorais and classmate Knute Rockne spending their summer as lifeguards at Cedar Point. When they weren't saving lives, they practiced their pass routes on the sandy Lake Erie beach.

What many don't know is that Dorais was the first and only four-year starter at quarterback for Notre Dame until Blair Kiel came along in 1980. He also led Notre Dame to three undefeated seasons and 24 career wins. Also a kicker, Dorais still owns the all-time Notre Dame individual record for most field goals attempted in a single game with seven (he made three) against Texas in 1913.

After his collegiate career ended, Dorais played for several professional teams, including the Massillon Tigers. He coached at Columbus College in Iowa from 1914 to 1917 and returned to his alma mater for a brief period as a coach after World War I. He also spent 17 years as head coach of Detroit University, posting a 150-70-13 mark. He also coached the Detroit Lions from 1943-47.

In 1954, Dorais was inducted into the National Football Foundation Hall of Fame as a coach.

Irish Lore

After its dazzling offensive display against Army, Notre Dame traveled to State College, Pennsylvania, the following week to play Penn State. This time the offense sputtered and clanked and looked as dreary as the gray rain that fell on that brisk November day. Still, Notre Dame managed to survive a 14-7 scare, handing Penn State the first defeat on its home field since 1894.

Ironically, the Notre Dame players spent the Friday night before the game in one of the campus dormitories. Quarters were cramped, and wind whistled through the walls and windows. No one got a good night's sleep, and most of the 19 team members spent the night tending their stomachs. No one ever said dormitory food was fine cuisine. But sometimes it helps slow down the enemy.

1914-15

Irish Moment

Many fans would be happy with a 6-2 record but never at Notre Dame.

After the stellar seasons of 1912 and 1913, Notre Dame wanted more of the same.

Although the team had lost Gus Dorais and Knute Rockne, many expected Notre Dame to keep climbing the football ladder of success.

The schedule included three prestigious teams from the East—Yale, Army, and Syracuse. And new coach Jesse Harper brought consistency and experience into the fold. Notre Dame was laying the foundation to be a real national power—not just a state and regional force.

Notre Dame won its first two games of the season in blowouts, but two of those Eastern powerhouses—Yale and Army—handed Notre Dame convincing defeats. Notre Dame did salvage the season with a 20-0 rout of Syracuse, which had beaten Notre Dame's old foe Michigan. Fans took great solace in that fact—convincing themselves that had Notre Dame played a truly regional schedule, the team might have gone undefeated.

Irish Legend

Rev. John Cavanaugh, who served as Notre Dame's president from 1905 to 1919, would have been perfectly happy to drop intercollegiate football. As Notre Dame's football reputation grew in stature, Cavanaugh was asked about the team's prospects everywhere he went—by alumni, fans, prospective students, businessmen, politicians, and distinguished guests who visited the University. He would smile and answer their questions politely, but underneath it all he must have bristled at the thought of his University becoming known as a "football school."

Time Capsule

- On January 12, 1915, the U.S. House of Representatives rejected a proposal which would have granted women the right to vote.

- D.W. Griffith's controversial film, *The Birth of A Nation,* premiered on February 8, 1915 in Los Angeles. The film would later be shown in Washington Hall on the Notre Dame campus.

- The first stop sign appeared on a road in Detroit, Michigan.

- Jess Willard defeated defending champion Jack Johnson for the world heavyweight boxing title on April 5, 1915, in Havana, Cuba.

- Knute Rockne played the role of Wockle in the senior class production of *The Girl of the Golden West* on April 24 in Washington Hall.

RIGHT:
COACH JESSE HARPER.

Cavanaugh would have preferred a program of intramural athletics that encouraged participation by all students, no matter the depth of their athletic prowess. He felt a healthy body aided a creative mind. Cavanaugh worried that coaches in intercollegiate athletics spent too much time focusing on players with impressive athletic potential, while ignoring other students who might have progressed with more attention and tutelage.

But Father Cavanaugh was also a realist. He knew the fame and attention football brought to Notre Dame, especially outside Catholic circles, gave the University an opportunity to tell its story and attract new students to the small Midwestern school. Plus, Notre Dame became a drawing card, and teams in both the East and the far West wanted the "Catholic" school on their schedules because a game with Notre Dame meant a huge return at the gate—profits shared with the University.

Irish Lore

Yale was added to the 1914 schedule, and students were thrilled about the opportunity to challenge the Ivy League school that ranked as one of the East's perennial football powers. If Notre Dame could beat Yale, well, just about anything in life might be possible.

Notre Dame had scored 158 points in its first two games of the season, while keeping its opponents from scoring. There was hope—Yale could be beaten. But the Notre Dame offensive onslaught was stopped cold by the Elis. When the game ended, Notre Dame found itself on the short end of a 28-0 score. The players felt embarrassed and humiliated, believing they had dashed the hopes of their classmates and failed to bring honor to their University.

But when the 23 players returned to campus after the loss, they were greeted warmly by their fellow students. Classes had been cancelled so students could cheer the team after a disappointing defeat, a tradition that continues today.

Time Capsule

- Pancho Villa led 1,500 Mexican raiders in an attack against the United States Cavalry in Columbus, New Mexico, on March 8, 1916. Eleven days later, the U.S. embarked on its first air combat mission to hunt the Mexican rebel.

- On January 28, 1916, Louis D. Brandeis became the first Jewish judge appointed to the Supreme Court of the United States.

- A Great Lakes excursion steamer overturned in the Chicago River leaving 812 people dead in July 1915.

- On January 17, 1916, the Professional Golfers Association of America was formed.

- Reverend Charles O'Donnell, a professor of rhetoric at the University of Notre Dame, published a book of poetry, *The Dead Musician*.

RIGHT:
COACH JESSE HARPER.

Irish Moment

Coach Jesse Harper continued his quest to make Notre Dame a national power by venturing into the West. Nebraska, Creighton, Texas, and Rice joined more traditional Notre Dame opponents on the 1915 schedule.

Notre Dame tuned up for its showdown with Nebraska by shutting out its first two opponents, Alma and Haskell. The team then headed to Lincoln to challenge the Cornhuskers who had not lost a game in three years.

Halfback Stan Cofall, who would earn All-America honors in 1916, scored Notre Dame's first two touchdowns, and the second "Dutch" Bergman brother (Arthur) added another score. But Notre Dame failed on two of those conversion attempts. Nebraska used a limited passing game to help its offense score three touchdowns to eek out a 20-19 win over the visitors from South Bend.

Many Notre Dame fans felt the officials played a significant role in the outcome. Several drives were stopped by penalities. End Harry Baujan appeared to have scored the winning touchdown for Notre Dame after picking up a loose ball on a punt. But the officials ruled the whistle had blown.

The loss to Nebraska was the only blemish on Notre Dame's 7-1 record in 1915.

Irish Legend

Reverend John Cavanaugh decided he wanted one coach for all four varsity teams at the University of Notre Dame and in 1912 offered that job, as well as the task of athletic director, to Jesse Harper.

Harper played football for Amos Alonzo Stagg at the University of Chicago from 1902-06. He then coached for three years at Alma College. After compiling a 10-4-4 record, he moved to Wabash College. He guided Wabash to a 15-9-2 mark over four seasons. One of those losses was a 6-3 defeat at the hands of his future employer.

Young, energetic, and innovative, Harper moved Notre Dame football forward on a number of fronts. He added national powers to the schedule so Notre Dame could enhance its reputation and give its players a chance to play the best teams in collegiate football. His offensive schemes balanced passing skills with physical strength and often drove opposing coaches batty. He also was smart enough to make Knute Rockne his assistant coach after Harper's former end graduated.

During his five years as football coach, Harper led Notre Dame to a 34-5-1 record in football. He never lost more than two games in a single season.

The Papaw, Illinois, native experienced success in his other Notre Dame duties as well. Under his guidance, the Notre Dame basketball team compiled a 44-20 record, while the baseball team stood 68-21.

Harper retired from coaching at the age of 33 and moved to a cattle ranch in Sitka, Kansas, leaving Notre Dame in the hands of his protégé, Knute Rockne.

In 1931, after Rockne died in a plane crash, Harper returned to Notre Dame for a two-year stint as athletic director.

Irish Lore

Coach Jesse Harper knew how to multi-task even before it was fashionable.

After coaching the football team to a 7-1 record, he turned his attention to the hardwood and led Notre Dame to a 9-3 mark in 1915-16. Two of those losses came back-to-back at the end of the season to perennial state powerhouse Wabash, Harper's former employer.

Harper may have been distracted by his responsibilities as coach of the track team, which competed during the basketball season ... or by his duties as athletic director ... or by his need to prepare his baseball squad for its spring campaign.

In Harper's first two seasons, the Notre Dame basketball squad played 33 games. Over the last three years of his tenure, the team played just 31. Maybe the guy was just tired.

1916-17

Time Capsule

- On April 6, 1917, the United States declared war on Germany and officially entered World War I.

- The Great Atlanta Fire destroyed over 300 acres on May 21, 1917.

- Thousands of men are required to register for duty in the U.S. Army on June 5, 1917.

- Boston pitcher Ernest Shore pitched a perfect game against Washington on June 23, 1917. Shore replaced starting pitcher Babe Ruth, who was ejected after walking the first batter. That base runner was thrown out trying to steal, and Shore retired all 26 batters he faced.

- Students at the University of Notre Dame were encouraged to register for military preparedness training.

Irish Moment

Jesse Harper entered the 1916 football season with several legitimate All-America candidates on a squad that would face a challenging, but not particularly difficult schedule. Since Notre Dame had beaten Michigan in 1909, the Western Conference teams (now the Big Ten) refused to schedule games with the small Catholic school that was morphing into a national football powerhouse.

The offense was still built around speed, speed, and more speed—with a little brawn thrown in for good measure. Notre Dame won its first four games by an average score of 46-0!

But a trip to Army provided the only disappointment of the season. Former Purdue quarterback Elmer Oliphant now played for the Cadets. Against Notre Dame he threw for three touchdowns and kicked two field goals to lead Army to a 30-10 victory. Those 30 points would be the only ones allowed by the Notre Dame defense that year.

Notre Dame shut out its last three opponents and notched a season-ending 20-0 win over Nebraska, avenging the disappointing one-point loss in Lincoln a year earlier.

Although halfback Stan Cofall earned first-team All-America honors, the best player on the Notre Dame team in 1916 didn't see action as a freshman, even though he drop kicked a 62-yard field goal in a freshman game against Western Normal. The player's name was George Gipp.

ABOVE:
JAKE KLINE.

RIGHT:
NOTRE DAME HALFBACK STAN COFALL.

Irish Legend

Third baseman Clarence "Jake" Kline captained the Notre Dame baseball squad as a senior in 1917. The Williamsport, Pennsylvania, native helped the Irish to a 10-4 mark that spring. He earned three monograms, hitting at least .300 every year. Kline still shares the team record of three home runs in a single game.

After a stint in World War I and a playing career in various professional leagues, Kline returned to his alma mater in 1931 as freshman baseball coach. He would not leave again until his retirement in 1975.

Assuming the head job in 1934, Kline guided Notre Dame on the diamond for over 40 years. He won more than 55 percent of the over 1,000 games he coached.

Notre Dame made its first NCAA post season tournament appearance under Kline in 1949. The Irish also competed in the 1956 and 1957 College World Series in Omaha.

In 1968 Kline was inducted into the College Baseball Hall of Fame, and in 1975, Cartier Field was renamed in his honor. He died in 1989 at the age of 94.

When the Notre Dame baseball program moved to its present headquarters at Frank Eck Stadium in 1994, "Jake" wasn't left behind. The official title of the playing area is Kline Field at Eck Stadium.

Irish Lore

On May 5, 1917, pitcher George Murphy threw a no-hitter against St. Viator, the third in the University's history.

LEFT:
JAKE KLINE.

BELOW:
GEORGE MURPHY.

1917-18

Time Capsule

- Congress established time zones and approved daylight savings time on March 19, 1918.

- On July 9, 1918, two trains collided in Nashville, Tennessee, killing 101.

- General Motors acquired the Chevrolet Motor Company of Delaware in May, 1918.

- The National Hockey Association dissolved on November 22, 1917, only to be replaced four days later by the National Hockey League.

- As the University celebrated its diamond (75th) jubilee, 600 Notre Dame students and 18 priests registered for service in World War I.

Irish Moment

The war took its toll on Notre Dame athletics. Students were leaving to join the Army, and Jesse Harper, who was still coaching three varsity teams, often had to rely on underclassmen to fill a void left by more experienced players.

After losing its starting quarterback to the draft after the third game of the season, Notre Dame regrouped for an impressive home win over South Dakota. But the following week was a road trip to Army, and no one thought Notre Dame could defeat the Cadets this time around. The teams had split their four previous meeting, and it looked like Army would claim bragging rights.

But Harper, who had rested his starting linemen against South Dakota, surprised the Cadets once again with his offensive game plan. Instead of the expected aerial assault, Harper installed a more balanced attack, mixing off-tackle runs with a short passing game.

Joe Brandy intercepted an Army pass and returned it 23 yards to set up the game's only touchdown, a seven-yard run he handled himself. He also recovered a fumble late in the game to preserve the 7-2 Notre Dame win.

RIGHT: JIM PHELAN.

In the defensive struggle, Army was held to eight first downs, five of them coming in the last quarter. Notre Dame did not substitute once, and George Gipp punted 11 times. The next week Gipp would suffer a broken leg in a game against Morningside.

Despite the obstacles, Notre Dame finished the year with a 6-1-1 mark. Coach Jesse Harper would leave later that year to take over his family's ranch in Kansas.

Irish Legend

One of the most versatile quarterbacks in Notre Dame history, Jim Phelan could pass, run, kick, and tackle equally well. His reserve performance as a freshman in 1915 propelled him into the starting role in just his second week as a collegian.

The 5-11, 182-pound native of Portland, Oregon, directed Notre Dame's sensational offense that scored 293 points in the 1916 season.

Elected captain by his teammates in 1917, Phelan scored the season's first touchdown, plus two others, in a 55-0 rout over Kalamazoo.

The following week against Wisconsin, he nearly beat the Badgers by himself. But his 61-yard field goal attempt, drop-kick style, hit the crossbar, and the game ended in a 0-0 tie.

Nebraska was next on the Notre Dame schedule, and the Cornhuskers handed the visitors a 7-0 setback, their only loss of the season. But Phelan and his teammates could be forgiven for being a bit distracted in Lincoln. Immediately after the game, Phelan, who had been drafted by the Army, left for Camp Taylor in Louisville. Bigger battles laid ahead.

Irish Lore

Jesse Harper had to attend a football conference so he asked his right-hand man, Knute Rockne, to coach the Notre Dame basketball team in its season opener at Purdue.

The Irish trailed 37-2 at halftime.

Although Notre Dame scored 10 points in the second half, while holding the Boilermakers to just 11, the game ended in a 48-12 defeat for Rockne's "head" coaching debut.

The loss marked the beginning of six straight losing seasons for the Notre Dame basketball program.

Rockne had better luck coaching the track team that year.

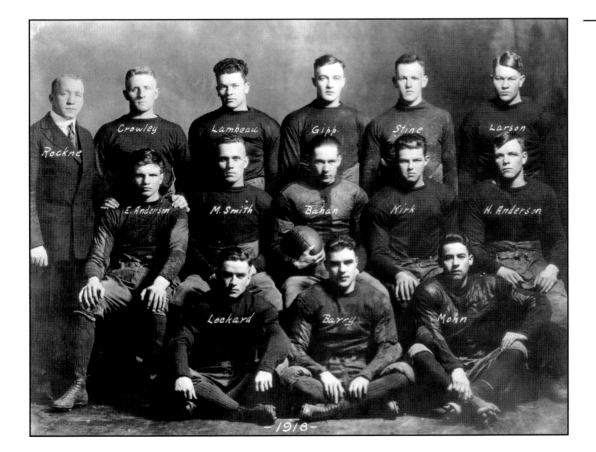

LEFT:
1918 FOOTBALL TEAM.

1918-19

The 1910s

Time Capsule

- On November 11, 1918, World War I ended when Germany signed an armistice agreement with the Allies in a railroad car outside of Compiegne, France.

- During the final months of 1918, 25 million people died of the "Spanish Flu," a worldwide pandemic that killed almost twice as many as died during World War I.

- Congress approved the 19th Amendment to the U.S. Constitution, which would guarantee women the right to vote if ratified by the states. The Amendment was passed on August 18, 1920.

- The Boston Red Sox defeated the Chicago Cubs in the 1918 World Series. The Red Sox would not win another title until 2004.

- Every student-athlete who earned a Notre Dame monogram in 1914, 1915, and 1916 served in the Armed Forces during World War I.

Irish Moment

Some say Knute Rockne became Notre Dame's head football coach over Gus Dorais with the flip of a coin. But most historians agree that Rockne was handpicked by his former coach, Jesse Harper, as his successor.

Rockne, who had passed up an opportunity to attend medical school in St. Louis, became Notre Dame's head football coach in 1918. But his first season was wracked with difficulties. Most of the best athletes in the country were away at war, and many colleges had trouble fielding complete teams. Even when Notre Dame did find a worthy opponent, the game was cancelled because of a flu epidemic—twice. Rockne managed to convince just one team to come to South Bend to play that year. Great Lakes handed the team, now routinely referred to in *The Scholastic* as the Fighting Irish, a 7-7 tie.

Nearly every game that season was played in bad weather, and Notre Dame had more than its share of injury and illness.

Perhaps the most positive event during that 1918 season was the return of traditional intrastate rival Purdue to the Irish schedule. After not playing for 11 years, the Boilermakers and Notre Dame set aside their differences and reopened a series that has now spanned 77 years.

Notre Dame finished the year at 3-1-2.

Irish Legend

With Knute Rockne as his track coach, Earl Gilfillian emerged as one of the best all-around performers in the Midwest as a member of the 1918 and 1919 Notre Dame track teams.

After serving in the Navy, Gilfillian returned to school to brighten the 1918 team's prospects.

Gilfillian specialized in the high and low hurdles and also participated in the shot put and discus. On occasion, he also entered the high jump.

In 1918, he won the Western Conference title in the discus.

Irish Lore

A flu outbreak in October killed tens of thousands of people across the United States and played havoc with Notre Dame's football schedule.

A game against Municipal Pier was cancelled by medical authorities. The medical personnel at Notre Dame were so worried about an outbreak on campus that the University doctor ordered that practices be cancelled as well.

1919-20

The 1910s

Irish Moment

The skies cleared for Knute Rockne in 1919.

The war had ended, and several former players who had left school to join the service returned to the University bigger, stronger, and more mature.

Many players from Jesse Harper's 1916 squad were back in the fold and ready to play for Rockne. Dutch Bergman, Frank Coughlin, Cy DeGree, Slip Madigan, Grover Malone, and Walter Miller provided stability and leadership for the promising young stars—George Gipp, Hunk Anderson, Eddie Anderson, and Pete Bahan.

Although the nine-game schedule was challenging, Rockne knew his team was capable of having an extraordinary season.

The Irish opened the season with a 14-0 win over Kalamazoo. George Gipp, who had been hampered in 1918 by injuries, rushed for 148 yards and one touchdown. Two other scoring runs of 80 and 68 yards were called back.

Gipp continued to dazzle Notre Dame fans the following week against Mt. Union. He ran for a pair of 30-yard touchdowns, threw two passes for 49 yards, rushed for 63 yards, and returned two kickoffs for 56 yards.

There seemed no end to Gipp's incredible talents on the football field. Against Nebraska, he tossed a lateral to Bergman, who then ran 90 yards for a touchdown. He also finished the day completing five of eight passes for 124 yards.

No one could stop Gipp for long. Notre Dame plowed through one opponent after another. When the season was over, the Irish owned a 9-0 record and had played before more than 56,000 fans. Although most football experts still considered Harvard, with its 9-0-1 mark, the mythical national champion, Notre Dame, and Rockne, served notice to the college fooball world that they would no longer be willing to settle for second best.

Time Capsule

- On January 16, 1920, the 18th Amendment of the Constitution, better known as "Prohibition," went into effect. Many Americans protested by moving to Paris, France.

- Congress refused to ratify the Versailles Treaty on March 19, 1920.

- During the summer of 1920, the U.S. Postal Service ruled that children could not be sent via parcel post.

- The "Black Sox" scandal tainted the 1919 World Series. The Cincinnati Reds were declared the winners over the Chicago White Sox.

- Women were routinely allowed to take summer school courses at the University of Notre Dame, although nearly all of the female students were nuns.

RIGHT:
KNUTE ROCKNE (IN CHAIR).

Irish Legend

"Hunk" Anderson came to Notre Dame with a friend from his high school days, George Gipp.

Despite weighing only 168 pounds as a freshman in 1918, Anderson earned a starting spot that year as a left guard, a position he commandeered until he graduated.

The Hancock, Michigan, native earned All-American honors as a senior and after graduation played four seasons for the Chicago Bears. Since professional football didn't pay much in those days, Anderson took a second job—as Knute Rockne's assistant coach.

Although he spent two years as the head football coach at St. Louis University, he returned to his alma mater as an assistant in 1930. After Rockne's death in 1931, Anderson coached the Irish for three seasons, compiling a 16-9-2 mark.

He then coached at North Carolina State, Michigan, and Cincinnati before moving to the NFL Detroit Lions in 1939. He moved to the Chicago Bears the following year and spent 11 seasons as the team's line coach.

LEFT:
HUNK ANDERSON (LEFT) WITH KNUTE ROCKNE.

Irish Lore

Rumor has it that Knute Rockne actually asked the referee in a Kalamazoo game to call a penalty on George Gipp after a long run.

It seems the head football coach wanted to teach his young star a lesson for slacking off during practice. The refs were more than accommodating, nullifying two runs of 80 and 68 yards.

Gipp, not one to waste energy or time, supposedly told the official, "Next time, give me one whistle to stop and two to keep going."

1920-21

Time Capsule

- Warren G. Harding defeated James Cox in the 1920 presidential election, the first in which women had the right to vote.

- More than 85 people died in the Tulsa Race Riot during two days of violence May 31-June 1.

- On November 2, 1920, radio station KDKA in Pittsburgh signed on the air as the first commercial radio station, broadcasting results of that day's presidential election.

- Bill Tilden won the first of two back-to-back singles championships at Wimbledon.

- The University of Notre Dame announced an ambitious $2 million endowment campaign in the spring of 1921.

ABOVE:
FRANK COUGHLIN.

Irish Moment

Nearly 10,000 Cornhusker fans, most adorned in red, packed their stadium, convinced that their team could stop Rockne and his talented star, George Gipp.

The Friday night before their homecoming game, 5,000 Nebraska students had paraded through the streets of Lincoln before gathering for a rally in front of the Hotel Lincoln, Notre Dame's headquarters. Rockne thanked the students for their warm welcome, and Notre Dame captain Frank Coughlin told the crowd that he knew their support would help Nebraska in its battle. But he ended his speech by saying, "Men and women of Nebraska, we are going to be true to them (Notre Dame fans). We are going to whip you tomorrow!"

Notre Dame, dressed in light blue jerseys, scored first on a safety. Nebraska then took a 7-2 lead after scoring in the second quarter, but the advantage didn't last long as Gipp scored in the fourth quarter to seal Notre Dame's 16-7 win.

Two weeks later Notre Dame traveled to Army to take on the undefeated Cadets. Although Army held a 17-14 halftime lead, Gipp put together a brilliant rally that showcased his versatile athletic talents. In the fourth quarter, he set up the go-ahead touchdown by Johnny Mohardt. On another drive, he broke loose for a 50-yard gain and then threw three short passes to move to the 20-yard line. Gipp had rushed for 150 yards and passed for 123 more against Army. He had also returned kicks for 207 yards.

Gipp wasn't feeling well so Rockne tried to rest him in the Homecoming game against Purdue. He played sparingly, yet still threw for 128 yards, rushed for 129 yards, kicked three conversions, and scored on a 35-yard run. A week later he played against Indiana with a separated shoulder.

Notre Dame played Northwestern on November 20 in Chicago. The stands were filled with Notre Dame alumni, who had come to see Gipp, many proclaiming it "George Gipp Day." Gipp was ailing, but Rockne let him play in the fourth quarter. He completed five of six passes for 157 yards and two touchdowns. But that would be his last game. He missed the season finale against Michigan State. During the team's season-ending banquet at the Oliver Hotel, Gipp left early and checked into a South Bend hospital. Three weeks later, the player who many historians still consider the best to ever play the game, died at the age of 25.

Irish Legend

No one ever mistook George Gipp for a saint. But Knute Rockne, and many of his teammates, felt he was the savior of Notre Dame football.

The stories surrounding Gipp's arrival on the South Bend campus are legendary, and every Notre Dame fan knows the tale of how Rockne "discovered" his young star by watching him punt a football "just for the fun of it." The clever coach must have sensed Gipp's natural athletic ability and convinced him to try football.

Never much of a student, Gipp originally came to Notre Dame from his home in Laurium, Michigan, to play baseball with a high school teammate. Since Gipp had never graduated from high school, he was admitted to Notre Dame as a "conditioned freshman." Football was a perfect fit for Gipp. He could run, he could throw, he could pass, and he could knock other people down. In his last three seasons, he led the Irish in rushing and passing, and his career mark of 2,341 rushing yards lasted more than 50 years until Jerome Heavens broke it in 1978. Perhaps more impressive is the fact that not one pass was completed in the territory he covered as a defender—ever. During his four years on the varsity, Notre Dame went 27-2-3, going undefeated and untied in his last 17 games. Honored by Walter Camp as the outstanding college player in America in 1920, Gipp was voted into the National Football Hall of Fame in 1951.

Gipp's teammates, and his coach, knew he frequented South Bend's pool halls, made his "spending" money by playing poker and gambling and lived off campus in the luxurious Oliver Hotel. He rarely came to practice and attended class even less frequently. Right or wrong, Gipp's coaches and teammates accepted his foibles. On March 8, 1920, Gipp was expelled from Notre Dame, supposedly for poor attendance habits. Other colleges, including the University of Michigan, tried to "recruit him." Several prominent local citizens, including many who were instrumental in the University's fund-raising efforts, pressured Notre Dame president Rev. James Burns to readmit Gipp. He did—on April 29, 1920.

The officially accepted version of Gipp's cause of death is a streptococcic throat infection. Many accounts say doctors had advised him the summer before to have his tonsils removed. Others think he died of pneumonia. Some blame it on his lifestyle. Gipp's death cast a gray pallor over the Notre Dame campus and the world of college athletics. But it also sealed his fate as perhaps the greatest legend in Notre Dame athletics.

ABOVE AND BELOW:
GEORGE GIPP.

LEFT:
FOOTBALL PRACTICE.

Irish Lore

During the 1921 track season, five Notre Dame competitors earned All-America honors—Gus Desch, who placed first in the low hurdles; Johnny Murphy, who won the high jump; Eugene Oberst, the top finisher in the javelin; Billy Hayes, who competed in the 100 and 200-yard dashes; and Chet Wynne, a hurdler. The five, guided by Irish head track coach Knute Rockne, were the first from Notre Dame to earn the All-America moniker in the sport.

The previous summer Desch and Murphy had represented Notre Dame and the United States at the 1920 Summer Olympics in Antwerp. Writing about his experiences as an Olympian in *The Scholastic,* Desch confided that luck had played a significant role in his ability to win his event in the preliminary round while tying the world record. "The more I pondered over my good fortune, the more I commenced to understand why it is nobody gets killed in the rush for the gates after football games on Cartier Field. Some people say there is no such thing as luck, but I have still to be convinced."

1921-22

The 1920s

Time Capsule

- In April 1922, the Teapot Dome Scandal marred the presidency of Warren G. Harding.

- The Lincoln Memorial was dedicated May 30 in Washington, D.C.

- The first Miss America was crowned in Atlantic City on September 7, 1921.

- Manager John McGraw and his New York Giants won the all-New York City World Series, besting the Yankees five games to three.

- Over 1,100 students at Notre Dame lived in the South Bend city limits because there were no dormitory rooms for them on the University's campus.

Irish Moment

Football continued its dominance during the 1921 season, although Notre Dame's 20-game win streak came to an end October 8 with a 10-7 loss at the University of Iowa.

The Irish recovered to claim victories in their last eight games, outscoring their opponents, 255-21, and playing before almost 72,000 fans, an average of nearly 9,000 a game. Rockne once again went against conventional wisdom and scheduled four football games in two weeks. His team beat Army, 28-0, on November 5 at West Point. Three days later, the Irish crushed Rutgers, 48-0, before 12,000 at New York City's Polo Grounds. After a 42-7 victory at home over Haskell, Rockne took his troops to Marquette for a 21-7 win before 11,000 fans.

Six Notre Dame football players—Eddie Anderson, Hunk Anderson, Paul Castner, Roger Kiley, Johnny Mohardt, and Buck Shaw—were tabbed All-Americans. Notre Dame might have made its first trip to the Rose Bowl after the 1921 season, but several players were caught playing semipro ball. That trip would have to wait.

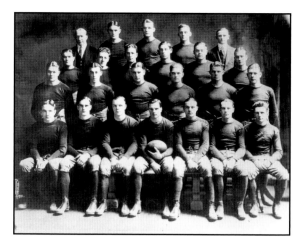

ABOVE:
1921 FOOTBALL TEAM.

RIGHT:
PAUL CASTNER.

Irish Legend

A native of St. Paul, Minnesota, Paul Castner left his mark on three Notre Dame sports—football, baseball, and hockey.

Although he had never played the sport in high school, Castner came to Notre Dame after Knute Rockne received a recommendation from a mutual friend. He made the varsity team as a second-string fullback in 1920. The following year he started at halfback and averaged 27.8 yards during eight kickoff returns. As a senior, he moved back to fullback and led the team in scoring with 64 points. He scored all of Notre Dame's points in a 27-0 win over Indiana in 1922. He earned All-America recognition as a junior and senior.

Castner might have been one of the Four Horsemen, but a back injury gave his spot to Elmer Layden.

In baseball, Castner earned three monograms. The 5-11, 175-pound left-handed pitcher and outfielder compiled an impressive 14-7 record for the Irish and threw a no-hitter at Purdue on May 17, 1922.

But Castner's first love was hockey. He put together his own Notre Dame team in 1919 and served as a player-coach for two seasons. He stayed on after graduation and coached for two more years. During his four seasons, he guided Notre Dame to an 18-4-0 record against Michigan Tech, Carnegie Tech, Michigan, Michigan State, Wisconsin, Culver Academy, St. Thomas, and Assumption.

Castner used his football connections to recruit hockey players. All-America offensive lineman Hunk Anderson was the goaltender on his 1920-21 team, and halfback Jim Crowley compiled an 8-1 record and an impressive 1.33 goals against average as a freshman goaltender. Crowley's brilliant career in the net ended when his football coach put his hockey career "on ice."

After graduation, Paul Castner played one season of professional baseball for the Chicago White Sox.

CAPT. CASTNER

Irish Lore

Johnny Mohardt played four seasons at halfback for Notre Dame, primarily as George Gipp's backup.

The Gary, Indiana, native would have started anywhere else. Relegated to second string early in his career, he made the most of what little opportunity he had to showcase his talents, scoring one touchdown in a romp over Mount Union. His playing time increased as a junior, and as a senior he started at left halfback. Mohardt, who would earn second-team All-America recognition, led Notre Dame in rushing, passing, and scoring in 1921. He ran for 781 yards on 136 carries, completed 53 of 98 passes for nine touchdowns and 995 yards, and scored 12 touchdowns for 72 points.

Mohardt also played three seasons of Irish baseball as a pitcher, catcher, and outfielder and served as captain as a senior. The 5-foot-10, 165-pounder compiled a 6-1 win-loss record on the mound.

After graduation, Mohardt spent one season with the Detroit Tigers before playing for the Chicago Bears in the National Football League. After retiring from sports, he earned his medical degree.

But perhaps Mohardt's most impressive claim to fame is that throughout his collegiate and professional career, he played with George Gipp, Red Grange, and Ty Cobb.

Irish Moment

The Four Horsemen, one of the most famous backfields in college football history, made their debut in 1922.

Don Miller, Elmer Layden, Jim Crowley, and Harry Stuhldreher would not acquire the nickname until two seasons later. But in 1922, coach Knute Rockne recognized their talents, teamwork and chemistry and tried to blend this young unit into a quartet that could produce plenty of offense and keep Notre Dame at the forefront of college football.

Rockne used three different backfield combinations in the season opener against Kalamazoo. He continued to tweak the offense as the Irish won their first seven games.

But Notre Dame's old nemesis, Army, figured out Rockne's game plan and forced several Notre Dame turnovers to create a 0-0 deadlock.

A week later star fullback Paul Castner, playing with a broken nose and sprained ankle, finally went down when he broke his hip in a game against Butler. The injury would sideline Castner for the rest of his Notre Dame career. But Rockne was forced to reconfigure his backfield. Layden switched to fullback, Crowley moved up to halfback, Stuhldreher stayed at quarterback, and Miller remained at the other end spot.

Although Notre Dame dropped its final game of the season at Nebraska, Rockne had finally found a combination in the backfield that would take Notre Dame to new heights in the next two seasons.

Irish Legend

Football tackle Tom Lieb earned All-America honors twice despite breaking his leg against Purdue as a senior.

Luckily he recovered in time for the spring track season when he also won All-America distinction. The Faribault, Minnesota, native won the NCAA championship in the shot put during the 1923 and 1924 seasons. Lieb is considered the "inventor" of the spin-style delivery, still used today, which he perfected under the watchful eye of his football and track coach, Knute Rockne.

Time Capsule

- On August 7, 1923, Calvin Coolidge succeeded President Warren Harding, who died in office.

- Howard Carter and Lord Carnarvon entered the tomb of Egyptian King Tutankhamun on November 26, 1922, becoming the first people in over 3,000 years to do so.

- *Time Magazine* published its first edition on March 2, 1923.

- As an amateur, Bobby Jones won the first of his four U.S. Open golf championships in a playoff.

- Reverend Matthew Walsh began his tenure as president of the University of Notre Dame.

ABOVE:
ADAM WALSH.

RIGHT:
TOM LIEB.

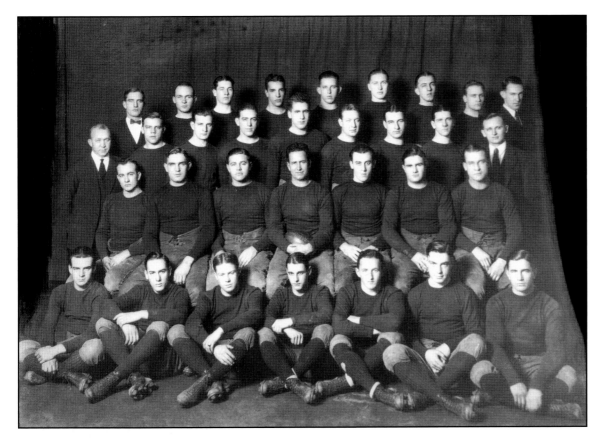

Lieb also thought he knew his way around the hockey rink. He coached Notre Dame's "unofficial" hockey team for three seasons, compiling a 3-8-3 record from 1923-26.

Irish Lore

In 1888, University vice president Rev. John Zahm and future Notre Dame president Rev. Andrew Morrissey formed a lawn tennis club for faculty members. The sport was taught in physical education classes, and by 1891, dormitories sponsored tennis teams in an interhall league. By 1910, the Notre Dame Tennis Club played a few matches against other colleges and universities. But the University did not grant tennis varsity status until the spring of 1923.

Six players made up that first team under coach C.P. Van Ryper. The Irish took the court just twice that season, losing both matches. But athletic director Knute Rockne was a firm supporter of Notre Dame's new varsity sport and did what he could to ensure the growth and eventual success of tennis on the Irish campus.

1923-24

Irish Moment

Notre Dame football continued to dominate the athletic spotlight at the University in 1923-24, and the "Rockmen" were the hottest ticket in town, especially when the Fighting Irish played on the road. Crowds of 30,000 showed up to see Notre Dame play Army at Ebbets Field in Brooklyn, Princeton on its campus, Nebraska at Lincoln and Carnegie Tech in Pittsburgh. Over 20,000 were on hand for home games against Georgia Tech and Purdue.

Rockne's offense was potent and his defense particular stingy. In the first six games Notre Dame outscored its opponents, 195-16. The biggest challenge came from Army, which wore bright yellow jerseys instead of its customary blue, for the high-profile contest. But Notre Dame's speed neutralized the Cadets' bulk and brawn, and the Irish walked away with a 13-0 victory.

The only thorn in Notre Dame's side in 1923 was the same prickly opponent from the 1922 season. Nebraska had Notre Dame's—and Rockne's—number. The Cornhuskers' defense frustrated the Irish passing game, and only a third quarter touchdown pass from Harry Stuhldreher to Bill Cerney kept Notre Dame from being held scoreless for the first time since the 1922 0-0 tie with Army.

Notre Dame and Rockne would still have to wait for the anticipated perfect season—but not for much longer. Football wasn't the only big news on campus that year. Notre Dame formally awarded varsity status to the cross-country team, a group that had been competing under the Notre Dame banner for several seasons with Rockne as its coach.

And after six consecutive losing seasons, the Notre Dame basketball team posted a 15-8 record under first-year coach George Keogan.

Keogan has previously coached football and basketball at Valparaiso, a Lutheran college less than an hour west of South Bend. In 1920, Keogan's Valpo football team had given the Irish a run for their money, and Rockne remembered the competitive spirit and preparedness of the Crusaders. As athletic director, Rockne needed a new basketball coach to turn around a floundering program in quick fashion. He didn't have to look very far.

Time Capsule

- Native Americans born within the territorial limits of the United States were granted U.S. citizenship on June 2, 1924, when President Calvin Coolidge signed the Indian Citizenship Act into law.

- J. Edgar Hoover was appointed head of the Federal Bureau of Investigation on May 4, 1924.

- The first state execution by gas was carried out in Nevada on February 8, 1924.

- On January 25, 1924, the first ever Winter Olympic Games opened in Chamonix, France. Less than four months later, the Summer Olympics began in Paris.

- On May 17, 1924, Notre Dame students disrupted a Ku Klux Klan rally held in downtown South Bend.

RIGHT:
1923–24 BASKETBALL TEAM.

66

Irish Legend

Clem Crowe began a Notre Dame and family tradition on December 8, 1923. The 6-9 sophomore forward started in a 22-21 loss to the University of Minnesota, a game which also marked the Irish coaching debut of George Keogan.

Over the next 15 years, the family from Lafayette, Indiana, would send six more brothers to play basketball for Notre Dame. Between 1923 and 1938, only one season (1934-35) did not feature the name "Crowe" on the roster.

Clem played from 1923 to 1926, Edward from 1924 to 1925, Francis from 1926 to 1929, Norbert from 1929 to 1932, Leo from 1931 to 1934, Michael from 1935 to 1938, and Emmett from 1936 to 1938.

Norbert and Francis both served as captains of their teams as seniors.

Irish Lore

LEFT:
1923 TENNIS TEAM.

In the early '20s, *The Scholastic* advocated for a course on campus that would attract nearly every student's attention and diligence—the history of football.

"Football is not scholarship, but neither is war," wrote *The Scholastic*. The anonymous article encouraged University administrators to realize that offering a class in the suggested subject matter would spread the word of Notre Dame's dominance in the football world and help tell the tale of the school's mission and purpose. The students argued that those who knew of Notre Dame's achievements in true scholarly and religious fields had only heard of the University because of its notoriously popular football team and its stars.

For some strange reason, the director of curriculum didn't take the students' advice.

1924-25

The 1920s

Time Capsule

- Wyoming's Nellie Tayloe Ross was elected the first woman governor in the United States in November 1924.

- Macy's held its first Thanksgiving Day Parade in New York City on November 27, 1924.

- The infamous Tri-State Tornado killed almost 700 people in Missouri, Illinois, and Indiana on March 18, 1925.

- Driving a Dusenberg Special, Peter DePaolo averaged 101.30 miles per hour at the 1925 Indianapolis 500, marking the first time a driver had maintained a speed over 100 miles per hour.

- Faced with a growing student population, the University of Notre Dame added 17 classrooms and seven laboratories to the Science Hall.

ABOVE:
JIM CROWLEY.

Irish Moment

The football planets finally aligned in Notre Dame's heavens in 1924.

Notre Dame and Knute Rockne secured that elusive consensus national championship, a title they had seen slip away in losses to Nebraska in both 1922 and 1923. But this year, Rockne's genius in scheduling, motivation, play calling, and training produced a magnificent undefeated season that solidified Notre Dame's place in football lore forever.

Back in 1924, the football team could make more money playing on the road than in relatively small Cartier Field which could hold only 22,000 fans. And hard as it is to believe, the first two home games of that championship year were far from sell-outs. Only 8,000 attended the season opener against Lombard, and just 10,000 saw a 34-0 win over Wabash.

But Rockne knew he could make money and gain exposure for his team and its stars by playing in huge venues all over the country.

A packed house of 55,000 saw Notre Dame defeat Army in the Polo Grounds. 40,000 more watched the Irish beat Princeton a week later. Nearly 30,000 showed up in Madison, Wisconsin; 45,000 braved the chilly Chicago wind in November at Soldier Field; and another 35,000 in Pittsburgh were there when Notre Dame downed Carnegie Tech, 40-19.

Rockne's 1924 unit did not have a weakness—or at least one that opponents could find. The offense, led by quarterback Harry Stuhldreher, fullback Elmer Layden, and halfbacks Jim Crowley and Don Miller, was a seasoned group that performed like a well-oiled machine. Immortalized by sportswriter Grantland Rice, "The Four Horsemen" still rate as one of the more proficient backfields in college football history. The defense that year allowed only 54 points in 11 games.

For the first time in history, Notre Dame agreed to play in the Rose Bowl, its first postseason appearance. Stanford, coached by the legendary Pop Warner, was undefeated and had tied one game during its impressive season. Concerned about the toll a long trip and the west coast heat could take on his team, Rockne tried to prepare his troops by taking them on a long train trip through Louisiana, Texas, and Arizona. The team stopped often for practices, winning fans through the south by participating in community celebrations.

Notre Dame earned its first bowl win in a January 1 game by taking advantage of eight Stanford turnovers and a critical goal-line stand in the fourth quarter. Notre Dame's offense, the bread and butter throughout the season, took a back seat to the defense, which scored two touchdowns on interception returns. The 27-10 Irish victory secured the national crown Rockne and Notre Dame wanted so desperately to wear.

Irish Legend

Even the most casual sports fan knows the story of "The Four Horsemen," Notre Dame's accomplished backfield, immortalized by *New York Herald Tribune* sportswriter Grantland Rice in his account of the 1924 Army-Notre Dame game at the Polo Grounds.

"Outlined against a blue-gray October sky, the Four Horsemen rode again.

"In dramatic lore, they are known as famine, pestilence, destruction and death. These are only aliases. Their real names are Stuhldreher, Miller, Crowley and Layden. They formed the crest of the South Bend cyclone before which another fighting Army team was swept over the precipice at the Polo Grounds this afternoon as 55,000 peered down on the bewildering panorama spread out on the green plain below."

George Strickler, a student publicity aid for Knute Rockne, made sure the name stuck. After arriving back in South Bend, Strickler borrowed four horses from a local livery stable and had a photographer take a picture with the four players—Don Miller, Elmer Layden, Jim Crowley, and Harry Stuhldreher—perched rather uncomfortably on the animals' backs. The wire services picked up the now famous photo, which ran in newspapers all across the country.

Stuhldreher, Crowley, Miller, and Layden played together for three seasons. As a unit, the Four Horsemen won 30 games and lost only twice—to the same opponent, Nebraska. After graduation their career paths took similar routes—all entered the coaching profession, and Layden, Crowley, and Stuhldreher became successful head coaches. Miller coached for four years as an assistant before beginning a law career in Cleveland.

All four were eventually inducted into the National Football Foundation Hall of Fame.

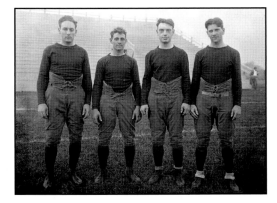

Irish Lore

The Four Horsemen might have stolen the thunder on that championship team, but Rockne relied just as much on his "Shock Troops" and "Seven Mules" to get the job done right.

Perhaps the most famous and competent second string in football, Rockne started his "Shock Troops" in every game of the 1924 season. They were indispensable to the innovative coach's game plan.

The "Seven Mules" made up an offensive line second to none. Its ability to block and hold off surging defenders allowed the Four Horsemen to rack up impressive offensive numbers.

The "Seven Mules" were center Adam Walsh, ends Ed Hunsinger and Chuck Collins, tackles Rip Miller and Joe Bach, and guards Noble Kizer and John Wiebel. Nothing stopped them—not even broken bones. Walsh played the Army game with two broken hands, and Bach played in the Rose Bowl with two cracked ribs. Who was tougher? It's hard to tell, although Walsh did leave the field during the Carnegie Tech game—after getting knocked unconscious six times.

LEFT:
THE FOUR HORSEMEN.

ABOVE:
IMAGES FROM NOTRE DAME'S FIRST ROSE BOWL APPEARANCE.

RIGHT:
1925 FOOTBALL TEAM.

Irish Moment

Knute Rockne was hoping to spend the money his football team made on the 1925 Rose Bowl to help replace Cartier Field. After all, more and more fans were clamoring for tickets, the team had just won a national championship, and the Fighting Irish were quickly becoming "America's team."

Even though he was athletic director and football coach, Rockne must have been a bit disappointed that the powers that be at the University decided the bowl money would be better spent on expanding and upgrading the Fieldhouse, home to the Irish basketball and track teams.

At the time, basketball was played on a clay court that had to be rolled and watered daily. But the bowl profits allowed the University to make the Fieldhouse larger and install an honest-to-goodness wooden floor.

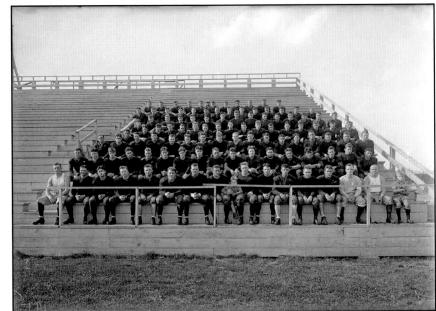

The rejuvenated facility with its shiny new floor was inaugurated in the season's opening game on December 7 with a 53-26 victory over Armour.

Notre Dame, which had not played a home game in the Fieldhouse for two seasons, finished the season with a 19-1 record, thanks in part to a 13-0 slate on its home court.

Fans surrounded the court, just two feet away from the action, making it a noisy and difficult place for opponents to play. Notre Dame did not lose a game in the updated Fieldhouse until the third contest of the 1928-29 season.

The Fieldhouse, which opened its doors to the basketball team in 1899, served as the squad's home until the opening of the Athletic and Convocation Center (now known as the Joyce Center) in the fall of 1968.

Notre Dame lost only 91 games in the Fieldhouse while winning 474 for an .839 winning percentage.

Irish Legend

Knute Rockne knew he needed the students on his side if he was ever going to achieve and maintain the sort of success he and the University both wanted in football.

Early in his career, he unofficially "employed" student managers to handle some of the less glamorous chores involved in taking care of a football team. Known as the Notre Dame "bums," these students staffed practices, took care of equipment, worked on travel arrangements, lugged baggage, and occasionally provided a "psychological" profile on a particular player to the head coach.

LEFT:
1925–26 BASKETBALL TEAM.

Since the team often traveled by train, the "bums" would stow away beneath the players' berths. Rockne claimed to be oblivious to the practice.

On a trip to Penn State in 1925, a suspicious conductor locked the compartments and turned up seven stowaways. Rockne publicly chastised the students for their behavior, but he never sent them home.

Irish Lore

Perhaps because his prayers had been answered, Knute Rockne became a Catholic.

His wife was a Catholic, as were his children. He was also surrounded by Catholics almost everywhere he looked. Yet, the Norwegian native never talked much about his religious beliefs or convictions.

In 1925, Rockne approached one of his former baseball players who had become a priest. He asked Father Vincent Mooney to give him instructions. Rockne was baptized on November 20 in the Log Chapel but didn't tell a soul.

The following day, Rockne's son, Knute Jr., was scheduled to make his First Communion at St. Edward's Hall. Father and son walked to the altar, with the son whispering in a low but stern voice that he could not participate in Communion because he wasn't Catholic. Rockne assured his son that things would be ok.

As father and son were kneeling at the Communion rail, Father Mooney saw the puzzled look on the young Rockne's face. He learned over and told young Knute, "Everything's all right, Junior; your dad was baptized yesterday."

Time Capsule

- Aviator Charles Lindbergh completed the first solo non-stop transatlantic flight in *The Spirit of St. Louis* May 20-21.

- Over 700,000 people were displaced by the Great Mississippi Flood from April 22 through May 5, 1927.

- The NBC Radio Network, created by Westinghouse, General Electric, and RCA, opened on November 15 with 24 stations.

- On September 23 in Philadelphia, Gene Tunney beat reigning title holder Jack Dempsey for the World Heavyweight Boxing championship.

- A flurry of building activity continued on the Notre Dame campus. Construction began on two dining halls which would have a combined seating capacity of 2,200.

RIGHT:
GEORGE KEOGAN.

Irish Moment

Notre Dame won a national championship in 1926-27—but it wasn't in football.

The fourth edition of coach George Keogan's Irish basketball team breezed through its 20-game schedule. The only setback was a 34-22 loss at Franklin College in mid-January. There were two close calls against Iowa and Detroit, but Notre Dame pulled out two one-point victories over those foes.

Senior captain John Nyikos averaged a team-high 8.6 points a game at the center position. A native of South Bend, Nyikos' team-mates included forwards Joe Jachym and Vince McNally and guards Ray Dahman and Louis Conroy. Only Conroy scored more than four points a game.

During the season, the Irish played several teams from the Big Ten as well as the region's other top basketball powers. Minnesota, Northwestern, Michigan State, Wisconsin, Marquette, Franklin, Wabash, Pittsburgh, and Detroit all fell to the Notre Dame five. The Irish clinched the "Western" championship with back-to-back season-ending wins at Creighton on March 4 and 5.

Although most basketball sportswriters thought Notre Dame was the best team in the land, there would be no cutting down the nets, no hoisting a big trophy, no huge community celebration. Keogan and the players didn't find out they were crowned national champions by the Helms Foundation until years later.

Founded in Los Angeles in the mid-1930s by Bill Schroader and Paul Helms, the Helms Foundation researched records to rank the nation's top teams dating back to 1901.

Nyikos was named All-American by the Helms Athletic Foundation, but not until 1943.

Irish Legend

Ed Walsh Jr., spent three seasons as a pitcher on the Notre Dame baseball team. The 6-1, 180-pounder from Meridian, Connecticut, posted an 18-6 record on the mound, while helping the Irish finish 51-27 from 1926 through 1928.

During his sophomore year, Walsh's dad, Ed, who had won two World Series games for the White Sox in 1906 and once recorded 40 victories in one season with the Chicago club, spent most of the spring helping George Keogan coach the baseball squad.

In 1933, the young Walsh, pitching in the minor leagues, stopped the 61-game hitting streak of an 18-year-old phenom, Joe DiMaggio.

Irish Lore

LEFT:
FOOTBALL TEAM COLLAGE.

Knute Rockne should have known better.

His 1926 football team looked as if it was cruising to its second national championship. Playing before capacity crowds in every venue but their own, the Irish had allowed just one touchdown in their first eight games while scoring 197 points. Beloit, Minnesota, Penn State, Northwestern, Georgia Tech, Indiana, Army, and Drake went down with barely a fight, even though the schedule, which took Notre Dame from coast to coast, was the toughest one Rockne could put together. Only two games remained— a trip to Carnegie Tech and a visit to the University of Southern California for the first game in what would become college football's signature rivalry.

Rockne was not worried about Carnegie Tech. He was so confident that his team would record its eighth shutout of the year that he sent his assistant Hunk Anderson to Pittsburgh while he went to Chicago to scout Navy, an opponent for 1927.

There was a shutout in the Steel City that late November day. But the Irish had the goose egg in that 19-0 blanking.

Rockne had subbed for head basketball coach Jesse Harper in 1920 while he went to a convention, and Notre Dame suffered a 48-12 drubbing at the hand of Purdue.

And some say the head coach doesn't make the difference.

Time Capsule

- Amelia Earhart became the first woman to pilot a plane across the Atlantic Ocean in June 1928.

- The Holland Tunnel, which linked New Jersey to New York City, opened to vehicular traffic on November 12, 1927.

- Mickey and Minnie Mouse made their debut in the animated short film, *Plane Crazy*.

- Norway's Sonia Henje won the first of her three Olympic gold medals in figure skating at the 1928 Winter Games in St. Moritz, Switzerland.

- By 1928, the number of faculty at the University of Notre Dame had grown to 175.

Irish Moment

November was not kind to Knute Rockne and his Irish in the fall of 1927.

After an exhilarating five straight victories, Notre Dame traveled to Minneapolis for a date with the Golden Gophers and their star guard Bronko Nagurski. Played in the snow, the game turned into a defensive struggle early on. Notre Dame recovered a fumbled punt at the Minnesota 18 and scored on the next play. The score stayed 7-0 until Nagurski fell on a misdirected snap at the Irish 15. Four plays later, Minnesota scored as time expired to tie the game.

The next week Army handed Notre Dame an 18-0 defeat before a capacity crowd of over 63,000 in Yankee Stadium.

However, the season ended on a high note. This time USC traveled east to play Notre Dame at Soldier Field in Chicago.

NOTRE DAME *vs* SOUTHERN CALIFORNIA

SOLDIER FIELD, CHICAGO
SATURDAY, NOVEMBER 26, 1927
PRICE 25 CENTS

The game a year earlier had ended in a 13-12 Irish win. Even though this was only the second time the two powerhouses would meet on the football field, expectations were high and so was the hype.

The official attendance is listed at 120,000, one of the largest crowds to ever watch a college football game. But many who were there said the crowd was much, much bigger. Fans were everywhere—on top of the colonnade and in the aisles.

Fans might have been packed in like sardines, but they got their money's worth. Notre Dame held on for a thrilling 7-6 win.

A Notre Dame-USC football game decided in the last minute became an ending that would become almost commonplace in this terrific national rivalry.

ABOVE:
NOTRE DAME GAME PROGRAM.

RIGHT:
SPRING-GAME STAR CHARLES WALSH.

Irish Legend

Halfback Christy Flanagan ran for over 1,800 yards and 15 touchdowns during his three years on the Notre Dame varsity.

A native of Port Arthur, Texas, Flanagan earned first-team All-America honors after leading the 1927 team in rushing with 731 yards on 188 carries.

Flanagan's running style and workmanship caught the attention of legendary sportswriter Grantland Rice with a 70-yard touchdown run which gave Notre Dame a 7-0 win over Army. Rice, who had dubbed Notre Dame's backfield the Four Horsemen just two years earlier, described Flanagan as the "lone horseman."

Irish Lore

On January 7, 1928, the Notre Dame basketball team defeated Pennsylvania, 30-28, at the Palestra, a brand new facility that held over 9,000 spectators in Philadelphia

That trip marked the first time an Irish basketball squad had played a game in a major city on the East coast.

But over the years, Notre Dame began making annual swings through that part of the country, and the Palestra became a favorite road haunt of the Irish, especially during the Digger Phelps' era.

Eventually, the popularity and sophistication of college basketball forced teams into bigger venues. But the loud, raucous crowds in gyms like the Palestra would be hard to duplicate.

RIGHT:
NOTRE DAME – ARMY GAME PROGRAM.

Irish Moment

Things were not going well for Knute Rockne.

To say his football team was struggling was perhaps an understatement. The Irish had lost two of their first six games. Hampered by injuries, the three toughest opponents on the schedule—Army, Carnegie Tech, and USC—were on the horizon. If Notre Dame did not beat Army, the odds were pretty good that Rockne would suffer his first losing season.

The critics were already saying he'd lost his touch. Rockne knew he'd need to dig deep in his bag of tricks to pull off the upset of the Cadets, who had won six straight.

It didn't take him long to come up with a plan. . .or the most famous pep talk in football history.

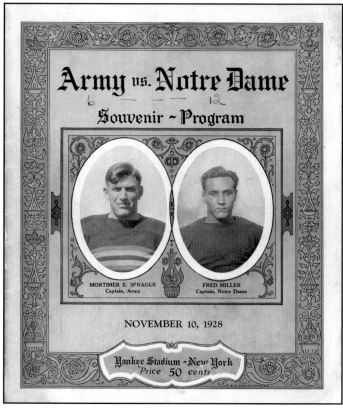

Before the game, Rockne gathered his players in the locker room. Instead of focusing on tactics and strategy, he talked about a former player—one who had died with just one game left in his senior season. That player was George Gipp.

These players had not known Gipp, but they knew of him. And they had been told over and over again that he might have been the greatest college football player who had ever lived.

Rockne told his players that he was with Gipp when he died. And that just before he passed, Gipp had asked his coach for one last favor. Rockne repeated Gipp's dying wish:

I've got to go, Rock. It's all right. I'm not afraid. Sometime, Rock, when the team is up against it, when things are wrong and the breaks are beating the boys—tell them to go in there with all they've got and win just one for the Gipper. I don't know where I'll be then, Rock. But I'll know about it, and I'll be happy.

Rockne then added his own words.

The day before he died Georgie Gipp asked me to wait until the situation seemed hopeless—then ask a Notre Dame team to go out and beat Army for him. This is the day and you are the team.

The rest, as they say, is history. Notre Dame came from behind with two touchdowns to eek out a 12-6 victory.

Over 3,000 students and local residents met the team at the New York Central train station in South Bend when Rockne and his players returned from the tremendous win. Each player was introduced to a deafening roar. Team captain Fred Miller thanked the crowd for its support, and finally the Notre Dame band led the crowd in a march back to campus.

Unfortunately, the night ended on a sad note. One student, John Gleason of Canadaigna, N.Y., died after being injured when a freight train knocked a baggage wagon down an embankment. Gleason, and three other fans, had been standing in front of the wagon and were hit when it came off the tracks.

Irish Legend

South Bend native Ed Smith became Notre Dame's first contemporary All-American in basketball after the 1928-29 season. The Christy Walsh Syndicate named the defensive specialist to its 11-man team.

He averaged 3.5 points per game that year and directed Notre Dame's offense from the guard position. Notre Dame finished the season at 15-5.

The following year, as a senior, Smith earned another spot on the All-America team after scoring 4.1 points per game. He helped the Irish to a 14-6 mark, including wins over Iowa, Marquette, Indiana, Michigan State, Butler, and Pennsylvania.

Irish Lore

Notre Dame track coach John P. Nicholson, who led the Irish from 1927-40, is considered one of the greatest innovators in the sport.

The starting block, which he created in the late '20s, added interest and ease to the short distance, hurdle and relay events.

Later in his career, Nicholson was injured by a wild discus throw in practice. Not about to miss time away from his team, the coach sat on the roof of a car and shouted instructions to his runners through a megaphone during training.

The roof top of the car worked so well Nicholson continued to use it after he recovered from his injury.

LEFT:
ED SMITH (CENTER).

BELOW:
CAPTAIN JOE ABBOTT AND COACH JOHN NICHOLSON.

1929-30

Irish Moment

Home field advantage is overrated—or at least it was during Notre Dame's 1929 national championship run.

Knute Rockne was finally getting what he wanted—a spanking new stadium. So while the bricks were being laid on what would later become known as "the house that Rock built," his teams played nine games at either the home fields of the opponents, a neutral site, or Soldier Field.

Rockne's Ramblers played in Bloomington, Baltimore, Pittsburgh, Atlanta, Chicago (four times) and New York ... and on six occasions, they left their head coach behind.

Rockne had developed phlebitis in October and was in constant pain. The doctors told him his life was in danger and urged him to stay in bed until the blood clot dissipated. He stayed away when he could, but more often than not, he went to practice and games, sitting in a wheelchair or resting in an ambulance. And when he couldn't go to practice, he had the team come to him.

"Practice" or at least some form of it was held at Rockne's house the week the Irish played Navy. He also telephoned every player to go over the game plan—again and again.

Still, the team seemed to respond to adversity. True, there were no huge blowouts like in past years. Instead, Notre Dame turned in solid performances week after week against a gritty schedule for close, but decisive victories.

When Notre Dame faced USC in mid-November at Solider Field, Rockne had himself wheeled into the locker room at halftime. The score was tied 6-6. However, after Rockne's pep talk, the Irish held on for a 13-12 win. A 7-0 victory at Army two weeks later secured the second national championship for Notre Dame and its legendary coach.

Irish Legend

Some quarterbacks are great passers; others are great runners; and a few are great leaders.

Frank Carideo, who stood just 5-7 and weighed 175 pounds, led Notre Dame to two national titles and a 19-0 record in the 1929 and 1930 seasons. He became Notre Dame's first con-

ABOVE:
KNUTE ROCKNE.

RIGHT:
FRED CARIDEO.

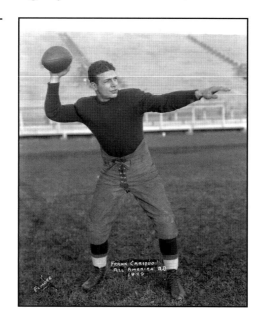

sensus All-American after both his junior and senior seasons. And he did it while never leading the team in passing.

A native of Mt. Vernon, New York, Carideo was a versatile natural athlete who also played defensive back and punted for the Irish.

Carideo was a multidimensional threat—he could throw a touchdown pass, catch a touchdown pass, rush for a touchdown, or return an interception, punt, or kick for a touchdown—and he could kick the extra point. He still ranks second on the all-time list for most total kick returns in a career with 96.

After graduation, Carideo served as an assistant coach at Purdue before becoming the head coach at the University of Missouri from 1932-1934. Two years later, he switched sports and coached basketball at Mississippi State while also serving as a football assistant. His coaching career at Iowa was interrupted by a stint in the navy as a lieutenant during World War II.

Carideo was inducted into the College Football Hall of Fame in 1954.

Irish Lore

Notre Dame added golf as a varsity sport in 1930, shortly after the opening of the University's first golf course, named after the land's donor, William J. Burke.

In 1922, two students from the South introduced their Northern peers to the sport, and golf took off as many students became "addicted" to the game. Student organizers put together a golf team in 1923, and it played two matches. A year later, the squad played six matches, winning five and losing the sixth to Northwestern by just one point.

Even though the University granted varsity status to golf in 1930, the sport went three years without a head coach. During that time, Notre Dame won 17 straight meets. The Irish golfers also claimed two state championships and twice finished among the nation's top three.

No one knows why the University finally instituted a serious search for a head coach. Things seemed to be going so well.

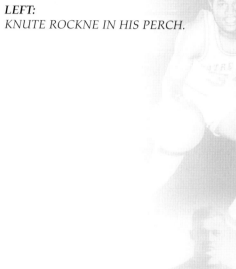

LEFT:
KNUTE ROCKNE IN HIS PERCH.

1930-31

ABOVE:
1930 NOTRE DAME VS. NAVY FOOTBALL PROGRAM.

Irish Moment

Knute Rockne's last team might have been his best.

Now in his 13th year as coach, Rockne had no way of knowing that the 1930 season would mark the end of a remarkable career in which he revolutionized college football, established standards few others could match, and became an American icon. In fact, the outlook for Rockne was particularly bright as the Irish prepared to defend their 1929 national title.

After playing the entire season away from home, Notre Dame now had the new 50,000-seat stadium that Rockne had wanted for so long. The coach's health, suspect at best through 1929, seemed on the upswing. And while his 1929 squad was awfully good, this one would be great.

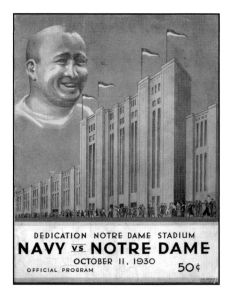

DEDICATION NOTRE DAME STADIUM
NAVY vs NOTRE DAME
OCTOBER 11, 1930
OFFICIAL PROGRAM   50¢

All-America quarterback Frank Carideo returned along with backs Marchy Schwartz, Marty Brill, and Joe Savoldi. Plus, the line of tackles Nordy Hoffmann and Joe Kurth, guards Tom Kassis and Bert Metzger, ends Ed Klosky and captain Tom Conley, and center Tommy Yarr made Irish fans forget—at least temporarily—about the Seven Mules.

Notre Dame played its season opener against Southern Methodist in the new stadium on October 4. The Irish won 20-14 but only 14,751 fans showed up—far less than what the new stadium could hold.

A week later, the stadium was dedicated during a game against Navy. This time over 40,000 fans attended, and the contest, which Notre Dame won 26-2, was also broadcast nationally on radio. Joseph Casasanta, a 1923 graduate of the University, composed an alma mater, "Notre Dame, Our Mother," as part of the ceremony. The Band of the Fighting Irish still concludes its game-day performances with the song at every home game.

The Irish breezed through their schedule, beating Carnegie Tech, Pittsburgh, Indiana, Pennsylvania, Drake, and Northwestern. The week of the Pennsylvania game, Charles Otis of Cleveland gave Rockne an Irish terrier dog named Brick Top Shuan-Rhu. The dog would be the first in a long line of terriers to act as the team's mascot.

For the season finale, Notre Dame traveled to USC, a team that most football experts felt was destined to wrestle the national championship away from Notre Dame and Rockne. But the game wasn't even close. Playing what Rockne himself called an almost perfect game, Notre Dame handed the Trojans a 27-0 loss and kept the national championship crown in South Bend for another year.

But the win at Notre Dame wasn't the last time Rockne was on the sidelines. On December 14, as a favor to his friend Jimmy Walker, the mayor of New York City, Rockne coached in a charity football game at the Polo Grounds to raise money for those left destitute by the Great Depression.

Irish Legend

Many in the late 1920s and early 1930s considered traveling by plane risky business, but Knute Rockne was a busy man and hated to waste time. An innovator in his own profession, he liked new things and airplane travel suited his lifestyle.

Approached by Universal Pictures about appearing in a movie about Notre Dame, Rockne agreed to come to Los Angeles to take part in the filming. After spending some time in Florida with his wife Bonnie, Rockne returned to South Bend and then traveled to Chicago and Kansas City by train. He would fly the rest of the way.

The plane, a Fokker Super Trimotor, carried two pilots, a steward, and six passengers. It left Kansas City in a light snow and encountered fog shortly after takeoff. The plane then crashed into a wheat field near Bazaar, Kansas. There were no survivors. The campus and the nation were stunned.

Rockne's funeral was held at the Church of the Sacred Heart on Holy Saturday. Hundreds of mourners, including nearly all of his former players, packed the church, while the overflow crowd waited outside. CBS Radio broadcast the funeral mass live across the nation.

The president of the University, Rev. Charles O'Donnell, delivered the sermon. "It is fitting that he [Rockne] should be brought here to his beloved Notre Dame and that his body should rest awhile in this church where the light of Faith broke upon his happy soul. ... He might have gone to any university in the land and been gladly received and forever cherished there. But he chose Our Lady's School, he honored her in the monogram he earned and wore, he honored her in the principles he inculcated and the ideals he set up in the lives of the young men under his care. He was her own true son."

During 13 years at Notre Dame, Knute Rockne won six national championships and five of his teams posted perfect records. He was inducted into the National Football Foundation Hall of Fame in 1951, its first year of existence.

Irish Lore

Rockne's death continued to cast a dark shadow over the campus during the last few months of the 1930-1931 school year. But one Notre Dame athlete and another Irish team gave the University something to celebrate with impressive performances at their respective NCAA championships.

Alex Wilson, who would later become Notre Dame's longtime track coach, captured an NCAA title at the outdoor championship meet with a win in the 400-meters and a second-place finish in the 880-yard dash. Wilson, who had placed fourth in the 400 the previous season, won All-America recognition for the second consecutive year.

Still without a coach, the Notre Dame golf team placed third in the NCAA Tournament played at the Olympia Fields Country Club outside of Chicago. Bill Redmond advanced to the third round and received second-team All-America honors. A year earlier, his teammate Larry Moller was named to the first team, becoming Notre Dame's first All-American in golf.

1931-32

Time Capsule

- United States citizens were required to pay a gas tax (1 cent on the gallon) with the passage of the Revenue Act of 1932.

- On March 1, 1932, the infant son of Charles Lindbergh and Anne Morrow Lindbergh was kidnapped. The child was found dead 10 weeks later.

- Former Olympic gold medal swimmer Johnny Weissmuller starred in the title role of *Tarzan the Ape Man*.

- On February 4, the 1932 Winter Olympics opened in Lake Placid, N.Y. Los Angeles hosted the Summer Olympics in July.

- The University opened a new building for the College of Foreign and Domestic Commerce.

RIGHT:
FRANK "NORDY" HOFFMAN.

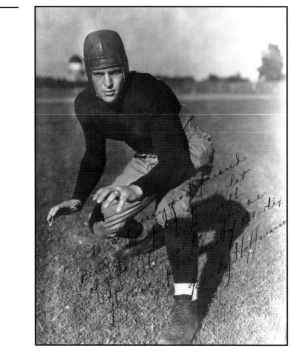

Irish Moment

A familiar face returned to campus to help the Notre Dame community move forward after Rockne's death. And another one was given the almost impossible task of filling the football coaching legend's shoes.

Former football and basketball coach and athletic director Jesse Harper left his Kansas ranch and came back to South Bend for his second go-round as athletic director. Heartley "Hunk" Anderson, who had earned All-America honors as a guard for Rockne in 1921, assumed the head coaching duties. Anderson had served as an assistant for his former mentor from 1922-26 while he played for the Chicago Bears. He then coached at St. Louis University for four years before he re-joined Rockne as his assistant for the 1930 season.

In 1931, Anderson's team shut out six of its first seven opponents for a 6-0-1 record. Then, USC came to town. For the first time in its short history, Notre Dame Stadium boasted a capacity crowd of 50,731. Ironically, more fans watched the Irish on the road than at home in the late '20s and early '30s. Tickets in South Bend were normally relatively easy to find, but not on this November day.

Interest in the game was high. An estimated 10 million fans listened to the game on radio. The Irish controlled the action early, but as is typical in a Notre Dame-USC contest, the tide turned very quickly. In the fourth period, USC's substitute quarterback led the Trojans to a pair of touchdowns, then kicked a field goal in the last minute of the game that gave the visitors a 16-14 win.

The following week, Notre Dame traveled to Yankee Stadium for the season finale against Army. This time, the Irish were on the short end of the shutout stick as the Cadets won, 12-0.

Four players earned All-America recognition—Marchy Schwartz, Joe Kurth, Tommy Yarr, and Nordy Hoffmann. But things were not the same without Rockne and wouldn't be again for a long time.

Irish Legend

Frank "Nordy" Hoffmann never played football while in high school in Seattle, Wash. But his size, 6-foot-2, 224 pounds, seemed suited for the sport, and he decided to give it a try as a walk-on.

He made the varsity in 1930 as a junior and earned his first letter, along with a

82

national championship. The next year he moved to right guard and received All-America honors even though he was banged up most of the season. He played the entire game against Army with torn knee ligaments.

An excellent shot putter, Hoffmann was awarded three monograms as a member of the Notre Dame track team.

Hoffmann's work ethic, passion, and drive, which had helped him excel on the athletic field, served him well in his professional career after graduation. After serving as head of the United Steel Workers legislative office, he worked as executive director of the Democratic Senatorial Campaign Committee. He then became sergeant-at-arms of the United States Senate before retiring in 1984.

Hoffmann was inducted into the National Football Foundation Hall of Fame in 1978.

Irish Lore

The legendary Edward "Moose" Krause would eventually leave an indelible mark on Notre Dame and intercollegiate athletics in many ways.

Recruited by Rockne, Krause was a freshman in 1930, Rockne's last season, and first-year students were ineligible to play in varsity games in those days.

Although he started at tackle on the 1931 football team, the 6-3, 217-pound sophomore really stood out on the basketball court. On December 31, 1931, he came off the bench to score 12 points in a 22-21 victory at Northwestern.

He became the team's starting center and led the Irish to an 18-2 mark. Krause averaged 7.7 points that season and

became Notre Dame's first consensus All-American in basketball. He would repeat the feat as a junior and senior, becoming only the second player in NCAA history to be named to three consensus All-America teams. The first player to earn that honor was John Wooden.

1932-33

The 1930s

RIGHT:
EDWARD "MOOSE" KRAUSE.

Irish Moment

Notre Dame's golf team finally got a coach.

Rev. George Holderith took over the program and promptly led the Irish to a 6-0 record and a third-place finish in the NCAA tournament, held at the Buffalo (New York) Country Club. Notre Dame golfer Johnny Banks, a sophomore from La Grange, Illinois, shared medalist honors at the championship event.

Known as the "father of Notre Dame golf," Holderith and his teams dominated the sport in the 1930s. Under his direction, the Irish won eight state titles and put together seven consecutive top-10 finishes in the NCAA Tournament. In 1934, Notre Dame became the first school to ever qualify all five of its team members for the NCAA match play championship.

Irish Legend

Arch Ward never played baseball, or any other sport for that matter. But he created a concept that turned into an annual mid-summer classic, an idea whose format has been tweaked and twitched in nearly every major and minor sport from professional leagues to youth programs.

Ward had served as Notre Dame's first sports publicity director while a student in 1920. After graduating, he worked for the newspaper in Rockford, Illinois, before moving to the *Chicago Tribune*, first as a sports writer, then as a columnist.

Chicago was the host city for the 1933 World's Fair, and the mayor of the Windy City asked Ward to come up with an idea for a sporting event. Ward knew that every team in both the National and American leagues had a day off on July 6, so he suggested an all-star game.

Although many owners expressed resistance, Ward finally won them over to the idea. *The Tribune* would pay expenses and donate any earnings to the Professional Ball Players of America, a charity organization.

The first Major League Baseball All-Star game was played July 6, 1933, in Chicago's Comiskey Park.

Today, the most valuable player award bears Arch Ward's name.

A year after creating the Baseball All-Star classic, Ward put together a college football all-star game, also sponsored by the *Chicago Tribune*, in Soldier Field. That game, which continued on an annual basis through 1976, featured several Notre Dame participants throughout the years.

Irish Lore

As a junior, Moose Krause continued to dominate at the center position in college basketball.

The team had struggled during the first half of the season, posting a 6-6 record through the third week of January. However, Coach George Keogan had turned the team's fortunes around, and the Irish were working on an eight-game winning streak when they traveled to Hinkle Fieldhouse in Indianapolis for a game with Butler. The Bulldogs had taken the first meeting between the two teams earlier in the year in South Bend. And when Notre Dame missed a shot with less than a minute to go, it appeared that Butler would make a clean sweep of the Irish that year.

In the scramble for the rebound, "Moose" had been knocked to the floor. He picked up the loose ball, and shooting from the supine position, heaved the ball through the hoop to send the game into overtime. Notre Dame finally won, 42-41.

When Keogan entered the Fieldhouse for practice the following day, he found his players practicing shots while lying on the floor.

Time Capsule

- On October 10, 1933, a United Airlines Boeing 247 exploded near Chesterton, Indiana, west of South Bend. It was the first proven case of air sabotage in commercial airline history.

- On January 1, 1934, Alcatraz became a federal prison.

- Public enemy number one, John Dillinger, was mortally wounded by FBI agents outside a Chicago theatre.

- On August 19, 1934, boys competed in the first All-American Soap Box Derby in Dayton, Ohio.

- Reverend John O'Hara, C.S.C., became the 13th president of the University of Notre Dame in the summer of 1934.

RIGHT:
COACH HUNK ANDERSON RECEIVES A
TROPHY FROM MRS. KNUTE ROCKNE.

Irish Moment

Never follow a legend.

Perhaps no one ever passed that advice along to Hunk Anderson. Perhaps he knew that, when he stepped into the head coaching job after Knute Rockne's death, he was taking on an impossible task. As a former player and assistant coach for Rockne, Anderson probably knew he had to at least try to carry on the tradition and keep the legendary coach's legacy alive.

Anderson's first two teams—in 1931 and 1932—were average, by Notre Dame standards. His first squad won six games and the second one had seven victories. But in 1933, the Irish hit bottom with a disappointing and unacceptable 3-5-1 mark, Notre Dame's first losing season since 1888.

Defense was always a strong point under Anderson, but the prolific offenses Irish fans had come to expect with Rockne were gone. In 1933, Notre Dame scored only 32 points in nine games and were shut out six times, including a second consecutive blanking by arch rival USC. As a head coach, Anderson failed to deliver one win in three tries against the Trojans.

Notre Dame traveled to Yankee Stadium for its season finale against Army. The Cadets had rolled up 33 points to Notre Dame's zero over the last two seasons. In 1933, Army was undefeated and appeared to have a lock on the national championship. With just five minutes to go in the game, the Cadets held a 12-0 lead over the Irish.

But Notre Dame worked its magic just one more time for Anderson. Moose Krause jump-started the rally by blocking an Army punt at the Notre Dame 48-yard line. End Wayne Millner scored the first Irish touchdown . The defense held Army and forced the Cadets to punt again. This time it was Millner who blocked the punt and scored on the recovery. Time was running out for Army, and Red Tobin snagged an interception to ice the incredible come-from-behind victory for Notre Dame and Anderson.

After the game, however, athletic director Jesse Harper and Anderson announced their resignations. They had moved Notre Dame through its mourning period. It was time to pass the torch to someone else.

Irish Legend

Wayne Millner had a habit of being in the right place at the right time.

The Salem, Massachusetts, native came off the bench as a sophomore in the season finale against Army. His heroics—including scoring one touchdown and blocking a late Cadet punt—pushed him into the spotlight.

As a senior, he caught the game-winning touchdown pass from halfback Bill Shakespeare in the 1935 Notre Dame-Ohio State matchup, which was often billed as the "game of the century."

Selected as an All-American after that season, the three-time monogram winner also competed in the College Football All-Star Game the following summer in Chicago.

Drafted by the Boston Redskins in the first-ever NFL draft in 1936, he moved with the team to Washington, D.C. In the 1937, he caught two touchdown passes from quarterback Sammy Baugh to help the Redskins beat the Chicago Bears in the NFL Championship game.

Millner served as an assistant coach for his alma mater for one season under Frank Leahy. He was elected to the National Football Foundation Hall of Fame in 1990.

Irish Lore

Although the Notre Dame basketball team had its 22-game winning streak snapped with a 39-34 loss at Pittsburgh, the Irish finished the season at 20-4. Moose Krause capped off his playing career with his third consecutive selection as a consensus All-American. The 6-3 center averaged 8.5 points and captained the squad as a senior.

Krause was so dominant in the paint that the NCAA implemented the three-second rule to keep him out of the lane. But even that couldn't completely stop the big guy from Chicago.

1934-35

The 1930s

Time Capsule

- The FBI killed the notorious Ma Barker and her gang in a shootout on January 16, 1935.

- The world's first parking meters appeared in Oklahoma City.

- A great dust storm devastated areas in Eastern New Mexico, Colorado, and western Oklahoma on April 14, 1935.

- The Detroit Tigers' Mickey Cochrane and the St. Louis Cardinals' Dizzy Dean were named most valuable players in their respective leagues for the 1934 season.

- With the Depression "over," the University reactivated its building expansion plan. A new infirmary would become the first in the area generally referred to as the northeast quad.

ABOVE:
ELMER LAYDEN WITH HIS STAFF.

RIGHT:
WILLIAM SHAKESPEARE.

Irish Moment

One of the Four Horsemen returned to save the day.

Summoned by the good fathers at his alma mater, Layden knew it would take time to restore the football program to the level of success it had attained under Rockne.

But Layden, who had been a head coach at Columbia College in Iowa and at Duquesne in Pittsburgh, used his experience, savvy, and eye for detail to restore the winning tradition at Notre Dame in his first season.

The Irish lost their first game, 7-6, to Texas, a team coached by former Notre Dame star Jack Chevigny. But the Irish then reeled off three straight wins over Purdue, Carnegie Tech, and Wisconsin. Two losses on the road to Pittsburgh and Navy followed. But Layden revived fans' hopes with season-ending wins at Northwestern, against Army at Yankee Stadium, and best of all, over USC in Los Angeles.

The 6-3 record was not spectacular by any means. But to most Irish followers, Notre Dame football appeared headed in the right direction.

Left tackle Joe Sullivan, who had replaced Moose Krause at tackle, was elected captain for the 1935 season. However, tragedy struck the football squad again in March, just four short years after Rockne's death. Sullivan died from complications of pneumonia. Once again, the Irish had to bury one of their own.

Irish Legend

Bill Shakespeare probably became a good football player so people wouldn't confuse him with that other Shakespeare guy.

Although best remembered for the touchdown pass he threw in 1935 that gave Notre Dame a win over Ohio State in the "game of the century," Shakespeare was indispensable to Elmer Layden's Irish offense in a variety of ways.

The native of Staten Island, New York, was Notre Dame's top passer and kickoff returner as a junior and senior. He also led the team in rushing with 374 yards and four touchdowns his final season. The 5-foot-11, 179-pound Shakespeare averaged over 40 yards a punt throughout his career and still owns the record for the longest punt, an 86-yard boot against Pittsburgh in 1935.

Selected as a consensus All-American in 1935, Shakespeare became the first Notre Dame player selected as the top pick in the NFL draft in 1936 when the Pittsburgh Steelers chose him.

There were no multimillion-dollar signing bonuses in those days, so Shakespeare went into business instead of playing professionally. He also served in World War II, winning four battle stars and the Bronze Star. He was inducted into the National Football Foundation Hall of Fame posthumously in 1983.

Irish Lore

Time was not on George Keogan's side—at least during a home game against Pittsburgh on February 16, 1935.

After losing Moose Krause to graduation, the Notre Dame basketball team struggled to find its offensive identity in 1934-35. The Irish had lost four games by four or less points and owned a 10-6 record heading into the contest with Pitt, who had beaten Notre Dame by four just a month earlier in Pittsburgh.

Keogan, however, had the home court advantage this time—Notre Dame was playing in the Fieldhouse, where

LEFT:
KEOGAN TALKS STRATEGY WITH HIS TEAM.

BELOW:
KEOGAN WITH TEAM MEMBERS MIKE AND EMMETT CROWE.

the Irish had lost just 14 times over the last 10 seasons. What he hadn't expected, however, was to play the longest game of his life.

There were no electronic scoreboards in those days, so time was kept at the scorer's table by an official with a stopwatch. At some point in the second half of the see-saw game, the referee, Frank Lane, was told by the timekeeper that there were 12 and a half minutes left to go in the game. When Lane sensed the game was nearing its end—time wise—he asked the timekeeper again, how much time remained. When the timekeeper looked at his stopwatch—it still read 12 and a half minutes.

Lane decided the only fair thing to do was to play the rest of the game by restarting the clock at 12 and a half minutes. The Panthers came from behind and handed Notre Dame a 27-25 defeat.

Don't ask what Keogan did to that stopwatch. At least its operator walked out without a scratch.

Time Capsule

- On August 14, 1935, President Franklin Roosevelt signed the Social Security Act into law.

- Three tornados killed 203 people and injured over 1,800 in Gainesville, Georgia, on April 6, 1936.

- Parker Brothers unveiled the board game Monopoly on November 5, 1935.

- The University of Chicago's Jay Berwanger won the first Heisman Memorial Trophy, presented by the Downtown Athletic Club of New York to the nation's top collegiate football player.

- On December 9, 1935, President Franklin Roosevelt came to the University to accept an honorary degree before 5,000 students and visitors in the Fieldhouse.

ABOVE:
NOTRE DAME UPSETS OHIO STATE.

Irish Moment

"Game of the Century" might have been an understatement.

The 1935 Notre Dame and Ohio State contest had all the earmarks of being a classic. Both teams were undefeated, each had legions of fans all across America, and the two schools boasted rich and proud histories in college football.

No one thought the game would be a toss up. Anyone who knew anything about college football thought the No. 1 ranked Buckeyes would manhandle the Irish—partly because the game was in Columbus and probably because Ohio State was just that good.

Ohio State's offense was indeed unstoppable in the first half. The Buckeyes took an early 13-0 lead, and their defense completely stymied Notre Dame's ability to move the football.

But Layden didn't panic—even though his troops were playing before 81,000 fans, mostly of the Scarlet and Gray persuasion. In his halftime talk, he told his team, "They won the first half. Now it's your turn. Go out and win this half for yourselves."

Neither team scored in the third quarter, but quarterback Andy Pilney moved the Irish to the Ohio State 12-yard line. Three plays later, Steve Miller finally found the end zone, but Notre Dame couldn't convert the extra point.

Miller went from hero to goat when he fumbled what looked like a go-ahead touchdown in the fourth quarter. Ohio State got the ball back but couldn't retain possession and had to punt with just three minutes left.

Starting from his own 20-yard line, Pilney eluded several would-be tacklers to get the Irish across midfield. He then threw a 33-yard touchdown pass to Mike Layden. But Notre Dame missed the conversion kick—again—and Ohio State clung to its 13-12 lead.

Ohio State recovered the onside kick, but once again the Buckeyes could not hang onto the football. Second-string Irish center Henry Pojman fell on the ball just across midfield on the OSU 49-yard line.

Pilney scrambled 30 yards on a broken play to Buckeyes' 19-yard line where he was forced out of bounds. But the scrappy quarterback could not get up. He had torn cartilage in his knee and had to be carried off the field on a stretcher.

Bill Shakespeare took his place. He promptly threw the ball—right into the hands of an Ohio State defender who dropped what would have been a game-winning interception. Shakespeare had another chance.

This time, with 32 seconds left, the ball was snapped to the fullback who handed off to Shakespeare. He then fired the ball to Wayne Millner, who caught the pass in the end zone for the improbable 18-13 victory.

No doubt about it ... Notre Dame football was back.

Irish Legend

Sophomore forward John Moir led the Notre Dame basketball team to a 22-2-1 record and the Helms Foundation National Championship in 1936.

A 6-foot-2 native of Niagara Falls, New York, Moir averaged 11.2 games that season and was named national player of the year by the Helms Foundation. He almost outscored one opponent by himself—tallying 25 points in a 43-35 win over Pittsburgh.

Although he had never played basketball until enrolling at Notre Dame, Moir paced the Irish in scoring all three seasons on the varsity. He also was named a consensus All-American in 1935-36, 1936-37, and 1937-38. During his tenure, Notre Dame posted a 62-8-1 mark.

The lone tie, almost unheard of in basketball, occurred during Notre Dame's annual New Year's Eve date with Northwestern. The scorekeeper failed to record Ray Meyer's free throw so the teams left the court thinking the Wildcats had claimed a 20-19 victory over the Irish. By the time someone realized the mistake, the players had already showered and dressed. The teams had to settle for a tie.

Irish Lore

Jim McKenna, one of Notre Dame's backup quarterbacks, did not make the travel squad for the game in Columbus.

Disappointed, but not deterred, McKenna snuck aboard the team train and hid in a berth with the help of his teammates. Once in Columbus, however, McKenna could not find a ticket anywhere, and scalpers wouldn't settle for anything less than $50, an exorbitant amount in those days. Somehow he talked his way into the locker room, and when coach Elmer Layden spotted him, he told McKenna to get dressed. He obliged, but without his pads.

McKenna did not see action until late in the game. Out of subs, Layden pulled McKenna aside and sent him in with what turned out to be the winning play.

Not a bad way to watch the "Game of the Century."

1936-37

Time Capsule

- Adolph Hitler refused to shake Jesse Owens' hand after the African-American won two gold medals in the 1936 Olympic Games in Berlin.

- The United Auto Workers Union staged its first sit-down strike on December 30, 1936.

- Howard Hughes set an air record by flying from Los Angeles to New York City in seven hours, 28 minutes, and 25 seconds on January 19, 1937.

- Owner Samuel D. Riddle's horse War Admiral won the Triple Crown in 1937.

- Students moved into Cavanaugh Hall, the first of three new dormitories built in the late '30s by Father O'Hara. Zahm Hall opened its doors in 1937, and Breen-Phillips accepted occupants two years later.

ABOVE:
GEORGE KEOGAN DIAGRAMS A PLAY.

RIGHT:
PAUL NOWAK.

Irish Moment

A longtime Notre Dame basketball tradition took root in 1935-36 and solidified one of the sport's best collegiate rivalries in 1936-37.

Although Notre Dame and Kentucky had played in 1929, Irish coach George Keogan and the Wildcats' young mentor Adolph Rupp struck a deal to play each other on a home-and-home basis from 1936 through 1942. But Kentucky did not have a facility big enough to support the number of fans who wanted to see the games. So when Notre Dame played Kentucky "away," the games would occur in Louisville.

In its first trip to the Southern city, Notre Dame downed the Wildcats, 41-28, at the Armory. Paul Nowak scored 16 points, while John Moir added 12 in the Irish victory.

Over the years, Notre Dame and Kentucky would play in Louisville on 31 occasions. Only nine times was the bus trip back to South Bend a happy one.

Irish Legend

Paul Nowak, a 6-foot-6 center from South Bend, anchored the middle on a Notre Dame basketball team that would go 62-8-1 during his three seasons as a starter.

During his first varsity season, Nowak averaged 7.0 points per game, which marked improvement to 7.2 his junior year and 7.5 his senior season. Nowak, and teammate John Moir, became the school's second and third three-time consensus All-Americans in basketball. Moose Krause had been the first. Over a seven-season span, from 1931-32 through 1937-38, a Notre Dame center earned All-America acclaim six times.

Those two centers were almost single-handedly responsible for two rule changes. The three-second rule was meant to neutralize Krause's dominance in the lane.

Before 1937-38, teams gathered at center court for a jump ball after every score. Now, the team that had given up a basket was awarded the ball out of bounds. Notre Dame coach George Keogan vigorously opposed the new guidelines, meant to keep his talented centers in check.

After graduation, Nowak played four seasons for the Akron Firestones in the National Basketball League

Irish Lore

Pedro DeLandero became Notre Dame's first tennis coach in 1934. In his six years at the helm, the Irish never produced a winning season.

However, DeLandero laid the foundation for enviable success in another Notre Dame sport—fencing.

A 1911 graduate of Notre Dame, DeLandero left his native Mexico during the revolution and returned to his alma mater as a full-time Spanish professor and part-time tennis coach.

Injured in a 1934 car accident, DeLandero's doctor recommended he take up swimming to help the rehabilitation process. But DeLandero, who had a fear of water, gravitated to fencing instead.

He started a small fencing club for students, and in 1936, the sport was granted varsity status.

DeLandero, however, returned to Mexico and turned over the coaching reins in both tennis and fencing to Walter Langford, who would build both sports into nationally respected programs.

LEFT:
PEDRO DeLANDERO.

93

1937-38

RIGHT:
RAY MEYER.

Irish Moment

The 1937-38 collegiate basketball season added a new wrinkle. The Metropolitan Basketball Writers Association of New York had put together a postseason tournament that would feature six teams—three from New York area colleges and universities and another trio from the top basketball squads in the country. Dubbed the National Invitation Tournament, the games would be played in Madison Square Garden.

Notre Dame's dazzling 20-3 record for the 1937-38 season grabbed the invitation committee's attention. All three losses had come on the road and two were by

less than two points. The only significant loss was a 12-point defeat at the hands of Big Ten champion Minnesota. Plus, the Irish-Catholic team was sure to be a big draw in the Garden. It was there Notre Dame had beaten NYU, 50-38, in the last week of February.

However, University officials had instituted a ban on postseason play after the football team's participation in the 1925 Rose Bowl.

So, Notre Dame, which would have been a sure-fire contender for the title, had to say, "Thanks, but no thanks."

Irish Legend

Chuck Sweeney, an end on Elmer Layden's 1935-37 teams, played both football and basketball during his first season of eligibility at Notre Dame. But the 6-foot, 179-pound native of Bloomington, Illinois, decided to concentrate on football after his sophomore year. The decision proved to be a good one as Sweeney became a starter on both offense and defense as a junior.

During his senior year, Sweeney almost single-handedly beat Northwestern. The Irish were ranked 12th at the time, but the Wildcats had held Notre Dame scoreless through much of the contest in Evanston. So Sweeney took matters into his own hands. After blocking a Northwestern punt, he recovered the ball in the end zone for the only touchdown of the day. He also intercepted a pass, downed a Notre Dame punt at the Wildcat one-yard line, and recovered two fumbles—although he needed help with one of them. About the only thing Sweeney did not do that day was kick the extra point.

But heroics were nothing new to the All-American. Earlier in what would be a 6-2-1 season for Notre Dame, Sweeney had tackled a Navy running back in the end zone to record a game-winning safety in the final two minutes.

Sweeney participated in the 1938 College All-Star and the East-West Shrine games following his final campaign at Notre Dame.

LEFT:
CHUCK SWEENEY.

BELOW:
RAY MEYER.

Irish Lore

The Notre Dame basketball team's 15-game winning streak that spanned two seasons was in danger of being snapped by Wisconsin on a cold December night in the Fieldhouse.

The Badgers, not exactly a powerhouse in the Big Ten, were leading the Irish at halftime. Disgusted by his team's play, coach George Keogan turned the coaching reins over to his captain, Ray Meyer, who was injured and could not play. Keogan then disappeared into the stands and watched what would become the beginning of a hall of fame coaching career for the senior from Chicago. Under Meyer's tutelage, Notre Dame stormed back for a 33-31 win over Wisconsin.

The 15-game winning streak was extended to 18 before Illinois downed the Irish, 33-32, in overtime in late December.

1938-39

Time Capsule

- The Thousand Islands Bridge, connecting the United States with Canada, opened on August 18, 1938.

- The New England Hurricane of 1938 killed 600 people on Long Island on September 21, 1938.

- On October 30, 1938, the radio broadcast of Orson Welles' adaptation of *The War of the Worlds* caused mass panic in various parts of the United States.

- The University of Oregon won the first NCAA men's basketball championship.

- The Rockne Memorial Building, which featured an indoor swimming pool, handball and squash courts, basketball courts, and weight rooms, was dedicated in memory of the late Notre Dame football coach during commencement exercises in June.

RIGHT:
ELMER LAYDEN.

Irish Moment

This might have been Elmer Layden's year. Things certainly started off well.

Notre Dame sent Kansas reeling with a 52-0 victory to open the season. Five substitutes scored touchdowns, and the offense ran for 392 yards, the best total in years.

However, the Irish would not find the going that smooth again that season. The offense would never again score more than 19 points in a game. Thank goodness the defense was that good.

Although every game was close, Notre Dame marched through the slate. Beating Georgia Tech and Illinois by identical 14-6 scores, the 3-0 Irish headed into the game against 13th-ranked Carnegie Tech as the fifth team in the rankings. Notre Dame notched a less-than-impressive 7-0 win but rebounded the following week to beat Army 19-7 before a capacity crowd in Yankee Stadium. Two shutouts against Navy and 12th-ranked Minnesota moved the Irish to number one in the polls.

Notre Dame survived a 9-7 nail biter, setting up a season finale in Los Angeles between the top-ranked Irish and USC, ranked number eight.

The Irish offense turned the ball over five times that day, and USC notched a 13-0 win. The national championship, which Rockne had managed to claim six times, still eluded his former pupil.

Irish Legend

Two-time All-American Ed "Beefy" Beinor played left tackle and anchored the Notre Dame line during his junior and senior seasons.

A native of Harvey, Illinois, Beinor also earned three monograms as a member of the Notre Dame track team. He participated in the 1938 Lithuanian Olympics and won the shot put event with a distance of 47-11.

After graduation, Beinor played in the 1939 College All-Star game. He continued playing professionally with the St. Louis Gunners, the Washington Redskins, and the Chicago Cardinals. He retired from football in 1942 to enter the Marine Corps and serve in World War II.

Irish Lore

George Keogan knew his 1938-39 basketball squad would be hard pressed to duplicate the success of its three previous predecessors.

Keogan had lost his All-Americans and gutsy captain Ray Meyer had finally graduated. Still, he had a strong nucleus of players with experience.

After going 3-3 in the first six games of the season, the Irish put together an impressive 10-game win streak that included a 42-37 win over Kentucky in Louisville, marking the fourth straight time Keogan had taken the upper hand in a battle with Adolph Rupp. The Irish had shot an incredible 22-for-24 at the free throw line, which stood as a team record for several years.

Keogan's squad finished the 1938-39 and 1939-40 seasons with identical 15-6 records.

1939-40

Irish Moment

Notre Dame had come oh-so-close to a national title in 1938.

Although Elmer Layden's squad had lost three All-Americans, his entire backfield returned, which helped raise expectations for another run at the crown.

The Irish won their first three games, all at home, by the slimmest of margins. Third-string quarterback John Kelleher's field goal beat Purdue in the season opener. Notre Dame hung on for a 17-14 victory over Georgia Tech and came from behind to hand feisty Southern Methodist a 20-19 setback.

Although the kicking game was the highlight of the Irish offense, Notre Dame had moved to No. 2 in the polls by the October 21 game against Navy at Cleveland. The Irish barely won, 14-7, and the next week managed to squeak by Carnegie Tech, 7-6.

Those two close calls dropped Notre Dame to fourth, but a 14-0 shutout of Army at Yankee Stadium pushed the Irish back up to No. 3.

But whatever championship hopes Notre Dame fans were harboring went out the window the following week when the Irish traveled to Iowa City to play the Hawkeyes and their eventual Heisman Trophy winner, Nile Kinnick. Kinnick accounted for all seven Iowa points, scoring a touchdown and kicking the extra point. Notre Dame scored late in the third quarter, but its kicking game, which had pulled a win out of the hat so many times before, failed when the PAT missed the uprights.

Notre Dame ended the season with 7-0 win over Northwestern at home, scoring in the last 3:30 of the game, and a 20-12 loss to No. 4 USC.

There were too many close calls on both sides of the win-loss ledger for Notre Dame to take great satisfaction from a 7-2 season.

Irish Legend

Greg Rice, a three-year member of the Notre Dame track and cross-country teams, was recognized as the nation's top amateur athlete in 1940 when he won the prestigious Sullivan Award. That honor capped an incredible career that saw him go undefeated in 65 major indoor and outdoor races.

During a three-year span, Rice set 10 world records in six different events.

In 1940, his time of 13:51 in the three-mile run at the national championships obliterated the previous standard.

Rice earned All-America recognition three times in both cross-country and track at Notre Dame, winning the NCAA two-mile title in 1937 and 1939 and finishing second in 1938.

He also captured first place at the inaugural NCAA cross-country championships in 1938 with a time of 20:12.9 over the four-mile course. Rice's performance helped Notre Dame to a runner-up team finish at the event.

Because of his endurance and versatility, Rice is often considered by many track experts as the greatest distance runner in U.S. track history.

Despite Rice's impressive record of success, his collegiate track coach, John Nicholson only watched him race once. When Rice traveled to away meets, Nicholson stayed in South Bend, somehow thinking he would jinx his speedy long-distance runner.

Nicholson, however, did see Rice win the 1940 three-mile duel with Taisto Maki and Don Lash. But just hours before the race, Nicholson had suffered a heart attack. He died from complications two days later.

Irish Lore

Walter Langford took over the tennis and coaching reins from Pedro DeLandero in 1940 and enjoyed success in his initial seasons with both sports.

The Irish tennis team had fallen on particularly tough times, having failed to produce a winning record in nine seasons.

But Langford convinced his players that the tennis team could win if they worked together. The Irish won their first two matches over Wabash and Kentucky and then shut out Indiana after a 6-3 loss to Western Michigan.

In late May, Notre Dame capped its quick resurgence by winning the Indiana Collegiate Championships in Lafayette for its first official state title. The Irish competed in the NCAA Tournament in Haverford, Pennsylvania, but did not place.

It didn't matter. Langford had worked a minor miracle on the Notre Dame tennis courts. Things were looking up.

1940-41

ABOVE:
KNUTE ROCKNE ALL-AMERICAN
PREMIERE.

Irish Moment

It was obvious that Notre Dame football fans were growing frustrated with Elmer Layden's inability to lead the Irish back to the mountaintop. His teams were good, his coaching staff strong, his players well prepared. But Notre Dame had won six national championships under Rockne, and Layden had come close just once in six years. The natives, as they say, were restless.

Plus, Notre Dame's new president, Rev. J. Hugh O'Donnell, had been the team's starting center in 1915. Football was close to his heart.

Notre Dame opened the 1940 campaign on October 5 against the College of the Pacific, coached by the legendary Amos Alonzo Stagg, who owned a 4-0 record over the Irish. *Knute Rockne — All-American* had premiered in South Bend the previous evening, and many of the stars and dignitaries stayed over to watch the game. Although Pacific scored first, Notre Dame reeled off 25 straight points for the victory.

Layden's team then won its next five games. The Irish were 6-0 and ranked seventh in the country with just three games left.

The dream died in a home game against Iowa. The Hawkeyes, who had lost four straight outings, held Notre Dame scoreless and forced the Irish into four fumbles in the game's final five minutes. Iowa capitalized on the last miscue and scored with five minutes left for the upset win in Notre Dame Stadium.

That loss might have sealed Layden's fate. Northwestern shut out the Irish the next week at Evanston. Notre Dame salvaged a season-ending win over USC in Los Angeles, but for the second year in a row, the Irish finished 7-2.

In late January, Layden resigned. His 47-13-3 record as head coach just wasn't good enough—at least not at Notre Dame. A year later he became commissioner of the National Football League.

Irish Legend

As a guard on the 1936-37 and 1937-38 basketball teams, Ray Meyer was the supreme floor commander. His coach, George Keogan, trusted Meyer's instincts and intelligence, as well as his ability to motivate his teammates. Those qualities would serve Meyer well in what would become his chosen profession—coaching.

Meyer became Keogan's first full-time assistant just prior to the 1940-41 season. In February, Keogan's health problems forced him to turn the coaching reins over to Meyer for the last seven games of the campaign. Under Meyer's guidance, the Irish won five of those contests.

The following year, Keogan's doctors forbid him to travel, so Meyer handled head coaching duties on the road. Although the Irish were just 4-5 during those games, he orchestrated wins over Michigan, Northwestern, and Detroit.

With Keogan's blessing and recommendation, Meyer left his alma mater to take the head coaching job at DePaul before the start of 1942-43 schedule. He would stay there for 42 years, taking the Blue Demons to two NCAA Final Fours and one NIT championship. His DePaul teams appeared in 21 postseason tournaments and put together 12 20-win seasons. Under Meyer's guidance, DePaul landed on the national basketball radar screen and became a model of consistency. "The Coach" was inducted into the Basketball Hall of Fame in 1978.

Ironically, Keogan died midway through that 1942-43 season. Had DePaul not come calling for Meyer, Notre Dame's athletic history may have written a somewhat different tale.

Irish Lore

The glamour and excitement of Hollywood came to South Bend in the fall of 1940 for the world premiere of *Knute Rockne – All-American.*

Starring Pat O'Brien as the legendary coach and a young actor named Ronald Reagan as George Gipp, the Warner Brothers production brought a somewhat sanitized version of Rockne's life and career to the big screen. Reagan didn't win any acting awards for the deathbed scene, but the film immortalized Gipp as a gifted young athlete and turned Rockne's "Win One for the Gipper" speech into the most famous pep talk of all time.

Thousands of Notre Dame students and South Bend residents gathered outside the Palais Royale Theatre to cheer the stars as they walked down the red carpet on October 4 before the film's showing. O'Brien and Reagan were there, along with singer Kate Smith, Ed Sullivan, and other celebrities.

Over 40 years later, Reagan, then president of the United States, returned to Notre Dame on May 17, 1981, to deliver the commencement address and receive an honorary degree. It marked his first public appearance since an assassination attempt the previous March. Also receiving an honorary degree that day was O'Brien. The actors reunited on the podium, and O'Brien recited the locker-room speech several times that weekend.

Reagan, a former sportscaster, spoke often of his fondness for Notre Dame and Knute Rockne. When the 1988 national championship football team visited the White House just days before Reagan left office, coach Lou Holtz presented the outgoing president with George Gipp's monogram sweater.

LEFT:
LOCKER-ROOM SCENE FROM KNUTE ROCKNE.

1941-42

Irish Moment

When Frank Leahy took over as head coach of the Fighting Irish in 1941, his task was simple—win football games.

He didn't need to rebuild—the nucleus was there—just retool. That he did. A taskmaster extraordinaire, Leahy drove his players physically and mentally. He drilled them in football fundamentals and passed on his passion, drive, and intensity. Leahy strove for perfection—in himself and in his players.

That first season proved a remarkable one. The Irish won every game except for a 0-0 standoff with Army before a capacity crowd at Yankee Stadium. Best of all, the offense, under the direction of sophomore quarterback Angelo Bertelli, was exciting and prolific. The Irish scored 21 more points than they did the previous season, and Bertelli completed 70 of 123 passes for 1,027 yards.

The Irish ended the season with a 20-18 victory over USC before a sellout crowd of 54,967 in Notre Dame Stadium, the first since 1938. Only Minnesota and Duke ranked ahead of Leahy's team in the final polls. End Bob Dove was named a consensus All-American.

Notre Dame football was definitely on the upswing, but two weeks later, the Japanese bombed Pearl Harbor. Winning took on an entirely new meaning for Irish fans everywhere.

ABOVE:
FRANK LEAHY.

RIGHT:
MARIO TONELLI.

Irish Legend

Chicago native Mario Tonelli played fullback for Notre Dame from 1936-38.

Injuries curtailed his junior season, but in 1938, the 5-11, 188-pound senior ranked as the team's second-leading rusher with 259 yards on 42 carries.

Tonelli's biggest battles were yet to come.

Tonelli played professional football for the Chicago Cardinals but left in 1941 to enlist with the armed forces. In the spring of 1942, Tonelli was stationed, along with 75,000 other American and Filipino soldiers, on the Bataan Peninsula off the coast of the Philippines. The Japanese Army had invaded the peninsula and attacked from the north. The allied soldiers were trapped. There was no way to escape and no way to replenish supplies. Rationed food soon disappeared. The soldiers were literally starving to death. On Good Friday, the Japanese attacked the camp, and although they outnumbered the Japanese, the emaciated American and Filipino soldiers surrendered. The soldiers were forced to march out of Bataan without food or water. Over the course of the week, the men were tortured and humiliated. Many were suffering from malaria, dehydration, dysentery, and died along the way. Some who showed signs of failing were killed— often beheaded by the Japanese soldiers. Only 54,000 survived the 100-mile march to Camp O'Donnell, then a prison camp. Tonelli was one of the lucky ones. He survived the Bataan Death March as well as a three-and-a-half-year stay in a Japanese prison camp.

Although he had lost 60 pounds in captivity, Tonelli returned to the Cardinals and played one more season before retiring. He wore number 58—his number at Notre Dame and at his Japanese prisoner of war camp.

Irish Lore

Frank Leahy started at tackle during his playing days at Notre Dame.

But an injury during the 1930 season forced him out of football. Sent to the Mayo Clinic for treatment, Leahy discovered his hospital roommate was his college coach Knute Rockne. Both patients were forced to recuperate in bed. The two passed the time by talking football. The experience convinced Leahy to make coaching his life's work. After graduation, he coached at Georgetown, Michigan State, Fordham, and Boston College. As the head coach of the Golden Eagles, Leahy led Boston College to a 20-2 record and a 1941 upset over Tennessee in the Sugar Bowl.

The Eagles obviously wanted to keep their head coach to themselves so Boston College offered Leahy a five-year extension on his contract. He accepted and signed the deal on the same day Elmer Layden resigned.

Leahy, who made a practice of outthinking his opponents, had been smart enough to add an out clause—rendering his contract null and void if his alma mater ever beckoned.

1942-43

The 1940s

Time Capsule

- Enrico Fermi and his colleagues began collaborating on the development of an atomic bomb, a task designated as the Manhattan Project. They worked in an area below the bleachers of Stagg Field at the University of Chicago.

- On November 28, 1942, nearly 500 people died when a fire swept through Boston's Coconut Grove Night Club.

- General Dwight D. Eisenhower was appointed commander of the Allied armies in Europe.

- The Detroit Red Wings won their second Stanley Cup.

- The University of Notre Dame celebrated the 100th anniversary of its founding. As part of the festivities, Notre Dame served as host of the NCAA Golf Tournament, held at the South Bend Country Club.

ABOVE:
OLIVER HUNTER.

Irish Moment

The war was taking its toll on Notre Dame athletics. Many football players left school to join the service, and nine of 10 members of the Irish basketball squad either graduated or enlisted.

Sports provided a diversion from the hostilities in Europe and the Pacific. Students, fans, athletes, and coaches suddenly had a different perspective on the importance and relevance of college athletics.

Even *The Scholastic* wrote in a sports column, "Victories are incidental; the real object is to get these men into condition for the various service organizations which they will enter upon graduation. It will instill the players with the same fighting spirit that has been one of the basic reasons for our successes on the battlefields of the world."

Still, there were plenty of victories for Notre Dame to brag about in 1942-43.

The football team went 7-2-2, while the basketball team won 18 of 20 games. Baseball turned in a 5-3 record with a shortened schedule, and tennis chalked up a 5-2 mark.

Notre Dame track star Oliver Hunter won the 1942 NCAA cross-country championship and finished second in the NCAA two-mile outdoor race to earn All-America recognition. Hunter also won All-America honors in 1940, 1941, and 1943, making him Notre Dame's first four-time All-American.

Irish Legend

Sophomore running back Creighton Miller's sealed his fate before he ever picked up a football. The family connections were just too strong.

Miller, a native of Wilmington, Delaware, had no choice but to attend Notre Dame. After all, his father had played running back for the Irish from 1907-09; his uncle Walter blocked for George Gipp; his other uncle Don won fame as one of the Four Horsemen; his uncle Ray was Knute Rockne's backup at left end; and another uncle, Gerry, played for Notre Dame in the 1920s. His older brother, Tom, also played for the Irish. The only football team in Creighton's Miller's periscope was Notre Dame.

Leahy thought Miller's work ethic was suspect. During a routine physical, Miller's doctor told him he had high blood pressure and encouraged him to stay away from strenuous exercise. When Miller relayed the news to Leahy, the Irish coach thought the diagnosis was poppycock. He thought Miller was lazy and spoiled, but Leahy kept him on the team anyway.

Miller also drove his coach crazy with his outgoing personality. He'd spend a good deal of time at practice cheering on his brother instead of focusing on the task at hand.

But Miller's talents were too impressive to overlook. In 1942, he earned a starting position and showed versatility and speed, qualities so lacking in the previous Irish offenses.

In the summer of 1943, Miller tried to enlist in the Army, but doctors confirmed the previous diagnosis and sent him home after six weeks in a military hospital. Finally, Leahy believed his star halfback.

The two worked out an arrangement that allowed Miller to "rest" when he felt dizzy or tired. The plan worked.

Miller ran for more than 911 yards and scored 13 touchdowns to help lead Notre Dame to the 1943 national championship, its first title in 13 years. Miller became a consensus All-American— he by-passed professional football to attend Yale Law School. In 1976, Miller was inducted into the National Football Foundation Hall of Fame.

Irish Lore

Basketball coach George Keogan's health had not been good for years, but the veteran coach loved the game and his players and was not about to retire. After all, he was only 52.

Keogan's team had won 12 of its first 13 games. The only loss was a 60-55 defeat at the hands of Kentucky in Louisville. The second week of February, Notre Dame made a successful swing through New York, beating NYU, 74-43, at Madison Square Garden and downing Canisius, 55-37, for Keogan's 327th win as Notre Dame head coach. It would be his last.

Four nights later, Keogan closed up shop after practice and went home. He sat down to read the newspaper and never got up. He had suffered a massive heart attack.

On February 20, Keogan's players served as pallbearers at his funeral. They then tried to get one more win for their coach. A game against Great Lakes went on as scheduled, mostly because Keogan's widow insisted, saying that's what her husband would have wanted. The Great Lakes team featured two former Notre Dame stars serving in the Navy as well as Butler's head coach, Tony Hinkle.

Notre Dame gave the talented Great Lakes squad a fight, but the Irish, playing with heavy hearts, lost 60-56 in overtime in Chicago Stadium.

1943-44

Time Capsule

- President Franklin Roosevelt closed the Works Progress Administration and declared the Great Depression over. Employment figures rose rapidly because of World War II-related jobs.

- The CBS radio network broadcast Edward R. Murrow's "Orchestrated Hell" report, describing a Royal Air Force nighttime bombing raid on Berlin.

- On June 6, 1944, over 155,000 Allied troops landed on the beaches of Normandy, France, to begin the largest amphibious military operation in history.

- The Chicago Bears defeated the Washington Redskins, 41-21, for the National Football League Championship.

- During World War II, the U.S. Navy used the Notre Dame campus as a site for Midshipmen School, a program which trained NROTC students who had graduated from various colleges. Between 1942 and 1946, almost 12,000 members of the Navy completed their officers' training at the University.

ABOVE:
ANGELO BERTELLI.

Irish Moment

Frank Leahy loved a challenge, and the 1943 season provided a plethora of obstacles for the Irish to tackle.

World War II played havoc with rosters. Players were called up during the season or shifted to colleges offering military training for their particular arm of the service. Only two starters were back from the 1942 team. Freshmen were now allowed to participate on the varsity, but Leahy never liked playing a raw rookie. In addition, the schedule was the most challenging one in years, featuring seven opponents that had finished the 1942 season ranked in the Associated Press top 13. And, because of a scheduling quirk, seven games were away from Notre Dame Stadium.

The previous season Leahy had installed the T-formation after seeking advice and input from the Chicago Bears' George Halas and Sid Luckman. It was designed to provide more pass protection for Leahy's emerging star quarterback, Angelo Bertelli. The strategic move also represented a shift away from Notre Dame's traditional "Box Formation." Rockne's legacy would live on, but not his game plans.

After two quick victories to open the season, Notre Dame moved to the top spot in the polls. The Irish then manhandled No. 2 Michigan, 35-12, in Ann Arbor. Notre Dame shut out Wisconsin, coached by Harry Stuhldreher, the former quarterback of Four Horsemen fame, and Illinois, 47-0.

Next up was a date with third-ranked Navy in Cleveland, but the game would be Bertelli's last for the Irish. The Marine Corps was calling and he would leave after the game to join his unit. The prolific passer led the Irish to an impressive 33-6 victory, scoring the final touchdown on an eight-yard run.

Sophomore John Lujack replaced Bertelli at quarterback the following week against Army, now the nation's third-ranked team. He completed two touchdown passes, ran for another, and intercepted a pass. Notre Dame shut out the Army, 26-0.

Notre Dame beat two more top 10 teams the following week to boost its record to 9-0.

The perfect Irish season was ruined in the season finale against Great Lakes. With just 33 seconds left, Great Lakes scored a touchdown to claim a 19-14 victory.

The loss didn't matter. The Associated Press made Notre Dame its national champion, the first in a string of titles to come for the "Leahy Lads."

Irish Legend

Angelo Bertelli became Notre Dame's first Heisman Trophy winner in 1943, even though he missed the final four games of the 1943 national championship season to join the Marines.

The "Springfield (Massachusetts) Rifle" came to Notre Dame in the fall of 1940 after turning down offers to play hockey for several prestigious Eastern schools. Coach Frank Leahy thought the 6-1, 173-pounder had lead in his feet but gold in his arm. Leahy started Bertelli at tailback and his sophomore season, as a single-wing tailback, and he promptly threw for 1,027 yards, leading the Irish to a 9-0-1 record. He moved to the quarterback slot as a junior and completed 72 of 159 passes for 1,039 yards and 10 touchdowns.

As a senior, he threw just 36 passes, completing 25 for 512 yards but an amazing 10 touchdowns. Helped by Bertelli's leadership, Notre Dame averaged 43.5 points per game before he left for military service.

After returning from to civilian life, Bertelli played three seasons with the Los Angeles Dons and the Chicago Hornets in the All-American Football Conference. A knee injury ended his professional career. Bertelli was inducted into the National Football Foundation Hall of Fame in 1972.

Irish Lore

National titles seemed easy to come by on the Notre Dame campus during the 1943-44 school year. Football claimed the first championship, but the Irish tennis and golf teams brought home their own trophies in the spring.

Walter Langford's tennis team won nine straight matches that season before heading to the NCAA Championships at Northwestern. Each team could enter four players, and the total team score was determined by the number of wins of those players from the quarterfinals on.

Jerry Everett, Jim Griffin, Charles Samson, and Bill Tully made up the Notre Dame quartet. They had combined for just one loss the entire season.

Only Samson survived the second round. But, the unranked player advanced to the title match , eventually losing to Miami's top-seed Pancho Segura, who won the second of three straight NCAA singles' crowns.

The doubles team of Everett and Samson moved through the competition and made it to the semi-finals. That performance guaranteed Notre Dame a share of the tennis title, along with Miami and Texas.

Not to be outdone, the Notre Dame golf team traveled to the Inverness Country Club in Toledo and brought home its own NCAA championship hardware. The Irish foursome of James Besenfelder, Jack Fitzpatrick, Bob Terry, and captain Mel Wilkie turned in a team score of 311. Ironically, none of the Notre Dame golfers earned All-America recognition.

The Irish track team also picked up some medals of its own at the NCAA Outdoor Championships. Phil Anderson won the pole vault, and Frank Martin finished first in the two-mile event.

ABOVE:
1944 NCAA TENNIS CHAMPIONS.

BELOW:
1944 NCAA GOLF CHAMPIONS.

Irish Moment

World War II was in full swing, and many Notre Dame coaches and players were serving their country.

Football coach Frank Leahy and basketball coach Moose Krause both left for two seasons of military duty.

Ed McKeever stepped in as interim football coach and led the Irish to an 8-2 mark and a ninth-place standing in the Associated Press final poll.

McKeever had attended Notre Dame as a freshman in 1930-31 but transferred to Texas Tech. He returned to South Bend several years later as Leahy's assistant.

The 1944 team won its first five games and moved to the top of the rankings by the third week of the season. But a 32-13 loss to Navy in Baltimore, which marked the first time the Midshipmen had beaten Notre Dame in eight tries, dropped the Irish from that lofty spot. Army embarrassed Notre Dame a week later with a 59-0 thrashing before a capacity crowd in Yankee Stadium. But the Irish rebounded to win their final three games.

Former Notre Dame player Clem Crowe, the head coach at Xavier, took over the basketball program (Xavier had suspended basketball during the War) and guided the Irish to a 15-5 mark, a remarkable accomplishment since he did it without a returning letterman on his squad. He did have sensational freshman Vince Boryla and sophomore Johnny Dee, who would later run the Irish basketball program as coach. The highlight of the season was the 59-58 overtime win over Kentucky in Louisville.

Although football and basketball had temporarily lost their leaders, student-athletes in those sports still played a full schedule against strong competition.

Notre Dame's young fencing team, however, was forced to take a three-year hiatus from competition because the sport's weapons were not being produced during the War.

Time Capsule

- On November 7, 1944, President Franklin Roosevelt was elected to his unprecedented fourth term in office with a victory over Republican challenger Thomas E. Dewey. He died unexpectedly in Warm Springs, Georgia, five months later, and Vice President Harry S. Truman took the oath of office.

- The Allied Forces liberated their first Nazi concentration camp at Buchenwald on April 10, 1945.

- German rocket scientist Wernher von Braun and 120 of his associates surrendered to U.S. forces. They later formed the nucleus of the United States space program.

- In an all-St. Louis World Series, the Cardinals of the National League beat the Browns of the American League, four games to two.

- Notre Dame football coach Frank Leahy took a leave of absence to join the U.S. Navy as a commissioned officer.

RIGHT:
ED McKEEVER.

Irish Legend

The NCAA began allowing freshman student-athletes to compete in intercollegiate athletics because World War II had depleted the rosters of teams everywhere.

A 17-year-old freshman from East Chicago, Illinois, Vince Boryla stepped in and made an immediate impact on the Irish basketball fortunes. He led Notre Dame in scoring, averaging 16.1 points per game to shatter the previous record set by future All-American Leo Klier. He tallied 18 points in an overtime win at Kentucky.

At the end of his rookie season, Boryla's teammates elected him honorary captain, an unheard of accolade for a freshman.

Boryla's scoring pace dipped just a bit to 15.3 his sophomore year, but Klier had returned from the war to help shoulder the load. Boryla and Klier both posted double-digit scoring averages in 1945-46 to lead the Irish to an impressive 17-4 mark.

Boryla left the following season to join the Army. He never returned to Notre Dame, although he did play on the 1948 U.S. Olympic basketball team. Boryla ended up at the University of Denver, and on January 22, 1949, the Irish held their former star to just five points in a 49-46 win over the Pioneers.

Irish Lore

Only a handful of football players from South Bend ever made their way to the Notre Dame Stadium turf, and Pat Filley may have been one of the best.

A starter at left guard, Filley captained the Irish as a junior and senior, becoming the first Notre Dame player to earn that honor twice. A two-time All-American, Filley was the smallest player on the 1943 national championship team. However, size was not important to the 5-8, 175-pounder.

The Cleveland Browns drafted Filley in 1944, but he decided to accept a job as an assistant coach at Cornell in 1945. Nine years later he began a seven-year tenure as athletic director at the Ivy League school.

Time Capsule

- At 8:16 a.m., August 6, the United States dropped an atomic bomb on Hiroshima, Japan. Three days later, a U.S. bomber detonated another atomic bomb over the city of Nagasaki, Japan. The country offered its surrender terms the following day.

- The United States Senate voted 65 to 7 to approve the membership of the United States in the United Nations.

- On May 2, 1946, six prisoners tried unsuccessfully to escape from Alcatraz, a prison located on an island in San Francisco Bay.

- Wimbledon resumed after a six-year hiatus during World War II.

- Admiral Chester Nimitz received an honorary degree from the University of Notre on May 15, 1946 in the Navy Drill Hall on campus.

ABOVE:
HUGH DEVORE.

RIGHT:
LEO KLIER.

Irish Moment

Changing coaches in football and basketball just a year later seemed to have little effect on both the football and basketball teams in 1945-46.

Ed McKeever, who had handled the football duties in Leahy's military absence, left to take the head job at Cornell, while Clem Crowe, who was subbing for Moose Krause, departed for the head football, yes, football, position at Iowa. Hugh Devore stepped in for football, while Elmer Ripley took over the basketball program.

Devore, a 1934 Notre Dame graduate, led the Irish to a 7-2-1 record. At one point in the season, Notre Dame ranked as high as No. 2 in the polls. However, No. 1 ranked Army again shut out the Irish in Yankee Stadium, this time by a 48-0 score. In the two seasons Leahy was gone, Army outscored Notre Dame, 107-0!

Ripley, eventually inducted into the Naismith Memorial Basketball Hall of Fame in 1973, guided the Irish to 13 straight wins. Notre Dame ranked No. 1 for six consecutive weeks in the AP poll. Getting a ticket to a basketball game, both at home and on the road, was almost impossible.

Interest in Notre Dame basketball had never been so high.

But the bubble burst late in the season as the Irish lost four of their last eight games to finish with a still impressive 17-4 record.

The Irish baseball team turned in a 13-6 mark, while tennis finished at 6-3. Irish golfer Dick Whitting capped the year by earning All-America accolades.

Irish Legend

Leo Klier first earned consensus All-America honors as a junior scoring sensation for the Irish basketball team in 1943-44. The 6-1 forward averaged 15.4 points per game which obliterated the previous Notre Dame mark.

The Washington, Indiana, native left school the following season to serve in the Navy. He returned a year later and picked up right where he left off, setting a single season record for field goals attempted (513). He averaged almost 17 points per game as a senior and led Notre Dame to a 17-4 record. Klier's efforts were rewarded with his second consensus All-America designation.

Following graduation, Klier played in the National Basketball League, first for the Indianapolis Katuskys and then for the Fort Wayne Pistons.

Irish Lore

Ray Meyer returned to the Fieldhouse on January 5, 1946. But this time, the former Notre Dame captain was coaching the enemy.

The game marked the beginning of a home-and-home series with DePaul that would run through 1968-69.

The Irish, under interim coach Elmer Ripley, had won their first six games, including a 50-48 win over in-state rival Purdue in West Lafayette.

But Meyer had All-America center George Mikan. The Blue Demons led almost the entire game, although Notre Dame's defense kept it close and held Mikan in check.

Notre Dame All-American Billy Hassett, who had transferred from Georgetown when the Hoyas suspended their program because of the War, turned in an awful offensive performance, failing to hit a shot in 11 tries. The 5-10 senior captain threw up a prayer as time expired, and the ball somehow went through the hoop, giving Notre Dame a 43-42 victory.

Meyer beat his alma mater later that season in the Chicago Stadium, but he would not get his first win in the Fieldhouse as the DePaul coach until the two teams met in 1948-49.

111

1946-47

Irish Moment

World War II had ended, and life was getting back to normal on the Notre Dame campus. The year would be one of the most successful in its athletic history.

Frank Leahy returned to his head football coaching job, and he promptly led the Irish to an 8-0-1 record and another national championship. Five Irish players—George Connor, Leon Hart, John Lujack, Jim Martin, and Emil Sitko—were named All-Americans, while Connor became Notre Dame's first Outland Trophy winner.

Moose Krause resumed his basketball coaching duties, and his team went 20-4. The NCAA extended a tournament invitation to the Irish, but the Notre Dame administration held fast to its ban on postseason competition.

Not to be outdone, the baseball team improved its record to 16-5, and the tennis squad won all eight of its matches.

Fencing began competing again, and Notre Dame placed 13th in the first NCAA Tournament that winter.

Life on campus was indeed good.

ABOVE:
JOHN LUJACK CARRIES AGAINST PURDUE.

RIGHT:
1947 TENNIS TEAM.

Irish Legend

Brothers Jim and Jerry Everett combined for 100 dual-match victories during their three years on the Notre Dame tennis team.

Jim, the older of the two Chicago natives, posted a 7-0 dual mark in singles and a similar record in doubles in 1943 before leaving for the service. Jerry first played in 1944, going 9-0 in singles and 9-0 in doubles. His only losses in open play came during the NCAA Tournament. Still, Everett and doubles partner Charles Samson advanced to the semifinals to ensure a tie for the NCAA title with Miami and Texas. Jerry and Samson were named second-team All-Americans for their effort, marking the first time a Notre Dame tennis player had achieved that honor.

Both Jim and Jerry returned to Notre Dame after the war and led the Irish to a 14-3 match play record for the 1946 and 1947 seasons. Both were undefeated in singles and doubles match play during that time. Jim matched his brother's All-America accolade in 1947.

Jim Everett remained in tennis, eventually helping coach his daughter Chris to the world's number-one ranking and 18 Grand Slam singles titles.

Irish Lore

George Connor, Notre Dame's 1946 Outland Trophy winner, was such a familiar figure on campus even after graduation that few forgot that the 6-3, 225-pound lineman had first earned All-America honors at Holy Cross College—in Massachusetts.

Connor had been a standout football player at DeLaSalle High School in Chicago and was heavily recruited by Notre Dame. His uncle, also named George Connor, was a monsignor at Holy Cross and felt he could keep a close eye on the 17-year-old George if he came East for college.

Connor played there for two years, winning the George Bulger Lowe Award, given annually to the best college football player in New England and garnering All-America recognition.

But Connor, a member of the Navy's V-12 program, was ordered to active duty in 1944 and sent to Pearl Harbor Naval Base. His commander just happened to be Frank Leahy.

The NCAA had relaxed its eligibility standards after the war to help veterans return to college, so Connor decided to enroll at Notre Dame. The gifted tackle led the Irish to two national championships in 1946 and 1947, and Connor earned All-America status both years.

A first-round draft pick by the New York Giants, Connor wound up playing eight seasons for the Bears in his native Chicago. He played on both offense and defense even though the NFL was in the process of phasing out the two-way system. Named All-Pro several times, Connor was inducted into the Professional Football Hall of Fame in 1975. He had entered the College Football Hall of Fame in 1963.

1947-48

Time Capsule

- The United States Supreme Court ruled that religious instruction in public schools violated the Constitution on March 8.

- Stanton Friedman claimed that a downed UFO was found in Roswell, New Mexico.

- Warner Brothers presented the first color newsreel on January 5. The mini film featured the 1948 Tournament of Rose Bowl Parade and the Rose Bowl.

- Mildred "Babe" Didrikson Zaharias won the first of her three U.S. Open golf titles.

- Mike DeCicco, a name that would become synonymous with Notre Dame fencing, placed 12th in the foil for the Irish in the 1948 NCAA Fencing Championships.

ABOVE:
FRANK LEAHY ON THE SIDELINES.

RIGHT:
JOHN LUJACK.

Irish Moment

Frank Leahy's Nineteen Forty-Seven national championship team may have been the best ever in college football history. Three players earned consensus All-America nods, and six would eventually be inducted into the National Football Hall of Fame. The roster included two players who would win the Heisman Trophy, one that had captured the Outland Trophy and another who would eventually become the team's head coach. An incredible number of players on that team—42 to be exact—would eventually play in the NFL.

Notre Dame's talented squad was barely challenged throughout the course of the season, despite playing ninth-ranked Army at home in November and taking on the No. 3 Trojans December 3 in Los Angeles. The Irish outscored their opponents, 291-52, and recorded three shutouts. Only Northwestern seriously tested Notre Dame's resolve, becoming the only team to score more than one touchdown against the Irish that year. Notre Dame won, 26-19, but the victory failed to put a smile on Leahy's face.

The Notre Dame-USC series had been suspended during the World War II, but games between the two national powers resumed in 1946 when the Trojans returned to Notre Dame Stadium.

1947 marked the football team's first trip to Los Angeles since 1942, but the Hollywood high life didn't distract the War veterans from their mission. The Irish never trailed and effectively dismantled the home team, 38-7.

Leahy now had his third national championship in five years.

Irish Legend

It was hard to tell who was the bigger star on campus during 1947-48—Johnny Lujack or Kevin O'Shea.

Lujack, of course, led the football team to its second consecutive national championship and became Notre Dame's second Heisman Trophy winner in four years.

A versatile athlete who had played basketball for the Irish as a freshman, Lujack earned his stripes on the football field in 1943 when he replaced quarterback Angelo Bertelli, who left to join the Marines. Lujack also went into the service after that season but returned to Notre Dame three years later and didn't miss a beat. In addition to his quarterbacking duties, Lujack punted and played defensive back. Amazingly consistent, he threw for 778 yards and six touchdowns as a junior and for 777 yards as a senior. Alongside the Heisman Trophy, Lujack was voted Male Athlete of the Year by the Associated Press.

Lujack, who played four seasons with the Chicago Bears, returned to South Bend in 1952 for a two-year stint as an assistant coach. He was inducted into the National Football Foundation Hall of Fame in 1960.

Kevin O'Shea became the sixth Notre Dame basketball player named a consensus All-American in 1947-48 as a sophomore. He would be the last Irish star so honored until Austin Carr in 1970-71.

The 6-1 guard averaged 11.5 points per game as a sophomore, but his play-making skills helped Notre Dame win 17 of 24 games that season. During his three years on the varsity, the Irish posted a 54-17 record.

Although he never led the team in scoring, O'Shea ranked as Notre Dame's scoring leader when he graduated in 1950. He finished with 1,065 career points.

O'Shea became Notre Dame's first-ever top draft pick in the NBA in 1950. He played professionally with the Minneapolis Lakers, the Milwaukee Hawks, and the Baltimore Bullets.

Irish Lore

Adolph Rupp hated playing in the Notre Dame Fieldhouse. The band, which sat behind the opposing coach's bench, bothered him. The priests, dressed in their black cassocks and sitting across the floor, made Rupp uneasy. The students, loud, raucous, and energetic, were his worst enemy. Rupp felt he couldn't win at the Fieldhouse ... and he was right.

But in 1947-48, Rupp's Kentucky team was enormously talented and came to South Bend ranked No. 1 in the country. Alex Groza, Ralph Beard, and Wallace Jones led a Wildcat contingent that would eventually post a 38-3 record, win the NCAA Tournament, and capture the 1948 Olympic gold medal. If Rupp was ever going to beat Notre Dame on its home court, tonight would be the night.

But the Irish had other plans. February 2 was Notre Dame basketball coach Moose Krause's 35th birthday, and his players wanted to extend their 37-game home-court win streak to 38 as a present.

Thanks to Kevin O'Shea's 25 points, the Irish played an almost perfect game to upset Kentucky, 64-55.

The home victory string ended a week later in a 68-51 loss to Saint Louis, which would win the NIT Tournament later that year. But the Irish pulled their second shocker of the season on March 1 when they beat the new No. 1 team, NYU, 64-59, in Madison Square Garden.

1948-49

- President Harry S. Truman defeated challenger Thomas E. Dewey in the hotly contested 1948 presidential election.

- On January 11, 1949, snow fell in Los Angeles for the first time in recorded history.

- The Federal Bureau of Investigation released a report that named several Hollywood actors and movie celebrities as members of the Communist Party.

- After a 12-year hiatus because of the conflicts in Europe and Asia, the Olympics resumed in 1948 with the Winter Games in St. Moritz, Switzerland, and the Summer Games in London.

- Student enrollment at the University of Notre Dame topped 5,000 students for the first time in its history.

ABOVE:
LEON HART SCORES AGAINST USC.

RIGHT:
BILL "MOOSE" FISCHER.

Irish Moment

Notre Dame's football team won nine straight games in 1948, but a 14-14 tie at USC kept the Irish from claiming their third consecutive national championship. Coach Frank Leahy's squad ranked second in the final Associated Press poll behind Michigan.

After escaping a close call to Purdue in the season opener, Notre Dame ran the table, beating the likes of Pittsburgh, Michigan State, Nebraska, Iowa, Navy, Indiana, Northwestern, and Washington. The Irish were ranked either No. 1 or No. 2 all season long. The closest call was a 12-7 squeaker over Northwestern at home.

Because of a quirk in the scheduling, Notre Dame had to travel to Los Angeles again for the season finale against USC. Although the Irish scored first, Notre Dame fumbled the ball away six times to give the Trojans several scoring opportunities. After USC took a 14-7 lead late in the fourth quarter, Emil Sitko scored with :35 left. A PAT kick tied the game, and Notre Dame recovered the onside kick.

Unfortunately, the Irish couldn't find the end zone before time expired. It was a long train ride home.

Irish Legend

Two-time consensus All-American Bill "Moose" Fischer became Notre Dame's second Outland Trophy winner in three years. A Notre Dame player would not claim the award again for almost 30 years.

A 6-foot-2, 226-pound native of Chicago, Fischer captained the 1948 team, which barely lost out on its third straight national title. The Irish did not lose a game during the 1946, 1947, and 1948 seasons.

Fischer, who grew up near Wrigley Field, came to Notre Dame almost by accident.

Football letters of intent were not as binding in the late '40s as they are today. A man's word was his honor. Fischer had decided to stay in-state and play for Coach Ray Eliot at the University of Illinois.

But Frank Leahy was away at war, and Hugh Devore had stepped in as the interim coach. Notre Dame assistant Gene Ronzani approached Fischer just a few days before Illinois preseason practice was to begin and convinced him to at least take a look around the Notre Dame campus. Fischer obliged. He never left.

Ironically, Notre Dame played Illinois twice during Fischer's Irish career and downed the Illini both times, 7-0 in 1945 and 26-6 in 1946.

Fischer earned all-pro honors twice during his five seasons for the Chicago Cardinals. He also spent four years as an assistant coach at his alma mater under head coach Terry Brennan in the fifties.

He was inducted into the National Football Foundation Hall of Fame in 1983.

Irish Lore

Notre Dame's baseball program hadn't exactly set the world on fire during the 1940s. The teams were up and down, a winning season here and there, but sustaining success in a northern climate became harder and harder to maintain.

Yet, the 1949 squad compiled an impressive 20-6 regular-season record to become the first

LEFT:
1949 BASEBALL TEAM.

Notre Dame baseball team invited to participate in the NCAA Tournament.

Ironically, the Irish had dropped their first three games to Big Ten foes Indiana and Iowa. But coach Jake Kline's squad reeled off 18 wins in its next 21 contests to advance to the NCAA District 4 playoffs in West Lafayette. Pitcher Walt Mahannah threw a one-hitter in Notre Dame's first-ever NCAA tournament game as the Irish beat Purdue 1-0. A 9-1 win over Western Michigan two days later moved Notre Dame to a first-round NCAA appearance. Although the games were played at Notre Dame, the Irish were eliminated with back-to-back losses to Wake Forest.

First baseman Dick Gieldin led the Irish in hitting that year with a .328 batting average.

1949-50

Time Capsule

- In a speech to the Republican Women's Club in Wheeling, WV., on February 9, 1950, Wisconsin Senator Joseph McCarthy accused over 200 employees of the United States Department of State as being members of the Community Party.

- On June 24, 1950, 585 people died when a commercial airliner crashed into Lake Michigan.

- All six of the last surviving veterans of the U.S. Civil War met in Indianapolis on August 28, 1949.

- On June 29, 1950 in Brazil, the United States upset England, widely recognized as the "Kings of Football," 1-0 in the World Cup. Joe Gaetiens scored in the 37th minute of the first half, giving the United States its first win in its last seven international matches, including the 1934 World Cup and the 1948 Summer Olympics. The United States did not compete in the World Cup again until 1990.

- Rev. Theodore Hesburgh, C.S.C., was named executive vice president of the University of Notre Dame.

Irish Moment

Sometimes things happen when you least expect it.

After the disappointment of the 1948 season, many Notre Dame football fans didn't think the Irish had a chance at the brass ring in 1949.

It's not that the cupboards were bare. The team had experience, brain, and brawn. Four starters would emerge as All-Americans, and another would become only the second end in college football to win the Heisman Trophy.

Notre Dame crushed every team in its wake. Not one game was close ... at least at the end. Fourth-ranked Tulane barely put up a fight, losing 46-7 in Notre Dame Stadium the fourth week of the season. Two weeks later, the Irish traveled to East Lansing to take on a challenge from the 10th-ranked Spartans. Michigan State fell, 34-21. And in late November, Notre Dame returned USC's hospitality from the past season, shutting out the Trojans, 32-0.

The Irish traveled to Dallas for the season finale against SMU. That turned out to be the toughest contest of the year. Notre Dame jumped out to a 14-0 lead, but running back Kyle Rote eventually tied the game for the Mustangs.

Leahy moved Leon Hart to fullback on the last drive to distract the Mustangs who were tired and outmanned. Billy Barrett scored the winning touchdown for Notre Dame from the two-year line.

SMU took one last shot at the Irish, but middle lineback Jerry Groom intercepted Rote's pass to seal the victory.

Over the last four years, Leahy's record stood at 36-0-2. Would the Irish ever lose again?

ABOVE:
1949 CHAMPIONSHIP POSTER.

RIGHT:
LEON HART.

Irish Legend

Leon Hart didn't like to lose.

So, it's a good thing the Irish finished 36-0-2 with three national championships during his four seasons at Notre Dame.

One of the last of the two-way players, Hart harassed opponents with his blocking and pass rushing skills. The 6-4, 245-pound, native of Turtle Creek, Pennsylvania, also knew how to grab a football. He caught 49 passes for 751 yards and 13 touchdowns for the Irish.

Hart earned All-America honors as a sophomore, junior, and senior. In 1949, he won the Heisman Trophy as well as the Maxwell Award. He also beat out Jackie Robinson and Sam Snead as the Associated Press male athlete of the year.

A mechanical engineering major, Hart played professional football for eight seasons with the Detroit Lions. As a pro, he won three NFL titles and was named all-pro on both offense and defense. He was elected to the National Football Foundation Hall of Fame in 1973. Hart's son Kevin and grandson Brendan also played football for the Irish.

Irish Lore

Adolph Rupp finally had enough.

The legendary coach had brought six Kentucky teams to Notre Dame, and not one would win in the Fieldhouse.

This time his squad was ranked fifth, but it didn't matter. Irish senior Kevin O'Shea led the 64-51 rout of the Wildcats with 18 points.

After the game Rupp vowed to never return to South Bend. He didn't.

Although Notre Dame and Kentucky played off and on in Chicago, Louisville, Lexington, and Columbus, Ohio, throughout the years, the Wildcats did not make a return trip to South Bend until March 5, 1990. Digger Phelps' Irish won that game, 80-67. . Kentucky finally beat Notre Dame, 81-62, in the Joyce Center on February 13, 1993, for its first win in South Bend since 1929.

1950-51

ABOVE:
THE 1950 FOOTBALL TEAM IN ACTION.

Irish Moment

Notre Dame had not lost a football game since December 1, 1945. Some Irish fans thought Frank Leahy's lads might never lose again.

Although several key players from the 1949 national championship squad had graduated, Notre Dame headed into the new season ranked No. 1 in the Associated Press poll.

North Carolina was the first opponent in the slate, and the Tar Heels were making their first visit to South Bend. North Carolina must have heard the ghosts in Notre Dame Stadium because the Tar Heels fumbled the opening kickoff on their own 25-yard line. They stopped the Irish and got the ball back, but they lost it again—this time on their own 10. All-America quarterback Bob Williams threw a three-yard touchdown pass to James Mutscheller three plays later to give the Irish the lead.

Carolina tied the game in the third quarter. Late in the game Williams and Mutscheller hooked up again, and the top-ranked Irish kept their 39-game winning streak alive.

But the string snapped the next week against in-state rival Purdue. The Boilermakers, led by quarterback Dale Samuels, cruised to a 21-0 halftime lead. Notre Dame managed to find the end zone twice in the second half, but Purdue's unrelenting defense never broke. The Irish lost their first game in four seasons.

Although Notre Dame recovered the next week for a win against Tulane, the Irish struggled through the remainder of the season, finishing 4-4-1, by far the worst record in coach Frank Leahy's tenure.

Irish Legend

Des Moines, Iowa, native Jerry Groom captained the 1950 Notre Dame football squad and earned consensus All-America honors as a linebacker and center.

Groom, a two-way standout in high school, began his Irish career as the back-up center. He moved to middle linebacker as a junior and became the stalwart of the Notre Dame defense. He logged 465 minutes of playing time during his Irish career and was on the field 86 percent of the time Notre Dame played.

After graduation, Groom was selected to play in the 1951 East-West Shrine game and the College All-Star game in Chicago. He was the first player drafted by the Chicago Cardinals in 1951, and he played there for four years.

Groom was inducted into the National Football Hall of Fame in 1994.

Irish Lore

Road trips took on a new meaning when the Notre Dame football team traveled to New Orleans the second weekend in October to play Tulane.

For the first time in its history, the Irish boarded a plane, not a train, to their away destination. Players, coaches, and administrators traveled on the charter airplane that left South Bend for the trip south.

Although the players traveled in style, the Band of the Fighting Irish and scores of students made their way to New Orleans by rail.

A week before the game, Shep Pleasants, the sports editor of the *Tulane Hullabaloo*, welcomed Irish followers to the Crescent City with a special message that appeared in the *Notre Dame Scholastic*.

He wrote, "The Paris of America awaits you with open arms. We hope you have the time of your lives and are able to keep inside your budget. We know that with the prospect of a wild winter at South Bend, you will utilize all of your spare time scrutinizing such French Quarter attractions as the St. Louis Cathedral, the Cabildo, Jackson Square, and various other 'places of interest.' Tulane sends a hearty welcome."

Notre Dame, still smarting from a 28-14 upset loss at home to the Purdue Boilermakers, thoroughly enjoyed New Orleans. The Irish left with a 13-9 victory over the Green Wave.

ABOVE:
JOE BERTRAND.

RIGHT:
BASKETBALL COACH JOHN JORDAN.

Irish Moment

Former Notre Dame basketball player John Jordan returned to his alma mater when Moose Krause announced prior to the 1950-51 season that he would relinquish his head coaching duties after the year to concentrate on his job as Irish athletic director.

Jordan, who was coaching at Loyola, was named Krause's successor on February 20, 1951, but he did not coach his first game for the Irish until the 1951-52 season.

His debut was special for a number of reasons.

The Irish opened against St. Thomas in St. Paul, Minnesota, on December 1. Notre Dame's starting lineup included two African-Americans, marking the first time an African-American played basketball for Notre Dame.

South Bend native Entee Shine and Chicago's Joe Bertrand had broken ground at Notre Dame as well as nationally.

Bertrand played three seasons for the Irish, becoming the third member of the 1,000-point scoring club. Shine transferred to Tennessee State after his freshman year.

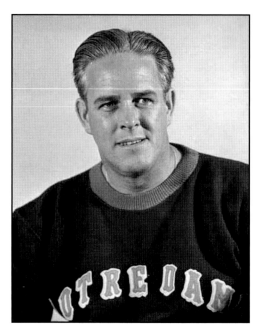

Both players were welcomed on the Notre Dame campus, but the administration was sensitive to the times and knew the two would not be given the red carpet treatment everywhere they went. Times being what they were, the administration avoided scheduling any games in the South for several years. The Irish never ventured farther south than Louisville for many seasons.

Irish Legend

Neil Worden helped Notre Dame football fans forget the disappointing 1950 season in his first game as a starter in 1951.

The sophomore fullback, nicknamed "Bull" by his teammates, earned the starting nod five games into the season. He promptly scored four touchdowns to lead Notre Dame to a 30-9 win over Purdue in Notre Dame Stadium. He finished the year as the team's leading rusher with 676 yards on 181 carries. He also paced the team in scoring with 48 points. The Irish finished 7-2-1, and Worden played a huge role in the turnaround.

A native of Milwaukee, Worden's ground game dropped off a bit his junior season, but he still scored 10 touchdowns, including two against Oklahoma, and retained the team scoring lead. Once again, the Irish finished 7-2-1, but this time they were ranked third in the final Associated Press poll.

Worden's senior season saw Notre Dame put together a stellar 9-0-1 record in coach Frank Leahy's final year at the helm. Once again Worden led the team in rushing, carrying the ball 145 times for 859 yards for a 5.9 yards-per-carry average. He also scored 11 touchdowns.

Irish Lore

First-year coach John Jordan was desperate. His team had won 11 out of 15 games, but injuries and grades were taking their toll. For the first time in school history, student-athletes were suspended for academic deficiencies, and Jordan lost three, including two starters, for the second semester.

Notre Dame had three games in four days, and guard Joe Bertrand was injured and would not make the trip. Jordan needed bodies. Sophomore football player Johnny Lattner was added to the team as a replacement.

The Irish had a date against NYU in Madison Square Garden. The game went into overtime, but the Violets held a three-point advantage with just moments remaining. Dick Rosenthal hit a shot to put Notre Dame within one, but then starter Leroy Leslie fouled out. Lattner entered the game with just 26 seconds left. With nine ticks left on the clock, Lattner scored a basket for a 75-74 Irish win.

RIGHT:
JOHN LATTNER.

Irish Moment

Over the last five years, Oklahoma had taken Notre Dame's place as the elite team in college football.

The Sooners, who boasted the best record in the sport over the past five seasons, were riding a 13-game winning streak and averaging 42 points per game.

And, they were coming to South Bend, along with 10,000 fans—all wearing red.

After that disastrous 4-4-1 season in 1950, Notre Dame had rebounded with a 7-2-1 record in 1951 and began the 1952 season ranked 10th.

By the time the Oklahoma game rolled around on the 8th of November, the Irish were 4-1-1. No one thought Notre Dame

stood much of a chance against the powerful Sooners, who stood fourth in the polls.

Eventual Heisman Trophy winner Billy Vessels scored two touchdowns in the first half to give Oklahoma a seven-point lead at halftime. Notre Dame tied the game in the third quarter after Johnny Lattner intercepted a Sooner pass and returned it deep into Oklahoma territory. Neil Worden tied the game a few plays later at 14-14.

Vessels showed he was worth his weight in Heisman gold by scoring his third touchdown of the day to push the Sooners ahead, 21-14. But the lead wouldn't last long. Notre Dame answered with two scores of its own, but a blocked extra point gave the Irish only a six-point lead.

The defense dug in and kept the Sooners' powerful offense at bay the rest of the afternoon, and Notre Dame won the first meeting between the two national powers, 27-21.

Irish Legend

Almost everyone said Dick Rosenthal was a nice guy.

But you would never believe it if you knew that he held the Irish record for most personal fouls in a season—104 (an average of four per game)—for 40 years.

The 6-foot-5 sophomore from St. Louis spent his first year on the varsity getting into foul trouble. He also finished tied for second on the team in scoring with a 12.7 average.

The following year, 1952-53, he led Notre Dame to a 19-5 record and its first appearance in the NCAA Tournament while averaging 16.3 points per game. In the second game of the season, Rosenthal and teammate Norb Lewinski upset Indiana, 71-70. The Hoosiers would avenge that loss three months later by beating Notre Dame in the Elite Eight and advancing on to win the NCAA championship.

Moving to center as a senior, Rosenthal captained the squad and became the first Irish player to average over 20 points per game in a season when he finished with a 20.2 mark. He was named to the Helms Foundation All-America team.

A 1954 Notre Dame graduate, Rosenthal enjoyed a remarkable business career before returning to his alma mater as athletic director in 1987. During his eight-year tenure, he orchestrated Notre Dame's affiliation with the BIG EAST conference and was a key figure in the University's negotiations with the NBC television network for the rights to television Irish home football games. Under Rosenthal's watch, a plan for enlarging Notre Dame Stadium was approved. Rosenthal also oversaw the increased commitment to Irish Olympic sports in terms of coaching, facilities, and opportunities.

He retired from the University in 1995.

LEFT:
DICK ROSENTHAL.

BELOW:
TV CAMERAS BECOME A FIXTURE AT NOTRE DAME.

Irish Lore

The Irish football team first appeared on national television in 1952. The ABC network, which broadcast a college football game of the week, selected the Notre Dame-Oklahoma game as a key matchup of the 1952 season.

Television was still a relatively new technology back then and being picked as the game of the week was a huge honor for the teams involved. The television coverage brought nationwide exposure for the schools and their players. However, many in the world of college athletics feared that television would hurt gate receipts.

Since that first appearance in 1952, Notre Dame football games have been a regular fixture on national television. NCAA rules limited appearances in those early days, but the Irish still managed to have at least one game televised nationally every year.

Since 1991, all Notre Dame home games have been televised nationally by the NBC (now NBC-Universal) network.

Irish Moment

Frank Leahy was only 46 years old, but the wear and tear of coaching the nation's favorite football team had taken its toll. The pressure to win, the drive to succeed, the commitment to excellence—those factors certainly played a role in the veteran coach's decision to leave the profession he so loved in January of 1954.

The 1953 Notre Dame football team began the season ranked No. 1. And after the Irish beat sixth-ranked Oklahoma, 28-21, in Norman to open the campaign, most observers thought Leahy would take Notre Dame to its eighth national title and his fifth.

After notching victories over Purdue and Pitt, Georgia Tech, ranked fourth in the country, brought the nation's longest winning streak (31 games) to South Bend. Although the Irish won 27-14, Leahy collapsed in the locker room at halftime with an attack of gastroenteritis and was taken to the hospital. It wasn't the first time he had fallen ill. During his career at Notre Dame, Leahy missed five games—the next contest against Navy would be his sixth. Both his doctors and his friends told him to quit coaching—it was killing him. He was still young and had a family, but Leahy was determined to go out a winner. He returned to the sidelines two weeks later.

The dream for another national championship ended at home November 21. The 20th-ranked Iowa Hawkeyes pulled off what amounted to a crushing "upset" by tying No. 1 Notre Dame, 14-14, before another Irish capacity crowd. Leahy's team was lucky to escape with a tie—the Irish scored with just six seconds left.

Notre Dame trounced USC, 48-14, in Los Angeles and then wrapped up the season with a rare December game at home against SMU. Although few suspected that the game would be Leahy's last, his team demolished the Ponies, 40-14, and carried the coach off the field on their shoulders. In his postgame press conference, Leahy remarked, "The 1953 football team is the greatest Notre Dame ever had."

Leahy's announcement that he was leaving the coaching profession on that late January 31 afternoon stunned his players, family, and friends. In 11 seasons at Notre Dame, he had won 87 games, lost 11, and tied nine. He guided the Irish to four consensus national championships—one more than his mentor, Knute Rockne.

Time Capsule

- Senator Joseph McCarthy accused over 200 employees of the U.S. State Department of being members of the Communist Party.

- Construction began on the Mackinac Bridge in northern Michigan.

- A disc jockey working for a radio station in Memphis, Tennessee, played a record by a new artist named Elvis Presley.

- Roger Bannister became the first runner to break the four-minute-mile barrier on May 6 in Oxford, England.

- The University of Notre Dame applied for a television license from the Federal Communications Commission. Under the auspices of the Michiana Telecasting Corporation, the University would eventually own and operate WNDU-TV, a commercial NBC affiliate, for over 50 years. The University sold the TV station in 2006.

RIGHT:
FRANK LEAHY.

Irish Legend

The resurgence was almost complete, and Irish fans had John Lattner to thank.

The talented right halfback didn't lead Notre Dame in any statistical categories in 1953. But he always seemed to be in the right place at the right time—whether on offense or defense—and he helped Notre Dame compile a 9-0-1 record in what would turn out to be coach Frank Leahy's last season. Lattner would also become Notre Dame's fourth Heisman Trophy winner.

Lattner, a native of Chicago, was a three-year starter at Notre Dame, but he didn't come into his own until his junior season in 1952. Named a consensus All-American, he averaged nearly five yards a carry and nearly 15 yards per catch. He also returned both kicks and punts and played defense, intercepting four passes.

As a senior, Lattner nearly duplicated those numbers. He finished his career as the Notre Dame record holder for all-purpose yards from rushing, receiving, and runbacks with 3,250 yards. The mark stood for 26 years until Vagas Ferguson passed Lattner in 1979. Lattner repeated as a consensus All-American his senior year.

In addition to the Heisman Trophy, Lattner received the Maxwell Trophy as the top collegiate player as a junior and senior.

Lattner was drafted by the Pittsburgh Steelers and played one year before entering the service. A knee injury in a military game ended his career.

He was inducted into the National Football Foundation Hall of Fame in 1979.

Irish Lore

During the 1953-54 season, the Notre Dame basketball team traveled to Bloomington to take on Indiana, the defending NCAA champion. Although the Irish held All-American Don Schlundt to just nine points, the Hoosiers handed Notre Dame a 66-55 setback. Eight days later, Notre Dame would lose at Bradley, but the Irish then went on a tear—winning the final 16 games of the regular season.

Making its second trip to the NCAA tournament in as many years, Notre Dame downed Loyola of Louisiana in its first-round game in Fort Wayne. The next opponent was top-ranked Indiana, but at least the game was in Iowa City and not Bloomington.

Dick Rosenthal scored 25 points and grabbed 15 rebounds to lead Notre Dame to a stunning 65-64 upset of the Hoosiers.

The celebration was short-lived. The next day it was Penn State's turn to be the spoiler as the Nittany Lions downed Notre Dame, 71-63, to end its incredible season at 22-3.

ABOVE:
COACH TERRY BRENNAN (LEFT).

RIGHT:
COACH TERRY BRENNAN (LEFT).

Irish Moment

Terry Brennan had big shoes to fill.

The former Irish halfback, who graduated in 1949, was handed the almost impossible task of following a legend—his former coach and mentor Frank Leahy.

Named as Leahy's successor on the same day as the coach's resignation, Brennan had spent the 1953 season as the coach of the freshman team. He would take over a varsity squad that ranked second in most preseason polls.

Although Brennan's squad shut out fourth-rated Texas in the season opener in Notre Dame Stadium, old nemesis Purdue pulled off another upset of the top-ranked Irish, 27-14, in the second game of the season.

From then on, Notre Dame posted victories over its next eight opponents to finish the season at 9-1-0. That mark was the best first-year mark of any coach in modern Notre Dame football history.

Brennan was in illustrious company on more than one occasion that first season. At halftime of the North Carolina game, Knute Rockne's last two teams—the national champions of 1929 and 1930—were honored at halftime. One of the former players present was Frank Leahy.

In the home finale against USC in late November, Leahy returned to the field again—this time to accept a bouquet of flowers from the Notre Dame student body—a small token of its appreciation for his efforts as head coach.

Leahy tried to keep a low profile that year, but he did attend Notre Dame games and sat in his stadium box.

Irish Legend

Three-year starting quarterback Ralph Guglielmi finally earned consensus All-America honors as a senior in 1954.

His heady, consistent play helped coach Terry Brennan's first Irish squad finish the year at 9-1. In the season opener against Texas, the six-foot, 180-pound native of Columbus, Ohio, was responsible for all three Notre Dame touchdowns. He rushed for two and threw for another score. Guglielmi also intercepted three Longhorn passes to seal the 21-0 shutout.

During his career, Guglielmi threw for over 3,000 yards and 18 touchdowns. He also crossed the goal 13 times himself, once on an interception return.

After playing in the 1955 College All-Star and East-West Shrine games, Guglielmi was the first-round draft pick of the Washington Redskins. He also played for St. Louis in 1961 and the New York Giants in 1962. He retired after the 1963 season with the Philadelphia Eagles.

Guglielmi was inducted into the College Football Hall of Fame December 2001.

LEFT:
RALPH GUGLIELMI.

Irish Lore

Notre Dame fencing and NCAA titles go together like bacon and eggs, macaroni and cheese, spaghetti and meatballs.

But, heading into the 1955 season, no Midwestern fencer had ever won an NCAA title in any weapon.

Notre Dame junior Don Tadrowksi changed all that. During the season, his first as a regular, the Chicago, Illinois, native posted a stellar 33-7 record.

At the tournament, held in East Lansing, Michigan, Tadrowski finished the first day of competition in a three-way tie for the lead in the epee. He won nine of his last 10 matches to win the championship by one bout.

Coach Walter Langford's team finished seventh overall. After the meet, Langford beamed over his star pupil. He told *The Scholastic*, "The odds of a Midwestern fencer taking a title in the NCAA competition are over 100-1 since Eastern schools have greater experience and competitive opportunities."

Tadrowski, like most Notre Dame fencers in the early years, did not take up the sport until enrolling in the University as a freshman.

1955-56

RIGHT:
PAUL HORNUNG INTERCEPTS A PASS
AGAINST INDIANA.

Irish Moment

For the first time in 20 years, Notre Dame added a varsity sport to its lineup.

Wrestling, which had competed as a club sport for years, began a 37-year run as a monogram sport in 1955.

Nearly 50 students attended try-outs in early November to vie for a spot on coach Tom Fallon's team.

By the end of the season, the Irish wrestlers had posted a respectable 6-4 dual match record. Jack Armstrong, who wrestled in the 177-pound class, posted a 10-0 individual mark for the season and advanced to the Case Tech 4-1 Tournament in Cleveland.

Irish Legend

Paul Hornung did just about everything but paint the helmets for coach Terry Brennan's teams in 1955 and 1956.

He played quarterback, halfback, fullback, and safety. As a junior he ranked fourth nationally in total offense with 1,215 yards (743 passing, 472 rushing, 109 kick returns) and earned All-America honors. Perhaps his best game came against fourth-ranked Navy. He ran for one touchdown, passed for another, and intercepted two passes to seal the 21-7 upset victory. In a loss to USC, the 6-2, 205-pound native of Louisville, ran and threw for 354 yards, the best performance in college football that year. Notre Dame finished 8-2.

In 1956, the Irish won only two games, their worst record in recent memory. Notre Dame might have been awful, but Hornung was brilliant. He ranked second in total offense with 1,337 yards and was responsible for more than half of the 130 points scored by the Irish that year. He capped his season senior by winning the Heisman Trophy, becoming the first and only player from a losing team to receive the award.

LEFT:
PAUL HORNUNG CARRIES AGAINST NAVY.

BELOW:
AUBREY LEWIS.

Hornung, who earned a monogram in basketball at Notre Dame, played professional football for the Green Bay Packers and led the team in scoring in 1959, 1960, and 1961. He retired from professional football in 1966 and was inducted into the National Football Foundation Hall of Fame in 1985. A year later he joined the Pro Football Hall of Fame.

Irish Lore

Things went Aubrey Lewis' way in 1955.

The second-string halfback rushed for over 200 yards and two touchdowns. He also intercepted four passes.

But the Montclair, NJ, native had an even better season with the track team. He finished first in the 400-meter hurdles at the NCAA Outdoor Championships.

As a junior, Lewis saw more playing time on the football field and rushed for 292 yards, and caught 11 passes for 170 yards. The following spring he finished third in the 400-meter hurdles at the NCAA Championships.

1956-57

Time Capsule

- President Dwight Eisenhower defeated Adlai Stevenson to win re-election to a second term.

- Hurricane Aubrey killed 400 people in Cameron, Louisiana.

- Marine pilot John Glenn set a transcontinental speed record by flying from California to New York in a supersonic jet. It took him three hours, 23 minutes, and eight seconds.

- Althea Gibson won her second consecutive singles titles at both Wimbledon and the U.S. Open.

- The University of Notre Dame awarded the 1957 Laetere Medal to Clare Boothe Luce, a member of the U.S. House of Representatives, who also enjoyed a career as an editor, playwright, social activist, journalist, and diplomat.

ABOVE:
IRISH BASEBALL COACH JAKE KLINE (LEFT).

RIGHT:
JOHN SMYTHE.

Irish Moment

Baseball stole the show at Notre Dame during the 1956-57 school year.

During the regular season, coach Jake Kline led the Irish to an 11-6 record—not spectacular but good enough to earn a bid to the NCAA Tournament.

Playing in Kalamazoo, the Irish won their first two games over Alma (18-2) and Western Michigan (4-2). After a 9-2 loss to Northwestern, Notre Dame and the Wildcats played for the trip to The College World Series in Omaha in the double-elimination tourney. This time the Irish came out on top, 6-1.

After losing its first World Series game to Iowa State, Notre Dame blasted Colorado State, 23-2. Right-hander Chuck Symeon threw a five-hitter the next day to blank Texas. But a 5-4 defeat at the hands of eventual runner-up Penn State ended the amazing World Series run for Notre Dame.

Infielder Jim Morris paced the Irish hitters in Omaha, collecting 10 hits in 14 at-bats for a .714 batting average, still a College World Series record.

Notre Dame's baseball team notched another milestone in 1957. Catcher Elmer Kohorst, who served as co-captain of the 1957 team, became the school's first baseball All-American.

Irish Legend

Center John Smythe knew how to persevere—in basketball and in life.

The 6-foot-5 native of Chicago came to Notre Dame to play basketball, but he was not on scholarship. Financial aid was not widely available in the early 1950s, so Smythe was scraping to get by.

A Notre Dame education cost much more than he could afford. After his first semester, Smythe told coach John Jordan he would most likely be heading back to Chicago because he could not pay his bills. Jordan worked a little magic, and the next thing Smythe knew, he had a basketball scholarship to stay and play for the Irish.

Smythe averaged 13.1 points per game as a sophomore and helped the Irish to a 14-10 record. Notre Dame dropped to 9-15 the following season, but Smythe scored over 16 points per game. He moved to center and captained the team as a senior. The Irish improved to 20-8 and finished third in the NCAA Mideast Regional. Smythe finished second in scoring that year, averaging 19 points per game.

Eventually Smythe found his calling and it wasn't on the basketball court. He entered the seminary and became a priest. At Maryville Academy in Des Plaines, Illinois, he founded a college scholarship program for at-risk children.

In 2002, Rev. Edward Malloy, C.S.C., president of the University, presented Rev. John Smythe the Laetare Medal during commencement ceremonies.

Irish Lore

Rev. George Holderith, C.S.C., celebrated his 25th anniversary as coach of the Notre Dame golf team by directing the squad to a 13-2 season. During Holderith's tenure, his teams won 152 matches, lost 59, and tied 11.

Holderith had organized golf as a club sport in 1933 and convinced Rev. John Cavanaugh to make golf a varsity sport in 1941.

1957-58

The 1950s

Time Capsule

- The bodies of unidentified soldiers killed during World War II and the Korean War were buried at the Tomb of the Unknowns in Arlington National Cemetery.

- A dog named Laika became the first animal in space as a "passenger" on *Sputnik 2*, launched by the Soviet Union.

- Bobby Fischer won the United States Chess Championship on January 8. He was 14 years old.

- Arnold Palmer captured his first Masters Tournament in 1958.

- As part of a $4 million expansion project, Keenan and Stanford halls offered rooms to a combined 600 residents. A new dining hall also opened on the east edge of campus.

ABOVE:
DICK LYNCH CARRIES
AGAINST OKLAHOMA.

Irish Moment

Oklahoma had not lost a game in 47 outings—the nation's longest winning streak. The last time the Sooners failed to celebrate after the final gun was when Notre Dame beat them, 28-21, in the 1953 season opener. They were the defending national champions, averaging 300 yards a game, and they had scored in 123 straight outings. Ranked No. 2 in the country, Oklahoma had manhandled the Irish, 40-0, the previous season.

Notre Dame was 4-2 heading into the game, but the Irish had dropped their last two contests to No. 16 Navy and No. 4 Michigan State. The offense had scored just 12 points in those two contests, while giving up 54. The only ones who gave Notre Dame any chance at all were the Irish players. "We went down there to win," wrote Irish halfback Dick Lynch in *The Scholastic* after the game. And win Notre Dame did. It wasn't easy, and it wasn't pretty. But it was perhaps one of the most improbable victories in Irish football history.

The Irish and Sooners battled to a scoreless tie through most of the game. Finally, with just 3:50 left and the Irish facing a fourth and goal at the Oklahoma three, Lynch took a pitch from quarterback Bob Williams, skirted around right end, and ran in for the touchdown. Notre Dame hung on for the 7-0 win.

After the game, hundreds of students packed the Notre Dame Grotto before gathering at the corner of Angela Boulevard and Notre Dame Avenue to welcome the Irish home. Nearly 5,000 fans cheered wildly when the team busses finally returned to campus.

Irish Legend

As a member of the 1930-32 Irish track teams, Alex Wilson earned All-America honors three times—quite a feat since he hailed from Canada. Competing in the quarter- and half-mile events, Wilson never lost a race while wearing a Notre Dame uniform. In 1932, he established a national indoor record in the 440 with a time of 49.3. He also won the Amateur Athletic Union 600 and the Millrose 600 twice.

Wilson represented Canada in the 1928 (Amsterdam) and 1932 (Los Angeles) Olympics, winning a silver medal in the 800 meters and a bronze medal in the 400 meters on his second trip to the Games. After graduating from Notre Dame, Wilson spent 18 years as a track and swimming coach at Loyola. In 1950, he returned to his alma mater and this time stayed for 23 years. During his tenure, the Irish track teams placed in the national top 10 a total of 11 times. Three of his athletes won national championships, while 28 earned All-America designations in track and another eight were cross country All-Americans.

In 1957, Wilson guided Notre Dame to the NCAA cross country title at East Lansing, Mich. His team was a balanced squad—the top Irish finisher that day was Ed Monnelly, who placed 19th. Not one Notre Dame runner earned All-America honors that year, but Wilson was more than happy to settle for the team trophy. Unfortunately, he and the team didn't stick around long enough after the race to pick it up. The weather was unseasonably cold that day, and Wilson figured his team's score of 121 points was much too high to contend for the championship. He rounded up his runners, and they left on the team bus for the drive back to South Bend. About halfway home, Wilson and his team were stunned to hear over the radio that Notre Dame had won the national cross-country title, upsetting heavily favored Michigan State by six points.

Wilson was inducted into the Canadian Track Hall of Fame in 1954. In 1967 he was honored by the Helms Athletic Foundation Hall of Fame for his contributions as a collegiate track coach.

The Alex Wilson Indoor Track and Field Invitational is annually held in his honor at the Loftus Center on campus.

Irish Lore

After a standout high school career in Southhampton, Long Island, Carl Yastrzemski accepted a scholarship offer to play basketball and baseball at the University of Notre Dame.

First-year students were not eligible for varsity competition in those days, so Yaz toiled for the freshman squads. During the spring, the baseball and football teams often practiced at the same time, on fields at least 500 feet apart. One day during practice, Yaz hit a ball that soared out of the baseball field and over the goal post on the football field before finally landing nearly a group of players. Irish assistant football coach Hank Stram, who would later guide the Kansas City Chiefs to the 1969 Super Bowl title, picked up the ball and said, "I guarantee Carl Yastrzemski hit this."

Yaz ended up leaving Notre Dame before ever playing in a varsity game. The Boston Red Sox offered him a professional contract for the then-unheard of sum of $112,000 after his freshman year.

Inducted into the Baseball Hall of Fame in 1989, Yastrzemski played 23 seasons in the major leagues—all with the Boston Red Sox. In 1967, he was the league's MVP and led the Red Sox to the pennant as well as a trip to the World Series. *Sports Illustrated* named him its Sportsman of the Year, and he won the Hickok Belt, which is awarded to the top professional athlete.

During his first three years as a professional player, Yaz returned to Notre Dame after the baseball season to take classes toward his degree. He eventually graduated from Merrimac.

1958-59

Time Capsule

- Alaska became the 49th state on January 3, while Hawaii joined the Union as the 50th state in August.

- NASA announced the selection of seven military pilots who would become the first astronauts in the Mercury space program.

- MGM's movie *Ben-Hur* won four Oscars for best picture, best director, best actor, and best supporting actor.

- Manager Casey Stengel guided the New York Yankees to their fifth World Series title in eight years, downing the Milwaukee Braves, four games to three.

- Bruce Babbitt was elected president of the Notre Dame student body. He would eventually serve as governor of his native Arizona as well as spend eight years as secretary of the interior in the cabinet of President Bill Clinton.

ABOVE:
MAX BROWN.

RIGHT:
TOMMY HAWKINS.

Irish Moment

Notre Dame claimed its second NCAA championship in tennis during the 1959 tournament, just two seasons after Tom Fallon had replaced former player Charles Samson as coach. The Irish shared the team title with Tulane.

During the regular season, the Irish won all 14 of its dual matches. Ten of those victories featured complete 9-0 sweeps of the opponent. Eventual Big Ten champion Michigan was the only team to challenge the Irish that year, but Notre Dame still prevailed, 5-4.

Ironically, the NCAA Tournament was held at Northwestern, the same site where the Irish had tied Miami and Texas for its first team tennis title.

Irish All-American Max Brown dropped the singles semifinals to eventual champion Whitney Reed of San Jose State. Brown then teamed with Bill Heinbecker in doubles but the pair lost to the top-seeded duo from Tulane of Crawford Henry and Ron Holmberg.

Brown, who was named second-team All-America in 1958, was accorded first-team honors in 1959. The Louisville, Kentucky, native posted a career mark of 52-7 in singles. Teammates Heinbecker and Don Ralph also gained second-team All-America recognition in 1959.

Irish Legend

Tommy Hawkins created quite a sensation when he became a starter for coach John Jordan's basketball team as a sophomore in 1956-57. The 6-foot-5 forward led the Irish in scoring with an impressive 20.6 scoring average. He also grabbed over 17 rebounds a game. Notre Dame finished with a 20-8 record and placed third in the NCAA Mideast Regional.

The following year, Hawkins was spectacular, leading the Irish to the NCAA Elite Eight and an eighth-place finish in the AP poll. As a junior, Hawkins ranked 11th in the nation in scoring, averaging 25.2 points per game. For the first and only time in nine appearances, Notre Dame finished 2-0 in the Hoosier Classic, an annual basketball tournament played in Indianapolis during the Christmas holidays. The Irish beat Purdue, 68-61, and then Indiana, 89-74, for the clean sweep of their in-state rivals. That season also marked the first time in history that a Notre Dame basketball team would score over 100 points in a single game.

Hawkins' senior season was somewhat disappointing because the Irish would win just 12 games in 25 tries. But Hawkins averaged 23.4 points per game and served as captain.

Hawkins, who twice earned All-America recognition, ended his Irish career as Notre Dame's all-time leader in scoring average (23.0) and rebounding average (16.7). Those numbers still rank him No. 3 and No. 2, respectively.

A 1959 graduate, Hawkins played 10 years in the NBA before embarking on a career in sports broadcasting. He also worked as vice president of communication for the Los Angeles Dodgers.

LEFT:
SWIMMING COACH DENNIS STARK.

Irish Lore

Swimming became a varsity sport in 1958-59, and coach Dennis Stark, a 1947 graduate of the University, led the Irish to a 5-5 dual meet record.

Stark, who also taught in the physical education department, was the face of the Notre Dame swimming program for 27 years until his retirement in 1983. In addition to teaching and coaching swimming, Stark directed swimming activities at the Rockne Memorial Pool and later the Rolfs Aquatic Center. He was instrumental in offering a learn-to-swim program for children of both faculty and staff at both pools and worked to create and expand the swimming program in Special Olympics.

Time Capsule

- President Dwight Eisenhower announced a plan to send 3,500 American military "advisers" to Vietnam.

- African-Americans began staging non-violent sit-ins at segregated restaurants throughout the country.

- *The Twilight Zone,* starring Rod Serling, debuted on the CBS network primetime lineup.

- Wilt Chamberlain of the Philadelphia '76ers was named most valuable player in the National Basketball Association.

- President Dwight Eisenhower became the first president to deliver a commencement address at the University of Notre Dame on June 5, 1960.

Irish Moment

For the second time in five years, Notre Dame had a new football coach.

Terry Brennan, who had led five Irish teams to a 32-18 record, was relieved of his duties in late December in 1958. South Bend native Joe Kuharich—who played under Elmer Layden at Notre Dame—was named head coach of his alma mater.

Kuharich certainly had the credentials to coach. Three years earlier, he had been named coach of the year in the NFL while with the Washington Redskins.

But Kuharich would learn quickly in his first season that college and professional football are two very different games. In 1959, with just 12 returning letterwinners on his squad, Kuharich led the Irish to a disappointing 5-5 record. The highlight of the season was a 16-6 win over seventh-ranked USC in the season finale.

Kuharich would coach at Notre Dame through 1962. Not once during those years did the Irish have a winning season.

ABOVE:
JOE KUHARICH.

RIGHT:
NOTRE DAME BENGAL BOUTS.

Irish Legend

Knute Rockne liked to box and he thought it would keep his football players in shape. So, in 1923, he started the Notre Dame Boxing Club.

In 1932, Dominic "Nappy" Napolitano, director of club and

recreational sports at Notre Dame, organized the Bengal Bouts Boxing Tournament to give students an opportunity to fight in a championship-like format and raise money for the Bengal Missions of the Holy Cross in East Pakistan. He incorporated the motto, "Strong bodies fight that weak bodies may be nourished," which carries on to this day.

For two months prior to the Bengal Bouts, Nappy worked with the students two hours a day five times a week. But he spent countless hours during his "down time," mentoring hundreds of young Notre Dame boxers who sought his counsel outside of the ring. Nappy directed the Bengal Bouts for 48 years, retiring in 1980.

In the 1950s, it was not unusual for the Bengal Bouts to draw 10,000 fans to the ring for what *The Scholastic* called "good, clean boxing."

In the winter of 1960, football player Nick Buoniconti, who would later play for the Miami Dolphins, was one of over 100 students who participated in the Bengal Bouts.

Irish Lore

Irish distance runner Ron Gregory set a world record in the 880-yard event on the dirt track of the Notre Dame Fieldhouse in a dual meet with Pittsburgh.

Gregory, a native of St. Louis, usually ran the mile and two-mile events and held school records in both. He also was the anchor leg on Notre Dame's distance medley relay team. His performance on that unit convinced Irish track coach Alex Wilson to give Gregory a chance to run the shorter distance as an individual.

Gregory, who won three monograms as a member of the track team, routinely established school and meet records during his career at Notre Dame.

LEFT:
RON GREGORY.

1960-61

Irish Moment

The 1960-61 school year was easily one of the worst in Notre Dame athletic history.

The football team, under the guidance of second-year coach Joe Kuharich, finished a dismal 2-8. The Irish sandwiched their season with victories over two California teams. Notre Dame downed the Bears of Cal-Berkeley, 21-7, at home on September 24 and then shut out USC, 17-0, on November 26 at the Coliseum. But in between, the Irish dropped eight straight—a school record—and scored only 73 points.

Somehow, guard Myron Pottios earned All-America honors. The football outlook was so bleak that Notre Dame's yearbook *The Dome*, titled its football section, "From Rock to Rock Bottom." Fans were openly accusing University president Rev. Theodore M. Hesburgh of trying to de-emphasize football.

Life didn't get much better during the winter months. The Irish basketball team compiled a 12-14 record, and only two players boasted scoring averages in double figures. The Notre Dame wrestling team went 1-8, and in the spring, the baseball squad won only 12 of 29 games.

Four Irish teams managed to put together winning seasons. The swim team finished 7-5 in dual meet action, the fencers went 14-2, and the golf team finished 10-3-1.

Tennis turned in the brightest performance of the year with a 17-2 dual match record and a fourth-place finish at the NCAA Tournament. Don Ralph, who ended his Notre Dame career with a 46-3 mark at singles and a 43-3 posting at doubles, was named All-American for the third consecutive year. He also won the University's Byron Kanaly Award.

ABOVE:
MYRON POTTIOS.

Irish Legend

Myron Pottios stood out in a crowd—at least on the Notre Dame football team in 1960.

The senior captain was the only Irish player to receive All-America recognition after a disappointing 2-8 season.

During his three years on the Notre Dame football team, Pottios played center, guard, and linebacker for the Irish. He came back from knee surgery as a junior and led the team in tackles with 74. He also blocked a punt. Pottios' teammates awarded him a game ball after the last outing of his career, a 17-0 victory over USC in the Los Angeles.

Pottios went on to play professional football with the Pittsburgh Steelers, the Los Angeles Rams, and the Washington Redskins. He played on the Redskins' 1973 Super Bowl team that lost to Miami, 14-7.

Irish Lore

Varsity sports offered little to cheer about in 1960-61 so students looked for other things to do on and off campus.

Several students formed a ski team that entered intercollegiate competition as a club sport. The bowling team, also a club sport, contended for the state title. There was a regatta in the spring, and inevitable games of catch on the Quad.

Many students simply buried themselves in their books.

1961-62

Irish Moment

Notre Dame won its first three football games to open the 1961 season, and fans cautiously hoped that the tide was finally turning. Two wins over Oklahoma and Purdue pushed the Irish to No. 8 in the polls, and a 30-0 trouncing of USC moved the Irish up to number six.

In week four, Notre Dame had to travel to East Lansing and the Spartans were ranked number one. Daryl Lamonica gave the Irish an early 7-0 lead, and the Notre Dame defense stymied Michigan State in the first half, but the Spartans erupted for 17 points in the last two periods. The victory put Michigan State in the Notre Dame record books—the Spartans became the first team to beat the Irish six consecutive times.

A pair of close losses the following two weeks dropped Notre Dame out of the polls, but the Irish recovered to beat Pitt on the road and Syracuse at home. However, Iowa and Duke handed Notre Dame setbacks in the final two games of the season, and the Irish were still looking for a record above the .500 mark.

Irish Legend

Guard Nick Buoniconti never played for a football team that turned in a winning record at Notre Dame. His perfect season with the 1973 Super Bowl champion Miami Dolphins may have helped ease that disappointment, however.

A native of Springfield, Massachusetts, Buoniconti played guard in 1959, 1960, and 1961. During his three years on campus, the Irish won just 12 games. After finishing third on the team in tackles as a sophomore, Buoniconti shared playing time with captain Myron Pottios as a junior. Pottios paced the team in tackles with 74; Buoniconti had 71.

Named an Irish co-captain as a senior, Buoniconti recorded 74 tackles—a team high—in 1961. He also blocked two kicks as Notre Dame improved to 5-5.

Although his name popped up on several All-America squads as a second or third team mention, Buoniconti was not drafted until the 12th round. After playing in the American Football League, Buoniconti joined the Miami Dolphins in 1968. There he won back-to-back Super Bowls. He retired from professional football after the 1976 season.

Irish Lore

According to Notre Dame fans, the officials got it right—at least this time.

Although the Irish had jumped out to a 14-0 lead over Syracuse, the visitors took a 15-14 lead late in the game when they successfully connected on the two-point conversion.

Notre Dame, however, had one last chance from its one 30-yard line with just 17 seconds left.

Finding his receivers covered, quarterback Frank Budka scampered 21 yards before going out of bounds to stop the clock. Now he had eight seconds. This time, he fired a

10-yard pass to George Sefcik, who quickly stepped out of bounds. The clock read 0:03. Joe Perkowski walked on to the field to attempt what would have been a 56-yard field goal.

Syracuse's Walt Sweeney rushed through the line and ran right into Perkowski. Flags flew, and the officials called a penalty for roughing the kicker. The ball was moved 15 yards forward, and Perkowski sent the 41-yard attempt through the middle of the uprights for the score and a 17-15 Irish win.

Syracuse protested, but the call held. Notre Dame got the win.

1962-63

Irish Moment

Basketball and baseball gave Notre Dame students and fans a reason to smile in 1962-63.

After two straight losing seasons, coach John Jordan had the Irish on a roll, winning their first six games. His excellent sophomore class of native Hoosiers—Walt Sahm of Indianapolis, Jay Miller of Goshen, and Ron Reed of LaPorte—helped herald the resurgence.

Prior to the mid-semester break, Notre Dame had posted a 12-4 record and were the talk of the basketball world, but grades burst Jordan's bubble. Two starters, responsible for nearly 30 points a game, were ruled academically ineligible for the second semester, and the Irish skidded through the rest of the way. Notre Dame did manage to wrangle an invitation to the NCAA Tournament, its first in three years, but the Irish lost, 77-72, to Bowling Green in the first round.

In the spring, the Notre Dame baseball team put together a 19-11 campaign and earned a bid to the NCAA Tournament even though the Irish lost their final four games of the season. Notre Dame was eliminated in its third game after a 4-0 loss to Illinois.

Irish Legend

No one knew just how good quarterback Daryle Lamonica could be until long after he left Notre Dame.

Lamonica came to Notre Dame as a highly touted four-sport athlete from Fresno, California. He chose the Irish after turning down an offer from the Chicago Cubs to play professional baseball.

As a sophomore, the 6-foot-2 Lamonica split quarterbacking duties with George Haffner as Notre Dame went 2-8. Lamonica also handled the punting chores and started at defensive back, recording 33 tackles. The next year coach Joe Kuharich played musical quarterbacks with Lamonica and Frank Budka, and the Irish "improved" to 5-5. Lamonica threw just 52 passes, completing only 20 for two touchdowns. He also rushed for 135 yards and three touchdowns. On defense, he had 29 tackles and a pair of interceptions.

As a senior, Lamonica finally got a chance to play quarterback for the entire season. He completed 64 passes of 124 passes for 821 yards. His favorite target was Jim Kelly, who made 41 catches that year. The Irish finished 5-5 again, and Kuharich's time had run out as head coach.

During the 1963 East-West Shrine game, Lamonica wowed the scouts by completing 20 of 28 passes for 349 yards. He was named the game's most valuable player.

Drafted by the Buffalo Bills in the AFL in 1963, he spent four seasons there as Jack Kemp's backup. Traded to the Oakland Raiders in 1967, he flourished in the Bay Area, leading his team to the Super Bowl in 1968. Nicknamed the "Mad Bomber," Lamonica threw for 3,228 yards and 30 touchdowns that year. He retired from football in 1974.

Irish Lore

Dean Smith is a very smart man.

But a few wondered what the future hall of fame coach was thinking when he agreed to play Notre Dame in the Fieldhouse during the 1962-63 season. True, the Irish were coming off two consecutive years under .500, and the Tar Heels owned a four-game winning streak over Notre Dame. Yet, they had not played in the Fieldhouse.

Even though Irish basketball had fallen on tough times, Notre Dame still owned an impressive 42-9 record at home over the last five years.

When Carolina came to town, students and fans packed the 4,000-seat Fieldhouse to the rafters. Many people who had braved the cold January night were turned away at the doors. Not one more soul could be squeezed in the building.

The game was a seesaw affair from start to finish, and when Jay Miller put Notre Dame up 63-61 with just six seconds left, the crowd went nuts. But the Tar Heels kept their cool, and Billy Cunningham threw up a 40-foot desperation shot at the buzzer that sailed through the net to send the game into overtime. Carolina then cruised to a 76-68 triumph—the Irish had run out of gas.

1963-64

Time Capsule

- On November 22, President John F. Kennedy was assassinated in Dallas. Vice President Lyndon Johnson, who was traveling with Kennedy that day, took the oath of office as the 36th president of the United States aboard Air Force One.

- Two days later, Jack Ruby shot and mortally wounded alleged assassin Lee Harvey Oswald. Millions of Americans saw the murder unfold live on television during network coverage of Oswald's transfer from the Dallas jail.

- On February 9th, the Beatles appeared on *The Ed Sullivan Show*. Two months later the British rock group owned the top five spots on the Billboard Top 40 singles list.

- Cassius Clay (Muhammad Ali) defeated Sonny Liston for the World Heavyweight Boxing Championship on February 25 in Miami Beach.

- The Memorial Library, now the Theodore M. Hesburgh Library and one of the most memorable landmarks on the Notre Dame campus, opened its doors to students and faculty. The Word of Life mosaic on the south façade of the building was added a year later.

ABOVE:
HEAD COACH HUGH DEVORE
TALKS WITH HIS TEAM.

Irish Moment

When Joe Kuharich resigned in March to take a job with the NFL, Notre Dame did not have a football coach. So, as the University had done once before, it turned to Hugh Devore to bail the Irish out of a tough spot.

A 1934 graduate of the University, Devore had filled in as head coach while Frank Leahy went to war. Now, he would step in again while University president Rev. Theodore Hesburgh, C.S.C., and executive vice president Rev. Edmund P. Joyce, C.S.C., looked for a football coach.

On paper, the Irish certainly seemed destined to improve its 5-5 record of a year ago. Kuharich had not left the cupboard bare.

Notre Dame lost its first two games of the season by less than six points. Sixth-ranked Wisconsin scored with just over a minute remaining to beat the Irish, 14-9, in the home opener, while Purdue edged Notre Dame, 7-6, in Ross-Ade Stadium.

The Irish came back to reel off two straight victories over seventh-ranked USC and UCLA, but the season quickly fell apart when Notre Dame lost its next four games.

After the Iowa game was cancelled because of the death of President John Kennedy, Devore's team let Syracuse take a 14-7 lead in the final three and a half minutes at Yankee Stadium. Notre Dame dropped its fifth straight game.

Over the last five years, Notre Dame had lost 30 of 49 games for an unspeakable .387 winning percentage. Could it get any worse?

A few months later, Irish officials would also be looking for a new basketball coach. After finishing 10-14, John Jordan tendered his resignation.

Irish Legend

Ron Reed won three letters in basketball and one in baseball as a student-athlete at the University of Notre Dame. Although he was a terrific two-sport athlete, most would have put their money on basketball as Reed's best and favorite sport.

The 6-foot-6 native of nearby LaPorte started as a sophomore for coach John Jordan's team that finished 17-9. As a junior, he averaged 20 points a game and ranked sixth in the nation in rebounding with 17.7 rebounds per game.

He capped his senior season with a 21.0 scoring average and helped Notre Dame to a 15-12-record and a return appearance in the NCAA Tournament.

A right-handed pitcher, Reed posted a 2-2 record and a 4.04 ERA in 1965 as a senior. He also struck out 47 batters in 64 innings of work.

After graduation, Reed signed a contract with the Detroit Pistons ... and the Atlanta Braves.

For two years, he played baseball in the summer and spent his winter months as the sixth man on the Pistons basketball team. The Braves finally told him he had to choose, and Reed picked baseball.

He played 19 years in the major leagues for Atlanta, St. Louis, and Philadelphia. He retired in 1984, spending his final season with the Chicago White Sox.

During his career, he posted a 146-140 mark and recorded 103 saves. He pitched in 751 games.

Reed, who became a reliever in 1976 while with Philadelphia, was the winning pitcher for the Braves the night Henry Aaron hit his home run to break Babe Ruth's record.

Irish Lore

At least the golf team had a rosy future.

Rev. Clarence Durbin, C.S.C., assumed the coaching reins from Irish golfing legend Rev. George Holderith, C.S.C., in 1962.

The sport of golf was changing on the collegiate level. Teams were moving away from the dual match format and gravitating to a schedule of invitational tournaments. Still, the Irish golfers finished 13-5 in competition and earned a bid to the NCAA Tournament at the Broadmoor Golf Club in Colorado Springs. Notre Dame finished fourth, and Mike O'Connell earned second-team All-America honors.

RIGHT:
ARA PARSEGHIAN.

Irish Moment

The Cavalry had arrived—and his name was Ara Parseghian.

Parseghian had been hired in early December after finishing his eighth season as head coach of the Northwestern Wildcats. Although he was the first non-Notre Dame graduate hired for the job, his credentials were impeccable. He had learned from the masters—Paul Brown, Woody Hayes, and Sid Gillman. Although Irish fans were skeptical of handing over the coaching reins to someone who had not played for or attended Notre Dame, they also were desperate for a winning football season. They had nothing to lose—except more football games.

Parseghian won them over early. Notre Dame obliterated Wisconsin, 31-7, in the season opener. A week later, Purdue fell, 34-15. The Irish rolled over Air Force, UCLA, Stanford, and Navy. The next thing Notre Dame fans knew their team was ranked No. 1—for the first time in 10 years. After a close win at Pitt, Parseghian closed out the season at home with lopsided victories over Michigan State and Iowa.

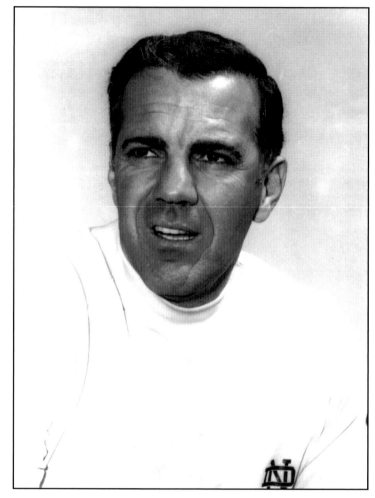

In nine games, Notre Dame had scored 270 points—more than twice its offensive output of the previous year, and the Irish defense had yielded just 57 points and had not given up more than two touchdowns in a game.

Only one obstacle stood in the way of Notre Dame and the national championship, but it was a big one. The Irish had to play traditional rival USC on Thanksgiving at the Coliseum.

Notre Dame owned the lead with just 1:33 to go, but USC scored a touchdown to dash Irish hopes for a perfect season. Although fans were disappointed with the loss, most couldn't wipe the smile from their faces. Notre Dame football was back. Parseghian had saved the day.

Irish Legend

John Huarte came out of nowhere to win the Heisman Trophy in 1964.

The Santa Ana, California, native missed more of his sophomore year because of an injury. As a junior he didn't accumulate enough playing time to earn a monogram.

But new coach Ara Parseghian didn't have much choice when making out the depth chart in his first season at the helm. He knew Huarte had been a highly recruited high school quarterback. The talent was there. It was Parseghian's job to figure out how to use it.

Huarte showed flashes of things to come when he threw for 270 yards and two touchdowns in the season-opening win at Wisconsin. By the time the season ended, Huarte ranked third nationally in total offense with 2,069 yards. He completed 114 of 205 passes for 2,062 yards and 16 touchdowns. He also scored three touchdowns himself. Huarte set 12 school records that season.

Huarte's numbers were hard to ignore. In addition to becoming Notre Dame's sixth Heisman Trophy winner, Huarte also won player of the year honors from UPI.

Irish Lore

Although Ara Parseghian stole most of the headlines in 1964-65, the other new kid on the Irish block also fared pretty well his first year on the job.

Former Irish football and basketball player Johnny Dee had taken over the basketball duties from his former mentor John Jordan. In his first season, Dee led the Irish to a 15-12 record and an appearance in the NCAA Tournament.

Notre Dame's cross-country team also had something to crow about in 1964. Senior Bill Clark placed second in the NCAA race in East Lansing to put Notre Dame fourth in the team standings. Clark's performance, which earned him All-America honors for the second straight year, remains the best individual finish in the NCAA Cross Country Championships by a Notre Dame runner.

1965-66

ABOVE:
ARA PARSEGHIAN.

Irish Moment

Notre Dame opened the 1965 season at home with a 48-6 thrashing of California. The win boosted the Irish to the top spot in the polls, but Ara Parseghian wasn't happy. His offense had accumulated almost 400 yards, but only 68 of those came from passes. Plus, the defense looked suspect. The secondary had given up to many completions.

A week later, Purdue, always a thorn in North Dame's side, welcomed the Irish to Ross-Ade Stadium. Notre Dame led late in the came, but Purdue sophomore quarterback Bob Griese orchestrated a 70-yard drive, scoring the final touchdown himself, to upset the Irish, 25-21.

Notre Dame won its next six games, but the season ended on a disappointing note. Michigan State, by then ranked No. 1, pinned a 12-3 loss on the Irish in the home finale. Notre Dame spent Thanksgiving in Miami. The Hurricanes couldn't score, but neither could the Irish. The game ended in a 0-0 time.

Notre Dame's offense had scored 250 points in its first seven games—20 in its last three. If Parseghian was going to get to the mountaintop, he needed to find a way to score—early and often.

At least one Notre Dame team had an undefeated season in 1965-66. Coach Tom Fallon's tennis squad breezed through its spring slate with a 15-0 mark and a first-place finish at the Eastern Collegiate Championships. But the Irish came up empty-handed in the NCAA Tournament and failed to place.

Irish Legend

Mike Wadsworth wore number 70 as a defensive tackle on the Notre Dame teams of 1963, 1964, and 1965, but his lucky number was likely three. His high school team lost three games during his career and the Irish compiled a 16-3-1 record with Wadsworth on the roster. Later in life, he would be blessed with three beautiful, intelligent daughters.

A native of Toronto, Canada, Wadsworth's first tour of duty at Notre Dame was hampered by knee injuries. But after a stellar career in a variety of fields, Wadsworth returned to his alma mater as athletic director and provided leadership, direction, and focus in a relatively turbulent period of college athletics.

Wadsworth graduated from Notre Dame in 1966 with a degree in political science.

He then returned to Toronto and spent five years in the Canadian Football League, earning rookie of the year honors. During his playing days he also attended the Osgoode Hall Law School and finished his law degree. He eventually became president of the CFL Players Association and helped his peers negotiate with their owners for better contracts and working conditions.

He moved into law after his professional playing career ended although he stayed in athletics by writing a column for the *Toronto Daily Star* and serving as a television color commentator for broadcasts of CFL games. Although he had argued several cases before the Canadian Supreme Court, Wadsworth took his litigating skills to the business world in 1981. Eight years later he was appointed to a five-year term as Canada's ambassador to Ireland.

Wadsworth succeeded Dick Rosenthal as Notre Dame's 10th athletic director in 1995. He moved the Irish into the BIG EAST Conference and oversaw the renovation and expansion of Notre Dame Stadium. As a former student-athlete at the University, Wadsworth was particularly aware of the demands and needs of those who try to excel on the field and in the classroom. He was instrumental in establishing a Life Skills Program.

Notre Dame also added two women's sports—lacrosse and rowing—under his watch and added 22 scholarships to the women's program.

During Wadsworth's tenure at Notre Dame, the athletic program ranked third in the nation in a review of all-around standards by *The Sporting News*.

Wadsworth returned to his native Canada in 2000. After a battle with cancer, he died on April 28, 2004, at the age of 60.

Irish Lore

The leprechaun became the official mascot of the University in 1965 when it was registered as an official University mark.

He joined the Notre Dame cheerleaders on the sidelines at football games, while "Clashmore Mike," represented by a series of terrier dogs since the 1950s, soon disappeared as part of the game day hoopla and promotion.

ABOVE:
THE "TICK" AND A TIE.

Irish Moment

Mention the year 1966 to a Notre Dame fan, and the odds are good the response will be one of two things—national championship or that dog-gone tie.

Ara Parseghian had tinkered with the offense and had Notre Dame rolling on all cylinders in the 1966 season. Quarterback Terry Hanratty and split end Jim Seymour had spent their winter "playing catch" and had worked their routine to near perfection.

The Irish cruised through the first eight games on the slate, outscoring the opposition, 301 to 28. Only Purdue and Bob Griese managed to score two touchdowns on the Irish in one game.

Heading into another "Game of the Century," Notre Dame owned the top spot in the polls and Duffy Daugherty's Spartans were right behind at number two. Hardly anything went Notre Dame's way once the team arrived in East Lansing. All-America halfback Nick Eddy slipped getting off the train and re-injured his shoulder. Backup quarterback Coley O'Brien, diagnosed with diabetes just a few weeks earlier, was still adjusting to his new regiment. And winter had come early for the November 19 game.

Injuries wiped out two starters early in the game. Spartan All-American Bubba Smith sacked Hanratty and sent him to watch from the sidelines. Two plays later center George Goeddeke sprained an ankle and joined him on the bench. The Spartans jumped out to a quick 10-0 lead, but the Irish fought back. O'Brien, who stepped in for Hanratty, directed Notre Dame 54 yards in nine plays. He capped the drive with a 34-yard scoring pass to Bob Gladieux, who had taken Eddy's place.

With the score tied and five minutes left in the game, Irish safety Tom Schoen intercepted a Spartan pass and returned it to the 18-yard line. After an eight-yard loss and an incomplete pass, Notre Dame had to try a field goal. This one—from 42 yards out—sailed wide right.

What happened next is still hotly debated 40 years later. The Irish, with less than three minutes to go, got the ball back on their own 30-yard line. Notre Dame managed one first down on four running plays. Coach Parseghian, to many of the fans' dismay, played it conservative—no Hail Marys, no trick plays, no desperation scrambles. With time running out, O'Brien kept the ball and ran straight into the line. The "Game of the Century" had ended in a tie but no one went home happy. Still, the tie might have preserved Notre Dame's No. 1 ranking and ultimately the national championship. The following week the Irish blasted USC, 51-0. Parseghian had his first title; Notre Dame had its first in 17 years.

Irish Legend

Commencement speakers are usually presidents, senators, poets, philosophers, or just plain old celebrities. Retired football players rarely get the nod.

But in 2004, Notre Dame could not have made a better choice when it selected Alan Page, a former All-American and All-Pro defensive end, to offer sage advice to the students it was turning loose on the world. Page, who earned monograms in 1964, 1965, and 1966, certainly had impressive football credentials.

A consensus All-America in 1966, the 6-foot-5, 230-pound native of Canton, Ohio, recorded 63 tackles as a senior to help Notre Dame win its ninth national championship. After participating in the 1967 East-West Shrine and College All-Star games, he was a first-round draft pick of the Minnesota Vikings.

Page, a member of the Vikings' famed "Purple People Eaters," played in four Super Bowls and eight Pro Bowls and became the first defensive player to win the league's most valuable player award in 1971. After retiring from professional football in 1981, Page sought a new challenge—law.

Page, a member of both the College and Pro Football halls of fame, has received two honorary degrees from his alma mater. He also was honored by the NCAA in 2004 as the recipient of its "Teddy" award, given annually to "a distinguished citizen of national reputation and outstanding accomplishment." Page and his wife Diane established the Page Foundation in 1988 to provide educational opportunities to students of color. The foundation has awarded over 4,000 grants, worth over $2.5 million, to nearly 2,000 students.

ABOVE:
ALAN PAGE.

BELOW:
IRISH CATCHER JOE KERNAN.

Irish Lore

Many college students end up following a professional path that has little to do with their major.

Not Joe Kernan. The catcher for the 1967 and 1968 baseball team used his Notre Dame degree in government to carve out a long and successful career in public service.

Originally from Washington, D.C., Kernan attended Notre Dame after graduating from Saint Joseph's High School in South Bend. After his 1968 graduation, he began his military service with the Navy in 1969 and was stationed as a flight officer on the *USS Kitty Hawk*. In 1972, while on a reconnaissance mission over North Vietnam, Kernan's plane was shot down. He spent 11 months as a prisoner of war.

After a career in business, Kernan decided to put his Notre Dame education to good use and ran for mayor of South Bend in 1987. He won three subsequent terms as mayor and was instrumental in bringing the College Football Hall of Fame to downtown South Bend.

In 1998, Kernan was elected to serve with Governor Frank O'Bannon as Indiana's lieutenant governor. He assumed the governorship in September 2003 when O'Bannon died in office.

Kernan returned to South Bend in 2005. He recently helped purchase the South Bend Silver Hawks, a single-A baseball team, and he teaches a course in government for the University.

1967-68

ABOVE:
DWIGHT MURPHY, BOB ARNZEN,
AND BOB WHITMORE.

RIGHT:
BILL HURD.

Irish Moment

Basketball coach John Jordan was getting what he wanted—a new arena. But the opening of the Athletic and Convocation Center was still one year away. The Irish basketball team wanted to send the Fieldhouse out in style.

Paced by the prolific scoring of a pair of junior Bobs—Arnzen and Whitmore—Notre Dame jumped off to an impressive 13-3 record by mid-January. The only losses were to three ranked teams—Indiana, UCLA, and Kentucky—on the road.

But after demolishing Butler at home, Notre Dame lost three straight to Illinois, Michigan State, and Detroit. An overtime win at home over DePaul snapped the losing skein, but two more defeats at the hands of Duke and St. John's sent the Irish to the NIT and not the NCAA.

The regular season ended with four wins, including the last two in the Fieldhouse.

Creighton would be the last opponent hassled in the old structure. The Blue Jays weren't fazed, however, and the Irish trailed at halftime. But George Restovich scored the game's last two baskets to give the Irish a 73-68 victory. Notre Dame had played in the Fieldhouse since 1899. The team had won 474 games there, losing just 91 for an amazing .839 winning percentage.

After accepting an NIT bid, the Irish traveled to Madison Square Garden for the second time that winter. They beat Army and Long Island in their first two contests, but dropped a 76-74 contest to nearby rival Dayton in overtime. Notre Dame beat St. Peter's, 81-78, in the consolation game for third place.

Whitmore led the team in scoring with a 22.0 average. Arnzen was close behind with a 21.5 mark.

Irish Legend

Bill Hurd ranked as one of the most accomplished athletes in Notre Dame history, both on and off the track.

As a collegian, he set eight Irish records and earned five All-America finishes at the 1968 and 1969 NCAA Track Championships. He was honored as the University's "athlete of the year" in 1967-68 after he broke the American indoor record in the 300-yard dash with a time of 29.8

He barely missed earning a berth on the 1968 U.S. Olympic team after a fifth-place finish in the 100 meters.

Hurd, who graduated with an electrical engineering degree, also earned a master's degree in management science from the Massachusetts Institute of Technology and his medical degree from the Meaharry Medical School in Nashville.

A noted eye surgeon, Hurd specializes in cataract, glaucoma and diabetic treatment, and keratorefractive surgery. He also spends two to three weeks a year providing voluntary eye surgery in Africa, Mexico, and Brazil.

Hurd has been honored with the Notre Dame Monogram Club's Moose Krause Distinguished Service Award as well as the Alumni Association's Harvey Foster Award.

In 1994, he was presented with the NCAA's prestigious Silver Anniversary Award, which recognizes the professional and community service accomplishments of former student-athletes.

Irish Lore

Rocky Bleier was as tough as his name.

The 5-foot-11, 195-pound, native of Appleton, Wisconsin, earned the starting job at halfback as a junior and helped Notre Dame win a national championship. He gained 282 yards on 63 carries and scored four touchdowns. He also caught 17 passes for 209 yards and a score.

Elected captain as a senior, he gained 357 yards on 77 tries and scored five touchdowns. Two of his 16 receptions were for scores. The Irish finished 8-2 that year, recovering from two early-season losses to win their last six games.

Small in stature but not in heart, Bleier became the 417th player picked in the 1968 NFL draft. The Pittsburgh Steelers were willing to take a chance. Determined to prove he could play in the NFL, Bleier worked harder than he had ever worked before—and that was hard. Making an NFL roster soon became the least of his worries.

LEFT:
ROCKY BLEIER.

In 1969, he was drafted into the Army and sent to Vietnam. He was seriously wounded in combat, and medical personnel told him he would be lucky to walk normally again. He could forget about football.

Bleier would not. His grit, toughness, and determination pushed him through grueling rehabilitation workouts. Finally, he gained a berth on the Steelers' roster in 1971. Three years later, he was Pittsburgh's starting halfback. He played an integral role in the team's four Super Bowl victories (1976, 1976, 1979, and 1980).

Bleier retired after that final Super Bowl championship. He had rushed for 3,864 yards on 928 carries and had caught 136 passes for 675 yards. Pittsburgh fans are grateful he didn't listen to his doctors.

Time Capsule

- Republican Richard M. Nixon defeated Hubert Humphrey in one of the closest presidential races in history.

- While aboard *Apollo 8*, astronauts Frank Borman, Jim Lovell and William Anders became the first humans to orbit the moon and view planet earth as a whole.

- Yale University announced plans to accept women students.

- Boston's Carl Yastrzemski won the American League hitting title for the third time with a .301 batting average.

- Students staged a rally to protest the Central Intelligence Agency's recruitment visit to Notre Dame.

Irish Moment

Completed over 29 months at a cost of nearly $9 million, the Athletic and Convocation Center gave the Notre Dame basketball team a much-needed new home.

The ACC (renamed the Edmund P. Joyce Center in 1987) also gave birth to a new varsity sport on campus—hockey.

The sport had deep roots at Notre Dame. In the early 1900s, a club team played on the lakes and at Culver Military Academy, some 45 miles away. Sporadically teams popped up through the years. Finally, in 1963, the University sanctioned a club team, which would play similar teams from other schools. South Bend's Howard Park, an outdoor rink, provided home ice.

In 1965, the University decided to elevate the sport to varsity status when the Athletic and Convocation Center opened three years later. One of the twin domes featured an ice rink and locker-room facilities. The athletic department began funding the team to help the transition. In 1966-67, the Irish icers finished with a 14-5-3 record and won the Air Force Invitational. The team had one more year to get ready for true intercollegiate play.

Charles "Lefty" Smith became the varsity team's first coach for the inaugural 1968-69 season. He retired from coaching 18 years later.

Notre Dame played its first hockey game in the Athletic and Convocation Center rink on January 9 and captured an 8-5 win over Ohio University. The Irish ended the year with a 16-8-3 record, and Dean Daigler served as captain. Notre Dame hockey was back.

ABOVE:
LEFTY SMITH.

RIGHT:
BOB ARNZEN.

Irish Legend

Bob Arnzen excelled on the basketball court, on the baseball diamond, and in the classroom.

A two-time captain for the Irish basketball squad, Arnzen became the Notre Dame basketball program's first and only three-time Academic All-American.

The 6-foot-5 native of Fort Thomas, Kentucky, led Notre Dame in scoring as a sophomore with a 21.4 scoring average. He also ranked 23rd in the nation that year with a .831 free throw percentage. The Irish finished 14-14, a significant improvement over the 5-21 mark of a year earlier.

As a junior—his first season as captain—Arnzen ranked second in scoring behind his classmate, Bob Whitmore, who averaged 22 points a game. Notre Dame posted a 21-9 mark and placed third in the NIT.

Arnzen captained the Irish again as a senior and led Notre Dame back to the NCAA Tournament on the strength of its 20-6 regular-season record. Arnzen and Whitmore tied for second in scoring with identical 17.7 averages. A 6-foot-3 sophomore guard named Austin Carr led the team that year with 22 points per game.

A right-handed pitcher, Arnzen posted a 6-3 win-loss record in three years with the Irish baseball team. He struck out 75 batters in 106.1 innings pitched.

Irish Lore

When the Athletic and Convocation Center opened in 1968, the building was state of the art.

Designed by Ellerbe Architects of St. Paul, Minnesota, the ACC featured 464,000 square feet of usable space, making it the largest exhibition center between Detroit and Chicago.

LEFT:
ATHLETIC AND CONVOCATION CENTER.

The ACC was meant to be versatile and serve as a venue to many different events. The north dome, which featured an ice rink and indoor track, could also be used for trade shows. The south dome, which seats over 11,000 for basketball, could also host concerts, banquets, lectures, and "graduation activities," as well as other special events.

During its almost 40 years of existence, the building has undergone several renovations. Its visitors have included a glamorous list of entertainers (Elvis Presley, Bruce Springsteen, Rod Stewart, Bill Joel, Bob Hope, Barry Manilow, James Taylor, Rod Steward, Neil Diamond, Elton John, Tina Turner, Garth Brooks, Bill Cosby, the Beach Boys, and U2), presidents (Jimmy Carter, Ronald Reagan, George H.W. Bush, and George W. Bush) and world leaders (Pierre Trudeau, Jose Napoleon Duarte, and Kofi Annan).

1969-70

Time Capsule

- Opposition to the war in Vietnam continued to increase even though President Richard Nixon began the first withdrawal of troops from Asia. In May 1970, four students at Kent State University were killed and nine others wounded by Ohio National Guardsmen during a demonstration.

- On July 20 astronaut Neil Armstrong became the first man to set foot on the moon. He was accompanied on the *Apollo 11* mission by Buzz Aldrin and Michael Collins. All three returned safely to Earth on July 24.

- The Woodstock Music Festival lasted three days in upstate New York.

- The Boston Bruins, led by Bobby Orr, became the first team in the United States to win the Stanley Cup in eight years.

- The College of Business announced plans to revise its curriculum and initiated a collaborative effort with the law school to offer a combined MBA/J.D. degree.

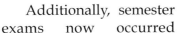

ABOVE:
JOE THEISMANN.

Irish Moment

For the first time since 1924, the University of Notre Dame changed its mind about postseason competition in football. If the Irish were lucky enough to earn a bowl invitation after the 1969 season, the University would accept it.

There were many reasons to make the change. Coach Ara Parseghian had resurrected the Notre Dame program from the dismal decade of the late '50s and early '60s. The exposure would help the program in recruiting and recognition, and participating in a bowl game would add to the coffers of the University's general fund.

Additionally, semester exams now occurred before the holiday break. Adding one more game to the schedule would not disrupt the players' academic pursuits.

Junior quarterback Joe Theismann had guided Notre Dame to a 8-1-1 regular-season mark. Purdue and quarterback Mike Phipps continued to be a thorn in the Irish side in early September by orchestrating the Boilers' third straight win over Notre Dame.

A 14-14 tie against third-ranked USC at home was the only other "blemish" on the schedule

Notre Dame headed to Dallas to take on top-ranked Texas.

The Irish had the Longhorns on the run early in the game. They jumped out to a 10-0 lead, thanks to Scott Hempel's 26-yard field goal in the first quarter and a 54-yard scoring pass from Theismann to Tom Gatewood in the second period.

Texas added its first touchdown in the second period and then took a short-lived lead on its second touchdown on the game in the fourth quarter. With six minutes left, Theismann threw another TD pass, this time to Jim Yoder, and Notre Dame clung to a 17-14 lead.

But the upset bid evaporated with just over a minute left to go in the game. The Longhorns drove 76 yards in 17 plays, scoring on a one-yard run by Billy Dale.

A Texas interception killed Notre Dame's final comeback attempt with 39 seconds left.

Texas earned the national championship that year, but the Irish made them earn it—the old fashioned way.

Irish Legend

Rick Wolhuter, the last man to qualify for the Olympic games in both the 800-yard and 1,500-meter events, brought an NCAA title back to Notre Dame in the spring of 1970 with a first-place finish in the 600-yard run.

A two-time All-American, Wolhuter also helped the Irish two-mile relay team take second place at the 1969 NCAA meet.

Wolhuter continued to improve on the track after graduation. In 1971, he won the IC4A 800-yard title and qualified for the Olympics in 1972. In 1974, he set the world record in the 1,000 meters and dominated that race the next three seasons at the national meet. In 1974, he won the prestigious Sullivan Award, presented annually to the nation's top amateur athlete.

Wolhuter finally added an Olympic medal to his collection when he won a bronze in the 800 meters at the 1976 Montreal Summer Games.

Wolhuter was inducted into the Track and Field Hall of Fame in 1971.

Irish Lore

Austin Carr, arguably the best basketball player in Notre Dame history, averaged 34.6 points per game during his Irish career. That mark still stands second on the NCAA all-time list behind Pete Maravich's incredible 44.2 average.

Ironically, while Carr paced the Irish in scoring three times, he never ever led the nation in scoring. He finished second behind Maravich as a junior and second to Mississippi's Johnny Newman as a senior. But coach John Jordan and Irish basketball fans never felt they had to settle for "second best."

Carr led the Irish to three 20-win seasons and three NCAA Tournament appearances.

ABOVE:
AUSTIN CARR.
Photo provided by Brother Charles McBride, C.S.C.

Irish Moment

What a difference a decade makes. While 1960-61 ranks as one of the lowest moments in Notre Dame athletic history, 1970-71 surely might be described as one of the best.

The Irish football team did not win the national championship but came awfully close.

In 1970 coach Ara Parseghian's team was loaded. Eleven starters returned, and four—Joe Theismann, Tom Gatewood, Larry DiNardo and Clarence Ellis—would win All-America honors.

Notre Dame moved up the ranks during the season by convincingly mowing down every team to get in its way. A pesky Georgia Tech squad and a stingy LSU defense provided close calls at home in November, but the Irish were still ranked No. 4 heading into their season finale against USC in Los Angeles.

Played in wet, sloppy conditions, the game showcased both teams' remarkable offenses. Theismann, who would finish second behind Jim Plunkett in the Heisman Trophy race, completed 33-of-58 passes for an incredible 526 yards. He also threw three interceptions that killed Notre Dame drives. Additionally, the Irish ground game was virtually nonexistent with 31 yards rushing. USC sent Notre Dame reeling, 38-28, and for the fourth time in history, the Trojans had ruined Irish hopes for a national championship.

The season didn't end there. Notre Dame made a repeat trip to the Cotton Bowl to face the defending national champion, Texas. The Longhorns, once again, were ranked No. 1 and were proud owners of a 30-game winning streak.

The Irish changed all of that—in a flash. Theismann accounted for three touchdowns in the first 17 minutes of the game, and the Notre Dame defense forced nine Texas turnovers.

A 24-11 victory, Notre Dame's second bowl win in history, kept Texas from claiming its second consecutive national title.

Less than a month later, the Irish basketball team also stopped an opponent's winning streak, and this one sent shock waves throughout the college basketball world.

Notre Dame had posted some impressive wins already that 1970-71 season. Senior Austin Carr pumped in 50 points to lead the Irish to a 99-92 victory over seventh-ranked Kentucky in Louisville, and the Irish had lost two close contests at Indiana and Marquette, ranked No. 2 at the time.

UCLA came to town on January 23. The Bruins had won four straight national championships and owned the country's top ranking. Coach John Wooden's Bruins had not lost a non-conference game in 48 tries.

UCLA never had a chance. Collis Jones scored the first two points of the game, and Notre Dame led almost the entire way. The Bruins tied the game once at 47 and cut the Irish lead to two twice. However, Carr scored 46 points to give Notre Dame an 89-82 victory in the nationally televised game. UCLA would not lose again for a very, very long time.

Irish Legend

By the time Joe Theismann graduated from the University of Notre Dame in 1971, he owned just about every passing record in the Irish history book. He may not have been the most decorated (winning All-America honors as a senior and finishing second in the Heisman Trophy voting), but there's no question he was one of the best.

Thanks to his leadership, enthusiasm, and incredible talent, the Irish compiled an 18-3-1 record during his two years as the starting quarterback.

A native of South River, N.J., Theismann received his baptism by fire as a sophomore, replacing the injured Terry Hanratty for three games at the end of the season. The pressure didn't faze him. Theismann completed 27 of 49 passes for 451 yards and two touchdowns.

As a junior, Theismann threw for over 1,531 yards and 13 touchdowns. His willingness and ability to scramble also helped him score six rushing touchdowns in each of his last two years.

His stats were certainly impressive—until compared to what he did his senior year.

In 1970, Theismann completed 155 of his 268 passes for 2,429 yards and 16 touchdowns.

Theismann also earned Academic All-America honors in 1970.

Although he never played baseball at Notre Dame, Theismann was selected in the 39th round by the Minnesota Twins. The Miami Dolphins used their fourth pick of the 1971 NFL draft on him, but since they had little use for him as a quarterback (they wanted him to play defensive back), he went to the Canadian Football League. He spent three seasons with the Toronto Argonauts, throwing for more than 6,000 yards and 40 touchdowns.

Theismann signed with the Washington Redskins in 1974, leading them to consecutive Super Bowl appearances in 1982 and 1983. He was named the league's most valuable player in 1983.

In 1985, Theismann suffered a severely broken leg when Lawrence Taylor sacked him during a *Monday Night Football* game. The injury ended his career.

ABOVE:
JOE THEISMANN.

Irish Lore

Notre Dame served as host of the 1971 NCAA Tennis Championships June 14-19.

The highlight of the five-day tournament was the championship singles match between UCLA freshman Jimmy Connors and Stanford's Roscoe Tanner. Both would become legendary players on the professional circuit. Connors beat Tanner at Notre Dame to win the individual title and lead UCLA to the team championship.

Although the Irish won 20 straight matches during the regular season to post a 26-5 mark and finished first in the Central Collegiate Championships, Notre Dame's tennis team failed to place in the NCAA Tennis Tournament.

1971-72

ABOVE:
DIGGER PHELPS.

Irish Moment

Digger Phelps became Notre Dame's basketball coach on May 4, 1971, five days after Johnny Dee had announced his resignation. Phelps, a brash young coach who made no secret of his desire for the job, had beaten the Irish, 94-88, three months before in front of a sellout crowd at Madison Square Garden. He was the talk of the town in basketball circles that year after leading Fordham to a 24-2 record during the regular season—his first at head coach.

Phelps' first year with the Irish offered little comparison to his inaugural season with the Rams. Team captain Doug Gemmell was sidelined with a leg injury suffered in a motorcycle accident. Sophomore John Shumate, penciled in as a starter, was diagnosed with a life-threatening blood clot, and Austin Carr had taken his game to the pros after graduation. Digger's first year was dismal. The 6-20 record included the worst defeat in Irish basketball history, a 94-29 loss to Indiana in the dedication game of Assembly Hall. Still, no one lost faith—Digger Phelps was where he wanted to be.

Digger wasn't the only story at Notre Dame in 1971-72.

Tom McMannon won the 55-meter hurdles at the NCAA Indoor Track Championships with a time of 7.2. That marked the last time Notre Dame would win an NCAA indoor event.

McMannon's teammate Greg Certins set a Notre Dame record in the shot put at 60 feet, 10 inches, a mark that still stands today.

And wrestler Mike Fanning pinned 20 opponents that season to establish a school record.

Irish Legend

Defensive end Walt Patulski, who shared captain duties with fellow All-American Tom Gatewood in 1971, became Notre Dame's first recipient of the prestigious Lombardi Award in 1971. He also was named UPI's lineman of the year.

Patulski, a native of Liverpool, New York, started every game of his Irish career. By the time he was finished, he had accumulated 186 tackles, including 40 for losses of 241 yards. He also recovered five fumbles, broke up 10 passes, and returned one blocked punt.

After playing in the College All-Star and Hula Bowl games, Patulski was the first pick in the 1972 NFL draft. Taken by Buffalo, Patulski spent three seasons there. But Patulski, who never missed a game at Notre Dame, was hampered by injuries and sat out the 1976 season with knee problems. He returned in 1977 with the St. Louis Cardinals. However, a back injury sidelined him in 1978, and he retired in 1979.

Irish Lore

Now the world's largest five-on-five outdoor basketball tournament, Bookstore Basketball debuted on the Notre Dame campus during An Tostal festivities in the spring of 1972.

The brainchild of student Tim Bourret, the first competition featured 53 teams comprised of students, faculty, and staff. The tournament took its name from the site of most of the action—basketball courts located on the parking lot behind the Hammes Bookstore near the center of campus. Games are played in the wind, the snow, the slush, and the mud. Only lightning stops a bookstore game.

Today, close to 600 teams and 3,000 players annually take part in Bookstore Basketball. Many famous Notre Dame football players have become "Bookstore Legends," including former Bookstore MVPS Tom Clements, Rusty Lisch, Tony Hunter, Justin Tuck, and Chindedum Ndukwe. Former Irish basketball players who earned MVP honors in Bookstore are John Shumate, Dave Batton, Bill Laimbeer, and Jimmy Dolan.

Former University president Rev. Edward "Monk" Malloy, C.S.C., was a long-time entrant with his team, "All the President's Men." Other "famous" Bookstore competitors included Lou Holtz and Gerry Faust.

Time Capsule

- President Richard Nixon defeated Democratic challenger George McGovern in an election that featured the lowest voter turnout in 24 years.

- The Federal Bureau of Investigation began hiring female agents in October.

- Members of the Arab terrorist group Black September took 11 Israeli athletes hostage at the 1972 Olympic Games in Munich. All 11 died the next day in a failed rescue attempt.

- On New Year's Eve, Pittsburgh Pirate star Roberto Clemente died when his plane crashed off the coast of Puerto Rico. Clemente was on a goodwill mission to deliver relief aid to victims of the Nicaragua earthquake.

- For the first time in its history, the University of Notre Dame accepted women as undergraduate students.

ABOVE:
JOHN SHUMATE.

Irish Moment

There must have been times when Digger Phelps wondered why he ever took the Notre Dame job.

His first team had gone 6-20, and now, the 1972-73 team had lost six of its first seven games. Three of those losses were by just two points and a defeat at the hands of Ohio State came in overtime. Still, Phelps must have wondered if his luck would ever change.

It would and it did—in a big way.

The tide started to turn on January 7. Kansas had brought its storied basketball program to the Athletic and Convocation Center for a Sunday afternoon game that was nationally televised. The game went into overtime, and somehow, someway, Notre Dame won, 66-64. Four days later, the Irish traveled to DePaul, and Digger Phelps posted his second straight win over Notre Dame alum Ray Meyer, who would become a close friend and colorful rival throughout the rest of their careers.

Now 3-6, the Irish continued north from Chicago to Milwaukee for a game at Marquette. Coach Al McGuire's Warriors were ranked No. 4 and boasted an 81-game home-court winning streak. Over the last five seasons, Marquette had competed in the NCAA Tournament four times and won the NIT in the NCAA off year.

Sophomore sharp-shooting guard Gary Brokaw poured in 28 points, while John Shumate, healthy and back on the court, added 21. But the game was still tied with just four seconds left on the clock. Sophomore guard Dwight Clay fired from the right corner to hit the shot that gave Notre Dame a 71-69 win and end Marquette's victory dance.

The Irish went on to finish the regular season with a 15-11 mark, winning their last four games, to earn a bid to the NIT. Notre Dame won its first three games over UCS, Louisville, and 11th-ranked North Carolina to advance to the championship against Virginia Tech.

The title game went into overtime, and a basket at the buzzer gave the Hokies the hardware with a 92-91 win to end Notre Dame's remarkable season turnaround.

Shumate, who had hit a record 20 straight field goals against Louisville and North Carolina, was named the tournament's MVP.

Irish Legend

Two-time All-American John Shumate scored 1,334 points in his Notre Dame career. Imagine what that number could have been if the 6-9 center from Elizabethtown, New Jersey, had played a full three years.

Recruited by Johnny Dee, Shumate put a sparkle in Irish fans' eyes when he averaged over 22 points and 13 rebounds on the freshman team in 1970-71. When Digger Phelps took over the head coaching job in the spring, he was counting on "Shu" to be the nucleus of his first team.

However, an infection and blood clot near his heart sidelined him in September and forced him to miss the entire year.

Shumate lost 45 pounds because of his illness, and many thought he would not be able to regain his strength. Those who questioned his determination underestimated Shumate's ability to persevere.

He came back his junior year to average 21 points and 12 rebounds a game and led Notre Dame to the championship game of the NIT where he was named most valuable player. As a senior Shumate dominated on both ends of the court, averaging 24 points and 11 rebounds a game. He was an integral part of Notre Dame's success that year as the Irish finished 26-3 and placed third in the NCAA Mideast Regional.

A bull's-eye shooter, Shumate still owns the Notre Dame record for field goal percentage (.610). In seven postseason games, Shumate shot an amazing 73 of 101 for a .723 percentage.

Although he could have applied for another year of eligibility, Shumate graduated from Notre Dame with his class and headed for the NBA. Phoenix selected him in the first round (fourth overall pick). Hampered by injuries, Shumate never quite found his niche as a player in the NBA.

He returned to his alma mater as an volunteer coach for two years. He then moved into a fulltime assistant's role for two seasons before becoming head coach at SMU.

ABOVE:
EDDIE BUMBACCO.

BELOW:
BILL NYROP.

Irish Lore

In just its second year as a member of the WCHA, the Notre Dame hockey team finished as the league's runner-up with a 19-9-0 league record (23-14-1 overall).

Coach Lefty Smith was named WCHA coach of the year, and left wing Eddie Bumbacco, who led the league in scoring, was rewarded with its MVP trophy. The Irish, who had swept No. 1 ranked Wisconsin in a two-game series during the regular season, lost to the Badgers, 8-7, in the second round of the total goal WCHA playoffs. Wisconsin went on to win the national championship.

Two Irish players—Bumbacco and defenseman Bill Nyrop—became the first All-Americans in the Notre Dame hockey program

A native of Sault Ste. Marie, Ontario, Bumbacco paced the Irish in scoring with 43 goals and 47 assists for 90 points, a school record that still stands today. During his four years with the Irish, he totaled 103 goals and 117 assists.

Nyrop, from Edina, Minn., scored 17 goals and added 72 assists during his four years with the Irish. Selected by the Montreal Canadiens in the fourth round of the 1972 NHL draft, the 6-2 defenseman spent seven years in the NHL with Montreal and the Minnesota North Stars.

1973-74

Irish Moment

When Notre Dame students chanted, "We're No. 1," in January 1974, they weren't kidding.

The football team gave Ara Parseghian his second national championship with a 24-23 victory over Alabama in the Sugar Bowl on New Year's Eve.

The hockey team upset top-ranked Michigan Tech, 7-1, on January 18.

The following day, the basketball team upended No. 1 ranked UCLA, 71-70, in the ACC to end the Bruins' incredible 88-game winning streak. Following the win, the Irish moved to the top spot in the basketball polls for the first time in its history.

Still smarting from a 40-6 loss to Nebraska in the 1973 Orange Bowl, the Notre Dame football team tackled the 1973 slate with a vengeance. The closest any team came to the Irish during the regular season was perennial rival Michigan State, but Notre Dame kept the Spartans in check with a 14-10 win. The Irish, ranked eighth at the time, also made USC pay for its 45-23 victory the year before with a 23-14 upset win over the No. 6 Trojans in late October.

Even though Notre Dame finished the regular season at 10-0-0, the Irish went into their Sugar Bowl matchup with No. 1 ranked Alabama, which was placed three in the polls.

No one expected the contest to match the pregame hype, but it did. The lead changed hands six times. Heading into the final five minutes, Alabama clung to a 23-21 lead. Starting at its own 21-yard line, quarterback Tom Clements moved the Irish downfield, but the drive stalled at the Alabama 15-yard line. Kicker Bob Thomas, who had missed two attempts earlier in the game, nailed a 19-yard field goal to give the Irish, the 24-23 win.

Notre Dame's hockey team struggled in 1973-74 after finishing second in the WCHA the previous season. Heading into the first night of a two-game series with top-ranked Michigan Tech, the Irish were just 8-11-1, although they had started the month with three straight wins over Minnesota-Duluth and St. Louis. Coach Lefty Smith's team came out firing and upended Michigan Tech, 7-1.

The following day was one of the most anticipated matchups of the college basketball season. Notre Dame, ranked No. 2 in the country, was 9-0. UCLA was, of course,

ABOVE:
DWIGHT CLAY "ICES" THE BRUINS.

RIGHT:
STUDENTS CELEBRATE WIN OVER UCLA.

No. 1 with a 13-0 record. Was the Bruins' 88-game winning streak in jeopardy?

Considering Notre Dame was ranked No. 2 and the game was at home, maybe the upset win over UCLA was not that surprising. Perhaps the most improbable aspect of the Irish victory was the way it came about.

UCLA dominated throughout most of the game. All-American Bill Walton had hit 12 of 13 shots, and with just 3:22 remaining, the defending national champions had a 70-59 lead. Neither Walton, nor any of his teammates, would score again on that frantic afternoon.

After calling timeout, Notre Dame scored 10 straight points to cut the seemingly insurmountable UCLA lead to just one. With 29 seconds left, junior Dwight Clay, nicknamed the "Iceman," tossed up a fadeaway shot from the corner to give the Irish the lead.

The game wasn't over yet. Two Bruin shots went awry, but Notre Dame's Gary Brokaw lost the rebound out of bounds, and UCLA had the ball with six seconds left. After a flurry of shots, John Shumate finally ... finally ... hauled in the rebound and the comeback was complete. It was, as Digger Phelps liked to say, "a Notre Dame moment."

Irish Legend

Kicker Bob Thomas led the Irish in scoring as a sophomore and senior, finishing second in that category as a junior.

During his three seasons at Notre Dame, Thomas connected on 98 of 101 extra points, including a streak of 62. He also made 21 of 28 field goals, including the 19-yarder to help the Irish win the 1973 Sugar Bowl and national championship.

After graduation, Thomas played for the Chicago Bears, the Detroit Lions, and the San Diego Chargers.

Perhaps his most significant and rewarding accomplishments have come in his latest endeavor. Thomas was elected to a three-year term as chief justice of the Supreme Court of Illinois in September, 2004.

Irish Lore

What most people don't remember is that UCLA avenged its loss to Notre Dame just a week later in Pauley Pavilion. A quirk in scheduling put dates of the home-and-home series just a week apart in 1973-74. After losing to the Bruins, 94-75, the Irish would not lose again until the season finale at Dayton.

Notre Dame won its first game in the NCAA Tournament against Austin Peay, but five days later were upset, 77-66, by Michigan. The Irish demolished Vanderbilt, 118-88, in the consolation game, but that didn't ease Notre Dame's pain. Neither did Digger Phelps' coach of the year award. Three teams who fell victim to the Irish in the regular season were going to the Final Four—Notre Dame was not.

1974-75

Time Capsule

- On August 8, Richard Nixon announced his resignation as president of the United States. Vice president Gerald Ford took the oath of office the following day.

- The Vietnam War officially ended on April 30 when Saigon fell to Communist forces.

- Teamsters' Union president Jimmy Hoffa was reported missing in Detroit, Michigan, on July 31.

- UCLA won the NCAA Basketball Tournament for the 10th time in 12 years. The only other schools to win an NCAA title in the same era were Texas Western in 1966 and North Carolina State in 1974.

- The Notre Dame Theatre presented the plays *Look Homeward, Angel; Fellows,* and *Medea* as part of its 1974-75 production schedule.

RIGHT:
ARA PARSEGHIAN.

Irish Moment

Notre Dame was still in the national championship hunt when the Irish traveled to USC for the 1974 regular season finale. A stunning 31-20 loss to Purdue earlier in the year had ruined Irish hopes for an undefeated season. But, if Notre Dame could beat USC and win a bowl game, maybe, just maybe, a national title would come its way again.

The Irish had a two-touchdown lead, but USC scored an incredible 49 unanswered points in the second half to wallop Notre Dame, 55-24.

No one wanted to see Ara Parseghian end his career with a loss. Although the Irish would face No. 1

ranked Alabama in the Orange Bowl, Notre Dame players were determined to send their coach out a winner. The Irish drew first blood in the first quarter on a four-yard run by Wayne Bullock. Mark McLane added another score on a nine-yard dash in the second period, but kicker Dave Reeve missed the extra point, and Notre Dame led, 13-0.

With less than two minutes to go in the half, Alabama finally cracked the scoreboard with a 21-yard field goal.

Neither team scored in the third quarter, and the Irish defense managed to strangle The Tide's prolific running game.

In the fourth quarter, Alabama went to the air and scored its first touchdown with just over three minutes left in the game.

Coach Bear Bryant's squad got the ball back, along with a chance to win, with just under two minutes remaining. But Reggie Barnett intercepted a Richard Todd pass to thwart the comeback attempt and give Ara Parseghian one final victory as the Irish head coach.

Notre Dame notched its 1,000th win in basketball on December 9 in superb fashion. Sophomore forward Adrian Dantley, who would go on to earn All-America honors and finish second in the nation in scoring, pumped in 30 points to lead the Irish to a 75-59 upset of seventh-ranked Kansas. The Irish also beat UCLA, the eventual national champion, for the second consecutive year in the ACC, 84-78. That marked the last time John Wooden, former coach at the city's Central High School, coached in South Bend.

Irish Legend

Two Irish coaching legends decided to call it quits in 1974-75 after remarkable careers on the Notre Dame campus.

When football coach Ara Parseghian announced his resignation, Irish fans were stunned. In 11 seasons, he had led Notre Dame to two national championships as well as victories in the 1971 Cotton Bowl, the 1973 Sugar Bowl, and the 1975 Orange Bowl. He had won 95 games, lost 17, and tied four for a .836 winning percentage. But the constant pressure and stress was taking its toll on Parseghian's health. After 24 years as a college head coach at Miami of Ohio, Northwestern, and Notre Dame, Parseghian decided to walk away from the profession he so loved.

He stayed involved in football as a color commentator with ABC Sports and then CBS Sports. Parseghian was inducted into the National Football Foundation Hall of Fame in 1980.

Jake Kline, the face of Notre Dame baseball for 42 years, also decided to retire after the 1975 season. During his career, Kline led his alma mater to eight appearances in the NCAA Tournament. Two of those teams advanced to the College World Series. Kline coached in over 1,000 games, posting a 558-449-5 mark for a .554 winning percentage.

1974-75 was the end of an era in more ways than one.

Irish Lore

For a guy who spent most of his college career trying to beat Notre Dame, Pat Haden sure spends a lot of time in South Bend these days.

Haden quarterbacked the Trojans to victories over the Irish in 1972 and 1974. A former Rhodes Scholar, he also led USC to three Rose Bowls and two national championships.

But for the last several years, the former NFL rookie of the year has served as the color analyst for NBC's telecasts of Notre Dame home football games. He's always welcomed on campus with open arms.

Irish Moment

Notre Dame looked to the professional coaching ranks for a replacement for Ara Parseghian. Although Dan Devine had been successful as coach at Arizona State and Missouri, Irish fans were a little nervous that a man who had most recently served as coach and general manager of the Green Bay Packers was heading the most storied football program in the land.

Devine led the Irish to three straight wins to open the 1975 season, but losses to Michigan State, USC, and Pitt didn't endear the first-year coach to the Notre Dame faithful.

Although Devine would win a national championship in his third season with the Irish and take Notre Dame to four bowl games in six years as head coach, he was never fully embraced by Irish fans.

Rick Slager started the season as the No. 1 quarterback, but an injury forced him to the sideline in the Northwestern game. His backup, Joe Montana, led the Irish to three touchdowns.

Two weeks later, Notre Dame traveled to Chapel Hill to play North Carolina. The home team owned a 14-0 lead before the Irish could score late in the third quarter. With just over six minutes left in the game, Montana came in again to try to get the offense moving. He did. He directed two touchdown drives and successfully completed the two-point conversion for the 21-14 win. Although he didn't win the starting job, Montana did earn a well-deserved reputation as "the comeback kid."

Irish Legend

Adrian Dantley won just about every honor imaginable during his three seasons at Notre Dame.

The 6-foot-5 forward ranked second in scoring behind John Shumate as a freshman, averaging 18.3 points per game. The following year Dantley finished

ABOVE:
DAN DEVINE.

RIGHT:
ADRIAN DANTLEY.

second in the nation in scoring with a 30.4 average. He earned first-team All-America honors and helped the Irish to a 19-10 record and an appearance in the NCAA Tournament.

As a junior, Dantley's scoring pace fell off a bit to just 28.6. He served as captain of a team that went 23-6 and finished seventh in the Associated Press poll. Dantley ranked fourth in the nation in scoring and was named national player of the year by the United States Basketball Players' Association.

In three seasons, Dantley moved to the No. 2 spot on the Irish scoring list with 2,223 points behind Austin Carr. He made more free throws (615) than any other player in Irish history, and he is the last player to average 10 or more rebounds in back-to-back seasons.

Much to the disappointment of Irish fans everywhere, Dantley decided to pass up his senior season to turn pro. He was drafted by the Buffalo Braves in the first round (sixth pick overall). But the NBA would still have to wait. A member of the 1976 U.S. Olympic team, Dantley and his teammates won a gold medal in the Summer Games in Montreal.

Dantley was just as impressive in the NBA as he was with the Irish. He earned rookie of the year honors in 1977 with averages of 20.3 points and 7.6 rebounds. Yet, he still returned to Notre Dame and finished his degree requirements in 1978.

A five-time NBA all-star, Dantley paced the league in scoring twice—in 1981 and 1984. By the time Dantley retired from the NBA in 1991, he had scored over 23,000 points.

Dantley now serves as an assistant coach for the Denver Nuggets.

Irish Lore

Critically acclaimed as one of the best sports movies of all time, *Rudy* tells the true story of Daniel "Rudy" Ruettiger, whose dreams of playing in a Notre Dame football game came true in 1975.

A native of Chicago, Ruettiger worked in a factory after high school and spent two years in the Navy. When he was 23, he moved to South Bend and attended Holy Cross Junior College with hopes of transferring to Notre Dame. After two years at Holy Cross, Rudy was finally accepted, on his second try.

LEFT: "RUDY."

Ruettiger convinced coach Ara Parseghian to let him on the football team as a walk-on. He was on the scout team but was not on the sidelines because NCAA rules limited the number of players able to dress for home games.

In the last game of his senior year, Ruettiger's dream finally came true. His name showed up on the dress list. He got into the game with just 27 seconds left. In typical Hollywood cinema fashion, he sacked the Georgia Tech quarterback on the last play of the game. Two teammates carried him off the field on their shoulders.

The moment embodied the stuff dreams—and movies—are made of.

1976-77

ABOVE:
NOTRE DAME VS. SAN FRANCISCO.

Irish Moment

The ACC rocked, and Notre Dame students have an award to prove it.

On the 5th of March, the No. 1 ranked University of San Francisco basketball team brought its 29-0 record to South Bend. The Dons boasted the only unbeaten mark in the country.

Notre Dame was no slouch. The Irish were 19-6 with impressive wins over three ranked teams—Maryland, UCLA (the Notre Dame victory ended the Bruins' amazing 115-game win streak in Pauley Pavilion), and Indiana. After a four-game losing skein after the Christmas holiday, Notre Dame won 12 of its last 14 games.

The game was so big the NBC television network asked San Francisco, DePaul, and Notre Dame to rearrange their schedules so the matchup could be broadcast on national TV. The Notre Dame-San Francisco game was originally scheduled for Tuesday, March 1 with DePaul the home opponent on March 5. Luckily, DePaul coach Ray Meyer and athletic director Gene Sullivan were Irish alums and agreed to the switch.

Notre Dame students love a TV camera. They packed the ACC. Many were dressed in Friar outfits, while others held up signs predicting San Francisco's demise. An hour before the game, the students were chanting, "29 and 1!"

Guard Don "Duck" Williams scored 25 points and led the Irish to a 93-82 victory.

At the end of its telecast, however, NBC bypassed Williams and awarded its most valuable player of the game to the Notre Dame student body.

The loss demoralized the Dons who were demolished by UNLV in the first round of the NCAA tournament. The Irish beat DePaul in the season finale to finish 21-6 and gain its fourth straight bid to the NCAA Tournament. After winning its opening-round game against Hofstra, the 10th-ranked Irish were upset by unranked North Carolina, 79-77. The Tar Heels advanced to the Final Four.

Notre Dame did get one national title that year—in fencing.

Coach Mike DeCicco's fencers and perennial power NYU were tied for the team lead at the end of the competition. New NCAA rules provided plans for a tiebreaker. Mike Sullivan, the gold-medal winner in the sabre, won his event, 5-3, in the "overtime." Then foilist Pat Gerard, who had also claimed an NCAA individual title, won his bout, 5-0, to give Notre Dame the first of many NCAA team titles. DeCicco was named coach of the year.

Irish Legend

Notre Dame defenseman Jack Brownschidle became Notre Dame's first two-time hockey All-American in 1977.

The East Amherst, New York, native still ranks as the fourth-highest scoring defenseman in Irish history with 109 career points (31 goals, 78 assists). Also a two-time WCHA selection (1975-76, 1976-77), Brownschidle was named one of the league's top 50 players on its 50th anniversary team in 2002.

During Brownschidle's last two seasons, Notre Dame posted a 41-30-5 mark and placed second in the WCHA in 1976-77. After graduation, Brownschidle, who had been a sixth-round draft pick of St. Louis in 1975, spent nine years in the NHL with the Blues and the Hartford Whalers.

Joining Brownschidle on the All-America team in 1976-77 was center Brian Walsh, who also was named the WCHA's most valuable player that year.

Walsh, a native of Cambridge, Massachusetts, still owns several Notre Dame scoring records. He ranks first in career points (234) and is tied for career marks in assists (145) and hat tricks (eight). He stands fifth on the all-time career goal list with 89 and his season mark of 77 points as a senior places him second in that category.

Walsh played three years of professional hockey with Calgary of the WHA, San Francisco (PHL) and New Hamsphire/Cape Cod (NEHL).

Walsh's son Rory recently spent four years as a goaltender for the Irish hockey team, receiving his degree in English in May 2006.

LEFT:
JACK BROWNSCHIDLE.

BELOW:
1976 TENNIS TEAM.

Irish Lore

Four years after the University of Notre Dame admitted women to the undergraduate student body, two women's tennis players became the first to receive varsity monograms. Jane Lammers and Mary Shukis earned those letters on the tennis court.

In 1976, only 1,500 women were enrolled at Notre Dame. There had been little need or interest in fielding women's varsity teams. Several competed in club sports, but times were much different in the late seventies. Opportunities and encouragement for women in sports just weren't there.

Tennis became the first women's varsity sport in 1976. Coach Kathy Cordes led Notre Dame to a 6-3-1 record while competing at the Division III level. The NCAA did not sponsor women's sports then so the Irish became members of the AIAW (the Association for Intercollegiate Athletics for Women).

Fencing became the second women's sport to gain varsity status later that year. Captain Kathy Valdiserri led the Irish to a 13-1 record.

1977-78

ABOVE:
JOE MONTANA.

ABOVE:
VAGAS FERGUSON.

Irish Moment

Success seems to come in waves at Notre Dame, and a big one hit campus in 1977-78.

Most football fans thought the Irish had no hope of a national championship after losing in the final three minutes at Ole' Miss the second week of the season. But coach Dan Devine had circled the wagons, and Notre Dame won its last nine games to earn an invitation to play top-ranked Texas and Heisman Trophy winner Earl Campbell in the Cotton Bowl on January 2.

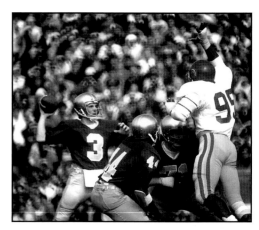

Joe Montana started out No. 3 on the depth chart but once again brought Notre Dame back from the brink of defeat at Purdue. He then pulled the same trick at Clemson. Vagas Ferguson and Jerome Heavens were almost unstoppable in the backfield, while Willie Fry and Ross Browner anchored the defense.

That defense would play a huge role in Notre Dame's amazing 38-10 thrashing of the Longhorns in the Cotton Bowl. So impressive was Notre Dame's victory that the wire service polls elevated the Irish, who had entered the game ranked No. 5, to the top spot. Devine had his first and only national championship.

Among the throng of Irish fans celebrating in Dallas that day was Notre Dame senior Charlie Weis.

Finally, after 72 seasons as a varsity sport, the Notre Dame basketball team earned a trip to the NCAA Final Four.

Ranked third in the preseason polls, Notre Dame's success in 1977-78 was truly a team effort. There were no superstars in Digger Phelps' system. A new "hero" stepped up to the plate almost every game: Captain Dave Batton led the team in scoring with a 14.0 average, but senior Duck Williams (13.3), freshman Kelly Tripucka (11.7), and sophomore Rich Branning (11.0) were right behind him. Bruce Flowers and Bill Laimbeer split time in the post. Sophomore Bill Hanzlik was the defensive specialist off the bench, while freshman Tracy Jackson and senior Jeff Carpenter were the top subs. During the regular season, the Irish had come from 17 points down to beat then-top-ranked Marquette, 65-59.

Notre Dame entered the tournament as the nation's 10th-ranked team. Laimbeer scored 20 points for the Irish in their first-round win over Houston. Notre Dame moved to the next round at the University of Kansas and posted a 13-point victory over Utah to advance to the regional championship against longtime foe, and friend, Ray Meyer and his DePaul Blue Demons. Phelps and Notre Dame showed no mercy toward the former Irish player and coach. The Irish won going away, 84-64. Notre Dame advanced to St. Louis and the Final Four.

But the Irish could not bring home bragging rights. They lost by four to Duke in the semifinal and then lost by two to Arkansas in the consolation game. Still, it had been a very good year.

Not to be outdone, the Notre Dame men's fencing team won its second consecutive NCAA championship. Two fencers won individual titles in their respective classes. Mike Sullivan repeated as sabre champion, while Bjorn Vaggo won the epee. Pat Gerard placed second in the foil.

Irish Legend

Ross Browner and Ken MacAfee took home two of college football's most prestigious trophies after the 1977 national championship season.

Browner, a two-time consensus All-American in 1976 and 1977, earned the Lombardi Trophy and Maxwell Award to complement the Outland Trophy he won as a junior. The 6-foot-3 defensive end still owns the career record for tackles (340) and fumbles recovered (12). A native of Warren, Ohio, Browner spent nine seasons in the NFL.

Tight end Ken MacAfee, a three-time All-American at Notre Dame, became the first lineman to receive the Walter Camp Trophy in 1977. During his career he caught 128 passes for 1,759 yards and 15 touchdowns. After participating in the Hula and Japan bowls, MacAfee was the first-round pick of the San Francisco 49ers in the 1978 NFL draft. Inducted into the College Football Hall of Fame in 1997, MacAfee attended dental school and now is an oral surgeon in the Boston area.

Irish Lore

Green and white accounted for three legendary stories in the history of Notre Dame athletics in 1977-78.

Football coach Dan Devine took basketball coach Digger Phelps' "suggestion" to help fire up his troops for a mid-season matchup with the fifth-ranked Trojans from USC. He ordered green jerseys but didn't tell the team. The Irish warmed up in their traditional blue. When the players returned to the locker room for the pregame talk, they found brand new green jerseys hanging in their lockers. The ploy must have worked because the crowd went berserk when the Irish emerged through the tunnel, and USC never had a chance. The Trojans lost, 49-19.

When the Irish played No. 1 ranked Marquette in basketball in late February, Phelps re-worked the gimmick for his team, providing green ... socks. Although most observers thought the green socks looked hideous, they worked. Notre Dame upset the Warriors, and the socks stayed until the last game of the Final Four.

White snow, and lots of it, fell in South Bend in the Great Blizzard of January 1978. The University shut down for three days. Notre Dame had a televised matchup with Maryland scheduled for January 29. Every road into South Bend was closed, but NBC would not reschedule the game. Somehow, the network arranged for the Terrapins and its crew to fly to South Bend.

The city was technically still under a snow emergency. Roads were barely passable, and many were still closed. Additionally, if someone managed to drive to the ACC, there was no place to park. The University decided to allow any student with an ID free admission to the ACC. Thousands showed up and created a raucous atmosphere. Notre Dame won, 69-54. Maryland had come all that way for nothing.

ABOVE:
ROSS BROWNER.

BELOW:
NOTRE DAME'S FINAL FOUR TEAM.

1978-79

Time Capsule

- Israeli Prime Minister Menachem Begin and Egyptian President Anwar Sadat signed the Camp David Peace Accord, an effort brought about by U.S. President Jimmy Carter.

- Peoples Temple cult leader Jim Jones orchestrated a mass suicide in Jonestown, Guyana. Over 900 people died, including 276 children.

- On May 9, a Northwestern University graduate student was injured by a Unabomber bomb.

- The Chicago White Sox forfeited their July 12 game against the Detroit Tigers after crowds went out of control during a "Disco Demolition Night."

- The University established the Holy Cross Associates program that provided opportunities for young lay people to serve the poor in the United States and Chile.

ABOVE:
JOE MONTANA.

Irish Moment

Notre Dame opened the defense of its 1977 national championship with two consecutive losses at home, something that had not happened since 1888! Missouri recorded a 3-0 shutout in the first game, holding the Irish scoreless for the first time since 1965.

The following week Michigan, ranked No. 5, returned to South Bend for the first time in 35 years. The Wolverines recorded a two-touchdown victory over the Irish.

Dan Devine's team found its heart and soul the following weekend at Purdue in a 10-6 comeback win in Ross-Ade Stadium. The Irish then won their next seven games to moveup to No. 8 in the polls. The season finale was a classic match up with USC in the Los Angeles Coliseum. Both teams' offenses were prolific, racking up a combined total of 949 yards and 52 points. The Trojans led most of the game, but Joe Montana threw a two-yard touchdown pass to Pete Holohan with just 1:35 left to give the Irish a 25-24 lead. The two-point conversion attempt failed. The defense would have to hold.

It didn't. USC kicked a field goal after a controversial official's call with just two seconds left to squeeze out a 27-25 win.

However, Notre Dame was still going to the Cotton Bowl for a January 1 matchup with ninth-ranked Houston.

Just days before the game, Dallas was hit by an unusual ice storm. The weather was better in South Bend. The ice was so thick, the temperatures so cold and the driving so hazardous that more than half of the people who bought tickets stayed home.

They missed the most incredible comeback in Irish football history.

Houston had a commanding 34-12 lead late in the third quarter. Many true-blue Irish fans brave enough to put up with the temperatures until then finally started to head for the exits. It was just too cold to watch their team lose. Plus, quarterback Joe Montana had disappeared.

The senior was in the locker room suffering from hypothermia. Team doctors were feeding him chicken soup in an effort to raise his body temperature. Finally, with five minutes left in the third period, he returned to the game.

Midway through the fourth period, Steve Cichy picked up a blocked punt and ran 33 yards for the first touchdown in the incredible comeback effort. The Irish went for two and Vagas Ferguson caught a two-yard pass from Montana. Notre Dame got the ball back, and Montana took the Irish 61 yards in five plays, scoring himself on a two-yard run. Again, the two-point conversion was successful.

The Irish were down by six points with just over four minutes remaining.

Houston had to punt again, and Montana moved the Irish to the Houston 20, but he fumbled the ball. Most thought it was over. Notre Dame got one more chance with just

20 seconds left after freshman Joe Gramke stopped Houston on a fourth-and-one from its own 29-yard line.

Montana, calm and obviously very cool despite the chicken soup, threw to Kris Haines in the corner but the ball was out of reach. Montana called for the exact same play, and this time he connected. Haines scored the touchdown to tie the game at 34. No time remained on the clock.

Dallas native Joe Unis kicked the extra point, but an illegal procedure call nullified the point. He had to kick it one more time, and he did. The Irish comeback was complete.

Irish Legend

Jerome Heavens became the most proficient runner in Irish football history when he passed the legendary George Gipp as a senior.

Never a 1,000-yard rusher, the East St. Louis native accumulated 2,685 yards on 590 carries for an average of 4.5 yards per carry. He also scored 15 touchdowns.

After leading the team in rushing as a freshman, a knee injury shortened his sophomore season and kept his numbers uncharacteristically low. He led the team in rushing again as a junior and senior.

Heavens' stay atop the career rushing list was short-lived, however.

The following season, his backfield mate, Vagas Ferguson, surpassed Heavens by ending his career with 3,472 yards. He still ranks third on that list behind Allen Pinkett and the leader Autry Denson.

Ferguson, a native of Richmond, Indiana, still owns the Notre Dame season rushing record with 1,437 yards on 301 carries as a senior. During his Irish career, he also scored 32 touchdowns. Ferguson also turned in two rushing performances that still rank among the best personal individual efforts in Notre Dame history. He gained 255 yards against Georgia Tech and 219 against Navy in 1978.

Heavens and Ferguson played together for three years and gave Notre Dame one of college football's most powerful one-two punch in the backfield.

Irish Lore

Notre Dame's 1978-79 basketball team may have been the best in Irish history.

It had experience in center Bill Laimbeer, leadership with junior guards Rich Branning and Bill Hanzlik, and an incredibly talented sophomore class that included Kelly Tripucka, Orlando Woolridge, Tracy Jackson and Stan Wilcox. Many thought the Irish were a sure fire bet to make a return appearance in the Final Four.

The Irish won eight of their first nine games. The only loss was a four-point decision to Kentucky in Louisville.

After beating Marquette, 65-60, in Milwaukee, the Irish moved to the top spot in the polls. Notre Dame spent four weeks there until the Irish dropped a four-point game to third-ranked UCLA at home on February 11.

Even though Notre Dame lost its last two games of the season, the Irish were confident they would get a chance to hang a championship banner in the ACC.

After advancing to the Elite Eight with early wins over Tennessee and Toledo, Notre Dame faced Michigan State in the regional final, losing to the eventual national champion Spartans and Magic Johnson in Indianapolis.

BELOW:
BILL LAIMBEER.

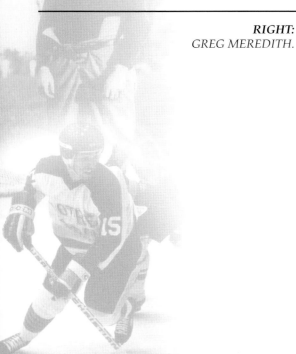

1979-80

Time Capsule

- On November 4, 3,000 Iranians invaded the U.S. Embassy in Tehran and took 90 hostages, including 53 Americans.

- Cable network ESPN broadcast its first programming on September 7.

- President Jimmy Carter announced that the United States would boycott the Summer Olympic Games in Moscow in response to the Soviet Union's invasion of Afghanistan.

- At the 1980 Lake Placid Winter Olympic Games, the United States hockey team, comprised of amateur players, pulled off a "miracle" by defeating the powerful Soviet squad. The U.S. would defeat Finland two days later to win the gold medal.

- University president Rev. Theodore M. Hesburgh, C.S.C., was appointed an ambassador to the United Nations Conference on Science and Technology.

RIGHT:
GREG MEREDITH.

Irish Moment

Notre Dame's 1979 football season was a disappointment to say the least. After beating Michigan, 12-10, in the season opener, the Irish took it on the chin at Purdue and then lost to USC at home in mid-October. Two losses in November to Tennessee and Clemson ended Irish hopes for a postseason invitation.

But the Irish were still going to a bowl game—far, far away.

The season finale between Notre Dame and Miami was scheduled to be played in the Mirage Bowl at the National Olympic Stadium in Tokyo.

Making the longest road trip in their history, the Irish spent almost a week in Japan, touring the sights, attending Mirage Bowl festivities, and practicing for their tilt with Miami.

The Japanese people knew of the legendary Notre Dame and had sent several reporters and television personalities to South Bend in weeks leading up to the game. The Irish players were minor celebrities in Japan, but the natives were more enamored with the Notre Dame cheerleaders who were booked at every event possible.

The game almost took a backseat to the hype. Played in a driving rain, Notre Dame ended up winning, 40-15.

Digger Phelps' basketball team pulled off the unthinkable on January 18, 1980. Native Californian Rich Branning led the Irish to their fourth straight win over the Bruins in Pauley Pavilion.

Although football and basketball had dominated the athletic spotlight at Notre Dame during the late seventies, many Irish Olympic sports were experiencing success as well.

Men's soccer, which attained varsity status in 1977, compiled an impressive 57-14-3 record through its first three campaigns.

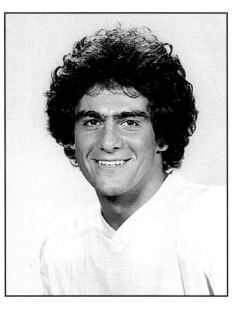

In 1979-80. the Notre Dame baseball team shrugged off three losing seasons to finish 29-8 and just miss receiving a bid to the NCAA tournament in coach Tom Kelly's final year as head coach.

On the women's ledger, field hockey and basketball became the third and fourth varsity sports. Coach Sharon Petro led the basketball team to a 49-10 mark in its first three years.

Irish Legend

Notre Dame's hockey team struggled through an inconsistent 18-20-1 season in 1979-80. About the only thing coach Lefty Smith could count on every game was that Greg Meredith would score a goal. As a senior, Meredith scored 40 goals, a total that still ranks second in the Irish record books.

The right wing from Toronto, Canada, became Notre Dame's first All-American in three years after finishing his career as Notre Dame's leading goal scorer. In four seasons with the Irish, he scored 104 goals and that number still stands atop the list over 25 years later.

Winner of the Byron Kanaley Award as a senior, Meredith also still ranks first in career power play goals with 43. He stands fourth in most points in a season with 71 and is tied for fifth in career game-winning goals with 10.

In 2005, Meredith was honored by the NCAA with a place on its prestigious Silver Anniversary team.

Irish Lore

Notre Dame's basketball team knocked off another top-ranked team in what many consider to be the greatest game ever played in the ACC.

This time DePaul was the team with No. 1 attached to its name. Coached by Irish alum Ray Meyer, the Blue Demons were 25-0. The Irish were ranked 14th with a 20-5 mark. The previous Saturday Notre Dame had lost at home, 77-74, to an unranked Marquette team.

Junior Tracy Jackson, who had hit a buzzer-beater in the ACC in early January to give the Irish a one-point win over Villanova, sent the game into overtime with two free throws. Senior Rich Branning extended the game to a second overtime, hitting a jumper with just seconds left.

Finally, Orlando Woolridge canned a pair of free throws with just 19 seconds left to give Notre Dame a 76-74 win. Kelly Tripucka had led all scorers with 28 points.

1980-81

Time Capsule

- California Governor Ronald Reagan defeated incumbent Jimmy Carter in the 1980 presidential election.

- Former Beatle John Lennon was shot to death outside his New York City apartment.

- Minutes after Ronald Reagan took the oath of office, Iran released the 52 American hostages the country had held for 444 days.

- Major League Baseball players went on strike, forcing the cancellation of 38 percent of the season.

- The Snite Museum of Art opened on the University of Notre Dame campus.

ABOVE:
KELLY TRIPUCKA.

Irish Moment

It was the year of stunning announcements and unbelievable endings.

During a live interview in the halftime segment of an ABC college football telecast in late August, Irish football coach Dan Devine shocked viewers — and the Notre Dame administration — he told the reporter he was resigning effective at the end of the season.

If that wasn't enough, athletic director Edward "Moose" Krause revealed weeks later that he was retiring as Notre Dame's athletic director after 32 years on the job.

Speculation centered on replacements for both men for weeks. Members of the media practically camped out on the doorstep of University executive vice president Rev. Edmund P. Joyce, C.S.C. And this was in the days before CNN and ESPN and the Internet.

Finally, at a press conference in the Athletic and Convocation Center "pit," Gene Corrigan, then current athletic director at the University of Virginia, was introduced as the eighth athletic director in Irish history. He would be the first non-Notre Dame alum to head the department since Jesse Harper in 1933.

Then, Corrigan introduced the new football coach — Gerry Faust, the legendary high school football coach from Cincinnati, Ohio.

Life, as Notre Dame fans knew it, had changed.

Devine's surprise announcement did not seem to distract his football players from the task ahead. The Irish "upset" ninth-ranked Purdue and Heisman Trophy candidate Mark Herrmann, 31-10, in the season opener at Notre Dame Stadium. The following week against Michigan, Harry Oliver kicked a 51-yard field goal as time expired to give the Irish a 29-27 win.

After claiming victory in its next five games, Notre Dame jumped to No. 1 in the polls. The top ranking did not last long — a frustrating 3-3 tie at Georgia Tech moved the Irish back down to sixth. Notre Dame added two more wins over fifth-ranked Alabama on the road and the home finale against Air Force. But a 20-3 loss at USC ended Notre Dame's hopes for a run at the national championship. The season ended with a 17-10 loss to eventual national champion Georgia and Heisman Trophy winner Herschel Walker in the Sugar Bowl.

The Irish basketball team, which finished the season at 23-6, never made it to the top of the rankings in 1980-81, but it beat two who did — within a span of just 36 days. Even more surprising was that neither of the wins came at home.

During its annual trip to Louisville during the Christmas holiday, Kelly Tripucka scored 30 points to lead Notre Dame to a 67-61 victory over top-ranked Kentucky for the first win over the Wildcats in eight years. Then, on Sunday, February 22, the Irish and No. 1 ranked Virginia met at the Rosemont Horizon outside of Chicago in a nationally televised contest. Orlando Woolridge helped hold Virginia star Ralph Sampson to just 10 points in the incredibly low-scoring game. Down by one with time running out, Woolridge picked up a loose ball and heaved a 16-foot shot that went in as time expired to give Notre Dame a 57-56 win.

It looked like the two might meet again in the final of the NCAA East Regional in Atlanta. After beating James Madison in its first game, the Irish faced Brigham Young, who had upset UCLA. With less than 12 minutes remaining, Notre Dame led 40-29. But the Cougars staged a furious rally to close the gap to one, 49-48, with 3:34 to go. BYU took the lead with one minute left, but Tripucka pumped in what seemed like the game-winner with just 10 seconds left. After a timeout, BYU's Danny Ainge drove the length of the court literally uncontested and laid in the game winner as the buzzer sounded. What many consider one of Digger Phelps' best teams went home empty handed again.

Irish Legend

The senior class of 1982 left an indelible mark on the Notre Dame basketball program. Marc Kelly, Tracy Jackson, Gilbert Salinas, Kelly Tripucka, Stan Wilcox, and Orlando Woolridge led the Irish to a record-setting 92-26 mark during their four years at Notre Dame.

Tripucka, whose dad had played quarterback for Notre Dame in the '50s, was by all accounts the star—both on and off the court. Named the MVP of Midwest Regional as a freshman, the 6-foot-7 forward played a key role in getting the Irish to their first—and only—Final Four. He led the team in scoring his next three years, earning All-America notice each season. Tripucka was hard to ignore, especially when he wore his fur coat on road trips.

Jackson and Woolridge weren't quite as colorful characters as Tripucka, but the two had their days in the sun as well. As a sophomore, Jackson averaged almost 12 points per game off the bench. He started his last two seasons, scoring 15.1 and 12.9 points, respectively.

Woolridge finished his senior season with a third-place ranking nationally in field goal percentage with a .552 mark. Tripucka, Jackson, and Woolridge are all members of Notre Dame's 1,000-point scoring club.

Salinas, Wilcox, and Kelly, who earned his spot as a walk-on, all played key roles in Phelps' rotating system throughout their careers.

Irish Lore

There were many firsts in 1980-81 at Notre Dame:
- Volleyball and men's lacrosse earned varsity status.
- Women's basketball moved into Division I under new coach Mary DiStanislao.
- Chuck Aragon became Notre Dame's first sub-four-minute miler with a time of 3:59.92 at the Illini Classic. It was only the fifth time Aragon had competed in the mile.
- A record crowd of 36,675 attended the annual Blue-Gold spring football game in Notre Dame Stadium.

ABOVE:
ORLANDO WOOLRIDGE.

BELOW:
MARC KELLY.

1981-82

ABOVE:
DAVE POULIN.

Irish Moment

Notre Dame's hockey team moved from the WCHA to the CCHA in 1981-82, and the newest kid in the neighborhood shook up the block.

The season turned out to be one of the most exciting in Irish history as Notre Dame posted its best record (23-1-2) in five years.

In late December, the Irish beat both Michigan and Michigan Tech to win the Great Lakes Invitational Tournament in Detroit's Joe Louis Arena before a crowd of 19,225.

Led by captains Dave Poulin and Jeff Logan, Notre Dame defeated Michigan in the first-round of the CCHA playoffs to advance to the conference finals at "the Joe."

Coach Lefty Smith's team, which had split a weekend series with Bowling Green in January, eliminated the Falcons with an 8-5 win and advanced to the title game. But, Michigan State notched a 4-1 win to keep Notre Dame from taking home the trophy and moving on to NCAA competition.

Poulin, a finalist for hockey's Hobey Baker Award in 1981-82, led the Irish in scoring that year with 59 points (29 goals, 30 assists). During his four years at Notre Dame, Poulin recorded 89 goals and 107 assists in 135 games. He ranks as the fifth best goal scorer in Irish history with 89 and eighth on the career assist list with 107. Poulin owns the Notre Dame record for most game-winning goals with 13. He is also tied for the lead in career hat tricks with eight.

After graduation, Poulin played one year in Sweden before signing as a free agent with the Philadelphia Flyers late in the 1982-83 season.

In the first game of his NHL career, he scored on his first two shots while playing before a hometown crowd at Toronto's Maple Leaf Gardens.

The following year, Poulin's first full season in the NHL, he won the league's rookie-of-the-year honor with 31 goals and 45 assists. He was named team captain a year later and led the Flyers to the finals of the Stanley Cup.

Poulin spent 12-plus years in the NHL with the Flyers, the Boston Bruins, and the Washington Capitals. An NHL All-Star in 1986, 1987, and 1988, he was awarded the league's Frank K. Selke Trophy as its best defensive forward in 1987. Poulin was presented the coveted King Clancy Memorial Trophy, given to the NHL player who best exemplifies leadership on and off the ice, in 1993.

After retiring from the NHL in 1995, Poulin returned to his alma mater and coached the Irish hockey team for 10 years. His 2003-04 squad made Notre Dame's first appearance in the NCAA Hockey Tournament.

Irish Legend

When John Paxson played basketball at Notre Dame, his family would often make the five-hour trip from Dayton, Ohio. But mom Jackie usually stayed in her room at the Morris Inn during the games because she would get too nervous watching her son play. She didn't care about winning necessarily. She just wanted John and his teammates to do well.

Jackie Paxson needn't have worried. The Irish were in good shape when her son had the ball.

The 6-foot-2 guard earned a starting spot as a sophomore, averaging nearly 10 points a game. But Paxson's primary role that year was to dish off to Tripucka, Jackson, or Woolridge. He led the team in assists with 112. His maturity and court presence made him a heady floor general Digger Phelps could trust.

After that superb class two years ahead of him graduated, Paxson was forced to persevere through the first losing season since Digger Phelps began at Notre Dame in 1971-72. Paxson paced the team in scoring with a 16.4 average and led Notre Dame to a pair of upsets of two top-10 ranked teams.

Help arrived in 1982-83 in the form of five freshmen, three of who would end up starting. Paxson led the team in scoring with a 17.7 mark and helped Notre Dame hand North Carolina State its last loss before the Wolfpack and coach Jim Valvano made their incredible run to the NCAA tournament title a month later. During his career at Notre Dame, Paxson earned All-America honors for his play on the court as well as his performance in the classroom.

After graduating, he spent 10 seasons in the NBA, including eight with the Chicago Bulls. He played a key role in the Bulls' record-setting three NBA championship seasons. In fact, he hit the winning shot in Game 6 with just under four seconds left to beat Phoenix and help Chicago, and Michael Jordan, win their third ring.

Paxson currently serves as general manager of the Bulls.

Irish Lore

California native Laura Lee became Notre Dame's first women's tennis national champion and All-American as a freshman in 1982.

Lee, who would eventually finish her career with a 70-28 mark at singles, and classmate Pam Fischette, led the Irish to AIAW titles at the state and regional levels to gain a spot in the AIAW National Tournament. Lee won the national singles title in the No. 5 flight, while Fischette earned runner-up honors at No. 3. She also earned All-America honors that year. Their performances helped the Irish to a sixth-place finish in the team standings.

ABOVE:
JOHN PAXSON.

BELOW:
LAURA LEE.

RIGHT:
GERRY FAUST.

Irish Moment

Let there be light!

Although Gerry Faust's first season had been a huge disappointment (5-6 record), Notre Dame football remained a national draw, and ABC Sports selected the season opener with Michigan as its national game. There was one problem, however: ABC wanted to air the game in primetime.

Enter Musco Mobile Lighting. The Iowa company could turn night into day with its portable lighting system. So, truckload after truckload of portable lighting fixtures arrived in South Bend to provide enough wattage to keep ABC and the University security department happy.

The game took on a carnival-like atmosphere, and some of the "electricity" must have seeped into the Notre Dame locker room as the 20th-ranked Irish upset the 10th ranked Wolverines, 23-17.

The Irish jumped 10 spots in the rankings, and three games later Notre Dame stood 4-0, although it needed a Mike Johnston field goal with 11 seconds left against Miami to stay undefeated.

The Irish weren't so lucky in their next two games. Arizona used a 49-yard field goal by Max Zendejas to pin a 16-13 defeat on Notre Dame at home, and the following week at Oregon, Johnston had to kick another field goal to escape with a tie.

After a win over Navy at Giants Stadium, the Irish entertained No. 1-ranked Pitt and Heisman Trophy contender Dan Marino at Notre Dame Stadium. Marino, a future member of the Pro Football Hall of Fame, completed 26 of 42 passes for 314 yards, but freshman Allen Pinkett scored two touchdowns and rushed for 112 yards as the Irish won, 31-16. It would turn out to be the highlight of the Faust era.

Notre Dame lost its final three games of the regular season (something that would happen twice in the next three years) to finish 6-4-1. It was an improvement over the previous year, but not by much.

Irish Legend

Lefty Smith knew the inevitable was coming, but that didn't ease the pain when the announcement finally came.

Title IX requirements had forced every athletic department in the country to scrutinize budgets and prioritize scholarship offerings. Hockey was an expensive sport to maintain, and student attendance at home games had been dwindling. So athletic director Gene Corrigan made a decision he wished he didn't have to make. The University announced near the end of the 1982-83 season that hockey would no longer compete at the varsity level at Notre Dame.

The plan was to compete one year at the club level—which allowed players to transfer to other schools without penalty—and then return to varsity status without conference affiliation and scholarships.

After the announcement, Smith's skaters went on a tear, posting a 7-2-1 mark to end the regular season. Forward Kirt Bjork became Notre Dame's sixth All-American. He was also the last for 16 years.

Smith continued to coach the Irish through the transition period. He retired from coaching in 1987 with a record of 307-320-30. During his tenure, every one of the 126 players who completed their college eligibility graduated.

ABOVE:
KIRT BJORK.

LEFT:
RICK CHRYST.

Irish Lore

Several Notre Dame Olympic sports teams and their athletes had plenty to brag about in 1982-83.

The men's fencing team finished second at the NCAA Tournament behind Ola Harstrom's first-place individual finish.

Steve Dziabis earned All-America designation with a sixth place in the 600-yard run at the NCAA Indoor Championships. The Irish track team also won the cross country and track championships in the Midwestern City Conference, a league Notre Dame Olympic sports joined prior to the season to help ease scheduling woes.

The Notre Dame wrestling team, under third-year coach Brother Joe Bruno, C.S.C., set a school standard for wins with its 18-2 record. Mike Golic, who also played football for the Irish, established an Irish record for fastest pin at 14 seconds.

In just its third year as a varsity sport, the volleyball team posted a 25-9 mark, its first winning season.

Coach Mary DiStanislao led the women's basketball squad to the 20-win mark for the second time in its short six-year history but did not advance to a postseason tournament.

The women's tennis team finished third at the NCAA Division II championships.

Outfielder Rick Chryst, now the commissioner of the Mid-American Conference, led the Irish baseball team with a .325 batting average and won the Byron Kanaley Award.

Notre Dame won the College Football Association's Academic Achievement Award.

1983-84

Irish Moment

Notre Dame finally made it to a bowl game under Gerry Faust—but it wasn't easy.

The Irish had plenty of talent and depth and were ranked No. 5 when they pasted a 52-6 thumping on Purdue in the season opener. But two straight losses, including being blanked 20-0 by eventual national champion Miami, dashed Notre Dame's hopes of a return to glory. Four straight wins pushed the Irish back into bowl consideration, but once again Notre Dame could not find a way to win in November, losing three games, the last two with under two minutes remaining.

At 6-5, the Irish accepted an invitation to play in the Liberty Bowl against Boston College and eventual Heisman Trophy winner Doug Flutie.

Notre Dame administrators saw several positives in participating in the bowl game. It would be an interesting match up between two premiere Catholic universities. The players and coaches would be rewarded for their efforts by getting one more chance at victory. It was an opportunity to showcase emerging running back Allen Pinkett and offensive guard Larry Williams, who both earned All–America recognition.

Pinkett and fullback Chris Smith both rushed for over 100 yards against the Eagles. Although Boston College had scored first, Notre Dame owned a 19-6 lead midway through the second quarter when Pinkett scored his record-setting 18th touchdown of the year.

Flutie drove the Eagles to a pair of scores, but missed on two two-point conversion attempts, leaving the Irish clinging to a 19-18 lead.

Could Notre Dame break its habit of giving away games at the end?

With just a little over a minute left on the clock, Boston College was driving toward the goal line. Faced with a fourth-and-four on the Notre Dame 35-yard line, Flutie tried to dodge the Irish blitz and unloaded the ball early. The pass fell incomplete, and the Irish had what they had come to Memphis for—a victory.

Men's soccer coach Rich Hunter had guided the team since its inception as a varsity sport in 1977. The program had made great strides, including beating sixth-ranked St. Louis in double overtime in 1981. In 1983, the Irish posted an impressive 18-4 record with 14 shutouts.

ABOVE:
ALLEN PINKETT.

RIGHT:
CHRIS SMITH.

Hunter, a Notre Dame alumnus who taught in the business school, left coaching to accept a faculty position at Seton Hall. His seven-year record, which included three 20-win seasons, stood at 128-32-8 for a .786 winning percentage.

Irish Legend

Trainer Gene Paszkiet had taken care of Irish athletes for over 31 years.

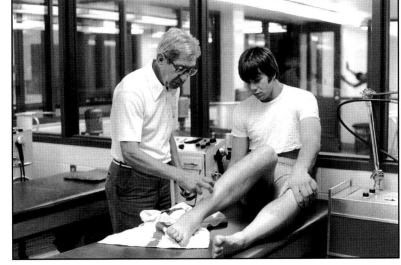

Although his name was never in the headlines, he was an integral part of the Notre Dame athletic operation. In fact, he was essential, and every Irish coach knew it.

A gruff, no-nonsense kind of guy, Paszkiet flat out refused to cooperate when the Notre Dame sports information office wanted to write a feature about him in a football program. He had no need for the spotlight, no need for public recognition. He just wanted to do his job, and he did. He did it very well.

A native of South Bend, Paszkiet played football at Washington High School and enrolled at Purdue after graduation, but he was called into military service and left school before completing a semester.

After a stint in the Coast Guard, Paszkiet attended Notre Dame and played on the 1946 freshman football team. But he left the playing field to work on the sidelines as a student athletic trainer, a position he held until his 1950 graduation.

Paszkiet spent two years as the athletic trainer for former Notre Dame coach Hugh Devore at NYU. Paszkiet returned to his alma mater in 1952 when athletic director Moose Krause named him head of the training staff.

Shortly after the 1983 football season, Paszkiet, who ironically never liked visiting doctors himself, died following a brief illness.

Irish Lore

Digger Phelps had friends all over the world, especially in Yugoslavia.

He had welcomed a few coaches from the communist country to South Bend on more than one occasion to watch and learn about the game. Basketball was growing in popularity in Eastern Europe, and Phelps was willing to do his part to spur that growth. He also traveled to the country several times for coaching clinics, and the Irish spent a week there during one summer break.

After a preseason game against the Yugoslavian National team in South Bend, Phelps signed its prolific shooter, Drazen Petrovic, to a letter of intent. The native of Sibenik, Croatia, had once scored 112 points in a Croatian League game.

Petrovic, however, never enrolled. He played in his native Croatia until joining the NBA's Portland Trailblazers in 1989. Two years later, he was traded to the New Jersey Nets. Petrovic was emerging as one of the NBA's newest stars when he was killed in a car accident in the summer of 1993.

LEFT:
GENE PAZSKIET (LEFT).

1984-85

The 1980s

Time Capsule

- President Ronald Reagan defeated Democratic challenger Walter Mondale to win re-election to a second term.

- Astronaut Kathryn Sullivan became the first American woman to perform a space walk aboard the space shuttle *Challenger*.

- Coca-Cola changed its recipe and began selling "New Coke." Months later the company declared the new product a "mistake."

- Villanova became the lowest seed in the 64-team NCAA Final Four to win the championship with an upset of Georgetown University.

- Jose Napoleon Duarte, the president of El Salvador and a Notre Dame alumnus, served as the commencement speaker during May graduation ceremonies.

Irish Moment

Notre Dame and Purdue had played each other every year since 1946, but in 1984, the game took on a different twist. Neither team had a home field advantage. The Irish and Boilermakers would be playing in the dedication game of the brand new Hoosier Dome in Indianapolis. Notre Dame could not get untracked, and Jim Everett completed 20 of 28 passes for 255 yards to lead Purdue to a 23-21 victory.

Notre Dame recovered to win three in a row, but a trio of back-to-back-to-back home losses to Miami, Air Force, and South Carolina doomed the Irish to another mediocre season. Still, there were bright spots. Notre Dame upset unbeaten and sixth-ranked LSU in Death Valley, where the Tigers rarely lost. Then, the Irish ended their regular season in Los Angeles with a 19-7 victory over USC, the first win in the Coliseum since 1966. That victory, Notre Dame's seventh of the season, earned the Irish a trip to the Aloha Bowl in Hawaii against 10th-ranked SMU.

Inconsistency had plagued the Irish all year, and that did not change in Honolulu. The Mustangs, who owned a 27-20 lead over the Irish with three minutes left to play, gave Notre Dame a last chance. Quarterback Steve Beuerlein, who had attempted only 12 passes all day, suddenly threw 11 in the next 2:19. But on fourth down from the SMU 16, Beuerlein just missed Milt Jackson in the end zone—another disappointing end to a frustrating season.

After losing to Michigan in the championship game of the 1984 NIT, Notre Dame set its sights on returning to the NCAA Tournament for the first time in four years.

Phelps' team had experience with a strong junior class of Tim Kempton, Ken Barlow, Joseph Price, and Jim Dolan in addition to the two smooth sophomores Donald Royal and Scott Hicks. Plus, a freshman named David Rivers dazzled fans everywhere with his passing and dribbling skills. He could score, too. In an early December game against Indiana, Rivers pumped in 23 points and added five assists to lead the Irish to a 74-63 upset of the 11th-ranked Hoosiers and their Olympic guard Steve Alford.

After finishing the season at 21-8, the Irish earned their trip back to the NCAA, but they didn't have to pack their bags. For the first time in its history, Notre Dame served as a host sight. The Irish won their first game against Oregon State but lost, 60-58, two days later to North Carolina.

ABOVE:
STEVE BEUERLEIN.

RIGHT:
KEN BARLOW.

Irish Legend

Many Irish fans often described the Gerry Faust offense as "Pinkett, Pinkett, Pass, Punt."

That wasn't far from the truth.

Allen Pinkett, a 5-foot-9, 181-pound tailback from Sterling, Virginia, became Notre Dame's leading rusher his senior year and held that spot until Autry Densen knocked him off the pedestal in 1988.

As a freshman, Pinkett didn't start. Yet, he still managed 107 attempts for 532 rushing yards and five touchdowns.

He more than doubled those statistics as a sophomore when he became a starter. That year he rushed 22 times for 1,394 yards and 16 touchdowns.

In 1984, his junior season, Pinkett carried the ball 275 yards for 1,105 yards and 17 touchdowns.

As a senior, Pinkett added 255 carries, 1,100 yards, and 11 touchdowns.

By the time he graduated, Pinkett owned Notre Dame records for touchdowns (53), rushing touchdowns (49), rushing yards per game (96.1), carries (889), and points (320).

A three-time All-American, Pinkett was drafted by the Houston Oilers after graduation and spent six seasons in the NFL. He now provides color commentary on the Westwood One radio broadcasts of Notre Dame games.

Irish Lore

Notre Dame's Olympic sports continued to make strides toward national prominence in 1984-85.

First-year wrestling coach Frank McCann led the Irish to an 8-4 record, while John Krug posted an individual mark of 26-7-2.

The field hockey team turned in the best record in school history with a 15-5-2 mark.

The men's cross-country squad breezed through the regular season unbeaten and placed 19th in the NCAA for the first time since 1966.

The women's basketball team finished 20-8 and won the first North Star Conference title but did not participate in postseason play.

The women's tennis team posted a 25-5 mark and earned a runner-up finish in the NCAA Division II tournament. Coach Sharon Petro was named coach of the year.

The men's fencing team went 23-0 and finished second in the NCAA Tournament, losing a chance at the title by one point.

1985-86

Time Capsule

- President Ronald Reagan met with Soviet Union leader Mikhail Gorbachev for the first time in Geneva.

- In January, the space shuttle *Challenger* exploded 73 seconds after launch, killing all seven astronauts aboard, including the first teacher in space, Christa McAuliffe.

- After an extensive renovation, the Statue of Liberty reopened to visitors on July 5.

- The Boston Celtics' Larry Bird won his third straight NBA most valuable player award.

- The Joan B. Kroc Institute for International Peace Studies at the University of Notre Dame opened in 1986.

RIGHT:
JERRY DURSO.

Irish Moment

Gerry Faust beat USC three straight times in his five-year tenure as Notre Dame football coach. But he just could not beat Air Force (the Irish lost four games to the Falcons), or enough other teams to keep his job. Five days before the season finale, Faust tendered his resignation. Two days later, Lou Holtz was introduced as the 25th head coach in Notre Dame history.

The Irish basketball team was big and strong and could outmuscle just about everybody in 1985-86. With a frontline of 6-foot-10 Ken Barlow, 6-foot-9 Tim Kempton, and 6-foot-7 Donald Royal, Notre Dame led the nation in rebounding margin with an 8.6 mark.

That muscle, along with the stellar backcourt play of sophomore David Rivers, pushed the Irish to seven wins in their last eight games (the only loss was by one point to second-ranked Duke in Cameron Indoor Stadium).

Disappointment continued to haunt Digger Phelps and his Irish basketball teams in the NCAA Tournament. Ranked 10th and seeded third in the Mideast Regional, Notre Dame lost its opening game to unheralded Arkansas-Little Rock, 90-83.

There were also moments of celebration for the Notre Dame athletic department that year.

In November, the University dedicated the $4.5 million Rolfs Aquatic Center, located at the east end of the Joyce Center. The 45,000-square foot facility houses a 50-meter Olympic pool, support and training facilities, and offices.

In his first year as Notre Dame swim coach, Tim Welsh led the men's team to its first MCC title and the women to their third North Star Conference championship.

The men's indoor track team won its fourth MCC title. Football player Tim Brown ran a .06:36 in the 60-yard dash to set an MCC record. Jim Tyler, who placed eighth in the 1,500-meters at the NCAA Outdoor Championships and led the 4x800 relay team to a third-place finish in the NCAA Indoor Championships, became the first Notre Dame athlete since 1968 to earn All-America honors both indoors and outdoors in the same year.

Wrestler Jerry Durso set a season record in wrestling with 38 wins.

Irish Legend

Trena Keys ended her career in 1986 as the top scorer in Notre Dame women's basketball history—a spot she owned until 1991.

A native of Marion, Indiana, Keys moved into the starting lineup midway through her sophomore year. Ironically, she scored five more points as a freshman coming off the bench.

As a junior, she shot 52 percent from the field and 70 percent from the free throw line. She totaled 483 points for a 17.3 average. She also joined the ranks of the Notre Dame 1,000-point club that season.

During her senior year she averaged almost 20 points a game and led the Irish to a 23-8 record as Notre Dame earned a bid to the women's NIT. She ended her career with 1,589 points. A starter in 78 straight games, Keys led the team in blocked shots each of her four seasons and was the leading scorer as a junior and senior.

Twice named player of the year in the North Star conference, Keys became the first Notre Dame player to earn all-conference honors.

Irish Lore

The Notre Dame men's fencing team returned to the mountaintop with its third NCAA title, the first since 1978.

Freshman Yehuda Kovacs earned the highest individual finish, placing second in the foil.

During the regular season, the Irish finished 26-0.

Sophomore Molly Sullivan became the first woman fencer to win a gold for the Irish in the 1986 NCAA Tournament, compiling a perfect 15-0 record in the foil. After placing third the following year, Sullivan recaptured the top honor at the 1988 NCAA Tournament. The North Andover, Massachusetts, native fin-

LEFT:
MOLLY SULLIVAN.

ished her Irish career with a 160-14 mark for an incredible .919 winning percentage, which ranks fourth in the Notre Dame record books.

Time Capsule

- The Tower Commission reprimanded President Ronald Reagan for his involvement in the Iran-Contra affair.

- Two more Unabomber bombs exploded in Salt Lake City.

- Aretha Franklin became the first woman inducted into the Rock and Roll Hall of Fame.

- The New York Mets defeated the Boston Red Sox four games to three to win the World Series.

- Rev. Edward "Monk" Malloy, C.S.C., became the 16th president of the University of Notre Dame. Rev. E. William Beauchamp, C.S.C., was appointed executive vice president.

Irish Moment

No one really knew what to expect under Lou Holtz his first year as the Irish head football coach. He had been considered a miracle worker at his previous college coaching stops—William and Mary, North Carolina State, Arkansas, and Minnesota. He liked having his back against the wall and enjoyed the challenge for turning an also-ran into a contender.

Holtz faced a daunting task in 1986, and although the cupboard was not bare, it wasn't fully stocked either. But in his first game in Notre Dame Stadium, he showed fans a fiery, competitive spirit that would endear him to Irish fans even today. Notre Dame lost a heartbreaker, 24-23, to Michigan, but the Irish accumulated 455 yards total offense, and Steve Beuerlein completed 21 of 33 passes for 263 yards to eclipse Joe Theismann's career passing yardage record. Notre Dame became the first unranked team ever to lose a game and THEN move into the top 20.

But the Irish could manage only one win in their first five games, and three of those losses were by five points or less. Still, Holtz's first year ended on a high note when John Carney kicked his record-setting 21st field goal of the season with no time remaining to upset 17th-ranked USC, 38-37, in the Coliseum.

Notre Dame finished the season at 5-6, and five of losses were by a total of 14 points. Tim Brown was honored as a first-team All-American. Irish fans could see the light at the end of the tunnel.

Digger Phelps earned coach of the year honors by *Basketball Weekly* after leading his team to a 24-8 record, including a run of 11 straight. The Irish also advanced to the NCAA Sweet 16 for the first time since 1981.

The Notre Dame women's fencing team won its first NCAA title in 1987 under the direction of first-year coach Yves Auriol.

There were also several coaching changes at Notre Dame in 1986-87.

Hockey coach Lefty Smith retired and was replaced by one of his former players, Ric Schafer.

Legendary Irish tennis coach Tom Fallon retired after 31 seasons and 517 wins. Navy's Bobby Bayliss was hired to take his place.

After seven seasons Mary DiStanislao resigned as the Irish women's basketball coach. She had posted a 115-79 record with three 20-win seasons and a pair of North Star conference titles.

Notre Dame athletic director Gene Corrigan also resigned in early summer to return to the Atlantic Coast Conference as its commissioner.

ABOVE:
LOU HOLTZ.

RIGHT:
JOHN CARNEY.

Irish Legend

David Rivers knew how to beat the odds.

The third youngest of 14 children, he had escaped the drugs and violence so prevalent in his Jersey City, N.J., neighborhood by dedicating himself to basketball at St. Anthony's High School.

After coming to Notre Dame, he became an immediate fixture in the starting lineup and led the Irish in scoring as both a freshman and sophomore and tied the single-season assist record his second year on the squad. With Rivers running the show, Notre Dame had posted season marks of 21-9 and 23-6 and returned to the NCAA Tournament both times.

In the summer before his junior year, Rivers and teammate Ken Barlow were on their way back to work after an assignment. The van Barlow was driving ran off the country road, and Rivers went flying through the windshield. He was taken to the hospital with a 15-inch gash in his abdomen — a cut doctors later would tell him came within an inch of ending his life. He would lose three pints of blood and undergo emergency surgery.

Nobody expected Rivers to play that season, and even fewer thought he could carry a full course load. But those "doubting Thomases" clearly underestimated his determination and drive. He worked diligently with trainer Skip Meyer the rest of the preseason and was ready to play when the Irish opened the season on November 21. He handled a 12-hour class schedule just fine.

Rivers ended up leading the team in scoring, steals, and assists — a feat he would accomplish all four of his years at Notre Dame. Former Notre Dame point guard Chris Thomas finally passed Rivers' as the Irish assist leader in 2004 with a total of 638. Rivers still ranks second with 586 career assists.

At the end of the 1986-87 season, Rivers earned the most courageous award by the United States Basketball Writers Association.

Irish Lore

It wasn't the luck of the Irish or the green carnation that helped the Notre Dame basketball team to an upset of top-ranked North Carolina in the ACC on February 1. It was the "fish tie."

Scott Dupree, an intern in the Notre Dame sports information office, had somehow gotten his hands on one of the hottest items in men's fashion that year — a tie with a print of a fish on it — not little fish, but one big fish. Most people thought it was the ugliest tie they had ever seen. But Dupree convinced most male members of the athletic department to wear it to just about every home game and it seemed to be a common thread in Irish victories that year. Athletic director Gene Corrigan wore it, trainer Skip Meyer wore it, and the assistant coaches wore it. But most everyone was afraid to suggest to the sartorially conscious head coach, one Digger Phelps, that he wear it.

Digger, even in the heat of the season, always liked to have a little fun, and he never wanted to be left out of anything. Digger wore the fish tie, and the Irish beat North Carolina — ironically Dupree's alma mater.

1987-88

Time Capsule

- Former pop star Sonny Bono was elected mayor of Palm Springs, California.

- The USS *Vincennes* launched missiles at an Iranian airbus, shooting it down.

- For three days, Americans watched live television coverage of the rescue of toddler Jessica McClure who fell down an abandoned well shaft.

- American swimmer Janet Evans won three individual gold medals at the 1988 Summer Olympic Games in Seoul.

- President Ronald Reagan visited the University of Notre Dame to celebrate the dedication of a U.S. postage stamp honoring Knute Rockne on March 3, 1988.

Irish Moment

Notre Dame finally returned to a major bowl game in 1987 by compiling an 8-3 record during the regular season.

The Irish opened the campaign by beating the ninth-ranked Wolverines on the road, 26-7. The only loss in the first nine games was a 30-22 defeat at Pitt.

After losing the last two games of the season on the road at Penn State and Miami, Holtz and his crew left for Dallas and the Cotton Bowl. Heisman Trophy winner Tim Brown would be returning to his hometown.

Notre Dame held a 10-3 lead midway through the second period, but Texas A & M's defense shut down the Irish after that. Notre Dame's defense, on the other hand, couldn't do anything to stop the Aggies who scored five straight times to put the game out of reach.

Irish fans were disappointed, but not daunted. After all, Notre Dame had returned to the major bowl picture and added another Heisman Trophy to its cache. Things were looking up.

The Irish basketball team posted another 20-win season and returned to the NCAA Tournament for its fourth consecutive appearance. In January, Notre Dame handed eventual national champion Kansas, coached by Larry Brown, an 80-76 defeat. The win would mark the fourth and final time under Digger Phelps that the team that would capture the national championship would lose during the regular season to the Irish.

But once again, the basketball season ended on a disappointing note with a first-round loss in the NCAA tournament.

ABOVE:
DAVID RIVERS.
Photo provided by Karen Croake Heisler

RIGHT:
TIM BROWN.

Irish Legend

Tim Brown's debut at Notre Dame elicited a lot of "oohs" but not many "aahs."

Notre Dame and Purdue opened 1984 as the dedication game for the Hoosier Dome in Indianapolis. Brown lined up to receive the opening kickoff, and he fumbled it at his own 12-yard line. The Boilermakers converted the miscue into a field goal.

Brown seldom made a mistake the rest of his Notre Dame career, and his electrifying punt and kickoff returns brought Irish fans to their feet and left opponents speechless.

The 6-foot, 195-pound flanker from Dallas, Texas, thrived his junior year under first-year coach Lou Holtz. He caught 45 passes for 910 yards and five touchdowns. He returned two kickoffs for scores and returned two punts for 75 yards.

Although he was on everybody's Heisman Trophy radar screen, his dazzling performance against Michigan State as a senior put Brown on the Heisman ballot.

In the opening quarter against the Spartans, he became the first player in college football history to return two consecutive punts for touchdowns. One was for 71 yards ... the other for 66.

His reputation preceded him. Teams feared him, and he was consistently the subject of double or triple coverage. As a senior he caught 39 passes for 846 yards; he also had 1,847 all-purpose yards.

Brown finished his career as Notre Dame's leader in pass reception yards with 2,493, but his most impressive catch might have been when he caught a football tossed into the audience by President Ronald Reagan at the March 1988, Rockne Stamp Dedication ceremonies.

A consensus All-American, Brown became Notre Dame's seventh (and last) Heisman Trophy winner in 1987. Although the vote was expected to be close, Brown ultimately ran away with the award, winning by over 600 votes.

A first-round pick of the Los Angeles Raiders, Brown played in 11 Pro Bowls.

Irish Lore

Mention Notre Dame lacrosse and the first name that comes to mind is Rich O'Leary.

A former All-American at Cortland State, O'Leary volunteered his time to coach Notre Dame's club lacrosse team for seven seasons, compiling a 111-91-1 record. When the sport gained varsity status in 1981, the only coach considered for the job was O'Leary.

Playing without benefit of scholarships, O'Leary won the first varsity game the Irish ever participated in and finished his initial year at 6-6. In 1985 and 1986, Notre Dame won back-to-back Midwest Lacrosse Association Great Lakes Conference titles. The Irish posted 10 wins in 1988 and tied for first in the MLA.

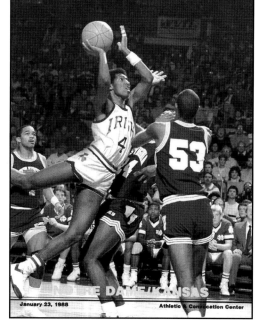

January 23, 1988   *Athletic & Convocation Center*

O'Leary, who also served as director of club sports, left coaching after the 1988 season. He had compiled a 64-42 record for a .604 winning percentage.

O'Leary turned the program over to his assistant, Kevin Corrigan. In 26 years as a varsity sport, O'Leary and Corrigan are the only two head coaches the sport has ever known.

1988-89

ABOVE:
RICKY WATTERS.
Photo by Bill Panzica-Sporting Shots

Irish Moment

Coach Lou Holtz entered the 1988 football season facing plenty of perplexing personnel questions. Heisman Trophy winner Tim Brown had graduated, and he had to replace the entire offensive line. But his running game was intact with Mark Green, Anthony Johnson, and Braxton Banks, and sophomore Tony Rice was adept at directing the option. Holtz had an experienced defense that liked to make opponents eat dirt. The potential to move into the national championship picture was there, but the chips would have to fall Notre Dame's way if the Irish were to climb back to the top of the charts. During Holtz's first two years, Notre Dame had lost 10 games—half of those were by two points or less.

Notre Dame opened the season at home in a night game against Michigan. The Wolverines were still smarting from their upset loss to the Irish the year before. The game see-sawed back and forth, and while the Notre Dame running game held its own, Rice did not complete a pass in his first nine attempts. In fact, the defense and kicking game accounted for all 19 Irish points. Ricky Watters returned a punt 81 yards for a touchdown, and field goal kicker Reggie Ho booted four field goals, the last one coming with just over a minute left. The Irish won, 19-17, but just barely.

Notre Dame crushed its next four opponents to head into a showdown with top-ranked Miami on October 15. The Irish had moved up to No. 4 in the polls, so the game was the toughest ticket in town.

The Hurricanes had humiliated Notre Dame in their last four matchups, winning by combined scores of 133-20.

Miami still managed to put points on the board and accumulate 481 yards of total offense. However, the feat wasn't enough to match Notre Dame's stellar defensive effort. The Hurricanes fumbled four times and threw three interceptions.

Notre Dame owned a 31-21 lead, but Miami came back. A field goal made the game 31-24, and with under a minute remaining, the Hurricanes scored on what looked like would be the game-tying or game-winning touchdown. But coach Jimmy Johnson decided to go for a two-point conversion and the win. Notre Dame's Pat Terrell, who had scored on a 60-yard interception return earlier in the game, batted down Steve Walsh's two-point conversion attempt, and the Irish had sweet revenge over the Hurricanes.

The Irish moved to the top spot in the polls two weeks later and finished the season undefeated after beating No. 2 USC, 27-10, in Los Angeles.

Only one thing stood in the way of a national championship—a confrontation with third-ranked West Virginia in the Fiesta Bowl. Notre Dame jumped out to a commanding 23-6 lead at halftime, and the Mountaineers never recovered.

When the polls were released the following day, Notre Dame stood at the top of each chart to claim its 11th consensus national championship.

Irish Legend

They called themselves the "Three Amigos."

Linebackers Michael Stonebreaker and Wes Pritchett and defensive end Frank Stams anchored a Notre Dame defense that allowed just 135 points in 1988 and played a key role in taking the Irish to the national championship.

Stams, a native of Akron, Ohio, came to Notre Dame as a fullback and started all 11 games there as a sophomore. But Holtz needed him at defensive end, and Stams made the switch. After the 1988 season, he earned consensus All-America honors and was named Lineman of the Year by the Moose Krause Chapter of the National Football Foundation Hall of Fame. He was selected as the MVP of the Miami game and was voted defensive MVP of the 1989 Fiesta Bowl after recording two sacks and three tackles against the Mountaineers.

Stams finished his career with 65 tackles and eight sacks for minus 63 yards.

Stonebreaker was a ferocious linebacker who earned All-America recognition three times, becoming a unanimous first-team selection as a senior in 1990.

During his career he had 220 tackles, five interceptions, and eight passes broken up. He also caused four fumbles, recovered two fumbles, and recorded five sacks for minus-29 yards. As a senior, he finished third in the balloting for the Butkus Award.

Pritchett, a native of Atlanta, Georgia, earned second-team All-America honors from *The Sporting News* after the 1988 season. He and Stams also participated in the 1989 Hula Bowl.

Irish Lore

Two Notre Dame Olympic sports teams made their first appearances in NCAA competition in 1988-89.

- In his fifth season as head coach, Dennis Grace led the men's soccer team to a 17 4-2 record, which included a 1-1 tie against perennial power Indiana in Bloomington. After winning the Midwestern Cities Conference title, the Irish were invited to the NCAA Tournament but lost their first-round match, 2-0, at SMU.

- The women's volleyball team, under the direction of coach Art Lambert, finished the regular season at 18-11 to advance to the NCAA Tournament for the first time in team history. The Irish upset 20th-ranked Penn State in the opening round at home to advance to the Sweet Sixteen. After dropping the first two games in the best-of-five match against fourth-ranked Illinois, Notre Dame won the next two games to tie the match. But Illinois won the tie-breaker, 15-9, to end the Irish season at 19-12.

TOP:
TONY RICE.

MIDDLE:
MICHAEL STONEBREAKER.
Photo by Bill Panzica-Sporting Shots

BOTTOM:
WES PRITCHETT.
Photo by Mike Bennett, Lighthouse Imaging

197

1989-90

ABOVE:
"ROCKET" ISMAIL.

RIGHT:
ANTHONY JOHNSON.

Irish Moment

A scheduling quirk put the defending national champions on the road for five of their first six games. In addition, Notre Dame had a 12th game on the docket with a season-opening matchup against Virginia in the Kickoff Classic—a daunting task for any team, especially one that had lost seven starters from its undefeated season of a year ago.

But the Irish responded to the challenge by winning all six in convincing fashion. Notre Dame had won 18 games in a row.

USC threatened to end that streak the following week after sophomore sensation Rocket Ismail fumbled on a kickoff return AND a punt return. The Trojans turned both of those miscues into touchdowns.

But Tony Rice engineered a skillful 80-yard touchdown drive, scoring on his own 15-yard run, with just over five minutes remaining to bring the Irish a 28-24 win to extend the winning streak to 19, keeping that No. 1 ranking.

Notre Dame won its next four games and went into the season finale at Miami with 23 straight wins. Unfortunately, it was payback time for the Hurricanes, and they ruined Irish hopes for a second consecutive national championship by winning, 27-10.

The Irish rebounded in the Orange Bowl by crushing top-ranked Colorado, 21-6.

After a scoreless first half, Anthony Johnson powered his way in from the two-yard line to put Notre Dame on top. Ismail added a second Irish touchdown with a 35-yard run on a reverse. The Buffalos finally scored with just one second left in the third quarter.

When Notre Dame gained possession after a punt with 10:27 left, Tony Rice engineered an 82-yard drive that took nearly nine minutes off the clock and sealed the win with Johnson scoring his second touchdown of the day from the seven.

Coach Lou Holtz had spent a lot of time trying to convince the press (and the voters) that since

his team had beaten the No. 1 ranked team, it deserved to win the national championship.

Few bought his arguments—the title went to Miami.

Irish Legend

For Monty Williams, life was sweet.

The 6-foot-7 freshman forward had averaged 7.7 points and helped the Irish to a 16-12 record that was just good enough to push the Irish into the NCAA Tournament for the sixth straight time.

Williams and coach Digger Phelps felt optimistic about the upcoming 1990-91 season because Williams, 6-9 sophomore LaPhonso Ellis, and veteran guards Elmer Bennett and Tim Singleton would be back along with forward Daimon Sweet.

But, on September 9, 1990, doctors told Williams he suffered from a rare heart condition called hypertrophic cardiomyopathy (HCM) which most likely would end his basketball career.

Williams, a native of Fredericksburg, Virginia, refused to accept the finality of the diagnosis and sought a second opinion. Finally, doctors gave him hope. Because he carried no other high-risk symptoms, Williams was finally given the all-clear to return to the court—two years later. Longtime trainer Skip Meyer learned to operate a defibulator, and he carried it everywhere the team went.

Elected co-captain by his teammates, Williams came back in 1992-93 for second-year coach John MacLeod. He led the team in scoring and rebounding with averages of 18.5 and 9.3 rebounds per game.

He also was selected to the U.S. Under-22 National Team that won the World Championship.

Captain again as a senior, Williams left little doubt in anyone's mind that he was healthy and happy. He paced the Irish in scoring and rebounding again with 22.4 points and 8.2 rebounds a game. He was selected as the 24th pick by the New York Knicks in the 1994 NBA draft.

Monty Williams had been given a second chance, and he made the most of it.

Irish Lore

Athletic director Dick Rosenthal had made a commitment to Irish Olympic sports when he assumed the job from Gene Corrigan in 1987, and the dividends were paying off in terms of postseason competition.

In 1989-90, the Notre Dame women's swimming team finished 39th in the NCAA Tournament based on the performance of freshman All-American Tanya Williams. She placed 11th in the 400-yard individual medley.

After 10 seasons as a varsity sport, second-year coach Kevin Corrigan led the Irish lacrosse team to its first appearance in the NCAA Tournament. Notre Dame lost, 9-3, to Harvard, but the Irish finished the season at 9-7 and ranked 17th in the final United States Intercollegiate Lacrosse Association poll. That marked the first time a Notre Dame lacrosse team had earned a national ranking.

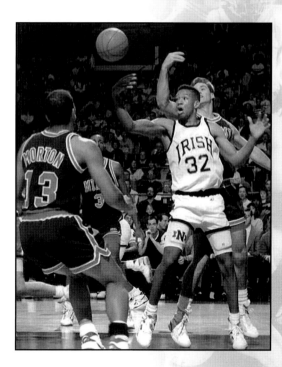

ABOVE:
MONTY WILLIAMS.

BELOW:
LaPHONSO ELLIS.

1990-91

ABOVE:
RICK MIRER.

RIGHT:
"ROCKET" ISMAIL.
Photo by Mike Bennett, Lighthouse Imaging

Irish Moment

The Notre Dame football team spent six weeks ranked No. 1.

Sophomore quarterback Rick Mirer led the Irish to three straight wins to open the season, but an unexpected 36-31 loss to Stanford pushed Notre Dame all the way down to the eighth spot in the polls. The Irish recovered to win five straight, including a 29-20 victory over Miami, which was ranked No 2. Penn State pinned a 24-21 loss on the Irish in the last 18 seconds to destroy Notre Dame's hopes for a national championship.

Still, the Irish finished 9-2 and headed to the Orange Bowl for a rematch with No. 1 ranked Colorado.

Irish Legend

Raghib "Rocket" Ismail was the most exciting football player in 1990.

Fans never knew what the 5-10 flanker from Wilkes-Barre, Pennsylvania, would do once he got his hands on the ball.

A first-team All-America selection as both a sophomore and a junior, Ismail earned the Walter Camp Player of the Year award in 1990 and finished second in the Heisman Trophy race.

Although he signed a professional contract after his junior year, Ismail accumulated over 4,000 all-purpose yards in his shortened Notre Dame career. He caught a total of 71 passes for 1,565 yards and four touchdowns; rushed 131 times for 1,015 yards and five touchdowns; returned 46 kickoffs for 1,271 yards and five touchdowns; and brought back 25 punts for 336 yards and one touchdown.

Ismail's final play with the Irish football team still leaves Notre Dame fans shaking their heads, but in frustration, not jubilation.

With Colorado owning a 10-9 lead over the Irish in the waning minute of the 1991 Orange Bowl, the Buffalos decided to risk a punt after being stopped on third down.

Ismail took the kick at his own nine-yard line and zigzagged through a bevy of defenders before breaking free for what appeared to be an electrifying 91-yard touchdown return. In the excitement, few fans noticed that an official had dropped a yellow flag in the backfield, and the Irish were called for clipping.

While at Notre Dame, Ismail also competed for the track team. He finished second in the 55-meter dash at the NCAA Outdoor Championships.

Where Ismail was exciting and unpredictable, nose tackle Chris Zorich was steady and dependable.

Zorich had grown up in a tough neighborhood on the south side of Chicago, and many predicted that the 6-1, 266-pounder would never succeed at Notre Dame, athletically or academically.

But after a difficult freshman year, he thrived. He started as a sophomore on the 1988 national championship team, making 70 tackles. As a junior, UPI honored him as its lineman of the year, and the Touchdown Club of Washington, D.C., made him its lineman of the year.

As a senior, Zorich missed the first two games of the season with a knee injury but returned to win the Lombardi Trophy, presented by the Houston Rotary Club to the top college lineman. He became the third Notre Dame player to win that award.

After playing the game of his life in the 1991 Orange Bowl, Zorich was named the game's most valuable player. He had made 10 tackles in Notre Dame's 10-9 loss to Colorado.

When Zorich returned home to Chicago the following morning, he discovered that his beloved mother had died of a heart attack shortly after watching her son turn in an incredible performance.

Zorich, who played professionally in his hometown for the Bears, later established the Chris Zorich Foundation to help others in the Chicago area. He also annually distributes Thanksgiving dinners in his old neighborhood.

Zorich graduated from law school at the University of Notre Dame in 2002.

Irish Lore

On April 10, 1991, Digger Phelps announced his retirement from coaching after 20 seasons of leading the Irish.

The winningest coach in Notre Dame history, Phelps posted a 393-197 mark for a .666 winning percentage. Fourteen times his teams won 20 games, and the Irish competed in 12 NCAA tournaments, advancing to the Final Four in 1978. Notre Dame played in the NIT three times, making it to the title game twice. Under Phelps, the Irish upset the nation's No. 1 ranked team seven times and defeated the eventual national champion four times during the regular season. Nine of his players earned some type of All-America recognition.

Even today, Phelps, a commentator for ESPN, still insists that his greatest achievement at Notre Dame was his perfect graduation rate. Fifty-four players spent four years with Phelps. All earned a Notre Dame degree.

1991-92

ABOVE:
DAVID DiLUCIA.
Photo by Mike Bennett, Lighthouse Imaging

RIGHT:
COACH BOBBY BAYLISS.

Irish Moment

Notre Dame had not competed in an NCAA Tennis Tournament for 14 seasons. Under coach Bobby Bayliss, the Irish returned to the field in 1990 and 1991, but Notre Dame did not place.

In Bayliss' fifth season, the Irish stunned the tennis world with a runner-up finish to Stanford in the 1992 NCAA Tennis Tournament.

After ending the regular campaign at 20-3, Notre Dame entered the tournament as its 10th seed.

The Irish split six singles matches with seventh-ranked Mississippi and took two out of three doubles matches to advance to the quarter-finals. Next up was No. 3 Georgia, also the tournament host.

Notre Dame took four of six singles matches, but lost at number-one and three doubles. However, the number-two doubles team of Will Forsyth and Andy Zurcher pulled off the upset win to move the Irish to the

semi-finals against top-ranked USC.

The Trojans owned a 21-2 season record, and most observers thought Notre Dame's incredible run would end here. The Irish took two of the first three singles matches and then won all three remaining matches in three sets to ruin USC's national championship hopes.

But Notre Dame's luck ran out against Stanford, and the Cardinal claimed a 5-0 win.

Two Irish tennis players earned All-America recognition in 1992.

Senior David DiLucia added to the accolades he had won as a sophomore and junior with both singles and doubles honors. He finished his Notre Dame career with a 90-11 mark in dual competition and a 25-11 record in dual doubles matches.

Junior Chuck Coleman, DiLucia's doubles partner, was also recognized for his play in 1991, 1992, and 1993. The Lake Wylie, South Carolina, native finished with a 75-35 ledger in dual singles matches and a 41-23 mark in doubles.

Irish Legend

Coach John MacLeod, who had left the NBA to return to the college ranks at Notre Dame, could only scratch his head and wonder.

This talented Irish squad, which featured a veteran lineup of Elmer Bennett, Daimen Sweet, and LaPhonso Ellis, had lost five of its first six games.

But thanks to the play and leadership of the ebullient Ellis, the 6-foot-8 senior captain responded to the challenge and helped engineer a quick turnaround. Notre Dame finished 18-15 with a second-place finish in the NIT.

A native of East St. Louis, Illinois, Ellis was recruited by Digger Phelps and former Notre Dame assistant John Shumate. His career had shown flashes of brilliance, including his first game in an Irish uniform when he scored 27 points against St. Bonaventure.

Ellis averaged 13.5 points that year followed by a 14.0 average his sophomore season. As a junior, he led the team in scoring with a 16.4 mark, and he scored 17.7 points as a senior.

During his four-year career, Ellis scored over 1,500 points and was credited with 200 blocked shots—a school record.

After graduation, Ellis was drafted in the first round of the 1991 NBA draft by the Denver Nuggets. During his injury-plagued NBA career, he also played for the Atlanta Hawks, the Minnesota Timberwolves, and the Miami Heat.

Irish Lore

Lou Holtz liked a good joke just as much as the next guy, but this one wasn't funny.

"What's the difference between Cheerios and Notre Dame?"

"Only Cheerios belong in a bowl."

Ouch!

Sure, the Irish had struggled through a particularly disappointing 9-3 season. Many thought Notre Dame, ranked 18th, had no business accepting an invitation to the Sugar Bowl to play third-ranked Florida.

But Holtz, always the master motivator, used the lack of respect for his team to his advantage. By the end of the game, after Notre Dame had staged a furious second-half comeback, Florida looked like soggy cereal.

Fullback Jerome Bettis scored three touchdowns in the fourth quarter to lead the Irish to a 39-28 victory.

1992-93

Irish Moment

It was Rick Mirer's senior year, and he had one last chance at a national championship.

The talented quarterback from nearby Goshen, Indiana, efficiently and effectively ran Holtz's offense, and in his three years at Notre Dame, the Irish stood 31-7. By the end of the season, he would pass Steve Beuerlein as the Notre Dame leader in total offense with 6,691 yards.

But a 17-17 tie in the home opener against Michigan and a 33-16 upset loss to Stanford in Notre Dame Stadium dashed Mirer's hopes for a ring. Still, there was plenty left to play for. The Irish won their last six regular-season games to go 9-1-1 and earn a trip to the Cotton Bowl against fourth-ranked Texas A&M.

On November 16, the Irish were scheduled to meet Penn State in the home finale. This would mark the last meeting between the two teams since the Nittany Lions were joining the Big Ten conference the following fall. It was uncharacteristically cold for November, even in South Bend, and the snow started swirling.

Notre Dame's offense was as frigid as the temperature. The Irish managed just three field goals by Craig Hentrich and took a 9-6 lead into the fourth quarter. Penn State added 10 points on a field goal and touchdown to put the Irish down, 16-9.

With 4:25 left in the game, Mirer guided the Irish through the snow, hitting Jerome Bettis for a 21-yard gain. After scrambling for 15 yards on his own, Mirer found Ray Griggs with a 17-yard completion. Reggie Brooks and Mirer ran the ball to the Penn State four-yard line, but the Nittany Lions' defense stopped Notre Dame on three straight tries. On fourth-and goal, Mirer found Bettis in the end zone for the touchdown.

No one was going for the tie. With just 20 seconds left on the clock, Mirer saw Brooks in the right corner and threw him the ball. Brooks dove and made the catch for the two-point conversion, and the Irish had a 17-16 win.

In the Cotton Bowl, Mirer completed eight-of-16 passes for 119 yards and Brooks ran for 115 yards on 25 carries to lead Notre Dame to a 28-3 victory. Bettis scored three of the four Irish touchdowns.

ABOVE:
REGGIE BROOKS.

RIGHT:
RICK MIRER VS. PENN STATE.
Photo by Mike Bennett, Lighthouse Imaging

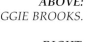

Irish Legend

Defenseman Mike Iorio became the first Irish lacrosse player to earn All-America recognition as a sophomore in 1993. He did it again in both 1994 and 1995.

A native of Chester, New Jersey, Iorio played in 55 games during his four years with the Irish. He was credited with 58 ground balls as a freshman, 45 as a sophomore, 55 as a junior, and 37 as a senior.

Outfielder Eric Danapilis notched consensus first-team All-America honors in 1993, becoming the first Irish player to win such acclaim.

Also named to the 1992 NCAA Atlantic Regional team, Danapilis still owns Notre Dame career records for RBI (221) and on-base percentage (.559). He ranks second in career batting average (.405) and doubles (61), third in hits (295), and slugging (.643).

In 1993, the St. Joseph's, Michigan, native batted .438, now the fourth best season average in history, totaled 85 RBI, and hit 24 doubles.

The 1994 Irish baseball team finished 46-16 and lost in the NCAA East regional.

Irish Lore

Women's tennis coach Jay Louderback took over the coaching reins in 1989, and in his fourth season, the Irish advanced to the NCAA Tournament for the first time in history.

Ranked 15th in the country with an 18-8 record, Notre Dame was eliminated in the round of 16.

In just her second year as head coach, Debbie Brown guided the women's volleyball team to its first appearance in the NCAA Tournament since 1988 after a 30-8 record during the regular season. Notre Dame has been every year since.

Coach Joe Piane, who had led his 1990 cross-country team to a third-place finish in the NCAA Championships, returned to the top 10 in 1992 when his Irish runners placed sixth. The following year, 1993, Notre Dame finished fifth. Mike McWilliams earned All-America honors four straight years.

1993-94

ABOVE:
JEFF BURRIS.

Irish Moment

It was time for another "game of the century."

Coach Lou Holtz had directed the Irish to 16 straight wins over the last two seasons. Although Notre Dame struggled in the first two games against Northwestern (a 27-12 win) and third-ranked Michigan (a 27-23 victory at Ann Arbor), the Irish rolled over everything that got in their way in the next seven games.

That set up a November showdown with top-ranked Florida State. Everybody wanted a ticket or a press credential. The Notre Dame sports information office issued a record 700 media passes for the game. At the Friday night pep rally, the Joyce Athletic and Convocation Center was packed ... and rocking two hours before the festivities were supposed to start.

Florida State opened the scoring with the game's first touchdown, but Notre Dame came right back on a 32-yard run on the reverse by Adrian Jerrell. The Irish scored again on a 26-yard run by Lee Becton. Jeff Burris added another rushing touchdown, and by halftime Notre Dame owned a 21-7 lead. A Kevin Pendergast field goal in the third quarter moved the Irish up 24-7, but with 10 minutes left to go in the game, Florida State had cut the Irish advantage to just a touchdown, 24-17.

Burris scored another touchdown to put Notre Dame back up by two touchdowns, but Florida State wasn't about to roll over and hand the Irish its No. 1 ranking without a fight.

Quarterback Charlie Ward, who finished the day with 297 yards passing and three touchdowns, showed the calm and poise that would help him win the Heisman Trophy later that fall. With just 51 seconds left and starting at his own 37-yard line, Ward moved his team to the Irish 14 in just three plays and 41 seconds.

There was no doubt he would try to throw the ball into the end zone for the touchdown. Defensive end Thomas Knight knocked down Ward's first attempt. Still, Ward had three seconds and one play left. This time Irish cornerback Shawn Wooden swatted the ball away, and the Irish student body swarmed the field.

Notre Dame appeared to be on track for its second national championship under Holtz, but the following week, the Irish were upset at home by Boston College. The Eagles' David Gordon kicked a 41-yard field goal as time expired for a stunning 41-39 upset of Notre Dame in its own stadium.

The Irish won their third straight bowl game with a 24-21 victory over Texas A&M in the Cotton Bowl. Notre Dame has not been successful in a bowl game since.

Irish Legend

Pat Murphy's dream was to take Notre Dame to the College World Series for the first time since 1957.

He was young, energetic, ambitious, and convincing. His recruiting skills brought a new level of talent to South Bend. His first team in 1988 had won 39 games. After that season, the Irish topped the 45-win mark each of the next five years. Plus, the MCC had an automatic bid to the NCAA Tournament, so the Irish became regulars in postseason play. During his seven-year tenure, Notre Dame won the MCC title four times.

Murphy almost lived his dream in 1992 and 1993 with 3-2 records in the NCAA regionals, but the Irish fell just short of advancing to Omaha. In 1994, Murphy directed Notre Dame to an 8-1 win over top-ranked Clemson in the East Regional.

Murphy was a hot commodity in the baseball coaching circles, yet his heart and soul were at Notre Dame. But, one day, after the 1994 season, Murphy received an offer he just couldn't refuse.

Perennial baseball powerhouse Arizona State needed a coach, and the Sun Devils wanted Murphy. Acknowledging that it was a gut-wrenching decision, Murphy knew the offer to coach one of the top baseball programs in the country was something he had to try.

Still an Irish fan, Murphy brought his Sun Devils to South Bend in 2002 for a three-game series. Because of the weather, the two teams played only once, with Notre Dame winning 9-4. The Irish traveled to Phoenix the following year in late February, and Murphy notched two wins over his former team.

Murphy has been a regular visitor to Irish football practices every time Notre Dame has made a bowl visit to Phoenix. His uniform may say ASU, but there's still some blue and gold running through those veins.

Irish Lore

The 1993-94 season marked several firsts in six women's sports.

- The cross-country team placed 15th in its first appearance in the NCAA Championships, and Sarah Riley became the sport's first All-American.

- The volleyball team upset third-ranked Nebraska in the Joyce Center and advanced to the quarterfinals of the NCAA Tournament. Junior Christy Peters became the first Irish volleyball player to earn All-America recognition.

- The Notre Dame soccer team made first appearance in the NCAA Tournament, losing 2-1 to eventual national runner-up George Mason.

- Coach Muffet McGraw led the Irish to its their first appearance in the NCAA tournament, losing a first-round game, 81-76, to Minnesota in the Joyce Center.

- Doubles partners Wendy Crabtree and Lisa Tholen became Notre Dame's first division I All-Americans. Crabtree also received All-America honors for her singles play.

- Pitcher Terri Kobata helped the Irish to a 41-20 record and became the first softball player to earn All-America honors.

To cap things off, the men's and women's fencing team won the NCAA fencing combined title.

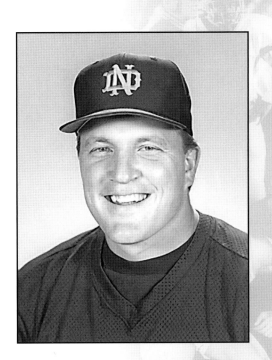

ABOVE:
PAT MURPHY.

BELOW:
SARAH RILEY.

1994-95

Time Capsule

- On April 19, a truck bomb exploded in front of the Murrah Federal Building in Oklahoma City, killing 168 people.

- Former President Ronald Reagan announced he had been diagnosed with Alzheimer's disease in November.

- U.S. astronaut Norman Thagard spent two weeks about the Russian Space Station Mir.

- Major league baseball players went on strike on August 12. For the first time in its history, the World Series was cancelled.

- During commencement activities, Chicago Cardinal Joseph Bernadin was awarded the Laetare Medal.

Irish Moment

It took five tries, but the Irish lacrosse program, one of just six in the nation making its fourth consecutive appearance in the NCAA tournament, finally proved it belonged with the sport's traditional powers.

On May 13, 1995, Notre Dame upset fifth-ranked Duke in Durham for its first-ever victory in the postseason.

The Blue Devils had won the ACC championship and expected to cruise over their Midwestern opponent, especially since they were playing on their own field. Duke owned a 7-4 lead at halftime, but as lacrosse fans know, a flurry of goals can turn a game around in a hurry.

The Irish scored seven straight goals in the second half to take an 11-7 lead. Duke added its first goal since the 1:29 mark of the second quarter with 8:25 left in the game. Notre Dame added its 12th goal of the day with 4:41 on the clock. The Blue Devils added two more goals, but freshman goalie Alex Cade made 18 saves that day, one shy of his career best, and Notre Dame hung on for the win.

Senior attackman Randy Colley tallied five goals and added an assist, while Tim Kearney scored three times for the Irish.

The following week Notre Dame took on Maryland in the quarterfinals at College Park. Despite a furious second-half rally, the Irish fell, 14-11, to the fourth-ranked Terrapins. No one would take the Irish lightly ever again.

RIGHT:
MIKE DeCICCO.

Irish Legend

Few people have had as big an impact in Notre Dame athletics as legendary fencing coach Mike DeCicco.

A 1949 graduate of Notre Dame, DeCicco arrived on campus as a freshman in 1945. Two years later, he joined the fencing team, which had resurfaced after taking a hiatus during World War II. He competed in all three weapons (the last Irish fencer to do so) and compiled a combined 63-20 record. His 45-4 career record in the foil still ranks third on the all-time list for career foil winning percentage.

DeCicco returned to his native New Jersey after graduation but came back to Notre Dame in 1954 to teach in the engineering department, finish work on his doctorate degree, and serve as an assistant to his mentor, Walter Langford. In 1962, he took over the head coaching duties after Langford retired.

By the time he retired from coaching in 1995, DeCicco's teams had compiled an unbelievable 680-45 record for a .938 winning percentage. His teams won five national championships, and he was named coach of the year four times. His fencers earned almost 100 All-America designations. He was also active in fencing on the national and international level, bringing the Junior World Championships to the Joyce Center in 1979.

DeCicco also served as a mentor to numerous Irish athletes as the head of the academic advising program for student-athletes—a forerunner to today's Academic Student Services for Student-Athletes. Founded in 1964, the program was ahead of its time and laid the groundwork for tutorial assistance programs, class monitoring, and degree progress reports.

Irish Lore

It took coach Chris Petrucelli just five years to turn the Notre Dame women's soccer program into a national power. After competing in their first NCAA tournament in 1993, the Irish almost climbed to the top of the mountain in 1994.

During the regular season, Notre Dame ended perennial power North Carolina's 92-game winning streak with a 0-0 tie in St. Louis. Goalkeeper Jen Renola made a career-high 11 saves. Later that month, after two more Irish wins and a Tar Heel loss, the Irish moved to the top spot in the polls—the first time Notre Dame had occupied that lofty position.

The Irish notched their first NCAA tournament win with 3-1 decision over

LEFT:
KATE SOBRERO.

George Mason in the first round. Future Olympian and World Cup team member Kate Sobrero scored on a corner kick to upend Portland, 1-0, to advance to the NCAA championship game against none other than North Carolina.

This time the Tar Heels won their 12th NCAA title with a 5-0 victory over the upstart Irish.

1995-96

ABOVE:
CHRIS PETRUCELLI.

Irish Moment

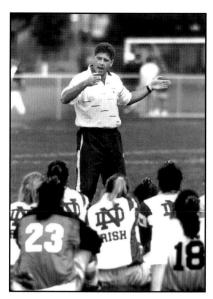

The Notre Dame women's soccer team opened the 1995 season by shutting out its first eight opponents and scoring a total of 36 goals. Coach Chris Petrucelli's squad might have been thinking that it would never lose.

But the second-ranked Irish began a mid-season slump in late September with a 2-2 tie with Cincinnati. Although Notre Dame won its next game, 2-1, in overtime against Ohio State, the Irish then lost to fifth-ranked Connecticut, 5-4. Notre Dame then edged Santa Clara, but a 2-2 tie at Duke and a 2-0 loss to North Carolina had the Irish reeling in mid-October.

The Irish regrouped and won the final seven games of the regular season. After avenging an earlier loss to Connecticut with a 1-0 victory to clinch the Big East title, Notre Dame entered the NCAA Tournament.

In the first game, freshman midfielder Shannon Boxx scored three goals to lead the Irish to a 5-0 victory over Wisconsin. The Irish faced Connecticut for the third time that season and won, 2-0. That set up another rematch with North Carolina in Chapel Hill in the semi-finals. The Tar Heels had won 31 straight NCAA tournament games over a 10-year period.

Playing before a crowd of 7,212, Notre Dame rattled North Carolina with its relentless pressure. In the 20th minutes of the game, Carolina's Cindy Parlow headed a cross out of the goal area. But Irish midfielder Cindy Daws headed it back toward the goal. Parlow tried to redirect it but the ball went into her own net to give the Irish a 1-0 lead.

Notre Dame's superb defense held the Tar Heels scoreless, and in what may be one of the biggest upsets in women's soccer history, the Irish moved into the finals.

In the title game against Portland, the teams battled through 125 scoreless minutes. Finally, Daws blew a direct kick into the back of the net for the overtime victory.

The Irish women's soccer team became the national champion.

Irish Legend

The Notre Dame roster in 1995 was literally a who's who of women's soccer.

Midfielder Cindy Daws, who had earned All-America honors as a sophomore, was named MVP of the NCAA Tournament. As a senior, she was again named a consensus All-America and was awarded the Honda-Broderick Cup, which honors the nation's outstanding collegiate woman athlete.

Three-time All-America goalie Jen Renola, who started all 98 games of her Irish career, was honored as the National Soccer Coaches Association of America Player of the

Year in 1996. Captain of the 1995 and 1996 teams along with Daws, Renola also won several academic citations, including an NCAA postgraduate scholarship.

Ragen Coyne became Notre Dame's first All-American in soccer after her freshman season of 1992. She missed her junior year with a stress fracture, but Coyne returned in 1995 and played in 22 of 25 games.

Rosella Guerrero earned All-America honors as a junior when she scored 21 goals and added nine assists. Although her goal production dropped in 1995, she was an integral part of the national championship team.

Midfielder Holly Manthei, who owns the NCAA record for career assists with 129, was a three-time All-American and led the nation in assists each of her four years at Notre Dame.

Defender Kate Sobrero was also a three-time All-American and was named Big East defensive player of the year in 1997.

Manthei played on the 1995 U.S. National team, while defensive midfielder Shannon Boxx and defender Kate Sobrero were starters on the U.S. Olympic team that won a gold medal in the 2004 Athens Games. Sobrero also was a member of the U.S. team that won the 1999 FIFA World Cup.

Irish Lore

Notre Dame had joined the Big East conference and 1995-96 marked the first season of competition for its teams.

If anyone thought the Irish couldn't hold their own, well, Notre Dame proved it belonged.

Coach Debbie Brown's volleyball team opened the season with an 8-0 run and won 14 of its first 15 games to earn its best national ranking to date — seventh. The Irish won their first Big East match against Georgetown on September 30, and Notre Dame did not lose a conference match until a little over three years later.

The women's tennis team won its Big East title and advanced to the quarterfinals of the NCAA Tournament.

Coach Liz Miller led the softball team to 48 wins and the Big East south championship.

1996-97

Irish Moment

Coach Muffet McGraw led the Notre Dame women's basketball team to its first appearance in the NCAA Final Four in 1996-97 even though the Irish were never ranked higher than seventh the entire season. In fact, Notre Dame entered the tournament ranked 15th in the country.

The Irish had finished the regular season with a 27-6 mark, and two of those losses were to top-ranked Connecticut and another one came at the hands of No. 2 Tennessee. Still, Notre Dame didn't seem to command much respect—at least not until the NCAA Tournament.

Katryna Gaither scored 24 points and grabbed 12 rebounds to help the Irish win their first-round game, 93-62, over Memphis in Austin, Texas. Two days later, Gaither and teammate Beth Morgan both scored 29 points as Notre Dame upset sixth-ranked Texas on the Longhorns' home court, 86-83, on St. Patrick's Day.

That moved the Irish into the regionals in Columbia, S.C., for a game against seventh-ranked Alabama. Although down by nine at the half, Notre Dame put together a second-half rally and ended up running away with an 87-71 win. Morgan hit a career-high 36 points, and Gaither added 26. In the regional final against George Washington, Gaither and Morgan once against paced the Irish with 25 and 15 points, respectively.

Gaither was named MVP of the East Regional. Notre Dame was on its way to its first Final Four.

But the Irish would have to wait for the national championship banner. An old familiar foe—Tennessee—ended Notre Dame's Cinderella season, knocking the Irish out of the running with an 80-66 victory.

Notre Dame compiled its best record in history with a 31-7 mark.

Irish Legend

Lou Holtz, one of the most popular and successful coaches in Irish football history, resigned on November 20, just three days before the home finale against Rutgers.

Perhaps the job, often called the toughest in America, finally got the best of him—just as it had

ABOVE:
MUFFET McGRAW.

RIGHT:
LOU HOLTZ WITH
QUARTERBACK JARIOUS JACKSON.
Photo by Mike Bennett, Lighthouse Imaging

worn down Frank Leahy, Ara Parseghian, and Dan Devine. During the 1995 season, he had to undergo corrective neck surgery after notching his 200th win as a college head coach at Purdue. He was forced to miss the Vanderbilt game at home the following week. Holtz had appointed Bob Davie as the interim head coach.

The 1996 season certainly was a successful one by all accounts. Two losses—to fourth-ranked Ohio State and an overtime defeat at the hands of Air Force—were disappointing, but no one had quite expected Holtz's sudden announcement.

In his 11 seasons at Notre Dame, Holtz guided the Irish to an overall record of 100-30-2. He owns the record for most games coached and ranks second to Knute Rockne in total victories. Holtz led Notre Dame to nine straight New Year's Day bowl games, winning one national championship and coming close on at least two other occasions. Five times his teams finished the season ranked sixth or higher.

Holtz spent two years as a college football analyst with CBS Sports after leaving Notre Dame, but coaching was in his blood. He returned to the sidelines in 1999 as head coach at South Carolina.

Irish Lore

The Notre Dame men's basketball team didn't exactly take to Big East competition. During the 1995-96 season, its first as a conference member, Notre Dame lost its first six games. In fact, the Irish finished a dismal 4-14 in league play.

Things got a little better the following year. The Irish improved to 8-10 in the Big East, an impressive enough turnaround to award the conference's coach of the year honor to John MacLeod. Plus, junior forward Pat Garrity, who became one of only two players in history to lead the Irish in scoring all four years of his career, was named the Big East player of the year. Garrity averaged 21.2 points per game and led Notre Dame to a 16-14 record and the quarterfinals of the NIT.

Other teams reveled in their success with conference competition.

The women's swim team, under the direction of Bailey Weathers, won the first of nine straight Big East titles.

The men's soccer team won the Big East tournament, and posted its first ever win in NCAA postseason play with a 1-0 upset of second-seeded UNC-Greensboro.

LEFT:
PAT GARRITY.

Time Capsule

- Actor Charlton Heston became president of the National Rifle Association.

- Tornadoes in central Florida killed 42 people and destroyed 2,600 structures.

- *Harry Potter and the Sorcerer's Stone* was published in the summer.

- Michael Jordan retired "again" after winning his sixth NBA title in eight years with the Chicago Bulls.

- Entertainer and educator Bill Cosby received an honorary degree from the University of Notre Dame and delivered its commencement address.

Irish Moment

The $50 million, 21-month renovation and expansion project of Notre Dame Stadium, one of the nation's most recognizable sports venues, was completed in August and ready for the season opener against Georgia Tech.

When the work began immediately following the final home game of the 1995 campaign, few Irish fans expected a new coach to be pacing the Notre Dame sidelines in the "rededication" game. Lou Holtz was gone, and his former defensive coordinator, Bob Davie, would be leading the Irish out of the tunnel against Georgia Tech.

Rededication festivities moved the Friday-night pep rally from the JACC to the Stadium for the first time in its history and more than 35,000 fans attended the celebration. Every former Notre Dame football player had been offered the opportunity to purchase tickets to the game, and those that came were invited to form a tunnel on the field for the team to run through as it emerged onto the playing field. That practice became a routine that continues today for the season home opener.

The first game of the Davie era turned out to be uncomfortably close. Although the Irish were ranked 11th in the preseason polls, George Tech owned a 13-10 advantage late in the fourth period. Finally, the Notre Dame offense put together a drive in the final three minutes to score the go-ahead touchdown. The defense hung on for a 17-13 win.

The Irish then lost five of their next six games to put them out of consideration for a major bowl bid. But Davie salvaged the season by directing Notre Dame to six consecutive wins to end the regular season at 7-5. However, the Irish lost their third straight bowl game—this one by a 27-9 margin to LSU at the Independence Bowl.

ABOVE:
BOB DAVIE.
Photo by Mike Bennett, Lighthouse Imaging

RIGHT:
TODD RASSAS.

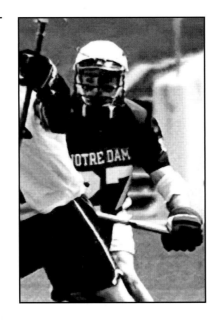

Irish Legend

Todd Rassas won All-America distinction three times as a defenseman for the Notre Dame lacrosse team.

Since professional lacrosse was just beginning to attract a following, most Irish players either had to put away their sticks or play on club teams after graduation. Rassas was one of the lucky ones, in more ways than he could have ever imagined.

A native of Chicago, Rassas was not invited to participate in tryouts for the 1998 U.S. team that would compete in the International Lacrosse Federation World Championships. Disappointed but not undaunted, Rassas continued to play club lacrosse and work on his game. He also began working for the U.S. Secret Service two years after graduating from Notre Dame with a degree in political science.

By the summer of 2001, Rassas, whose father Nick had earned All-America honors as a defensive back in the mid-sixties at Notre Dame, had finagled an invitation to the U.S. team tryouts for the 2002 squad. The 6-2 defenseman was a physical presence and impressed the coaches with his leadership and intelligence. Named to the 23-man squad, Rassas was one of only eight who had not played collegiate lacrosse the previous year. In fact, he hadn't played in four years!

On September 11, 2001, Rassas was working for the Secret Service at his office at the World Trade Center in New York City.

After the first plane hit, Rassas joined other agents in establishing a triage center. He was bandaging a woman's hand when the second plane struck the second tower.

Rassas survived the attacks and spent the next month working at Ground Zero while his 2002 U.S. Lacrosse team practiced without him. He played in the fall tournament but admitted his focus wasn't on the games.

The following summer, the U.S. team played a series of exhibition games before leaving for the tournament in Australia. Although no one gave the U.S. team much of a chance, Rassas and his teammates took home a gold medal.

Rassas, who didn't get into Notre Dame, the Secret Service, or the U.S. team on his first try, will compete on the U.S. team again in the 2006 World Championships in Canada.

Irish Lore

Baseball coach Paul Maineri had a major league pitching staff on his 1998 team, his fourth Irish squad.

Junior Brad Lidge, posted an 8-2 record, striking out 93 batters in 80.1 innings. Named Big East pitcher of the year, Lidge finished his career with a 13-5 mark over three years. Drafted by the Houston Astros in the first round of the MLB draft, Lidge, from Evergreen, Colorado, now ranks as one of the premier relievers in Major League Baseball. In 2003, Lidge pitched two innings of relief, striking out two, as the Astros became the first team to hold the New York Yankees hitless at home since 1952.

Freshman Aaron Heilman finished his first-year with a 7-3 mark, striking out 78 in 67 innings, and was honored as the national freshman of the year. During his four years at Notre Dame, Heilman won 43 games and lost just seven while striking out 425 batters in 393.2 innings. As a senior in 2001, he was undefeated at 15-0. The 6-foot-5 right-hander from Logansport, Indiana, was a first-round pick of the New York Mets in the 2001 draft.

Both players are still pitching in the major leagues for the teams that drafted them.

ABOVE:
BRAD LIDGE.
Photo by Pete LaFleur

BELOW:
AARON HEILMAN.
Photo by Pete LaFleur

Time Capsule

- President Bill Clinton was impeached by the U.S. House of Representatives. He was later acquitted by the U.S. Senate.

- Two students at Columbine High School killed 12 of their classmates and one teacher before turning their guns on themselves.

- Senator and former astronaut John Glenn returned to space as part of the space shuttle *Discovery* crew.

- St. Louis Cardinal slugger Mark McGwire broke baseball's single season home run record, previously held by Roger Maris, with his 62nd home run on September 8.

- Elizabeth Dole addressed members of the 1999 class at the University of Notre Dame commencement and received an honorary degree.

ABOVE:
JARIOUS JACKSON.
Photo by Mike Bennett, Lighthouse Imaging

Irish Moment

The Irish football team opened the 1998 season in impressive fashion by upending fifth-ranked Michigan, 36-20, in Notre Dame Stadium. The Wolverines had won the national championship the previous year, but the Irish, playing behind new quarterback Jarious Jackson, weren't intimidated. After falling behind 13-6 at halftime, Notre Dame put together five unanswered scoring drives to leave Michigan in the dust.

Notre Dame jumped 12 places in the polls (from No. 22 to No. 10) after that victory, but the Irish shouldn't have read their press clippings. The following week Michigan State knocked Notre Dame back to reality with a 45-23 loss. The win would be the second in a string of five over the Irish for Michigan State.

Escaping with a 31-30 win over Purdue in the waning minutes the following week seemed to right the ship. Notre Dame won its next seven games, including two thrillers over Boston College and LSU, and headed to the season finale against USC ranked ninth.

But Jackson damaged his knee on the last play of the game in Baton Rouge and would be watching from the sidelines.

Freshman Arnaz Battle earned the nod against the Trojans. But USC held record-setting running back Autry Denson to just 46 yards on 19 carries, and the offense could not find the end zone all day. Eventual Heisman Trophy winner Carson Palmer quarterbacked USC to only 10 points, but it was all the Trojans needed to end Notre Dame's hopes for a berth in a major bowl for the second time in three years.

Even though Jackson returned to lead the offense in the Gator Bowl against Georgia Tech, Notre Dame couldn't shake its bowl hex, losing 35-28. The Irish tied the game just seconds into the fourth quarter on a Denson run from the one-yard line. Unfortunately the Yellow Jackets scored on a 55-yard touchdown pass with eight minutes left, and Tech's defense kept the game out of reach. In three possessions, Notre Dame couldn't move past its own 28-yard line.

Basketball coach John MacLeod spent eight seasons at Notre Dame, but only three of those years produced winning records. The University's formerly advantageous status has an independent had turned into an albatross in recruiting and scheduling. Notre Dame, at MacLeod's urging, joined the Big East in his fifth year, but it wasn't soon enough to see an upswing in Irish basketball fortunes.

Shortly after Notre Dame's third consecutive first-round exit from the Big East tournament in as many tries, MacLeod resigned.

Irish Legend

Nearly every sport at Notre Dame boasted an outstanding athlete who brought home impressive honors in 1998-99.

- Erich Braun, a freshman forward from Frankfurt, Germany, was named the Big East soccer rookie of the year.

- Midfielder Anne Makinen was named collegiate MVP by Soccer America.

- Joanna Deeter, a member of the cross-country team, earned All-America designation in both cross country and track. She finished 14th in the NCAA Cross Country Championships and placed sixth in the indoor 5,000, fourth in the outdoor 5,000, and third in the outdoor 10,000 at the NCAA Championships.

- Marshaun West, a long jumper, was recognized as the Big East outstanding track performer. He and teammates Antonio Arce, Michael Brown, and Ryan Shay also earned All-America honors.

- Benoit Cotnoir became hockey's seventh All-American and led the Irish to a first-round home berth in the CCHA playoffs.

- Ryan Sachire finished fifth in singles at the NCAA Tennis Championships.

- Fencer Sara Walsh earned All-America honors for the fourth straight year.

- Freshman swimmer Carrie Nixon won the first of what would be 12 All-America awards.

- Ruth Riley was named Big East defensive player of the year and became the first women's basketball player at Notre Dame to achieve All-America status from the Associated Press.

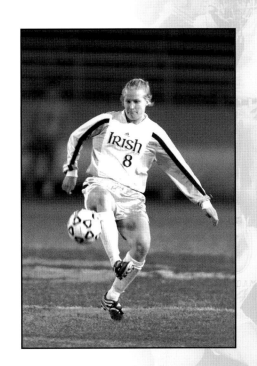

ABOVE:
ANNE MAKINEN.

BELOW:
RUTH RILEY.
Photo by Mike Bennett, Lighthouse Imaging

Irish Lore

The Notre Dame women's softball team began its domination of the Big East in 1999.

The Irish, under coach Liz Miller, breezed through its conference schedule with a 16-0 mark. Notre Dame's overall record stood at 42-20.

Since 1999, the Irish have claimed either the Big East regular season or the Big East tournament championships (or both) every year. Even when Miller retired and turned the coaching reins over to Deanna Gumpf in 2002, Notre Dame didn't miss a beat.

Over 45 players have earned all-conference recognition since 1996. Six players have earned Big East player of the year honors, while two have been named Big East pitcher of the year. Jennifer Sharron won that award four times—in 1998, 1999, 2000, and 2001.

1999-2000

- Seattle cancelled its massive public Millennium celebration for fears of a terrorist attack.

- Twelve students were killed and another 28 injured during the collapse of the traditional bonfire on the campus of Texas A & M.

- Fearing a massive shutdown of computer systems, millions of Americans prepared for the fallout of Y2K. Nothing happened.

- Lance Armstrong won his first Tour de France.

- After a two-year, $58 million renovation and restoration, the 120-year-old Main Building (the Golden Dome) reopened.

Irish Moment

Matt Doherty spent only one season as the head basketball coach at Notre Dame, but the former assistant at Kansas put the Irish back on the national map and turned in the first 20-win season in 11 years.

In his first game as a head coach, Doherty led the Irish to a 59-57 upset of fourth-ranked Ohio State in Columbus during the first round of the preseason NIT. Sophomore forward David Graves canned a buzzer beater for the win. Notre Dame won two more games to advance to the tournament's final four in Madison Square Garden, but a pair of ranked teams dashed Irish hopes for an improbable title.

During the season, Notre Dame beat four more ranked teams, including a home sweep of second-ranked Connecticut, the defending NCAA champion.

Doherty's team ended its season the way it started—by earning a trip to New York to participate in the finals of the postseason

NIT. The Irish won three straight games at home over Michigan, Xavier, and BYU to advance to the Big Apple.

After beating Penn State, 73-52, in the semi-final, Notre Dame lost to Wake Forest, 71-61, in the championship game for the fourth time.

Most Irish fans were excited about the future of Notre Dame basketball for the first time in years. Doherty seemed to have the magic touch.

But in July 2000 he left to take the head coaching job at the University of North Carolina, his alma mater.

Irish Legend

Mike Berticelli led the Irish men's soccer program through a new era during his 10 years as coach.

After taking UNC-Greensboro to national titles in 1982 and 1983, Berticelli moved to Old Dominion and coached there for six years.

ABOVE:
MATT DOHERTY.
Photo by Mike Bennett, Lighthouse Imaging

RIGHT:
MIKE BERTICELLI.
Photo by Mike Bennett, Lighthouse Imaging

When he came to Notre Dame, the Irish program was in its 14th season and moving onto the national scene.

Berticelli's first team in 1990 won just four games. But within three years, the Irish were back in the NCAA tournament.

Berticelli's best season at Notre Dame was in 1996. The Irish won their first ever Big East soccer championship and received an automatic bid to the NCAA tournament. Notre Dame posted its first-ever victory in the tournament with a 1-0 win over second-ranked UNC-Greensboro in the first round. The Irish lost 1-0 to eventual semifinalist UNC-Charlotte in the second round.

During his tenure, Berticelli won two straight conference titles in the Midwestern Cities Conference. His 10-year coaching ledger stood at 104-80-19.

On his way to a staff meeting in early January 2000, Berticelli suffered a heart attack and died.

Irish Lore

During 10 seasons in the Big East conference, the Notre Dame men's cross country team has won the title five times, including its second crown in 1999. The lowest Irish finish has been fourth.

In 1999, Ryan Shay took home individual honors in the race, earning All-America honors for the first time in cross country. Luke Watson finished third, Ryan Maxwell ninth, and Marc Striowski 11th. The Irish finished eighth in the 1999 NCAA Championships.

The following spring, coach Joe Piane led the Notre Dame men's track team to a Big East outdoor title. Six of his performers earned All-America recognition at the NCAA Indoor and Outdoor meets. The distance medley relay team—Chris Cochran, Tim Kober, Phil Mishka, and Luke Watson—finished sixth, while Shay came in seventh in the 10,000-meters, and Marshaun West placed seventh in the long jump.

LEFT:
LUKE WATSON.
Photo by Mike Bennett, Lighthouse Imaging

2000-01

ABOVE:
RUTH RILEY.
Photo by Mike Bennett, Lighthouse Imaging

Irish Moment

It was a magical season for Muffet McGraw. Although her last seven teams had posted 20-win seasons, the Irish had only been to the Final Four once before. But this team was loaded with talent at every position, and if all the pieces fell into place, Notre Dame had the ability to win it all.

The Irish were unbeatable through the first 23 games of the season. One of those victories was a 92-76 victory over top-ranked Connecticut before a record-crowd in the Joyce Center. That marked the first time in history that the Irish had beaten the perennial women's basketball power. In fact, Notre Dame would lose just two games in the regular season, both to Big East opponents.

Muffet and her team would have the last laugh, however. The Irish opened NCAA play at home on Saint Patrick's Day (not a good sign for the visitor). McGraw had borrowed a motivational tool from Irish football and basketball history and dressed her players in green jerseys for the first time in her 14 years at the helm. Five players scored in double figures, and Notre Dame won, 98-49.

After defeating Michigan to make the Sweet Sixteen, the Irish had to travel to Denver for a matchup with Utah. Riley recorded her ninth double-double with 24 points and 14 rebounds as Notre Dame coasted to a 69-54 win. Vanderbilt offered the toughest roadblock to the Final Four in the regional final. But Riley, Alicia Ratay and Kelley Siemon combined for 65 of Notre Dame's 72 points, and the Irish won, 72-64, to earn a berth in St. Louis.

Notre Dame and Connecticut squared off in the rubber match of what would be three games in 2000-2001. The Huskies led, 49-37, at halftime, and many fans thought it would be business as usual for Connecticut in the second half. But the Irish exploded for 53 points in the final period, while holding the Huskies to just 26 points, almost half of what they had scored in the first 20 minutes of the game. Notre Dame eventually ran away with a 90-75 victory.

Notre Dame and in-state rival Purdue squared off in the championship game. It was a seesaw affair that saw the Boilermakers take a 66-64 lead with just 1:22 left to play. Riley connected on a lay-up with 1:01 left to tie the game. After missing a shot, Purdue fouled Riley with just 5.8 seconds remaining. She iced them both. But the Boilermakers still had once last shot, and forward Katie Douglas, who led Purdue with 18 points, took it. It missed, and the Irish were national champs.

Irish Legend

Perhaps the best all-around player in Irish women's basketball history, Ruth Riley became a fan favorite just as much for her presence off the court as on.

A native of nearby Macy, Indiana, Riley started 26 games as a freshman, averaging 11.5 points and 7.3 rebounds per game. A little rough around the edges, she often got into foul trouble. Riley worked hard in the off-season to improve every aspect of her game, and when she returned as a sophomore, she became a fixture in Muffet McGraw's game plan.

The only Irish player to score over 2,000 points and haul down 1,000 rebounds, Riley scored almost 17 points a game as a sophomore. She also averaged over eight rebounds a game. She was fun to watch, and Irish fans loved chanting, "RUUUUUTH," when she was introduced or made a big play. More importantly, Riley sensed her appeal—particularly to young basketball players. She patiently signed every autograph, posed for every picture, and shook everybody's hand. She understood her role as basketball ambassador from very early on and accepted the "role-model" responsibility willingly.

During her junior year, Riley averaged 16.2 points and 7.2 rebounds a game. As a senior those numbers went up to 18.7 and 7.8, respectively.

Riley earned first-team All-America honors as both a junior and senior. She became the first Notre Dame player to win the Naismith Award, presented annually to the best college basketball player in the country. She owns seven career marks at Notre Dame: rebounds (1,007), blocked shots (370), field goal percentage (.632), highest blocks average (2.8), free throws made (518), free throws attempted (687), and most fouls (411).

The 2001 Big East player of the year, Riley also was named Big East defensive player of the year three times. She was also recognized as an Academic All-American twice from the College Sports Information Directors of America, earning its Academic Team member of the year in 2001.

She capped her career by connecting on two free throws in the final 5.8 seconds to give Notre Dame its first ever NCAA title. She was named the tournament MVP.

After graduation, Riley was drafted by the WNBA's Miami Sol. After that team dissolved, she went to the Detroit Shock. While playing for former Notre Dame and NBA star Bill Laimbeer, she led the Shock to the WNBA title in 2003. She also won the MVP trophy there as well. Riley also was a member of the U.S. team that won the gold medal at the 2004 Summer Olympics in Athens.

Irish Lore

The Notre Dame men's lacrosse team had a sensational run during the 2001 season. Led by first-team All-American Tom Glatzel and second-team All-American goalie Kirk Howell, the Irish posted their best-ever record at 14-2. Notre Dame beat four ranked teams during the regular schedule and headed into the NCAA Tournament as the nation's fourth-ranked team.

Eight different players scored for the Irish in their 12-7 opening-round win over Bucknell. The competition got even tougher the following week. Perennial power Johns Hopkins was Notre Dame's next opponent in College Park. The Blue Jays were ranked third, the Irish fourth. In three previous NCAA meetings, Notre Dame had never beaten Hopkins. The teams traded leads throughout the first three periods. The score was 8-8 when the fourth quarter began. A flurry of five goals by John Flandina (2), Steve Bishko, John Harvey, and Todd Ulrich gave the Irish a 13-9 victory, and a ticket to their first NCAA Final Four.

Syracuse, the defending national champion, held Notre Dame to a season low of five goals while puncturing the Irish defense for 12 goals of its own. Although the Irish fell short of reaching the title game, they turned in their most successful season to date.

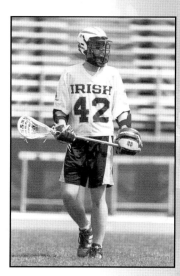

2001-02

ABOVE:
BRIAN STAVISKY.
Photo by Pete LaFleur

RIGHT:
CHRIS NIESEL.
Photo by Pete LaFleur

Irish Moment

Paul Maineri knew he would eventually take a Notre Dame team to the College World Series. He just didn't know when.

The Irish probably should have gone in 2001 when they posted a 49-13-1 record, won the Big East regular season and spent part of the year as the nation's top-ranked team. But a one-run loss in the regional in Frank Eck Stadium kept Notre Dame home.

In 2002, the Irish repeated as Big East regular-season champions with an 18-8 record. They also won the Big East tournament.

Notre Dame started on the road to Omaha in South Bend as the Irish again hosted a regional. Notre Dame beat Ohio State, 8-6, and then blasted South Alabama, 25-1. Grant Johnson threw a one-hitter, and second baseman Steve Sollmann went 6-for-7 with 7 RBI.

Another win over Ohio State, this one by a 9-6 count, sent the Irish to the Super Regional in Tallahassee to face top-ranked Florida State.

Notre Dame shocked the Seminoles by taking a 10-4 win in the first game. Florida State bounced back to take the second contest, 12-5. The third and deciding game turned into a pitcher's duel and freshman right-hander Chris Niesel, a Florida native who was credited with the first win over the Seminoles, earned his second victory of the weekend with a 3-1 decision. The Irish were on their way to Omaha.

Notre Dame lost its first game in the World Series, 4-3, to Stanford, but came from behind to beat Rice ,5-3, on Brian Stavisky's game-ending home run. Stanford eliminated the Irish in another close contest, 5-3.

Irish Legend

Ryan Shay ranks as the most decorated athlete in Notre Dame's illustrious track history.

In 2001, Shay won the 10,000 meters at the NCAA Outdoor Championships, becoming the first Irish athlete to win an outdoor event since 1954. The following year he placed second. He also had seven top-10 finishes at the NCAA Championships in various distance events, including the 3,000, 5,000 and 10,000 meters.

During his Notre Dame career, Shay won All-America honors 10 times—twice in cross country, twice in indoor track, and six for outdoor track.

In cross country, Shay won one Big East championship.

A nine-time Big East champion in various events, Shay was also named an Academic All-American in 2002.

Irish Lore

Tracy Coyne has coached the Notre Dame women's lacrosse team since it first gained varsity status in 1997.

In 2002, the Irish set a school record for wins with 13 and finished 5-1 in Big East play. During the regular season, Notre Dame beat seventh-ranked Syracuse, 12-7, 10th-ranked Vanderbilt, 10-9, and 12th-ranked Yale, 11-8. Two Irish losses during the regular season were overtime defeats to ranked teams by the same 10-9 score (Cornell and Duke).

Notre Dame earned its first berth in the NCAA tournament and won its first contest, 11-7, over Ohio State. But the following week, the Irish lost, 11-5, to top-ranked Princeton in the quarterfinals. Notre Dame ranked seventh in the final lacrosse polls that season.

Kathryn Lam and Danielle Shearer, both four-time monogram winners, became Notre Dame's first two All-Americans.

Shearer finished her career as the all-time leading scorer with 130 goals and 66 assists. At one point, she scored in 36 consecutive games.

Lam ranks as Notre Dame's career leader in ground balls with 193.

223

RIGHT:
MATT CARROLL.

Irish Moment

The long wait was finally over.

It had been 16 years since the Notre Dame men's basketball team had advanced to the Sweet Sixteen in the NCAA Tournament

But third-year coach Mike Brey had engineered three straight 20-win seasons and now, three consecutive NCAA tournament appearances. Notre Dame's storied basketball reputation had been restored. Notre Dame last played in the Big Dance in 1990, and the Irish had not won a game in the tournament since 1989. Now, Brey was 2-2 in NCAA play, and both losses in the second round were by less than seven points.

Most importantly, Brey convinced his Irish charges that they could win — and win in the Big East. Prior to his arrival in 2000, Notre Dame had posted a 35-53 mark in league play. By the end of Brey's third season, the Irish had won 31 of 48 games.

The unranked Irish made basketball observers stand up and take notice with an impressive performance in the BB&T Classic in the MCI Center in Washington, D.C., in early December. Notre Dame upset eighth-ranked Maryland, 79-67, and then shocked No. 2 Texas, 98-92, the following day.

Six days earlier, the Irish had trounced 10th-ranked Marquette, 92-71. Within a week, the Irish had beaten three ranked teams, something that had never happened in Notre Dame basketball history. That trio of wins boosted the Irish into the nation's top 10.

The Irish persevered through a late-season slump, losing four of their last five games before the NCAA Tournament began. Notre Dame survived a 70-69 upset bid by Wisconsin-Milwaukee in the first round at Indianapolis. Two days later, the Irish downed 10th-ranked Illinois, 68-60, to move to the Sweet Sixteen.

Second-ranked Arizona bounced Notre Dame from the tournament with an 88-71 loss.

However, Brey and his Irish gave fans reason to believe the best was yet to come.

Senior guard Matt Carroll led the Irish in scoring with a 19.5 average, while sophomore point guard Chris Thomas added 18.7 points per game.

Irish Legend

Shane Walton came to Notre Dame to play soccer.

As a freshman in 1998, he scored 10 goals and added seven assists, earning Big East Rookie-of-the-Week recognition three times and a place on the all-conference second team.

What Walton really wanted to do was play football.

So as a sophomore, he walked onto the football team. By the following season he was the starting cornerback.

Because he had not played football as a freshman, he was granted another year of eligibility. As a senior in 2002, Walton, a native of San Diego, earned consensus All-America honors and was a finalist for the Bronko Nagurski Award, given annually to the nation's most outstanding defensive player. Walton, elected captain in 2002, finished the season with 68 tackles and seven interceptions. He tied a school record with three interceptions in one game.

Irish Lore

Notre Dame's Olympic sports provided numerous highlights during the 2002-03 season.

- The women's cross-country team won the Big East title and placed third in the NCAA race. Molly Huddle, who finished sixth in the NCAA and second to teammate Lauren King at the Big East, and King both earned All-America honors and then were recognized as All-Americans later in the year in track.

- The men's soccer team advanced to the second-round of the NCAA Tournament after upsetting top-ranked Akron in the first postseason game hosted by the Irish.

- The women's swimming team finished 9-1 and won the Big East title.

- The fencing team won another NCAA title. Alicja Kryczalo won her second straight NCAA foil title, while Michal Sobieraj finished second in the epee.

- The hockey team advanced to the CCHA Super Six.

- Second baseman Steve Sollman earned All-America honors to lead the baseball team to its second consecutive Big East tourney championship.

- The women's rowing team won its 1st gold at the Central Regional (2nd varsity four) and won three golds at the Big East Challenge.

- Freshman golfer Katie Brophy, co-medalist at the Big East Tournament, set a season scoring mark at 78.44 and became the first Irish golfer to win two tournaments.

ABOVE:
SHANE WALTON.
Photo by Pete LaFleur

BELOW:
MEN'S BASKETBALL COACH MIKE BREY.
Photo by Mike Bennett, Lighthouse Imaging

Time Capsule

- On June 5, former President Ronald Reagan died at the age of 93.

- The Concorde made its last commercial flight on October 24.

- Fifty-two million viewers watched the last episode of the NBC sitcom *Friends*.

- American swimmer Michael Phelps won four individual gold medals at the 2004 Summer Olympic Games in Athens.

- The University received a $400,000 grant from the Office of Housing and Urban Development to create new outreach programs and initiatives at the Robinson Community Learning Center in the Northwest Neighborhood.

ABOVE:
DAVE POULIN.
Photo by Mike Bennett, Lighthouse Imaging

RIGHT:
JASON PAIGE.
Photo by Matt Cashore

Irish Moment

When Dave Poulin captained the Irish hockey team as a senior, Notre Dame came very close to making its first appearance in the NCAA Tournament.

He finally gained entry to the NCAA playoffs with the Irish—this time as head coach.

In his ninth season, Poulin led the Irish to a 20-15-4 record, Notre Dame's first 20-win campaign in 14 years. The Irish finished tied for fourth in the CCHA with a 14-11-3 mark.

Notre Dame earned home ice for the first-round of the CCHA playoffs and split the first two games of the best-of-three series with Western Michigan. The third game went into sudden death overtime. Freshman center Jason Paige scored to move the Irish to the CCHA Super Six at Joe Louis Arena in Detroit. A native of Saginaw, Paige scored 10 goals that year, and four of them were game winners. His goal at Lake Superior on the final day of reg-

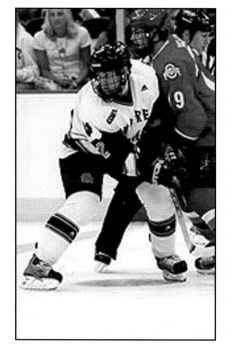

ular season gave Notre Dame a 2-1 win and home ice in the playoffs.

The Irish did not last long in the Super Six, losing to Ohio State, 6-5, in overtime.

But, during the regular season, Notre Dame had posted a 5-0-1 mark against teams ranked in the top five, and that convinced the selection committee to offer the Irish a bid

Notre Dame traveled to Grand Rapids to face two-time defending NCAA champion, Minnesota. Ironically, the Gophers were coached by Don Lucia, a Grand Rapids native, a 1981 Notre Dame graduate, and a former Irish teammate of Poulin's.

The Irish jumped out to a quick 2-0 lead on goals from Cory McLean and Aaron Gill, but the veteran Minnesota team came from behind with five uncontested goals to send Notre Dame home.

But the Irish hockey team had broken the hex. It will be back.

Irish Legend

It would be an understatement to say that coach Debbie Brown has taken the Irish volleyball program to new heights. Since she accepted the job in 1991, the former Olympian has molded Notre Dame into a consistent national power.

Her teams have won more than 75 percent of their games, captured 10 of 11 Big East titles, and competed in 14 straight NCAA tournaments. The Irish are almost unbeatable at home, winning over 85 percent of their games in the Joyce Center.

Brown's players have earned All-America honors 11 times, and seven have gone on to play professionally. Since joining the Big East in 1995, Irish players have won over 26 individual statistical conference championships.

A native of El Segunda, California, Brown captained the USC team and led the Trojans to national titles in 1976 and 1977. She received the Mikasa Award as the "nation's best all-around player" and earned All-America honors in both of those seasons.

She left USC before her junior year to train with the U.S. national team. She was also named to the 1980 U.S. Olympic squad and was elected co-captain. However, Brown never competed in the Moscow Olympics. President Jimmy Carter kept the U.S. teams from participating in the Summer Games to protest the Soviet Union's invasion of Afghanistan. However, Brown was elected to carry the Olympic torch during its run through northern Indiana prior to the 2002 Winter Olympics.

Brown, who received her degree from Arizona State, began her coaching career with the Sun Devils in 1980 as an assistant coach. She was named the school's head coach in 1983 and in six years, the Sun Devils finished 117-83. She left in 1988 to help coach the U.S. national team.

In 2003, Brown was honored by the NCAA with its Silver Anniversary Award, presented annually to six former student-athletes who have distinguished themselves professionally and through community service in the 25 years since their graduations.

Irish Lore

When Notre Dame men's soccer coach Bobby Clark talks, people listen.

A native of Glasgow, Clark's distinctive Scottish accent enthralls those who hear it. But, most importantly, Irish soccer players have paid attention to Clark's instructions which have engineered an amazing turnaround in the fortunes of the 27-year program.

Before Clark's arrival in 2001, the Notre Dame soccer team had suffered through two consecutive losing seasons. In his first year, Clark directed the Irish to a 12-7 mark. In 2002, he had the Irish back in the NCAA Tournament, and they advanced to the second round before losing, 1-0, to fifth-ranked Indiana.

In 2003, the Irish went 16-3-4, winning eight straight in the final weeks of the campaign—its best win streak in 16 years. During the regular season, Notre Dame beat 11th-ranked California and 19th-ranked Indiana in two overtimes. The Irish needed just one overtime to upend ninth-ranked Virginia Tech.

After winning the Big East Tournament, Notre Dame advanced to the NCAA Sweet Sixteen but lost in a shoot-out after two overtimes to Michigan. *Soccer America* ranked Notre Dame third in its final 2003 poll.

ABOVE:
DEBBIE BROWN.

BELOW:
BOBBY CLARK.
Photo by Matt Cashore

2004-05

The 2000s

Time Capsule

- President George W. Bush earned a second term in office by defeating Democratic challenger John Kerry in the presidential election.

- Condoleezza Rice, who received her master's degree from the University of Notre Dame, succeeded Secretary of State Colin Powell.

- Hurricane Charley killed 27 people after making landfall as a category 4 storm in Florida. Hurricane Frances struck a little over two weeks later.

- The Boston Red Sox came from three games down to defeat the New York Yankees in Game 7 to win their first World Series since 1918.

- The Marie P. DeBartolo Center for the Performing Arts was dedicated in the fall and became a major campus landmark in its first year of operation.

ABOVE:
RANDY WALDRUM.
Photo by Pete LaFleur

Irish Moment

Randy Waldrum took over the reins of the Irish women's soccer program in 1999.

In 2000, his second year at the helm, Notre Dame posted a 23-1-1 record, that included a 16-game winning streak and a 24-game unbeaten string. The Irish were ranked No. 1, and Waldrum and the Irish thought they had a pretty good shot at Notre Dame's second national title. But perennial power North Carolina, which the Irish had knocked out of the semi-finals in 1995 on their way to the championship, returned the favor, beating Notre Dame, 2-1.

The Irish would have to wait four long years to return to the Final Four.

Notre Dame won the first 15 games of the 2004 season, becoming the nation's top-ranked team by the fifth week of the campaign. After a scoreless overtime tie against Rutgers, the Irish won four more games before losing, 2-1, to Connecticut in the championship game of the Big East Tournament.

Notre Dame would not lose again. The Irish downed Eastern Illinois, 4-0, in the first round and then beat Wisconsin, 1-0, to set up a rematch with the Huskies in the third round. Notre Dame downed Connecticut, 2-0, and then downed Portland, 3-1, in the quarterfinals to advance to the College Cup in Cary, North Carolina.

In the semi-final match against Santa Clara, Candace Chapman scored on a give-and-go from Katie Thorlakson in the 73rd minute to give the Irish a 1-0 lead that turned out to be the final score.

Notre Dame met UCLA, ranked 11th, in the championship match. The Irish fell behind in the 60th minute when Gundrun Gunnarsdottir's intended back-pass slipped by goalkeeper Erika Bohn for an own goal

In the 74th minute, Notre Dame tied the game on a penalty kick by Thorlakson.

The Bruins had their own chance at a PK with five minutes left, but Bohn knocked the ball off its trajectory and made the save.

After a 20-minute scoreless overtime, the game went to a shootout and became the first ever needed in an NCAA title tilt. Waldrum let his players decide the order of the kicks.

But the game was still tied after the shootout, so the game went to a sudden-death shootout.

Jill Krivacek, whose only goal that season had been against Wisconsin, beat the UCLA goaltender in the lower right corner. Bohn made the save on the Bruin kick and the Irish were national champions again.

Waldrum didn't see it. The superstitious coach, who never watches penalty kicks, had his back turned. Oh, well, maybe he watched the videotape.

Irish Legend

Notre Dame track and cross country coach Joe Piane loves an adventure.

The former Peace Corps volunteer arrived on the Notre Dame campus in 1974 as an assistant track coach and physical education instructor. Piane had just received his master's degree from Western Illinois, and spending a year in South Bend would give him a chance to pad his resume before looking for a head coaching job.

Piane never left. He was named head track and cross country coach the following season and boasts the longest tenure of 31 years among active Irish coaches.

Recognized by his peers as a distance-coaching specialist, Piane's teams have accumulated enough plaques and trophies to fill a warehouse ... or two. His cross-country teams have finished among the nation's top 15 in 15 of the last 19 seasons, including a third-place standing in 2005. During Piane's tenure, his athletes have received All-America recognition over 90 times. Piane participated in both cross country and track at Loras College, captaining the cross country squad as a senior.

After his 1969 graduation, Piane coached track and field and cross country in Morocco while working for the Peace Corps. He returned to the United States in 1972 and served as an assistant at Western Illinois while completing his master's degree.

Piane and his staff have earned "coach of the year" awards on the district, conference, and national level 27 times.

The adventure continues.

ABOVE:
JOE PIANE.

BELOW:
PATRICK GHATTAS.
Photo by Pete LaFleur

Irish Lore

Olympic sports took the spotlight in 2004-05.

- Swimming coach Tim Welsh became the school's winningest coach after Irish swimmers posted a 10-2 dual meet record, set 12 Notre Dame records, won their first Big East title, and finished 21st in the nation. Tim Kegelman became the first swimmer in the Welsh era to participate in the NCAA Championships.

- South Bend native Jackie Batteast earned Kodak All-America honors and was named Big East player of the year after leading her team to a 27-6 record.

- The fencing team won another NCAA crown. Michal Sobieraj finished first in the epee, while four other fencers—Patrick Ghattas in saber, Alicja Kruczalo in the foil, Mariel Zagunis in saber, and Amy Orlando in epee—finished second.

- Karen Lotta led the Irish golf team to its second straight at-large berth and shared medalist honors at the Big East tournament.

- First-year coach Jim Kubinksi led the men's golf team to its second straight Big East title.

- The rowing team won the Big East's first championship meet.

- The baseball team won its fourth straight Big East crown.

2005-06

Time Capsule

- The space shuttle *Discovery* returned to space, marking the first "return to flight" after the explosion of the *Columbia* in 2003.

- Twelve miners died in the Sago Mine disaster in Buckhannon, West Virginia. Only one miner survived.

- Hurricane Katrina destroyed much of the coastal area of Louisiana, Mississippi, and Alabama and killed over 1,000 people. A month later, many of the same areas were hit by Hurricane Rita.

- The Chicago White Sox swept the Houston Astros in four straight games to win their first World Series title since 1917.

- Novelist Harper Lee, author of *To Kill a Mockingbird,* received an honorary degree during commencement at the University of Notre Dame.

ABOVE:
CHARLIE WEIS.
Photo by Mike Bennett, Lighthouse Imaging

RIGHT:
BRADY QUINN.
Photo by Mike Bennett, Lighthouse Imaging

Irish Moment

Notre Dame turned to one of its own to wake up the football echoes, and it didn't take long for Charlie Weis to prove he was back where he belonged.

A 1978 graduate of the University, Weis was named the head football coach at his alma mater in December 2004. He had spent the last seven seasons as an offensive coordinator in the NFL, winning four Super Bowls with the New York Giants and the New England Patriots.

Irish fans couldn't wait for the season to start.

In the first game at Pitt, Notre Dame exploded for 28 points in the second quarter and posted a 42-21 defeat on the Panthers. Quarterback Brady Quinn completed 18 of 27 passes for 227 yards and two touchdowns, while Darius Walker gained 100 yards and scored once.

Notre Dame finished the season 9-2 and earned a BCS bid to face Ohio State in the Tostidos Fiesta Bowl.

Nevertheless, the Buckeyes' tenacious defense kept the Irish offense in check, and Ohio State emerged a 34-20 winner.

In one season, Weis had restored the excitement, the anticipation, and the fun to Notre Dame football.

Irish Legend

Quarterback Brady Quinn must have hung on every word Charlie Weis said.

In 2005, the 6-foot-4 signal-caller led the Irish resurgence and became the most prolific passer in Notre Dame history.

He will be a leading candidate for the Heisman Trophy in 2006.

A native of Columbus, Ohio, Quinn started nine games as freshman, throwing for 1,831 yards and nine touchdowns. As a sophomore, he completed 191 of 353 passes for 2,586 yards and 17 touchdowns.

He blossomed under Weis' tutelage as a junior. He threw 450 passes and completed 292 of them for a 64.9 completion percentage and 3,919 yards. Just seven of his passes were intercepted—three less than his 2004 total when he threw 100 more passes. Quinn passed for at least one touchdown in every game, except in the Fiesta Bowl against Ohio State.

He threw six against BYU, five against Michigan State, and four against Navy.

Wide receiver Jeff Samardzija is hard to miss on the football field.

First, there's that flowing hair and then there are those hands.

The 6-foot-5 native of nearby Valparaiso will return as college football's top receiver in 2006. He currently owns Notre Dame single-season records for catches (77), receiving yards (1,249), and touchdown catches (15).

As a junior, he was named a consensus first-team All-American and was one of three finalists for the 2005 Biletnikoff Award. Samardzija and Quinn shared the team's most valuable player award for the 2005 season.

Samardzija also owned a spot in the starting rotation as a member of the Irish baseball team. The crowds at Frank Eck Stadium swelled on Friday nights, usually when Samardzija pitched during a homestand.

Irish Lore

The Notre Dame women's lacrosse team celebrated its 10th season as a varsity sport by posting a 15-4 record and earning its first-ever trip to the NCAA Final Four.

Although the Irish lost in the semi-final game against Dartmouth, Notre Dame's appearance among the sport's elite capped a remarkable turnaround for coach Tracy Coyne's squad. In 2005, the Irish struggled through a disappointing 3-12 campaign. Just a year later, Notre Dame was in the hunt for a national title, thanks to a determined group of veterans and freshman class generally regarded as the best in the nation. Ranked as high as seventh during the regular season, the Irish used a high-powered offense that left all but three opponents on the short end of the stick before the tournament. And two of the three teams to beat the Irish during the year—Duke and Northwestern—also advanced to the Final Four.

Senior Crysti Foote, an all-Big East selection, shattered Irish scoring records and became one of the top offensive threats in the nation. The Suffern, New York, native scored 74 goals and 40 assists in 2006 to make her Notre Dame's career leader in goals, assists, and total points. Foote and teammates Jillian Byers (54 goals/24 assists) and Caitlin McKinney (42 goals/22 assists) were selected to the Intercollegiate Women's Lacrosse Coaches Association all-West/Midwest Region team.

Another women's squad—rowing—also made its first appearance as a team in the NCAA Championships in 2006.

Coach Martin Stone's rowers won their third straight Big East title and qualified its varsity eight, second varsity eight, and varsity four boats for the NCAA team meet. The Irish placed ninth overall.

The Notre Dame baseball squad won its fifth consecutive Big East tournament to earn the conference's automatic bid to the NCAA playoffs, making the Irish one of just 12 squads to qualify for post-season play the last eight years.

Coach Paul Manieri's team finished the regular season at 45-15-1 and boasted one of the nation's top pitching rotations of Tom Thornton, Jeff Samardzija, Jeff Manship, Wade Korpi, and David Phelps.

Korpi, a sophomore lefthander, won two games during the Big East tournament and became the youngest player to win the Jack Kaiser Trophy, presented to the most valuable player in the league tourney.

Irish sophomore Sheeva Parbhu advanced to the final eight of the NCAA Men's Singles Championships, becoming the first Notre Dame player to move into the quarterfinals since Maxwell Brown did it in 1959. The Omaha, Nebraska, native, who was seeded 32nd in the tournament, posted a 33-8 mark during the season.

ABOVE:
SHEEVA PARBHU.
Photo by Mike Bennett, Lighthouse Imaging

Monogram Recipients

The list of monogram recipients was provided by the Notre Dame Monogram Club. Female athletes may be listed by their married name. Year indicates graduation class or last season monogram was earned. Every effort was made to find the year the recipient earned a monogram.

NAME	YEAR	GENDER	SPORT
ALEXY LYNN ELIZABETH	1986	F	Basketball
ASKIN DENISE MARIE	1986	F	Basketball
BARRON KATHARYN ANN	1988	F	Basketball
BATTEAST JACQUELINE MILES	2005	F	Basketball
BOHMAN ROSANNE MARIE	1997	F	Basketball
BORTON TERESA CAROL	2006	F	Basketball
BOTHAM SANDRA LEE	1988	F	Basketball
BOWEN LETITIA CAYE	1995	F	Basketball
BRAENDLY DIANA LYNN ELIZABETH	1999	F	Basketball
BROMMELAND KATHERINE KRISTINE	1988	F	Basketball
COLE KRISTIN LIANE	1994	F	Basketball
CONBOY MELISSA LOUISE	1982	F	Basketball
CUMMINGS CAROLA MARIE	1980	F	Basketball
CUNNINGHAM BETH ANN	1997	F	Basketball
DAVIS KRISTINA MARIE	1991	F	Basketball
DEYO KELLEY DONNELLY	2001	F	Basketball
DROZD CATHERINE	1990	F	Basketball
DUFFY MEGAN MARIE	2006	F	Basketball
DUNBAR IMANI MONIQUE	2001	F	Basketball
ELLIOTT CAROL ANN	1990	F	Basketball
ELY LAURA JANE	1985	F	Basketball
GAITHER KATRYNA RENEE	1997	F	Basketball
GAVIN MARY THERESA	1988	F	Basketball
GOMEZ AUDREY	1993	F	Basketball
GOSSARD HEATHER SUZANNE	1996	F	Basketball
GREEN DANIELLE LATRICE	1999	F	Basketball
HAIGH SHERRI MICHELLE	1994	F	Basketball
HAMILTON HEIDI ANN	1989	F	Basketball
HAMM MARJORIE MEAGHER	1978	F	Basketball
HANEY ERICKA LENAE	2002	F	Basketball
HART CARRIE A.	1985	F	Basketball
HAYSBERT COMALITA MICHELE	1992	F	Basketball
HEATH KELLY LYNN	1996	F	Basketball
HEBERT DEBRA ANN	1992	F	Basketball
HENDERSON JULIE MARIE	2000	F	Basketball
HENSLEY DEBORAH SUSAN	1983	F	Basketball
HUMS MARY AVITA DR.	1979	F	Basketball
HUTCHINSON KARI ANNE	1998	F	Basketball
IVEY NIELE DEIRDRE	2000	F	Basketball
JANICKI STACY LYNN	1995	F	Basketball
JONES KATURA MAZON	1994	F	Basketball
JORDAN ADRIENNE LOUISE	1997	F	Basketball
KAISER RUTH ANNE	1985	F	Basketball
KELLER SHEILA JEAN	1999	F	Basketball
KEYES KAREN MARIE	1991	F	Basketball
KEYS TRENA RENA	1986	F	Basketball
KLAUKE-KOLL JENNIFER L.	1984	F	Basketball
KRAKER MOLLY ANN	1990	F	Basketball
KRANDA MARY ELIZABETH	1988	F	Basketball
KUHNS LISA MARY	1989	F	Basketball
LAVERE COURTNEY ARLENE	2006	F	Basketball
LEAHY MEAGHAN ANN	2001	F	Basketball
LEARY KARA MS.	1994	F	Basketball
LIEBSCHER SARA CHRISTINE	1991	F	Basketball
LOHMAN SUSAN MARGARET	1995	F	Basketball
MALCOLM ANNE MARIAN	1990	F	Basketball
MARCINIAK MICHELLE MARIE	1992	F	Basketball
MAROUS MARGARET ROSE M.D.	1981	F	Basketball
MATVEY SHARI ANN DR.	1983	F	Basketball
MCCAFFERY MARGARET SUNDE	1992	F	Basketball
MOMONT SHEILA MARIE M.D.	1981	F	Basketball
MURPHY-SLEEPER J. BYRNE MRS.	1978	F	Basketball
ORION KELLY ANN MRS.	1980	F	Basketball
PEIRICK-BUSAM MOLLIE ELIZABETH	1998	F	Basketball
POLITISKI JANE KAY	1980	F	Basketball
RATAY ALICIA ANN	2004	F	Basketball
REISING PATRICIA J. MRS.	1982	F	Basketball
RILEY RUTH ELLEN	2001	F	Basketball
RUPE MAJENICA JILL	1993	F	Basketball
RYAN MOLLY ANNE	1984	F	Basketball
SCHEFFLER JEANNINE MARIE	1997	F	Basketball
SCHUETH-CAIN MARY ELIZABETH	1985	F	Basketball
SEBOLD MOLLY L.	1980	F	Basketball
SEVERE LETANIA PAULINA	2004	F	Basketball
SHIELDS CAROL ANNE DR.	1979	F	Basketball
SHOREY THERESA ANN	1984	F	Basketball
SMITH DIONNE	1993	F	Basketball
SMITH PATRICIA A.	1982	F	Basketball
SWANSON KAREN ELIZABETH	2003	F	Basketball
WALLEY CAREY LEE	1996	F	Basketball
WASHINGTON COQUESE MAKEBRA	1992	F	Basketball
WEESE ANNE PATRICIA	2005	F	Basketball
WHITESIDE DIONDRA MICHELLE	1989	F	Basketball
WILLIS LAVETTA CHERISE	1988	F	Basketball
ZAMET PATRICIA ANNE	1980	F	Basketball
ANZICK FRANCESCA MAE	1997	F	Cheerleader
BANKS CANDACE ANNE MRS.	1977	F	Cheerleader
BIOLCHINI JESSICA ANN	2000	F	Cheerleader
BOZZELLI HEIDI GORMAN	1999	F	Cheerleader
BRACKEN-MARLEY REBECCA	1977	F	Cheerleader
BRALY ANN E. MRS.	N/A	F	Cheerleader
CANTOLINO MARY ELIZABETH	2001	F	Cheerleader
CAPSHAW MEREDITH LEE	2004	F	Cheerleader
CARNESALE VIRGINIA POWELL	1997	F	Cheerleader
CERRITO JOCELYN ANGELA	2003	F	Cheerleader
CIARIMBOLI BETSY ANN DR.	1992	F	Cheerleader
CLARK STEPHANIE HILL	2003	F	Cheerleader
CRAIN LAURA LEWIS	1984	F	Cheerleader
CRONE KATHRYN TERRESA	2005	F	Cheerleader
DENVIR MARY M.	1993	F	Cheerleader
DOYLE ELIZABETH ANN	2005	F	Cheerleader
FINELLI NICOLE REED	1999	F	Cheerleader
GARCIA SONIA ANN	N/A	F	Cheerleader
GARKO RACHEL	N/A	F	Cheerleader
GILMARTIN MOLLY	1970	F	Cheerleader
GRAY MARY	N/A	F	Cheerleader
HARDING CINDY ANN	1999	F	Cheerleader
HARMON MARGARET	1978	F	Cheerleader
HOFFMAN HEATHER ANNE	2003	F	Cheerleader
JENKINS ALEXANDRA MICHELLE	2000	F	Cheerleader
JENKO HELEN MARIE	1986	F	Cheerleader
JONES ANGELA NICOLE	1993	F	Cheerleader
KINNAMAN STEPHANIE JO	1996	F	Cheerleader
KIZER REBECCA DAULTON	1998	F	Cheerleader
KOLLIG MICHELE A.	N/A	F	Cheerleader
LAHAM LISA CHAVEZ	1980	F	Cheerleader
LANKTREE JENNIFER KLEINE	2002	F	Cheerleader
LEWALLEN TERESA	1970	F	Cheerleader
LYDIATT CAROL ANN M.D.	1973	F	Cheerleader
MACQUARRIE MARGO MARY	1990	F	Cheerleader
MATHES AMY ELIZABETH	1981	F	Cheerleader
MCELWEE ELIZABETH MARY	1999	F	Cheerleader
MCLAUGHLIN SUSAN P. MRS.	N/A	F	Cheerleader
MILLER NICOLE I.	N/A	F	Cheerleader
MURRAY ANNE C.	1974	F	Cheerleader
NOGA PATRICIA KULIK MRS.	1978	F	Cheerleader
OCAMPO DENA MARIE	N/A	F	Cheerleader
OLIN SUSANNE MARIE	1979	F	Cheerleader
PAIGE JULIA H.	N/A	F	Cheerleader
PALUTSIS JOSEPHINE M. DR.	1984	F	Cheerleader
PIKAL AMY JANICE	1996	F	Cheerleader
REISING CASEY LORAINE	2006	F	Cheerleader
RISTO CHLOE ELISABETH	2004	F	Cheerleader
RIVERA KELLY MARIE	2000	F	Cheerleader
ROBINSON STACY WEAVER	1978	F	Cheerleader
ROMAN JESSICA CHIAPPETTA	1992	F	Cheerleader
RUHMAN SONDRA LYNN	1996	F	Cheerleader
RUSSELL MARY ROONEY	N/A	F	Cheerleader
RUTLAND DANA RENAE	N/A	F	Cheerleader
SANDERS SARA MARIE	1997	F	Cheerleader
SCHINDLER HEIDI ROSE	2006	F	Cheerleader
SHEEHAN KRISTIN LYNN	1990	F	Cheerleader
SHIEL CATHERINE ELIZABETH	2004	F	Cheerleader
SMITH KEILLEEN JANE	N/A	F	Cheerleader
SOBOLEWSKI MARY BETH	N/A	F	Cheerleader
STANKO KELLEY ANN	1996	F	Cheerleader
STONE PHYLLIS WASHINGTON	1980	F	Cheerleader
STUBBS ANNE THERESE M.D.	1986	F	Cheerleader
STUFFINGS AMBER LYNN	2002	F	Cheerleader
TOLLEY RACHEL KIRSTEN	2002	F	Cheerleader
TRAPPEY ALISON KAY	2005	F	Cheerleader
WALSH HEATHER HAZEL DR.	1997	F	Cheerleader
WARNER ELIZABETH MALAY	2000	F	Cheerleader
WHALEN JENNIFER COLLEEN	1993	F	Cheerleader
WILLIFORD CHRISTINE ELENA	2006	F	Cheerleader
WILSON MEGAN NICOLE	2005	F	Cheerleader
ALBERTSON PIA MONICA	1984	F	Fencing
ALOKOLARO PAULINE EBUN	2001	F	Fencing
AMENT ANDREA ERIKA	2005	F	Fencing
BACHHUBER MINDI ROSE	1996	F	Fencing
BEDNAR MARY MARGARET	1992	F	Fencing
BOUTSIKARIS LIZA ANN	2003	F	Fencing
BROL MICHELLE MARAFINO	1999	F	Fencing
BROWN ELIZABETH M.	1980	F	Fencing
BROWN MYRIAH HARRAH	1999	F	Fencing
BURNS ANNE MARIE	1983	F	Fencing
BUSTAMANTE NATALIE SUZANNE	2005	F	Fencing
CALL MEAGAN BAYARD	2004	F	Fencing
CAREY MARY KATHLEEN MRS.	1981	F	Fencing
CARNEY DOROTHY S.	1982	F	Fencing
CARNEY SUZANNA KAY	1979	F	Fencing
CARNICK ANNA NAOMI	2003	F	Fencing
CARROLL JANICE MARIE	1989	F	Fencing
CARROLL GINA LYNN	1999	F	Fencing
CHAPMAN MARCELLA LUCILE	1982	F	Fencing
CHIMAHUSKY REBECCA LOUISE	2005	F	Fencing
CLARK SUSAN MARIE	2002	F	Fencing
CONNOR MARIELLE AMELI	2006	F	Fencing
CORDELL AMEE MICHELLE	1998	F	Fencing
DAILEY ELIZABETH ANN	2000	F	Fencing
DAVIS DANIELLE ELIZABETH	2004	F	Fencing
DEMAIO KIMBERLY MARIE	2001	F	Fencing
DEMARCO CAROLE ANN	1984	F	Fencing
DEVORE JENNIFER ANN	1997	F	Fencing
DINICOLA SHARON ANNETTE	1984	F	Fencing
EMILIAN ELIZABETH ANNE	2004	F	Fencing
FARGO STEPHANIE MCNEILL	1989	F	Fencing
FERGUSON SARAH KIERSTEN	2001	F	Fencing
FISCHER MARIT MARTHA	1994	F	Fencing
FLANAGAN KATHERINE COURTNEY	2001	F	Fencing
FOLEY ANN THERESE	1980	F	Fencing
FOSTER JOANNE C.	1984	F	Fencing
FOULDS MARGARET LAUREN	1991	F	Fencing
GALLAGHER MAURA KATHRYN	1994	F	Fencing
GARCIA-BANIGAN DINAMARIE CRUZ DR.	1994	F	Fencing
GASE LINDA MARIE	1986	F	Fencing
HARADEM DENISE MISS.	1981	F	Fencing
HARTWIG ROSE MARIE	1997	F	Fencing
HAUGH RACHEL KRISTINE	1992	F	Fencing
HAYES ANNE FRANCES	1999	F	Fencing
HOOS HERR ANNE FRANCES	1998	F	Fencing
HOUSING KIRSTEN ANN	2002	F	Fencing
HUGHES LINDA D.	1982	F	Fencing
INGHRAM JILL MARIE	2003	F	Fencing
JACOBSEN CLAUDETTE LOUISE	1996	F	Fencing
JORDAN MARGARET RANDALL	2004	F	Fencing
KADRI LYNN ANN	1991	F	Fencing
KALOGERA AIMEE GRACE MRS.	2000	F	Fencing
KELLY E. TARA 1ST LIEUTENANT	1992	F	Fencing
KOWALSKI CELESTE	1985	F	Fencing
KRALICEK KRISTIN ANN	1989	F	Fencing
KROL EWA MAGDALENA	2000	F	Fencing
KRYCZALO ALICJA MARIA	2005	F	Fencing
LAMBERT BARBARA JOAN	1983	F	Fencing
LANDGRAF JOCELYN ANNE	2005	F	Fencing
LAPLANTE SALLY MARY MRS.	1973	F	Fencing
LECHNER NICOLE LEANNE	1999	F	Fencing
LEE KELLY RENEE	1992	F	Fencing
LEISER BRENDA ELAINE	1989	F	Fencing
LONGO KAREN JOAN MRS.	1979	F	Fencing
LUZI AMY SROMEK	1997	F	Fencing
MARCINIAK CHRISTINA MARIA M.D.	1977	F	Fencing
MARSHALL MARY THERESA	1983	F	Fencing
MAZELIN CECELIA ANN	1986	F	Fencing
MAZUR NATALIA ANNA	2004	F	Fencing
MCCULLOUGH CARIANNE	2002	F	Fencing
MCKENNA MARIA KATHLEEN	1997	F	Fencing
MILO DESTANIE	2004	F	Fencing
MORRISON KATHLEEN D. DR.	1984	F	Fencing
MOWCHAN DONNA MARIE	2001	F	Fencing
MULLER TIFFANY MONIQUE	2005	F	Fencing

NAME	YEAR	GENDER	SPORT
JONES MEGHAN PATRICIA	2005	F	Manager
KEANE MARITA CORRIGAN	2001	F	Manager
KERNS LEIGH ANN	1999	F	Manager
KING KRISTEN ANN	2002	F	Manager
LAMPE KRISTEN RANDALL DR.	1994	F	Manager
LANDERS KELLY CHRISTINE	2003	F	Manager
LAUER JESSICA LYN	2003	F	Manager
LEE HEATHER MEANEY	1992	F	Manager
LUCAS AIMEE MARIE	1993	F	Manager
LYONS MARTHA ELIZABETH	1998	F	Manager
MASON AMY	N/A	F	Manager
MCGILLICUDDY TRACI SUZANNE	1997	F	Manager
MCKERNAN SHELLEY	1981	F	Manager
MCLAUGHLIN MARGARET C.	N/A	F	Manager
MCNEILL YVETTE MELISSA	1993	F	Manager
MEIER ANN MARIE	1991	F	Manager
MERCADO JENNIFER KATHERINE	1993	F	Manager
METZGER LAURA ELIZABETH	2004	F	Manager
MICHALEC JENNIFER ANN	1996	F	Manager
MICHELENA MARILOU	N/A	F	Manager
MILLER ANN LOUISE	1981	F	Manager
MILLER KARA LYNN	1994	F	Manager
MODDE SARAH ARCHAMBEAULT	1995	F	Manager
MORELLI ANDREA LEE	1996	F	Manager
MORREL KATHERINE HARPER	2003	F	Manager
MOUSAW MEEGHAN BERNADETTE	1999	F	Manager
MURRY CHRISTINE ALLISON	1994	F	Manager
O'CONNOR MARY BOUVIER	1996	F	Manager
O'GORMAN MEGAN EILEEN	2001	F	Manager
ORTIZ NATALIE	2003	F	Manager
PARSLEY TRINA LANETTE	1992	F	Manager
PETERSON LINDSAY ANN	2006	F	Manager
PRIVITERA LAURIE ANN	2005	F	Manager
PUETZ ANN MARIE	1992	F	Manager
RADONA ZORAIDA PASCUAL	1996	F	Manager
REDDING KAITLIN MARGARET	2005	F	Manager
REEVES ELISABETH EILEEN	2004	F	Manager
RUFF SARA SUZANNE	2000	F	Manager
SCHAFF KAREN	N/A	F	Manager
SCHERER JENNY NICOLE	2005	F	Manager
SCHMIDT CAROLYN FINCH	2001	F	Manager
SCHUMER GRETCHEN G	N/A	F	Manager
SCOGGINS GRETCHEN DELORES	2001	F	Manager
SHIELDS CALLIE SUE	1997	F	Manager
SINCLAIR MARGARET ELIZABETH	2000	F	Manager
SMITH JULIA DAWN	1998	F	Manager
SNYDER KIMBERLY ANN	1995	F	Manager
SPRINGMAN RACHAEL ELIZABETH	1999	F	Manager
ST. GERMAIN ELLEN MARIE	1998	F	Manager
STEPHAN MELVINA EVELYN	2000	F	Manager
STONE TERESA MARY	1990	F	Manager
TALLMADGE KATHLEEN ELIZABETH	2005	F	Manager
TANSKI CHERYL MARIE	2002	F	Manager
TERASHIMA DAWN TOMOMI	2003	F	Manager
THOMASON AMY JEAN	1994	F	Manager
TRAINOR MELANIE SISSEL	1996	F	Manager
TREVINO SHANNON MARIE	2006	F	Manager
TRUITT LYNN MARIE	2006	F	Manager
TYNAN SARAH	N/A	F	Manager
VEACH KRISTIN MARIE	1995	F	Manager
VOSILLA KIMBERLY KLINE	1995	F	Manager
WALSH LAUREN ANDERSON	2003	F	Manager
WARD MOLLY CATHERINE	2003	F	Manager
WEST ERIN KATHLEEN	2002	F	Manager
WHITTINGTON KATHRYN KELLY	2000	F	Manager
WICH MARAH LEIGH	1997	F	Manager
WIEREMA MAUREEN ELIZABETH	2005	F	Manager
YUDT KRISTIN ELIZABETH	2000	F	Manager
BARTEK ALICE BERNADETTE	2004	F	Rowing
HAZEN JACQUELINE LOUISE	2004	F	Rowing
LADINE NATALIE MARIE	2004	F	Rowing
LONG KATHRYN ELIZABETH	2004	F	Rowing
MCCAFFREY KACY CHRISTINE	2004	F	Rowing
O'HARA KATIE SCARLETT	2004	F	Rowing
PROTASEWICH DANIELLE NICOLE	2004	F	Rowing
SANDERS MEGAN SUE	2004	F	Rowing
STARKS ANNE ELIZABETH	2004	F	Rowing
WELSH KATHLEEN ELIZABETH	2004	F	Rowing
ANDERSON MAUREEN L.	1992	F	Soccer
BAER EMILY KATHERINE	N/A	F	Soccer
BAKKER KERRI ELIZABETH	2001	F	Soccer
BEENE LAKEYSIA RENE	2005	F	Soccer
BENDER MIMI SUBA	1991	F	Soccer
BOERNER MARY KATHLEEN	2000	F	Soccer
BOHN ERIKA CRAY	2006	F	Soccer
BOLAND MARY ELIZABETH	2005	F	Soccer
BOXX SHANNON LEIGH	1999	F	Soccer
BRAUN MICHELLE KATHLEEN	1991	F	Soccer
BROWN KARA WHEATLEY	2001	F	Soccer
BRUMMELL MARTA ROEMER	1993	F	Soccer
BURKHART KATHLEEN FRANCES	1989	F	Soccer
CAHILL TANIA CHRISTA	1996	F	Soccer
CALLANEN ANDREA SOBAJIAN	1994	F	Soccer
CARPENTER KIMBERLY PATRICIA	2004	F	Soccer
CARTER JENNIFER ELIZABETH	2004	F	Soccer
CHAPMAN CANDACE-MARIE	2006	F	Soccer
CLINTON CAMILLE MELINDA	1997	F	Soccer
COYNE RAGEN ANN	2001	F	Soccer
DANIELSON KRISTIN JOAN	2003	F	Soccer
DOYLE HOLLY JEAN	2000	F	Soccer
DRYER ASHLEY RAYE	2003	F	Soccer
ERICKSON JENNIFER MICHELLE	2000	F	Soccer
ERIKSON MEOTIS MITBO	2001	F	Soccer
FORD MIRANDA JEANNINE	2006	F	Soccer
GAILLARD DEBORAH SKAHAN	1992	F	Soccer
GALLA MARY CATHERINE	1991	F	Soccer
GERARDO MONICA MARIE	2000	F	Soccer
GIOLITTO MARIANNE	1992	F	Soccer
GODINEZ TERESA ANNA DR.	1992	F	Soccer
GOLD KIMBERLY ANNE	1995	F	Soccer
GONZALEZ MONICA CHRISTINE	2002	F	Soccer
GOODWIN-KELLY MARY KATHLEEN	1994	F	Soccer
GRENNER JODI LYNN	1995	F	Soccer
GRUBB JENNIFER LEIGH	2001	F	Soccer
GUERTIN AMANDA LEIGH	2004	F	Soccer
GUNNARSDOTTIR GUDRUN SOLEY	2005	F	Soccer
HALING SUSAN MARIE	1989	F	Soccer
HALPENNY SARAH THERESA	2005	F	Soccer
HANRATTY KELLY ANN	1992	F	Soccer
HINOSTRO NICOLE MARIE	1998	F	Soccer
HUTA JEAN KEAVENEY	1993	F	Soccer
IORIO ASHLEY DRU	1996	F	Soccer
JENKINS SHANNON LYNDSEY	1993	F	Soccer
JONES LINDSEY LOFTUS	2002	F	Soccer
JONES REAGAN LEE	2005	F	Soccer
KARKOS DENISE JACQUELINE	1993	F	Soccer
KAYA DEBORAH ANN	1989	F	Soccer
KELLY ROSELLA	1996	F	Soccer
KLINE JULIE CAROL	1996	F	Soccer
KOCORAS ALISON ANN	1994	F	Soccer
KRAYER SUSAN ANNE	1992	F	Soccer
KUHN CAROLINE SARAH	2001	F	Soccer
KUREK SLAGH ANDREA NICOLE	1994	F	Soccer
KWIATKOWSKI GENNIFER MICHELE	1994	F	Soccer
LANCASTER IRIS KEALAWAIOLI	2000	F	Soccer
LINDSEY KELLY ANN	2001	F	Soccer
LIZARRAGA JOY KATHRYN	1990	F	Soccer
LODYGA MICHELLE RENEE	1993	F	Soccer
LYNCH ROBIN ELIZABETH	1995	F	Soccer
MAKINEN ANNE MAARIT	2001	F	Soccer
MANNING MARGARET COLLEEN	2006	F	Soccer
MARKGRAF KATHRYN MICHELE	1998	F	Soccer
MARTINOV KATHLEEN THERESA	1990	F	Soccer
MASCARO JENNIFER WHITE	2001	F	Soccer
MATESIC JILL	1995	F	Soccer
MAUND JULIE ELEANOR	1998	F	Soccer
MCCRYSTAL KELLY ANN	1992	F	Soccer
MCGREGOR JEAN VIDAL	1998	F	Soccer
MCLAUGHLIN MARGARET EILEEN	1993	F	Soccer
MCMILLIN AMBER RENAY	2006	F	Soccer
MCNEILL ALICIA ANNE	1991	F	Soccer
MILLER REBECCA WELBORN DR.	1991	F	Soccer
MITCHELL AMY MARIE	N/A	F	Soccer
MORREL KATHERINE HARPER	2003	F	Soccer
MOSLEY CYNTHIA ERIN	1997	F	Soccer
MOUNT BERNADETTE MARIE	1991	F	Soccer
MURPHY HEATHER ANN	1992	F	Soccer
MURRAY KATHLEEN FISHER	1997	F	Soccer
ORTWEIN CHRISTINE LEWIS MRS.	1994	F	Soccer
O'SULLIVAN MEGAN ELIZABETH	1997	F	Soccer
PAGE KHAMSIN BROOKE	1995	F	Soccer
PETERS CHRISTY SUZANNE	1995	F	Soccer
PORTER STEPHANIE DANIELLE	1994	F	Soccer
PRUZINSKY VANESSA MARIE	2003	F	Soccer
REISHMAN SARAH BRECKINRIDGE	1996	F	Soccer
RENOLA JENNIFER MARIE	1997	F	Soccer
RESTOVICH MICHELLE EILEEN	1996	F	Soccer
RICHARDS STACIA RAE	1997	F	Soccer
SARKESIAN MIA DEANNE	2002	F	Soccer
SCHEFTER ANNIE LEONE	2006	F	Soccer
SCHELLER RANDI JANE	2005	F	Soccer
SOENS INGRID WILHELMINA	1998	F	Soccer
STIEFEL COURTNEY ELISABETH	2000	F	Soccer
STRAWBRIDGE NATALIA KATHERINE	1994	F	Soccer
TANCREDI MELISSA	2005	F	Soccer
TATE MOLLY ELIZABET	2004	F	Soccer
THOMPSON TIFFANY LYNN	1995	F	Soccer
THORLAKSON KATIE MARIE	2006	F	Soccer
TORRES BRENDA LYNN MRS.	1994	F	Soccer
TUFTS MARGO MONTGOMERY	1995	F	Soccer
TULISIAK KATHRYN MARIE	2005	F	Soccer
TULISIAK KELLY ELIZABETH	2002	F	Soccer
VAN LAECKE AMY MICHELLE	1997	F	Soccer
VANDERBERG LAURA EILEEN	1999	F	Soccer
VANDEVENDER JULIE C.	1989	F	Soccer
WAGNER ALICE ELIZABETH	2002	F	Soccer
WALZ JENNIFER LYNN	2006	F	Soccer
WARNER AMY DEE	2004	F	Soccer
WEIGERT KAREN ROSE	1993	F	Soccer
WOOLSON BREAH KRISTEN	1994	F	Soccer
ZANKEL SUSAN MARY	1990	F	Soccer
ZANONI ELIZABETH ANN	2001	F	Soccer
ABELE KATHERINE A.	1987	F	Swimming
AMBROSE COLLEEN MARIE	1986	F	Swimming
AMICO MARY THERESE	1986	F	Swimming
ARTHURS MICHELE RENE	1997	F	Swimming
BAKER ALISON ELISE	1992	F	Swimming
BANKS LEE ANN	1983	F	Swimming
BARTON KELLI LYN	2005	F	Swimming
BEELER MARGARET MURPHY	1995	F	Swimming
BEELER MOLLY MALONE	2000	F	Swimming
BERINGER KAREN MADIGAN	1987	F	Swimming
BERNARD ELIZABETH MARIE	1981	F	Swimming
BOBEAR KAREN MAY	1984	F	Swimming
BOLATTINO CALLIE	1991	F	Swimming
BONNY ANDREA ELENA DR.	1988	F	Swimming
BOUVRON CHRISTEL MEI-YEN	2006	F	Swimming
BUCHINO SUSAN THERESA	1997	F	Swimming
BUSH KAREN K.	1984	F	Swimming
BUTCHER SHANNAH MARIE	1994	F	Swimming
BYORICK KAREN DAYLOR	1997	F	Swimming
CARRIGAN JULIE MARIE	1995	F	Swimming
CATENACCI VICTORIA ANNE DR.	1994	F	Swimming
CHOUDHARY JOAN PATRICIA	1986	F	Swimming
CHOURA COURTNEY AMANDA	2006	F	Swimming
CHRISTIE EVA JOANN	1988	F	Swimming
CLARK KATHERINE MAURA	1992	F	Swimming
COLEMAN CARA LOUISE	1995	F	Swimming
COLEMAN CHRISTINE RAE	1993	F	Swimming
COLLINS KATHERINE ALICE	1998	F	Swimming
CRAWFORD KATHERINE MARIE	2004	F	Swimming
DAILEY RITA H. MS.	1982	F	Swimming
DAVEY BROOKE TETHER	2002	F	Swimming
DE FOOR JOYA CHERYL	1977	F	Swimming
DEGER AMY CATHERINE	2003	F	Swimming
DEMARIA HALEY ADELLA	1995	F	Swimming
DENHAM BARBARA ANN	1988	F	Swimming
DEVINE SUZANNE LEE	1987	F	Swimming
DICAMILLO LORREINE KAY	1995	F	Swimming
D'OLIER LISA ELIZABETH	2004	F	Swimming
DORAN KRISTIN JANE	1992	F	Swimming
DUNN KRISTIN MIKAEL	1993	F	Swimming
DURBIN PORTIA JEAN	1987	F	Swimming
ECKHOLT KATHERINE JANE	2005	F	Swimming
ECKSTEIN MEGHAN CATHLEEN	1999	F	Swimming
EDDY ANNE MARIE	1988	F	Swimming
ELLIOTT HEATHER LEIGH	1992	F	Swimming
EMERY RAILI MARIE	1984	F	Swimming
EPPING KATHLEEN PATRICIA	1989	F	Swimming
FARRINGTON ALISA DIANE	1996	F	Swimming
FIEBER MONICA WALKER	1987	F	Swimming
GALLAGHER LIANE	1996	F	Swimming
GALLO LINDA NANCY	1998	F	Swimming
GAMBOA GINA MARIA	1984	F	Swimming
GARCIA ELIZABETH LOUISE	2004	F	Swimming
GATES ELIZABETH ANN	1997	F	Swimming
GERAGHTY BARBARA ELLEN DR.	1990	F	Swimming
GIBBONS KAREN L.	1995	F	Swimming
GODDARD RACHEL COUGHLIN	1996	F	Swimming
GRAZIANO KATHLEEN MARIE	2001	F	Swimming
GRINNEL MARY CLARE	1990	F	Swimming
GROYA KATHERINE LEIGH	1993	F	Swimming
GRUNEWALD BRENDA REILLY	2001	F	Swimming
HABEEB CHRISTINE NICOLE	2005	F	Swimming
HEALEY GEORGIA OLSIEWSKI	2005	F	Swimming
HEATH KRISTIN LEE	1994	F	Swimming
HECKING KELLY A.	2002	F	Swimming
HEGARTY KATHLEEN QUIRK	1990	F	Swimming
HENDERSON KAREN LYNN	1997	F	Swimming
HENDRICK HEIDI MARIE	2003	F	Swimming
HERZFELD JACQUELYNN DALE	1992	F	Swimming
HILLENMEYER MAUREEN ELIZABETH	2002	F	Swimming
HILLMAN JEAN ANN	1983	F	Swimming
HIPP COLLEEN MARIE	1995	F	Swimming
HOLLIS ALLISON MARIE	2000	F	Swimming
HOTCHKISS SHELLEY ANNE	1996	F	Swimming
HULICK DANIELLE MARIE	2004	F	Swimming
IACOBUCCI ANNE KELLY	1999	F	Swimming
ISAACS DEBRA KARLING DR.	1983	F	Swimming
JOEST SHEILA ANN	1983	F	Swimming

NAME	YEAR	GENDER	SPORT
NELSEN MARGARET HOGAN	2005	F	Track
NUSRALA LUCY MEGAN	N/A	F	Track
O'BRIEN BRIDGET LORRAINE	2001	F	Track
OLSON ERIN ELIZABETH	2001	F	Track
PEITERSEN ELIZABETH GROW	2002	F	Track
PETERSON KELLY MARIE	1999	F	Track
PETERSON MEGAN ALAINE	2004	F	Track
PINGEL KRISTEN LEIGH	1996	F	Track
POLANIECKI SHERRI ANDRE	2003	F	Track
REED ERIN JEANNINE	1999	F	Track
REICHENBACH HEIDI MARIE	1997	F	Track
REKLAU JANELLE MARIE	2001	F	Track
RICE DORAN PATRICIA MARY	2000	F	Track
RICHARDS KRISTINE LYN	1995	F	Track
ROBERTS TERESE MARIE	1991	F	Track
ROTATORI RENEE JEAN	1991	F	Track
SAMPSON SARAH KATHERYN	1992	F	Track
SCHMIDT JULIA ANN	2004	F	Track
SCHMIDT MELISSA MARIE	2003	F	Track
SCHMIEDT NADIA PRISKA	1999	F	Track
SHINNICK MAUREEN VIRGINIA	1996	F	Track
SHOWMAN EMILY SUSAN	2003	F	Track
SIQUEIRA VALERIE MAE	2000	F	Track
SLATTERY EMILY ANNE	1999	F	Track
STAPLETON DIANA CHRISTINE	1992	F	Track
STEWART-WHACK SHEILA DENISE M.D.	1992	F	Track
STOVALL KRISTIN MARIE	1994	F	Track
TATUM TIFFANI ROSE	2001	F	Track
TETER HEIDI ELAINE	1997	F	Track
TUGGLE ASHEA DIANE	1994	F	Track
TUTKO KELLY JOY	2000	F	Track
VAN WEELDEN JILL MARIE	2004	F	Track
VOLKMER JAIME ANNE	2003	F	Track
VOLLAND-CHAPLUK MARY RITA	1999	F	Track
WALES KATHERINE MARIE	2004	F	Track
WATERS KARMEN LATRICE	1994	F	Track
WEBSTER ELIZABETH MARIE	2006	F	Track
WEIHER GRETCHEN COLGAN	1998	F	Track
WILSON BETHANY VICTORIA	2001	F	Track
YORK KATHERINE ANNE	1997	F	Track
BAIMA JENNIFER ANNE	1997	F	Trainers
BECKSCHI HELEN CHANDRA	1987	F	Trainers
BEISENSTEIN-WEISS KELLY LYNN	1999	F	Trainers
BOURNAY RACHEL ANN	2006	F	Trainers
BRANDT PATRICIA MAUREEN	1989	F	Trainers
BUCCELLATO JEANNE MARIE	1995	F	Trainers
BUCKLE ROSEMARY M.D.	1985	F	Trainers
BUSCH KRISTA JO	2002	F	Trainers
CASTELLANO SHANNON L.	N/A	F	Trainers
CORBETT ERIN ELIZABETH	2000	F	Trainers
DAMMANN JACQUELINE MARIE	2005	F	Trainers
DAVIS KYLA AMA	2003	F	Trainers
DONOVAN KERRY ELIZABETH	2001	F	Trainers
DONOVAN MAUREEN ELIZABETH	1989	F	Trainers
EARLEY MONICA MACYS	1992	F	Trainers
EGAN NICOLE MICHELE	1994	F	Trainers
ESQUIVEL CYNTHIA	2006	F	Trainers
FITZGERALD SHANNON LEE	1990	F	Trainers
FORST HARTEY THERESA MARIE	1993	F	Trainers
HAINES JENNETTE CATHERINE	2005	F	Trainers
HARMON KIMBERLY MARIE M.D.	1989	F	Trainers
HARRIS ANDREA LANTZ	1988	F	Trainers
HICKEY LAINE ELIZABETH	1993	F	Trainers
HOCKENBERRY JANICE MARIE	1991	F	Trainers
JOHNSTONE KRISTEN ANN	1994	F	Trainers
KELLOGG ANN	2003	F	Trainers
LABIN TRACY ANNE	1991	F	Trainers
LAMBOLEY NICOLE JEANNE	1989	F	Trainers
LANDON KAYLENE INSOOK	2003	F	Trainers
LETHERMAN SUZANNE ELIZABETH	1996	F	Trainers
LONG JANCY MARIE	2002	F	Trainers
MASCA GIANNA MARIE	1990	F	Trainers
MAYGLOTHLING JULIE ANNE DR.	1995	F	Trainers
MILLER JOAN MARIE	1988	F	Trainers
MORAN MARCI JULE	1992	F	Trainers
NEVIN COLLEEN MAURA	1993	F	Trainers
O'REILLY CHRISTINE ELIZABETH	2001	F	Trainers
QUIGLEY KATHLEEN ELIZABETH	2005	F	Trainers
RAMOS RACHEL ANN	2005	F	Trainers
REGAN-PAUL AMY KATHLEEN	1991	F	Trainers
REPP KIM RUTH MRS.	1988	F	Trainers
RETTIG LAURAE DAWN	2004	F	Trainers
SCHLAFLY JEAN MARIE	1995	F	Trainers
SOWA CAROLINE ELISABETH	1997	F	Trainers
SPELLACY KRISTEN MARIE	2000	F	Trainers
SPIERING ELLEN CECILIA DR.	1992	F	Trainers
TERRY ALLISON JUDITH	2000	F	Trainers
TODD BRIANNE ELIZABETH	2004	F	Trainers
VANKOSKI PATRICIA MARIE	1990	F	Trainers
WALLIS NICOLE MARIE	2000	F	Trainers
WEBER KATHRYN ANNE	1993	F	Trainers
WIENEKE BROGHAMMER CARRIE LYNN	1998	F	Trainers
WILLIAMS JOAN RYAN	2004	F	Trainers
WILLIAMS SHERA SHIAN	2006	F	Trainers
WILLIAMS MARY THERESE KRAFT	1996	F	Trainers
YERGLER MICHELLE L.	N/A	F	Trainers
HOLMES JENNIFER LYNN	2002	F	Video Technician
OBERST CAITLIN ELIZABETH	2005	F	Video Technician
AKERS ANGELA MARIE	1998	F	Volleyball
ALDERETE JANE FITCH	2003	F	Volleyball
ALLEGRA EMILY MARIE	2000	F	Volleyball
ANDERSON JILL MARIE	1988	F	Volleyball
BAILEY TRACY JO MRS.	1986	F	Volleyball
BELANGER MARY LYNNE	1986	F	Volleyball
BENNETT ZANETTE LOUISE	1990	F	Volleyball
BIRCH WHITNEY ANNE	1989	F	Volleyball
BOMHACK MARCIE RAE	2002	F	Volleyball
BOYLAN-EGNER DENISE MARIE	2001	F	Volleyball
BRENNAN KATHLEEN ANNE	1988	F	Volleyball
BRENNAN KATHLEEN DAGES	1982	F	Volleyball
BREWSTER LAUREN CADE	2006	F	Volleyball
BRIGGS JENNIFER LEIGH	1997	F	Volleyball
BRODEN JO MATERNOWSKI	1985	F	Volleyball
BRUENING JENNIFER EILEEN	1992	F	Volleyball
BURRELL KELLY LYNN	2006	F	Volleyball
CHILES MICHELLE LORENE	2001	F	Volleyball
CLARK KATHLEEN MARY	1992	F	Volleyball
COOPER CAROLYN ANN	2006	F	Volleyball
CORBETT KELLY ELISSA	2005	F	Volleyball
COUGHLIN KEARA ANN	2003	F	Volleyball
CROWE KAREN E.	1987	F	Volleyball
DIBERNARDO MOLLIE TERESA	1987	F	Volleyball
DOYLE JULIA LINUS	1985	F	Volleyball
EIKENBERRY RACHEL JANE	1991	F	Volleyball
ERVIN KRISTINA LOUISE	1997	F	Volleyball
EVANS NANCY MARIE	1986	F	Volleyball
FLETCHER KIMBERLY RENEE	2004	F	Volleyball
FORD CHRISTINE NOELLE	1992	F	Volleyball
FRASER LAUREN ANNE	2000	F	Volleyball
GALLAGHER JENNIFER REBECCA	1997	F	Volleyball
GIBBONS JANET ELLEN MRS.	1982	F	Volleyball
GILLIN AMY ELIZABETH	1991	F	Volleyball
GIRTON CHRISTINE ELAINE	2001	F	Volleyball
GRECO LAURIE LYN	1990	F	Volleyball
HARRINGTON DYAN ELIZABETH	1994	F	Volleyball
HARRIS JULIE KRISTEN	1994	F	Volleyball
HART CAROL ANN	1984	F	Volleyball
HARTLAGE GRETCHEN MARY	1988	F	Volleyball
HEALEY JANE FRANCES	1984	F	Volleyball
HELT MARILYN ELIZABETH	1993	F	Volleyball
HENDRICKS AUDRA NATALIJA	1999	F	Volleyball
HENICAN MARGARET ANNE	2006	F	Volleyball
HOSFELD JAIMIE LEE	1998	F	Volleyball
JAMEYSON OLIVIA JO	2001	F	Volleyball
KAISER MAUREEN MARIE	1989	F	Volleyball
KASSON MARY TERESE	1984	F	Volleyball
KELBLEY LAUREN ELIZABETH	2006	F	Volleyball
KERR JESSICA ERIN	1993	F	Volleyball
KINDER JESSICA FRANCES	2004	F	Volleyball
KINDER KRISTEN ROSE	2004	F	Volleyball
KORDAS BRETT JANINE	1996	F	Volleyball
LAMBROS COLLEEN ANN	1991	F	Volleyball
LEAHY JENNIFER ROUSE	1997	F	Volleyball
LEFFERS MARY WELCH	2000	F	Volleyball
LETOURNEAU DEBORAH ANN MRS.	1981	F	Volleyball
LEZYNSKI JACQUELINE ANNE	1983	F	Volleyball
LITZAU KATHLEEN ANNE	1990	F	Volleyball
LOOMIS EMILY JANE	2005	F	Volleyball
LUND ALICIA ROSANNE	1993	F	Volleyball
MAY CAREY ELIZABETH	1998	F	Volleyball
MCCARTHY MOLLY VIRGINIA	1998	F	Volleyball
MEDLEY SUE ANN	1986	F	Volleyball
MILLER KATHLEEN MARIE	1988	F	Volleyball
MISCHLER KAREN ROBERTA	1986	F	Volleyball
NEFF KATHERINE ELIZABETH	2004	F	Volleyball
NI MAUREEN E.	1984	F	Volleyball
O'CONNOR CYNTHIA ANN	1993	F	Volleyball
PETERS CHRISTY SUZANNE	1995	F	Volleyball
POWELL AMANDA ROSE	2000	F	Volleyball
PRATT MARY JO MRS.	1985	F	Volleyball
RAY ROBIN LYNN	1985	F	Volleyball
RECKMEYER LAURA BETH	N/A	F	Volleyball
ROSENTHAL LINDSAY JT	1999	F	Volleyball
SANCHEZ JANELLE KATHRYN	1994	F	Volleyball
SAWYER MALINDA KAY	2002	F	Volleyball
SCHAEFBAUER NICOLE SUZANNE	1995	F	Volleyball
SHELTON TRACEY ANN	1991	F	Volleyball
SHIMMEL ADRIENNE CLAUDIA	2001	F	Volleyball
SMITH JENNIFER MELISSA	1993	F	Volleyball
STAHLMAN ANDREA A.	1993	F	Volleyball
STARK MOLLY ANNE	1994	F	Volleyball
SULLIVAN KRISTINE LOUISE	2002	F	Volleyball
TUTTLE SHANNON MARIE	1996	F	Volleyball
VAN OORT MARY KAY	1989	F	Volleyball
VAUGHN TARYN LEAH	1992	F	Volleyball
WATSON-WASHINGTON ANGELA	1981	F	Volleyball
ACKIL LAUREN LYONS	2001	F	Womens Rowing
AMONI ANDREA SUSANNE	2003	F	Womens Rowing
ARLETH BARBARA JOANNE	2001	F	Womens Rowing
ASHE LEAH MARIE	2001	F	Womens Rowing
BARTSH ALLISON ELIZABETH	2000	F	Womens Rowing
BENN JADA PERDITA	1999	F	Womens Rowing
BESSON KATHRYN ANNE	2002	F	Womens Rowing
BOSCO EMILY ELIZABETH	2001	F	Womens Rowing
BOUCHE MELISSA JEANNE	2001	F	Womens Rowing
BOYLE MEGHAN KATHLEEN	2006	F	Womens Rowing
BRAUN AMY MARIE	2002	F	Womens Rowing
BUCKSTAFF JULIET CASEY	2003	F	Womens Rowing
BULA CLAIRE ELIZABETH-G.	2001	F	Womens Rowing
BURNETT KATHERINE JENNIFER	2002	F	Womens Rowing
CAMPBELL REBECCA LEE	2003	F	Womens Rowing
CARR MAUREEN ELIZABETH	2002	F	Womens Rowing
CASUCCIO MARY LAMPE	2002	F	Womens Rowing
CHAPUT ANGELA MARIE	2001	F	Womens Rowing
CLUBB KATHERINE LOUISE FOX	1999	F	Womens Rowing
CUSHING ELIZABETH ANGELA	2002	F	Womens Rowing
DILLHOFF ANN MARIE	2003	F	Womens Rowing
DONNELLY CHRISTINE MARY	2005	F	Womens Rowing
DOUD ANDREA NICOLE	2006	F	Womens Rowing
DRENNEN ERICA RAE	2003	F	Womens Rowing
FEELY MEGAN ANNE	2002	F	Womens Rowing
FELKER MELISSA INGE	2006	F	Womens Rowing
FRANZOSA ELIZABETH GORMALLY	2005	F	Womens Rowing
GAUL ERIN KIERNICKI	2001	F	Womens Rowing
GIBBONS MAUREEN ELIZABETH	2005	F	Womens Rowing
GRIBBIN EILEEN MARIE	2001	F	Womens Rowing
HALE TRICIA LINNE	2005	F	Womens Rowing
HALEY JEANETTE MCKENNA	2001	F	Womens Rowing
HEGEMAN DEVON ROSE	2005	F	Womens Rowing
HENKEL KRISTIN ELIZABETH	2005	F	Womens Rowing
JEFSON PAMELA ANNE	2006	F	Womens Rowing
JENISTA ELIZABETH ROSE	2005	F	Womens Rowing
KUHN CAROLINE SARAH	2001	F	Womens Rowing
LETTIERI SHANNAN MARIE	2006	F	Womens Rowing
LOPEZ KATHLEEN LINDSEY	2005	F	Womens Rowing
MABBUTT KRISTIN VANDEHEY	2001	F	Womens Rowing
MARKSTAHLER CASSIE JANE	2003	F	Womens Rowing
MCCALDEN KATHERINE MARIE	2003	F	Womens Rowing
MERCER COURTNEY ELIZABETH	2002	F	Womens Rowing
MILLER KATHERINE TERESE	2002	F	Womens Rowing
MINER EMILY BRENNAN	1999	F	Womens Rowing
MOHAN SHANNON ELIZABETH	2005	F	Womens Rowing
MOREAU JOSLYN ANNA	2000	F	Womens Rowing
MURPHY KERRI MARGARET	2003	F	Womens Rowing
MYERS KOLLEEN SARA	2002	F	Womens Rowing
NARDI CHRISTINE MARIE	1999	F	Womens Rowing
NATTER KELLY KAINE	2000	F	Womens Rowing
NELSON SARAH EILEEN MS.	2000	F	Womens Rowing
NERNEY ELIZABETH JANE	2000	F	Womens Rowing
OLSGARD MICHELLE LEE	2002	F	Womens Rowing
PALANDECH SARAH ASHLEY	2006	F	Womens Rowing
POLINSKI RACHEL LYNN	2005	F	Womens Rowing
RACKISH CAITLIN ERKINS	2005	F	Womens Rowing
REDGATE JENNA MARIE	2006	F	Womens Rowing
ROOSA LEZLIE MORGAN	1999	F	Womens Rowing
SEDUN CATHERINE ELIZABETH	2005	F	Womens Rowing
SHANKS MELISSA JEAN	2002	F	Womens Rowing
STACER KATHRYN CHRISTINE	2000	F	Womens Rowing
STEALY DANIELLE MARIE	2006	F	Womens Rowing
STOREY ELIZABETH ANN	2002	F	Womens Rowing
TALBIRD SANDRA EILEEN	2001	F	Womens Rowing
TEN EYCK KATRINA FLORENCE	2000	F	Womens Rowing
THORNBURGH MEREDITH LEIGH	2005	F	Womens Rowing
VANDENBERG QUINN HELEN	2001	F	Womens Rowing
WARREN ASHLEE MEGHAN	2003	F	Womens Rowing
WHITE VIRGINIA JOSEPHINE	1999	F	Womens Rowing
ALFORD STACI SUZANNE	1993	F	Womens Softball
ALKIRE MELANIE LEANN	2001	F	Womens Softball
AUDETTE JOYLENE MAE	1997	F	Womens Softball
BAILEY KARA MICHELLE	1997	F	Womens Softball
BESSOLO ANGELA MARIE	1999	F	Womens Softball
BOOTH HEATHER MARIE	2006	F	Womens Softball
BOULAC DAWN MARIE	1989	F	Womens Softball
BOULAC DEBORAH ELLEN	1993	F	Womens Softball
BURKE TERRI LYNN	1989	F	Womens Softball
CIOLLI MEGAN GAIL	2005	F	Womens Softball
CONNOYER CHRISTY LYNN	1994	F	Womens Softball
COOK MELISSA MARIE	1994	F	Womens Softball
CROSSEN RACHEL ELIZABETH	1991	F	Womens Softball
CUNNINGHAM DAWN NICOLE	1999	F	Womens Softball

NAME	YEAR	GENDER	SPORT
DEBIASE LISA ROCHELLE	1993	F	Womens Softball
DEFAU NICOLE MURIEL	2004	F	Womens Softball
DILLON KATHRYN ANN	1991	F	Womens Softball
DONOVAN AMY NICOLE	1994	F	Womens Softball
DUMPMAN MICHELE RAE	1995	F	Womens Softball
EIMEN REBECCA LYNN	2000	F	Womens Softball
FOLSOM-MULLANEY AMY RENEE	1992	F	Womens Softball
GANEFF KRISTINA SUE	1999	F	Womens Softball
GIAMPAOLO JENNIFER ANNE	1998	F	Womens Softball
GODLEWSKI JENNA MARIE	1996	F	Womens Softball
GOETZ ELIZABETH ANN	1995	F	Womens Softball
GOODWIN TAMARA ANN DR.	1989	F	Womens Softball
GRIMMER ANGELA MARIE	2002	F	Womens Softball
HARRIMAN ANDRIA MARIE	2003	F	Womens Softball
HARTMANN ELIZABETH MARIE	2005	F	Womens Softball
HAYES SARA BETH	1995	F	Womens Softball
HOAG KATHLEEN ANN	2002	F	Womens Softball
KING TARA THERESE	2000	F	Womens Softball
KIRKMAN SARAH RHIANNON	2001	F	Womens Softball
KLAYMAN DANIELLE LEE	2001	F	Womens Softball
KMAK RUTH ANN	1992	F	Womens Softball
KNECHT MELISSA LINN	1992	F	Womens Softball
KNIGHT JOANNA	1998	F	Womens Softball
KOBATA TERRILYN AKIKO	1996	F	Womens Softball
KRIECH JENNIFER LEIGH	2002	F	Womens Softball
LABOE AMY ELIZABETH	1999	F	Womens Softball
LATIMER ELIZABETH MARIE	1997	F	Womens Softball
LEHMANN STEPHANIE JEANNE	1994	F	Womens Softball
LEMIRE ELIZABETH WALSH	2001	F	Womens Softball
LENN MALLORIE ERIN	2006	F	Womens Softball
LIDDY MARIE TERESA	1991	F	Womens Softball
LOMAN ANDREA DANIELLE	2003	F	Womens Softball
MACLEOD KARA LEE	1996	F	Womens Softball
MADRID ALEXIS CHRISTINA	2003	F	Womens Softball
MAHAN KATHLEEN ARMSTRONG	1997	F	Womens Softball
MATHISON SARAH ELLEN	2000	F	Womens Softball
MATSUDA HOLLY UILANI	2002	F	Womens Softball
MATTISON LISA ANNE	2003	F	Womens Softball
MCCURDY HEATHER MCMURRAY	1993	F	Womens Softball
MCGOFF MEGAN JANE	1991	F	Womens Softball
MIDDLETON KELLIE KRISTIN	2006	F	Womens Softball
MILLER BARICHIEVICH CAROLINE SUZANNE	1994	F	Womens Softball
MOONEY BARBARA FRANCES	1989	F	Womens Softball
MOSCHEL MICHELLE MORGAN	2002	F	Womens Softball
MURRAY MEGHAN LYNN	1997	F	Womens Softball
MYERS JARRAH ROCHELLE	2002	F	Womens Softball
NICHOLS-DULONG KELLY NAVA	1998	F	Womens Softball
O'BRIEN VERONICA RAE	1993	F	Womens Softball
PIERCE ANDREA SUSAN	1996	F	Womens Softball
PINEDA LAURA ANN	1992	F	Womens Softball
QUINN SHERI BETH	1993	F	Womens Softball
ROWE KELLY ANN	1998	F	Womens Softball
RUTHRAUFF MEAGAN LEIGH	2006	F	Womens Softball
SCHOONAERT SARA ELIZABETH	2006	F	Womens Softball
SEAVEY ANDREA KEYS	1995	F	Womens Softball
SHARRON JENNIFER MERKIN	2001	F	Womens Softball
SHARRON JESSICA LEAH	2003	F	Womens Softball
SOLAROLI MICHELE LYNN	1992	F	Womens Softball
SORENSEN PATRICIA ANN	1996	F	Womens Softball
STENGLEIN STEFFANY DANIELLE	2005	F	Womens Softball
SULLIVAN MARIA	1989	F	Womens Softball
TULLY LISA JENNIFER	2000	F	Womens Softball
WICKS NICOLE BRIANNE	2005	F	Womens Softball
WINKLOSKY SUSAN EILEEN	1993	F	Womens Softball
WISEN CARRIE JO	2005	F	Womens Softball
ZUHOSKI KORRIE	1998	F	Womens Softball
ABBATIELLO JAMES PAUL	1977	M	Baseball
ALLEN CRAIG QUENTIN	1996	M	Baseball
ALLEN THOMAS GEORGE	1992	M	Baseball
AMBREY TIMOTHY JAY	1982	M	Baseball
AMRHEIN MICHAEL KEVIN	1997	M	Baseball
ANDRES STEPHEN FROST	2006	M	Baseball
ARBOIT ENNIO BENJAMIN	1938	M	Baseball
ARNZEN ROBERT LOUIS	1969	M	Baseball
ASKEW J. HASKELL	1931	M	Baseball
AXFORD JOHN BERTON	2005	M	Baseball
BADER ROBERT JOSEPH	1978	M	Baseball
BALICKI MICHAEL SCOTT	1997	M	Baseball
BARRETT JOHN T.	1947	M	Baseball
BARROWS JOSEPH L.	1982	M	Baseball
BARTISH DAVID CHARLES	1980	M	Baseball
BARTLETT ROBERT JOHN	1981	M	Baseball
BAUTCH DANIEL JOHN	1992	M	Baseball
BEACH JOSEPH DEPAUL SR.	1935	M	Baseball
BEHE FRANCIS JAMES	1941	M	Baseball
BERGER ALVIN H.	1915	M	Baseball
BERTELLI ANGELO B.	1944	M	Baseball
BESSER PAUL THOMAS DR.	1957	M	Baseball
BESTEN ELMER W.	1927	M	Baseball
BICKFORD SCOTT EDWARD	2005	M	Baseball
BILLMAIER KRISTOPHER CARL	2003	M	Baseball
BINKIEWICZ JOSEPH ARTHUR M.D.	1992	M	Baseball
BIRK ROBERT CEBE	1994	M	Baseball
BLYTHE THOMAS E. JR.	1966	M	Baseball
BOBINSKI MICHAEL A.	1979	M	Baseball
BOBOWSKI STANLEY H. III	1977	M	Baseball
BOK MATTHEW AARON	2002	M	Baseball
BOLAND THOMAS MICHAEL	1951	M	Baseball
BONHAM E. DOUGLAS	1909	M	Baseball
BOROWSKI CHARLES CASIMIR	1938	M	Baseball
BOYLE HUGH J.	1910	M	Baseball
BRADDOCK JOHN PATRICK	1938	M	Baseball
BRADY J. ROBB	1940	M	Baseball
BRANSFIELD MATTHEW MILLER	2006	M	Baseball
BRAUN ROGER JOSEPH	1953	M	Baseball
BRAY JAMES F.	1929	M	Baseball
BRENNAN J. MICHAEL	1961	M	Baseball
BRETTING H. LYMAN JR.	1958	M	Baseball
BROCK JOHN ROY	1997	M	Baseball
BROEMMEL ROBERT TERENCE	1959	M	Baseball
BROOKS RANDALL HOXIE	1997	M	Baseball
BRUTVAN WILLIAM J. JR.	1962	M	Baseball
BUCHMEIER MATTHEW THOMAS	2002	M	Baseball
BUJNOWSKI ANTHONY THOMAS	1958	M	Baseball
BUSHEY ANDREW WILLIAM	2002	M	Baseball
CALLAHAN THOMAS FRANCIS	1943	M	Baseball
CAMERON JAMES MALCOLM	1983	M	Baseball
CAMPAGNA JOSEPH F.	1943	M	Baseball
CAPOZZI ANGELO DR. JR.	1956	M	Baseball
CARIDEO JAMES VINCENT	1957	M	Baseball
CARLIN JAMES T.	1947	M	Baseball
CARLIN JOHN MICHAEL	2001	M	Baseball
CARLIN THOMAS FRANCIS	1948	M	Baseball
CARLSON GARRET JOHN	1996	M	Baseball
CARMODY ARTHUR R.	1915	M	Baseball
CARMODY MICHAEL	1915	M	Baseball
CARNEY R. MARK MR.	1980	M	Baseball
CARPIN FRANK DOMINIC	1960	M	Baseball
CARRETTA JOHN VINCENT SR.	1960	M	Baseball
CARSON JAMES F.	1938	M	Baseball
CARUSO THOMAS NICHOLAS	1979	M	Baseball
CASTNER PAUL H.	1923	M	Baseball
CAVEY SCOTT TIMOTHY	2000	M	Baseball
CELMER DAVID ROBERT	1968	M	Baseball
CHENAIL KEVIN MICHAEL	1988	M	Baseball
CHLEBECK ANDREW JOHN SR.	1942	M	Baseball
CHRYST RICHARD WILLIAM	1983	M	Baseball
CIANCHETTI ROBERT M.	1949	M	Baseball
CIZON FRANCIS A.	1947	M	Baseball
CLARK DAVID DRAKE	1985	M	Baseball
CLEARY ROBERT KEVIN M.D.	1979	M	Baseball
CLEMENS PETER ANTON	1974	M	Baseball
CLEMENTZ MARK A.	1984	M	Baseball
CLEVENGER KASEY RYAN	1995	M	Baseball
COCCITTI THOMAS FRANCIS	1948	M	Baseball
COFFEY MICHAEL DAVID	1990	M	Baseball
COLEMAN PATRICK MICHAEL	1975	M	Baseball
COLLOTON RICHARD HAROLD	1954	M	Baseball
COLVILLE JOHN ELEAZER	1932	M	Baseball
COMBS ARTHUR HAMILTON M.D.	1972	M	Baseball
CONLIN THOMAS EARL	1984	M	Baseball
CONNELLY EUGENE E.	1912	M	Baseball
CONROY THOMAS EDWARD	1982	M	Baseball
CONWAY BRIAN DAVID	1992	M	Baseball
COOKE BENJAMIN MCKIM	2001	M	Baseball
COOPER ALAN JOHN DR.	1965	M	Baseball
COOPER CRAIG MICHAEL	2006	M	Baseball
CORBIN JOHN THOMAS	2000	M	Baseball
CORCORAN CHARLES G.	1917	M	Baseball
CORRAO ANDREW CHARLES	1954	M	Baseball
COSS MICHAEL PATRICK	1992	M	Baseball
COSTA DONALD JAMES	1959	M	Baseball
COSTIGAN DAVID	1953	M	Baseball
COUNSELL CRAIG JOHN	1992	M	Baseball
COUNSELL W. JOHN MR. JR.	1964	M	Baseball
CRANE HUGH THOMAS	1940	M	Baseball
CREEVEY JOHN FRANCIS	1948	M	Baseball
CRIMMINS CHARLES VINCENT	1941	M	Baseball
CROSS J. BRADFORD MR.	1986	M	Baseball
CROWLEY FRANCIS W.	1926	M	Baseball
CUGGINO THOMAS JOHN	1968	M	Baseball
CUMMINGS LEO JAMES	1933	M	Baseball
CUNHA DANIEL JOSEPH	1935	M	Baseball
CURTIN EGBERT LEO	1923	M	Baseball
CUSACK JAMES DONALD DR.	1957	M	Baseball
DALTON JAMES THORNTON	1954	M	Baseball
DANAPILIS ERIC JAMES	1995	M	Baseball
DAVIS PATRICK JOSEPH	1998	M	Baseball
DEASEY JOHN JOSEPH	1989	M	Baseball
DEASEY MICHAEL PATRICK	1981	M	Baseball
DEE JAMES MATTHEW	1984	M	Baseball
DEFACCI DAVID WAYNE	1978	M	Baseball
DEGRAFF MARTIN THOMAS	1994	M	Baseball
DELPRETE LOUIS JOHN	1932	M	Baseball
DESENSI W. CRAIG MR.	1995	M	Baseball
DESILVA MARK ANTHONY DR.	1981	M	Baseball
DINGLE PHILLIP STEPHEN	1983	M	Baseball
DOBOSH JOSEPH JAMES	1985	M	Baseball
DOEMEL DAVID STANLEY	1975	M	Baseball
DONNELLY PHIL LOSEE	1964	M	Baseball
DONOHOE EDWARD F.	1929	M	Baseball
DORNING MICHAEL DALLAS DR.	1985	M	Baseball
DOYLE LAWRENCE A. SR.	1939	M	Baseball
DREVLINE JOHN-PAUL WILLIAM	2002	M	Baseball
DUDLEY AMBROSE F. JR.	1943	M	Baseball
DUFF DENNIS ANDREW	2002	M	Baseball
DUFFY EUGENE RAYMOND	1959	M	Baseball
DUNN KIERAN LOUIS JR.	1935	M	Baseball
DURKIN HARRY PATRICK	1953	M	Baseball
DWYER JAMES FRANCIS	1926	M	Baseball
EBERT JOHN WILLIAM	1982	M	Baseball
EDGREN PAUL E.	1918	M	Baseball
EDWARDS MATTHEW MARCHETTI	2005	M	Baseball
EICH RICHARD JOHN	1973	M	Baseball
EILERS PATRICK CHRISTOPHER	1989	M	Baseball
FAILLA PAUL JOHN	1995	M	Baseball
FANNING KEVIN WARD	1974	M	Baseball
FARABAUGH G. ALOYSIUS	1904	M	Baseball
FARRELL CHARLES JOSEPH	1941	M	Baseball
FARRELL RICHARD JOHN	1955	M	Baseball
FARRELL SIMON THOMAS	1914	M	Baseball
FELKER JEFFREY ALDEN	2000	M	Baseball
FENZEL H. JEROME MR.	1972	M	Baseball
FERRYMAN JEAN FRANCIS	1951	M	Baseball
FIASCKI FRANK THOMAS	1977	M	Baseball
FINNEGAN ROBERT JAMES	1946	M	Baseball
FISH JAMES LEO	1911	M	Baseball
FITZ ROBERT MARK	1989	M	Baseball
FITZPATRICK JAMES BERNARD	1962	M	Baseball
FLANAGAN JOHN	1990	M	Baseball
FLYNN CHRISTOPHER FRANCIS	1988	M	Baseball
FRANCIS HARRY H. JR.	1930	M	Baseball
FROMHART WALLACE LEO	1936	M	Baseball
FRYE TODD MICHAEL	1998	M	Baseball
FUENTES JAVIER ROLANDO	1994	M	Baseball
GABERIK RICHARD PAUL	1955	M	Baseball
GAGNE JON-PAUL VERNE	2003	M	Baseball
GALLOWAY WILLIAM MICHAEL	1977	M	Baseball
GAROFALO EMIL VICTOR	1950	M	Baseball
GARVEY ARTHUR A.	1923	M	Baseball
GEHRING JOSEPH E.	1948	M	Baseball
GENESER JOSEPH DANIEL SR.	1958	M	Baseball
GENTEMPO JOHN MARTIN	1961	M	Baseball
GHIGLIOTTI EDWARD EUGENE	1944	M	Baseball
GIARRATANO ROBERT CHARLES M.D.	1959	M	Baseball
GIBBONS BRIAN J.	1984	M	Baseball
GIBBONS JAMES VINCENT	1953	M	Baseball
GIEDLIN RICHARD JOHN	1951	M	Baseball
GIESELMAN JAMES FREDERICK	1971	M	Baseball
GILHOOLEY FRANCIS PATRICK	1947	M	Baseball
GILLESPIE WILLIAM FRANCIS	1936	M	Baseball
GILLIS JAMES J.	1951	M	Baseball
GLEESON JOHN J.	1987	M	Baseball
GLEICHOWSKI JUSTIN EDWARD	1995	M	Baseball
GOETZ GERALD JOSEPH	1968	M	Baseball
GOLOM EDWARD MICHAEL	2003	M	Baseball
GONCHER JOHN STEPHAN	1938	M	Baseball
GONRING MARK LEROY	1966	M	Baseball
GONSKI RICHARD C.	1964	M	Baseball
GORE FREDERICK PETERS	1942	M	Baseball
GREENE CLAUDE ALLEN IV	1999	M	Baseball
GREENWELL RICHARD GLENN	1977	M	Baseball
GRIEVE DONALD CHARLES	1951	M	Baseball
GRIFFIN GERALD R.	1929	M	Baseball
GUILFOILE THOMAS EDWARD	1986	M	Baseball
HAAS MATTHEW EDWIN	1994	M	Baseball
HAGAN DANIEL YATES	1961	M	Baseball
HAMMETT JOHN B.	1957	M	Baseball
HANDRICH TIMOTHY GERARD	1980	M	Baseball
HANNAN JAMES JOHN	1960	M	Baseball
HANSEN THOMAS JOSEPH	1974	M	Baseball
HANSON DAVID JOHN	1963	M	Baseball
HARMON MICHAEL JOSEPH	1988	M	Baseball
HARRINGTON DANIEL J.	1984	M	Baseball
HARSHA TERRY EUGENE	1966	M	Baseball
HART THOMAS VICTOR	1929	M	Baseball
HARTVIGSON CHAD ALLEN	1990	M	Baseball
HARTWELL EDWIN DARYL	1993	M	Baseball
HASSETT WILLIAM JOSEPH	1947	M	Baseball
HEILMAN AARON MICHAEL	2001	M	Baseball

NAME	YEAR	GENDER	SPORT
HELLRUNG ROBERT THORNTON	1930	M	Baseball
HENEBRY GREGG CLARK	1997	M	Baseball
HENGEL EDWARD DONALD	1941	M	Baseball
HICKEY JOHN PATRICK	1944	M	Baseball
HILBRICH JOHN FRANCIS	1950	M	Baseball
HILLER JOHN MALCOLM	1948	M	Baseball
HOAG ROBERT JOHN JR.	1939	M	Baseball
HOLBA MICHAEL ANDREW	2003	M	Baseball
HORAN PAUL CHARLES	1971	M	Baseball
HOWARD THOMAS PATRICK	1989	M	Baseball
HRABCSAK EDWARD PAUL	1973	M	Baseball
HUGHES ROBERT C.	1977	M	Baseball
HUGHES THOMAS M. DR. JR.	1966	M	Baseball
HUISKING CHARLES LOUIS JR.	1934	M	Baseball
HUNTHAUSEN NORVALL MATTHEW	1940	M	Baseball
HURLEY EDWIN HENRY JR.	1957	M	Baseball
HUTSON TIMOTHY ROBERT	1988	M	Baseball
IAMS GEORGE E.	1981	M	Baseball
IAROCCI ANTHONY JOSEPH	1975	M	Baseball
JACOBS FRANCIS ALBERT	1995	M	Baseball
JAEB THOMAS EVERETT	1956	M	Baseball
JAEGER ROBERT JAMES	1970	M	Baseball
JAMIESON MICHAEL RAYMOND	1981	M	Baseball
JAUN GREGORY JAMES DR.	1983	M	Baseball
JOHNSON STEVEN ARNOLD	1957	M	Baseball
JONES ALLEN JAY	1996	M	Baseball
JONES TYLER GRANT	2005	M	Baseball
KALITA RYAN JOSEPH	2003	M	Baseball
KALITA TIMOTHY RYAN	2001	M	Baseball
KANE MICHAEL GEORGE	1923	M	Baseball
KANE PAUL RAYMOND	1934	M	Baseball
KARAZIM FRANK JULIUS	1965	M	Baseball
KARPOWICZ JOSEPH R. JR.	1978	M	Baseball
KEENAN JOSEPH D. III	1970	M	Baseball
KELLY MICHAEL DONATH	1942	M	Baseball
KELLY NEIL F.	1948	M	Baseball
KENAHAN MICHAEL PATRICK	1979	M	Baseball
KENNEDY LAWRENCE MICHAEL	1965	M	Baseball
KENT ROBERT MICHAEL	1994	M	Baseball
KERNAN JOSEPH EUGENE	1968	M	Baseball
KING ROBERT HAROLD	1952	M	Baseball
KISGEN RICHARD WILLIAM	1943	M	Baseball
KLEIN ROBERT ALVIN	1948	M	Baseball
KLINE CLARENCE JOSEPH	1921	M	Baseball
KNECHT MICHAEL SCOTT	1999	M	Baseball
KOBLOSH PETER	1950	M	Baseball
KOCMALSKI ROBERT PAUL	1968	M	Baseball
KOHORST ELMER J.	1957	M	Baseball
KOLASA GEORGE WILLIAM	1954	M	Baseball
KOLSKI ALVIN GEORGE	1931	M	Baseball
KONOPKA STANLEY J. JR.	1953	M	Baseball
KOT GREGORY P.	1982	M	Baseball
KOVZELOVE ALEXANDER S.	1938	M	Baseball
KOZAK GEORGE JOSEPH	1933	M	Baseball
KOZLIK BENEDICT R.	1950	M	Baseball
KRALL MATTHEW CHARLES	1992	M	Baseball
KRAUS TIMOTHY GIBSON	1995	M	Baseball
KREIS CHARLES COAKLEY	1951	M	Baseball
KRILL PHILIP DONALD	1971	M	Baseball
KRIVIK STANLEY E.	1949	M	Baseball
KWIATKOWSKI FRANK WALTER D.M.D.	1967	M	Baseball
LACKNER LAWRENCE STEVEN	1983	M	Baseball
LADD MARK WILLIAM	1979	M	Baseball
LAIRD MATTHEW HARRIS	2003	M	Baseball
LANGE EDWARD M.	1973	M	Baseball
LANGE HENRY FRANKLIN	1985	M	Baseball
LAPINSKAS MARK CHRISTOPHER	2000	M	Baseball
LAROCCA JOSEPH ANTHONY	1972	M	Baseball
LATHROP RALPH JEFFERSON	1916	M	Baseball
LAVALLE HAROLD VINCENT	1957	M	Baseball
LAVERY EUGENE ROBERT	1950	M	Baseball
LAVERY HUGH THOMAS	1919	M	Baseball
LAW JOHN B.	1930	M	Baseball
LAYSON GREGORY JOSEPH	1994	M	Baseball
LAZZERI DAVID JOSEPH JR.	1976	M	Baseball
LEAHY JOSEPH CHARLES	1978	M	Baseball
LEAHY PATRICK MICHAEL	1995	M	Baseball
LEATHERMAN DANIEL JOSEPH	1998	M	Baseball
LEDWIDGE JEREMIAH SEAMUS	1952	M	Baseball
LEGUS DAVID JOHN	1990	M	Baseball
LENNON CHARLES F. JR.	1961	M	Baseball
LEONARD JAMES RAYMOND SR.	1934	M	Baseball
LEROSE LEONARD JAMES SR.	1953	M	Baseball
LESSO MICHAEL ALBERT	1956	M	Baseball
LICINI RICHARD ALLEN	1969	M	Baseball
LIDGE BRADLEY THOMAS	1998	M	Baseball
LINBECK LEO EDWARD JR.	1956	M	Baseball
LISANTI ROBERT ANTHONY	1996	M	Baseball
LIVORSI ANTHONY PETER	1990	M	Baseball
LOMASNEY WILLIAM F. JR.	1933	M	Baseball
LOPES ROBERT A. JR.	1985	M	Baseball
LOPEZ GREGORY DAVID	2006	M	Baseball
LORDI JOSEPH JOHN	1930	M	Baseball
LOUGHRAN JOHN MATTHEW	1987	M	Baseball
LUCKE RICHARD PAUL	1970	M	Baseball
LUND EDWARD VICTOR	1990	M	Baseball
LUPTON EDWARD ROBERT	1965	M	Baseball
LUX THOMAS CLINTON	1969	M	Baseball
LYNCH ROBERT EMMETT	1903	M	Baseball
MACDONALD THOMAS LOUIS	1964	M	Baseball
MACHADO ROBERT F.	1949	M	Baseball
MADSEN ERIK ANDREW	1990	M	Baseball
MAGEVNEY HUGH MICHAEL JR.	1924	M	Baseball
MAHANNAH WALTER ELLSWORTH	1950	M	Baseball
MAHER RICHARD O.	1950	M	Baseball
MAHONEY JOHN M.	1931	M	Baseball
MAINIERI NICHOLAS GIANNI	2006	M	Baseball
MAISANO ADAM GOEPEL	1993	M	Baseball
MANDJACK MICHAEL M.	1940	M	Baseball
MANNING JAMES PATRICK	1952	M	Baseball
MANNING ROBERT EMMETT JR.	1960	M	Baseball
MANNIX CHARLES	1931	M	Baseball
MAPES MARK TODD	1994	M	Baseball
MARKEY THOMAS S.	1929	M	Baseball
MARTIN THOMAS JOHN	1950	M	Baseball
MARTINEZ JASON LEE	1992	M	Baseball
MASSA EDWARD CLEMENT	1933	M	Baseball
MATHEWS CHRISTOPHER FRANCIS	1936	M	Baseball
MATRE WILLIAM P.	1983	M	Baseball
MAUK PAUL EUGENE	1988	M	Baseball
MAYER GARY LEE	1974	M	Baseball
MAYO JOHN LEWIS JR.	1947	M	Baseball
MCGINN DANIEL MICHAEL	1966	M	Baseball
MCGRATH FRANK JAMES	1924	M	Baseball
MCGRATH JAMES H.	1933	M	Baseball
MCHALE JOHN JOSEPH SR.	1943	M	Baseball
MCHALE THOMAS EUGENE SR.	1950	M	Baseball
MCKEOWN CHRISTOPHER PATRICK	1999	M	Baseball
MCNAMARA JOSEPH JEREMIAH	1961	M	Baseball
MEE CORY THOMAS	1992	M	Baseball
METZGER JOHN BERNARD	1943	M	Baseball
METZLER MICHAEL P.	1984	M	Baseball
MEYER KENNETH TAYLOR	2002	M	Baseball
MIADICH MICHAEL CHRISTIAN	1993	M	Baseball
MICHALAK CHRISTIAN MATTHEW	1995	M	Baseball
MILES J. FRANK SR.	1922	M	Baseball
MILLER THOMAS PAUL	1975	M	Baseball
MITCHELL JOHN EDWARD	1961	M	Baseball
MOHS LAWRENCE FRANCIS	1997	M	Baseball
MONTAGANO JAMES ANTHONY	1981	M	Baseball
MOONEY VINCENT	1916	M	Baseball
MOORE DANIEL A.	1927	M	Baseball
MORAN JOHN FRANCIS JR.	1985	M	Baseball
MORAN JOHN THOMAS SR.	1930	M	Baseball
MORRIS JAMES RICHARD	1958	M	Baseball
MOSHIER MICHAEL PATRICK	1989	M	Baseball
MOTTL RONALD MILTON	1956	M	Baseball
MURPHY GEORGE LOUIS	1920	M	Baseball
MURPHY JOHN PATRICK	1985	M	Baseball
MURRAY PATRICK JOSEPH	1919	M	Baseball
MURRAY THOMAS MARTIN	1992	M	Baseball
MURRAY TIMOTHY KEVIN	2004	M	Baseball
MUSTO JOHN FRANK	1966	M	Baseball
NAUMANN MICHAEL TODD	2001	M	Baseball
NEMES ROBERT VINCENT	1951	M	Baseball
NESPO DANIEL NORMAN	1952	M	Baseball
NETTEY ALEXANDER EGYA-KOW	2006	M	Baseball
NEWBOLD WILLIAM M.	1932	M	Baseball
NOE JAMES HAMILTON	1974	M	Baseball
NOLAN CYRIL U.	1930	M	Baseball
NOLAN ROGER W. JR.	1953	M	Baseball
NOLAN ROGER W. SR.	1926	M	Baseball
NOWICKI SEBASTIAN JOHN	1942	M	Baseball
NUSSBAUM MATTHEW RICHARD	2000	M	Baseball
NUSSBAUM RICHARD ANTON II	1974	M	Baseball
OBERBRUNER KENNETH LOUIS	1940	M	Baseball
O'BOYLE HARRY W.	1927	M	Baseball
O'BRIEN PATRICK MICHAEL	1988	M	Baseball
O'CONNOR JAMES PATRICK	1932	M	Baseball
O'CONNOR RICHARD DANIEL	1934	M	Baseball
O'CONNOR THOMAS JOHN	1972	M	Baseball
O'DROBINAK JOHN MARION	1957	M	Baseball
OGILVIE PETER C.	2003	M	Baseball
O'HAGAN THOMAS VINCENT	2000	M	Baseball
O'KEEFE DENNIS JOSEPH	1933	M	Baseball
O'KEEFE PATRICK WILLIAM JR.	1997	M	Baseball
O'LEARY JOHN RICHARD MAJOR	1961	M	Baseball
O'NEILL LAWRENCE THOMAS	1934	M	Baseball
O'NEILL MICHAEL EUGENE	1975	M	Baseball
O'NEILL PATRICK WILLIAM	1953	M	Baseball
O'NEILL PHILIP BERNARD	1901	M	Baseball
ORGA FRANK MICHAEL	1968	M	Baseball
ORGA WILLIAM JAMES	1970	M	Baseball
OSGOOD WALTER JOSEPH	1962	M	Baseball
O'TOOLE PAUL JONATHAN	2003	M	Baseball
PAJA RONALD PHILLIP	1974	M	Baseball
PALERMO JOSEPH P.	1930	M	Baseball
PALIHNICH NICHOLAS J. JR.	1961	M	Baseball
PALT CHARLES I.	1932	M	Baseball
PARISIEN ARTHUR EMILE	1928	M	Baseball
PARKER CHRISTIAN MICHAEL	1996	M	Baseball
PASSILLA MICHAEL KENNEDY	1989	M	Baseball
PASSINAULT STEPHEN M.	1984	M	Baseball
PAVELA STEPHEN L. JR.	1948	M	Baseball
PAVLINA CRAIG STEVEN	1988	M	Baseball
PEARSON JAMES MARTIN	1926	M	Baseball
PELTIER DANIEL EDWARD	1991	M	Baseball
PERCONTE JEFFREY DAVID	2000	M	Baseball
PERRY VICTOR	1930	M	Baseball
PESAVENTO PATRICK EDWARD	1988	M	Baseball
PETERS BRIAN EUGENE	1968	M	Baseball
PETITCLAIR PAUL JOSEPH	1962	M	Baseball
PETRZELKA RAYMOND J.	1949	M	Baseball
PHELPS DAN EARL	1972	M	Baseball
PHELPS JAMES JOSEPH	1970	M	Baseball
PILNEY ANTON JAMES	1936	M	Baseball
PINELLI RALPH RAYMOND	1941	M	Baseball
PINELLI ROY WILLIAM M.D.	1940	M	Baseball
PIOTROWICZ BRIAN LEE	1990	M	Baseball
PITTMAN MARK FRANCIS	1974	M	Baseball
POLISKY JOHN	1928	M	Baseball
POLLOCK TIMOTHY SEAN	1977	M	Baseball
PONZEVIC JOSEPH JOHN	1936	M	Baseball
POPPLETON BRET PATRICK	1997	M	Baseball
PORZEL ALEC PAUL	2001	M	Baseball
POWELL STEPHEN GERARD	1986	M	Baseball
POWELL WILLIAM J. JR.	1934	M	Baseball
PRENDERGAST EDWARD M.	1927	M	Baseball
PRICE THOMAS ORVILLE	1994	M	Baseball
PRISTER TIMOTHY J.	1982	M	Baseball
PRYBLO PAUL PHILLIP	1997	M	Baseball
PULLANO RICHARD LOUIS	1979	M	Baseball
PUPLIS ANDREW JOSEPH	1938	M	Baseball
QUINLAN JOSEPH WEBER	1926	M	Baseball
RASCHER NORBERT H. SR.	1934	M	Baseball
RATTERMAN GEORGE WILLIAM	1949	M	Baseball
REARDON TIMOTHY ALOYSIUS SR.	1963	M	Baseball
REED RONALD LEE	1965	M	Baseball
REESE FRANK ALEXANDER	1925	M	Baseball
REGAN GEORGE JOSEPH	1914	M	Baseball
REILLY HAROLD F. DR. JR.	1954	M	Baseball
REITHER PHILIP H.	1947	M	Baseball
RESTOVICH GEORGE BRENNAN	1996	M	Baseball
RESTOVICH GEORGE FLOYD	1968	M	Baseball
REYNOLDS JOHN STEPHEN SR.	1954	M	Baseball
RICHARDS ROWAN ARTHUR	1996	M	Baseball
RIDDELL MICHAEL THOMAS	1973	M	Baseball
RIDGE JOSEPH STEPHEN	1953	M	Baseball
RIEDER MICHAEL JOSEPH M.D.	1964	M	Baseball
RIZZO CODY MICHAEL	2006	M	Baseball
RODEMS GREGORY JOHN	1980	M	Baseball
ROEMER ROBERT WALTER	1973	M	Baseball
ROGERS JOHN ARTHUR	1969	M	Baseball
ROGERS SCOTT DAVID	1987	M	Baseball
RONAY STEPHEN H.	1927	M	Baseball
ROONEY MICHAEL PATRICK III	1992	M	Baseball
ROTKIS MICHAEL CHARLES DR.	1990	M	Baseball
RUSSO J. ALBERT M.D.	1932	M	Baseball
RUST OSKAR D.	1929	M	Baseball
RUSTECK RICHARD FRANCIS	1963	M	Baseball
RYAN WILLIAM R. SR.	1911	M	Baseball
RYDELL OSCAR FERDINAND	1937	M	Baseball
SALMON LOUIS J.	1905	M	Baseball
SANCHEZ JAVIER ARMANDO	2004	M	Baseball
SANFILIPPO FRANCIS JOSEPH	1944	M	Baseball
SAUGET RICHARD ARNOLD JR.	1995	M	Baseball
SAUGET RICHARD ARNOLD SR.	1966	M	Baseball
SCAFATI ORLANDO MICHAEL	1936	M	Baseball
SCANLON RAYMOND JOSEPH	1909	M	Baseball
SCARPELLI LEONARDO ENRICO	1947	M	Baseball
SCARPELLI NICHOLAS P. JR.	1970	M	Baseball
SCARPITTO ROBERT FRANK	1961	M	Baseball
SCHLOEMER JAY BERT	1967	M	Baseball
SCHMALZ DARIN BLAINE	1997	M	Baseball
SCHMIDT PETER DAVID	1974	M	Baseball
SCHMITZ MARK RICHARD	1975	M	Baseball
SCHMITZ RONALD JOSEPH D.D.S.	1971	M	Baseball
SCHNEIDER GEORGE JOHN DR.	1947	M	Baseball
SCHOEN WILLIAM CLIFFORD	1971	M	Baseball
SCHOLL JUSTIN BLAKE	1997	M	Baseball

NAME	YEAR	GENDER	SPORT
SCHOMER JASON ROBERT	1985	M	Baseball
SCHRADER JOSEPH HERMAN	1965	M	Baseball
SCHRALL LEO S.	1929	M	Baseball
SCHUSTER KENNETH PAUL	1974	M	Baseball
SCRIVANICH CHARLES JOSEPH	1960	M	Baseball
SELCER RICHARD JAMES	1959	M	Baseball
SENECAL ROBERT JOSEPH DR.	1958	M	Baseball
SEPE THOMAS ANTHONY	1935	M	Baseball
SERENA MARTIN JOSEPH II	1976	M	Baseball
SHAUGHNESSY FRANK J.	1906	M	Baseball
SHAW THOMAS JOSEPH	1989	M	Baseball
SHEEHAN THOMAS JOSEPH	1948	M	Baseball
SHEEHAN WILLIAM F. SR.	1924	M	Baseball
SHERMAN WILLIAM HOWARD	1949	M	Baseball
SHIELDS THOMAS CHARLES	1986	M	Baseball
SHILLIDAY E. ALEXANDER MR.	2000	M	Baseball
SHOLL JAMES KENT	1977	M	Baseball
SILER SCOTT WILLIAM	1982	M	Baseball
SIMENDINGER MARK FRANCIS	1980	M	Baseball
SIMONE STEPHEN MICHAEL	1974	M	Baseball
SINNES DAVID ANTHONY	1993	M	Baseball
SISKO ZACHARY WALSH	2004	M	Baseball
SKUPIEN STEPHEN SEAN	1988	M	Baseball
SLAVINSKY THOMAS ALBERT	1977	M	Baseball
SMITH BRYAN LEE	1982	M	Baseball
SMITH DAVID JAMES	1978	M	Baseball
SMITH EDWARD P. IV	2006	M	Baseball
SMITH IRVIN MARTIN	1993	M	Baseball
SMITH JAMES LEE	1975	M	Baseball
SMITH RICHARD PAUL	1927	M	Baseball
SMITH WILLIAM GEORGE	1933	M	Baseball
SMULLEN HAROLD R.	1944	M	Baseball
SMULLEN RICHARD A.	1949	M	Baseball
SNIEGOWSKI DONALD CHESTER DR.	1956	M	Baseball
SNOW CHARLES THOMAS	1966	M	Baseball
SNYDER CASEY BEGGS	1984	M	Baseball
SNYDER H. JACK JR.	1976	M	Baseball
SOLLMANN SCOTT ALBERT	1997	M	Baseball
SOLLMANN STEVEN RICHARD	2004	M	Baseball
SOOS KENNETH JAMES	1988	M	Baseball
SPAETH GERALD LEO	1956	M	Baseball
STANLEY STEPHEN VANORMER	2002	M	Baseball
STARR WILLIAM GREGORY	1978	M	Baseball
STAVISKY BRIAN SCOTT	2004	M	Baseball
STAVISKY W. DANIEL MR. III	1998	M	Baseball
STEPHAN ANTON CHARLES	1904	M	Baseball
STEWART JOHN KEATING	1946	M	Baseball
STOLTZ MITCHELL THOMAS	1976	M	Baseball
STONIKAS WILLIAM JOHN	1983	M	Baseball
STOPPER ANTHONY JAMES	1906	M	Baseball
STOUFFER JAMES BLAKE	1963	M	Baseball
STRATTA ROBERT JOSEPH M.D.	1976	M	Baseball
STRICKROTH MATTHEW MICHAEL	2002	M	Baseball
SULLIVAN CHESTER NICHOLAS	1940	M	Baseball
SULLIVAN JOSEPH M.	1929	M	Baseball
SWEET GEORGE H.	1896	M	Baseball
SYMEON CHARLES S.	1958	M	Baseball
SZAJKO DANIEL KARL	1982	M	Baseball
SZAJKO RAYMOND ALLEN	1988	M	Baseball
SZAJKO THOMAS JOSEPH	1966	M	Baseball
SZCZEPANSKI STEVEN CRAIG	2000	M	Baseball
TALLETT JOHN HAROLD	1943	M	Baseball
TAMAYO IGNACIO DANIEL	2001	M	Baseball
TASCH CHARLES JOSEPH	1982	M	Baseball
TENCZA THOMAS JOHN	1967	M	Baseball
TESCHKE WILLIAM JOHN	1956	M	Baseball
THAMAN JOSEPH BENJAMIN	2004	M	Baseball
THORNTON THOMAS FREDERICK	2006	M	Baseball
TOMMASINI KEVIN PAUL	1994	M	Baseball
TOPHAM RYAN GEORGE	1996	M	Baseball
TOPOLSKI PATRICK JOSEPH	1967	M	Baseball
TRACY WILLIAM JOSEPH	1943	M	Baseball
TRAPP HAROLD JOSEPH JR.	1958	M	Baseball
TREMBLAY MARK CHRISTOPHER	1954	M	Baseball
TRUDEAU MICHAEL ANDRE	1985	M	Baseball
TURCO PAUL JOHN JR.	1997	M	Baseball
TWOHY JAMES F. JR.	1955	M	Baseball
TWOMBLEY DENNIS ALAN	1994	M	Baseball
UNDERKOFLER JOSEPH M.	1935	M	Baseball
UST BRANT STEVEN	2000	M	Baseball
VALENZUELA HENRY E.	1982	M	Baseball
VANTHOURNOUT RICHARD ALAN	1986	M	Baseball
VAUGHAN CHAMP C.	1927	M	Baseball
VELCHECK ARNOLD ANTHONY	1936	M	Baseball
VERDUZCO STEVEN BENJAMIN	1993	M	Baseball
VERHOESTRA ARTHUR JOSEPH	1939	M	Baseball
VILORIA BRANDON JONATHAN	2003	M	Baseball
VOELLINGER DANIEL D.	1980	M	Baseball
VOGELE GREGORY JOSEPH	1991	M	Baseball
VOITIER M. ROBERT JR.	1970	M	Baseball
VUONO CARL II	1984	M	Baseball
VUONO MARTIN JOHN	1981	M	Baseball
WAGNER JEFFREY CHRISTOPHER	2000	M	Baseball
WALANIA ALAN JOHN	1994	M	Baseball
WALBRUN THOMAS ALFRED	1976	M	Baseball
WALDRON JAMES ALBERT	1937	M	Baseball
WALDRON JOSEPH JOHN	1936	M	Baseball
WALKER MICHAEL EUGENE	1963	M	Baseball
WATZKE MARK GERALD	1986	M	Baseball
WEISS BRENT MITCHELL	2005	M	Baseball
WELCH THOMAS J.	1905	M	Baseball
WENTWORTH GEORGE ROLAND	1936	M	Baseball
WIDELSKI WALLACE MATTHEW	1997	M	Baseball
WILKINS STEPHEN CODY	2004	M	Baseball
WILSON FRANCIS JOSEPH SR.	1928	M	Baseball
WOJCIK EDWARD NICK	1960	M	Baseball
WOLFE DONALD FANNING JR.	1979	M	Baseball
WOOD HOWARD EDWARD	1974	M	Baseball
WOOLWINE JAMES ROY	1963	M	Baseball
WROBLESKI KOREY TODD	1992	M	Baseball
YAEGER JOSEPH LOUIS	1956	M	Baseball
YAWMAN DAVID MARNOC	1990	M	Baseball
YORE WILLIAM JOSEPH	1929	M	Baseball
ZABROSKI PETER JUDE	1978	M	Baseball
ZAPPIA ANTHONY MICHAEL	1972	M	Baseball
ZIEMIENSKI JOSEPH A.	1947	M	Baseball
ZIMONT LARRY VICTOR	2000	M	Baseball
ZOLNOWSKI RAYMOND MICHAEL	1967	M	Baseball
ADAMSON MATTHEW THOMAS	1993	M	Basketball
ALLEN DONALD LEWIS	1937	M	Basketball
ANDERSON ROGER EVERETT	1976	M	Basketball
ANDREE TIMOTHY PAUL	1983	M	Basketball
ANDREOLI JOHN WILLIAM JR.	1963	M	Basketball
ARNZEN ROBERT LOUIS	1969	M	Basketball
AUBREY LLOYD ROY	1956	M	Basketball
AYOTTE R. LEE	1957	M	Basketball
BAGLEY DANIEL MAURICE	1951	M	Basketball
BALDWIN JOHN ARTHUR	1933	M	Basketball
BARLOW KENNETH	1986	M	Basketball
BARNHORST LEO A.	1949	M	Basketball
BATTON DAVID ROBERT	1978	M	Basketball
BEDAN JACK WILLIAM SR.	1957	M	Basketball
BEEUWSAERT MATT	1986	M	Basketball
BEKELJA LEWIS MICHAEL	1960	M	Basketball
BELL GARY MCARTHUR	1997	M	Basketball
BENNETT ELMER JAMES	1992	M	Basketball
BENTLEY ROBERT CECIL	1967	M	Basketball
BERNARDI JOHN ARTHUR	1967	M	Basketball
BERTRAND JOSEPH GUSTAVIUS	1954	M	Basketball
BONICELLI ORLANDO A.	1944	M	Basketball
BORNHORST THOMAS LOUIS	1966	M	Basketball
BORYLA VINCENT J.	1948	M	Basketball
BOSL GREGORY PAUL	2005	M	Basketball
BOYER BROOKS CHRISTOPHER	1994	M	Basketball
BRADTKE ROBERT JOSEPH	1960	M	Basketball
BRANNING RICHARD D.	1980	M	Basketball
BRAY JAMES F.	1929	M	Basketball
BRENNAN JOHN R.	1949	M	Basketball
BRENNAN THOMAS BERNARD	1944	M	Basketball
BROKAW GARY GEORGE	1975	M	Basketball
BROUCEK WILLIAM MYLES	1956	M	Basketball
BROWN EARL MELVIN JR.	1939	M	Basketball
BURNS JAMES JOSEPH	1924	M	Basketball
BURNS THOMAS AMBROSE	1932	M	Basketball
BUSCH VINCENT DE PAUL	1931	M	Basketball
BUTLER CHARLES J.	1943	M	Basketball
CALDWELL THOMAS HALE	1967	M	Basketball
CARNES JAMES ROBERT SR.	1942	M	Basketball
CARPENTER ROBERT JEFFREY	1978	M	Basketball
CARR AUSTIN GEORGE	1971	M	Basketball
CARROLL DENNIS ARTHUR	1999	M	Basketball
CARROLL MATTHEW JOHN	2003	M	Basketball
CATLETT SIDNEY LEON	1971	M	Basketball
CLAY DWIGHT	1975	M	Basketball
CONNOR SEAN ERIC	1989	M	Basketball
CONROY JOHN LOUIS	1927	M	Basketball
CORNETT L. RICK II	2006	M	Basketball
CORNETTE JORDAN CHASE	2005	M	Basketball
COZEN CARL JOSEPH	1994	M	Basketball
CREEVY RICHARD CASSELL	1943	M	Basketball
CRIMMINS BERNARD ANTHONY	1942	M	Basketball
CROSBY WILLIAM HENRY	1961	M	Basketball
CROTTY PETER JAMES	1975	M	Basketball
CROUCH STEPHEN HUGH DR.	1988	M	Basketball
CROWE CLEM FREDERICK	1926	M	Basketball
CROWE FRANCIS A.	1929	M	Basketball
CROWE LEO JEROME	1934	M	Basketball
CURRAN FRANCIS H.	1944	M	Basketball
DAHMAN RAYMOND J.	1928	M	Basketball
DANTLEY ADRIAN	1978	M	Basketball
DEARIE JOHN CHARLES	1962	M	Basketball
DECOOK RAYMOND LAPEER	1932	M	Basketball
DEE JOHN FRANCIS JR.	1952	M	Basketball
DEMOTS JOHN EDWARD	1937	M	Basketball
DERRIG JAMES RICHARD	1969	M	Basketball
DEVINE ROBERT THOMAS	1958	M	Basketball
DIENHART JOSEPH STANLEY	1926	M	Basketball
DILLON JAMES RICHARD	2000	M	Basketball
DOLAN JAMES ARTHUR	1986	M	Basketball
DONOVAN CLARENCE JOSEPH	1931	M	Basketball
DREW WILLIAM G.	1975	M	Basketball
DUCHARME PAUL EDMUND SR.	1939	M	Basketball
DUDGEON PATRICK EDWARD	1965	M	Basketball
DUFF DAN A.	1985	M	Basketball
EGART JOHN JOSEPH	1972	M	Basketball
ELLERY KEVIN LEON	1991	M	Basketball
ELLIS H. REX MR.	1940	M	Basketball
ELLIS LAPHONSO DARNELL SR.	1992	M	Basketball
ELSER DONALD LEWIS	1936	M	Basketball
ENRIGHT REX EDWARD	1926	M	Basketball
ERLENBAUGH RICHARD ALBERT	1964	M	Basketball
ERTEL MARK ANTHONY	1940	M	Basketball
FABIAN CHRISTOPHER A. M.D.	1979	M	Basketball
FANNON JOHN JOSEPH	1956	M	Basketball
FAUGHT ROBERT EDWARD	1944	M	Basketball
FEHLIG VINCENT JOSEPH	1934	M	Basketball
FICHTEL NEAL DAVID	1951	M	Basketball
FISH JAMES LEO	1911	M	Basketball
FLOWERS BRUCE D	1979	M	Basketball
FOLEY JOHN PATRICK	1950	M	Basketball
FORD JOHN FRANCIS	1937	M	Basketball
FRANCIS TORIN JAMAL	2006	M	Basketball
FRANGER MICHAEL CRAIG	1969	M	Basketball
FREDRICK JOSEPH BARTON	1990	M	Basketball
FRIEL KEITH MCFADDEN	1998	M	Basketball
GAGLIONE FRANCIS JOSEPH	1939	M	Basketball
GALLAGHER JOHN FRANCIS JR.	1970	M	Basketball
GARRITY PATRICK JOSEPH	1998	M	Basketball
GATENS DONALD JOSEPH	1949	M	Basketball
GEMMELL DOUGLAS GEORGE	1972	M	Basketball
GIBBONS JAMES VINCENT	1953	M	Basketball
GILHOOLEY FRANCIS PATRICK	1947	M	Basketball
GILLESPIE C. JOSEPH	1941	M	Basketball
GLEASON EDWARD JAMES	1958	M	Basketball
GLEASON JOSEPH THOMAS	1938	M	Basketball
GOONEN JOHN J. DR. SR.	1948	M	Basketball
GORDON PAUL C.	1949	M	Basketball
GOTSCH MATTHEW JAMES	1997	M	Basketball
GOTTLIEB DOUGLAS MITCHELL	1996	M	Basketball
GRANEY MICHAEL ROBERT	1960	M	Basketball
GRANT DONALD CHESTER	1922	M	Basketball
GRAVES DAVID RHODE	2002	M	Basketball
HAEFNER J. RANDALL	1978	M	Basketball
HAMILTON ROBERT ANTHONY	1928	M	Basketball
HANSEN THOMAS JOSEPH	1974	M	Basketball
HANZLIK WILLIAM H.	1980	M	Basketball
HASSETT WILLIAM JOSEPH	1947	M	Basketball
HAWKINS KEVIN JEROME	1981	M	Basketball
HAWKINS THOMAS JEROME	1959	M	Basketball
HEALY TIMOTHY JOSEPH	1980	M	Basketball
HICKEY PHILIP EDWARD	1999	M	Basketball
HICKS SCOTT LAMONT III	1987	M	Basketball
HILLER JOHN MALCOLM	1948	M	Basketball
HINGA JAMES DOUGLAS	1971	M	Basketball
HINGA WILLIAM T. JR.	1973	M	Basketball
HONINGFORD RICHARD HENRY	1954	M	Basketball
HOOVER RYAN JAMES	1996	M	Basketball
HOPKINS JOHN ANDREW	1936	M	Basketball
HORNUNG PAUL V.	1957	M	Basketball
HOST PAUL ANTHONY	1933	M	Basketball
HUMPHREY RYAN ASHLEY	2002	M	Basketball
INGELSBY MARTIN EDWARD	2001	M	Basketball
IRELAND GEORGE MARTIN	1936	M	Basketball
IRELAND MICHAEL PATRICK	1959	M	Basketball
JACKSON JAMERE	1990	M	Basketball
JACKSON TRACY C.	1981	M	Basketball
JASTRAB ROBERT JOSEPH D.D.S.	1956	M	Basketball
JESEWITZ LAWRENCE PHILLIP	1965	M	Basketball
JOHNSON H. CLAY	1932	M	Basketball
JONES J. COLLIS MR.	1971	M	Basketball
JONES TORRIAN D'ANDRE	2004	M	Basketball
JORDAN JOHN JOSEPH	1935	M	Basketball
JORDAN THOMAS GEORGE	1938	M	Basketball
JUSTICE LAMARR EDWARD	1995	M	Basketball
KANE MICHAEL GEORGE	1923	M	Basketball
KAUFMANN A. FRANK MR. SR.	1949	M	Basketball
KEATING LEO DANIEL	1933	M	Basketball
KELLER BRIAN MICHAEL	1968	M	Basketball
KELLY JOHN EDWARD JR.	1947	M	Basketball
KELLY JOHN HAROLD	1947	M	Basketball

NAME	YEAR	GENDER	SPORT
KELLY M. MARC MR.	1982	M	Basketball
KEMPTON TIMOTHY JOSEPH	1986	M	Basketball
KING PAUL LOUIS	1956	M	Basketball
KIZER MARSHALL FORCE	1929	M	Basketball
KLIER EUGENE PAUL DR.	1940	M	Basketball
KLIER LEO ANTHONY	1946	M	Basketball
KLUCK RICHARD J.	1949	M	Basketball
KNIGHT TOBY THOMAS	1977	M	Basketball
KRAUSE EDWARD W.	1934	M	Basketball
KUKA RAPHAEL EUGENE	1944	M	Basketball
KUKA RAPHAEL EUGENE DR. JR.	1967	M	Basketball
KUROWSKI KEITH MICHAEL	1996	M	Basketball
KUZMICZ DAVID P.	1977	M	Basketball
LAIMBEER WILLIAM JR.	1979	M	Basketball
LATIMORE DENNIS MARION	2005	M	Basketball
LESLIE LEROY EDWARD	1952	M	Basketball
LEWINSKI NORBERT EDWIN	1953	M	Basketball
LEY THEODORE NOONAN	1926	M	Basketball
LOFTUS JOHN R.	1949	M	Basketball
LOGAN F. LESLIE	1923	M	Basketball
LOVE KARL FRANZ DR.	1983	M	Basketball
LUCAS WILLIAM PHILLIP	1973	M	Basketball
LUEPKE HENRY FRANCIS JR.	1957	M	Basketball
LUNGREN JOHN CHARLES M.D.	1938	M	Basketball
LUSTIG DANIEL JOSEPH	2003	M	Basketball
MACURA JERE	2003	M	Basketball
MAHONEY PHILIP SHERIDAN	1925	M	Basketball
MALLOY EDWARD A. REV. CSC	1963	M	Basketball
MANNER DEREK GLENN	1998	M	Basketball
MANNING JOHN JOSEPH M.D.	1937	M	Basketball
MARTIN RAY A.	1977	M	Basketball
MATTHEWS J LT.COL. USMC RET.	1963	M	Basketball
MAYL EUGENE A.	1924	M	Basketball
MCCARTHY EMMETT DANIEL	1960	M	Basketball
MCCARTHY JOHN F.	1958	M	Basketball
MCCLOSKEY GERALD LEO	1954	M	Basketball
MCGANN JAMES CHARLES	1966	M	Basketball
MCGINN EDWARD JOSEPH	1954	M	Basketball
MCGRAW THOMAS EARL	1972	M	Basketball
MCGUFF ALBERT L.	1934	M	Basketball
MCKENNA JOSEPH W.	1918	M	Basketball
MCKIRCHY JAMES ROSS	1968	M	Basketball
MCNALLY VINCENT A. SR.	1927	M	Basketball
MEEHAN JOHN FRANCIS JR.	1971	M	Basketball
MEHRE HARRY J.	1922	M	Basketball
METTLER VICTOR HERBERT	1935	M	Basketball
MEYER RAYMOND JOSEPH	1938	M	Basketball
MILLER DANIEL BRIAN	2003	M	Basketball
MILLER JAY MR.	1965	M	Basketball
MILLER PETER MICHAEL	1997	M	Basketball
MITCHELL MICHAEL THOMAS	1982	M	Basketball
MOIR JOHN WILLIAM	1938	M	Basketball
MONAHAN JAMES EDWARD	1967	M	Basketball
MOORE DANIEL A.	1927	M	Basketball
MORELLI JOSEPH PETER	1957	M	Basketball
MURPHY CHRISTOPHER JOHN	2006	M	Basketball
MURPHY DWIGHT EUGENE	1969	M	Basketball
MURPHY TROY BRANDON	2000	M	Basketball
NANNI CHRISTOPHER	1988	M	Basketball
NARDONE JOSEPH R.	1939	M	Basketball
NEUMAYR JACK WALLACE	1952	M	Basketball
NEWBOLD ROBERT G.	1929	M	Basketball
NEWELL CASEY JEROME	1985	M	Basketball
NICGORSKI STEPHEN JOHN	1988	M	Basketball
NICKOL BENJAMIN THOMAS	2006	M	Basketball
NIEMIERA JOHN RICHARD	1944	M	Basketball
NOONAN WILLIAM FRANKLIN	1961	M	Basketball
NOVAK GARY JAMES M.D.	1974	M	Basketball
NOWAK PAUL THOMAS	1938	M	Basketball
NYIKOS JOHN J.	1927	M	Basketball
OBERBRUNER KENNETH LOUIS	1940	M	Basketball
O'CONNELL MICHAEL PAUL	1971	M	Basketball
O'CONNOR MARTIN RICHARD	1951	M	Basketball
O'HALLORAN JAMES E. JR.	1949	M	Basketball
O'KANE JOSEPH CORNELIUS	1936	M	Basketball
O'NEILL KEVIN MICHAEL	1966	M	Basketball
O'SHEA KEVIN C.	1950	M	Basketball
OWENS SKYLARD BRASHAWN	2000	M	Basketball
PADDOCK SCOTT MILAN	1990	M	Basketball
PALMER TODD WILLIAM	2000	M	Basketball
PATERNO WILLIAM ROBERT	1977	M	Basketball
PAXSON JOHN MACBETH	1983	M	Basketball
PERRINE ALFRED JEROLOMAN	1941	M	Basketball
PETERS JEFFREY SCOTT	1988	M	Basketball
PLEICK JOHN CLINTON	1971	M	Basketball
POPE ARTHUR W.	1942	M	Basketball
PRICE JOSEPH PAUL	1986	M	Basketball
QUINN CHARLES F. JR.	1934	M	Basketball
QUINN CHRISTOPHER JAMES	2006	M	Basketball
QUINN DANIEL BRIAN	1969	M	Basketball

NAME	YEAR	GENDER	SPORT
QUINN FRANCIS BERNARD	1942	M	Basketball
RAINEY VERNELL PAUL	1998	M	Basketball
RASMUSSEN HANS GUNNAR	2001	M	Basketball
RATTERMAN GEORGE WILLIAM	1949	M	Basketball
REARDON THOMAS A.	1924	M	Basketball
REBORA STEPHEN RICHARD	1955	M	Basketball
REED RONALD LEE	1965	M	Basketball
REGELEAN JAMES D.	1972	M	Basketball
REINHART THOMAS JAMES	1959	M	Basketball
RENSBERGER ROBERT LAMAR	1943	M	Basketball
REO ARMAND JOSEPH	1962	M	Basketball
RESTOVICH GEORGE FLOYD	1968	M	Basketball
REYNOLDS JOHN STEPHEN SR.	1954	M	Basketball
RISKA EDWARD JOSEPH	1941	M	Basketball
RIVERS DAVID LEE	1988	M	Basketball
ROBINSON KEITH LEON	1990	M	Basketball
ROESLER KARL EDMUND SR.	1962	M	Basketball
ROMANOWSKI THEODORE ANTHONY	1962	M	Basketball
RONCHETTI PETER JOHN	1918	M	Basketball
ROSENTHAL RICHARD A.	1954	M	Basketball
ROSS JON ANDREW	1994	M	Basketball
ROSS JOSEPH FRED	1994	M	Basketball
ROYAL DONALD A. JR.	1987	M	Basketball
RUCKER CECIL ELWOOD JR.	1984	M	Basketball
RUSSELL MALIK NAKI	1993	M	Basketball
RYAN F. LARRY MR.	1948	M	Basketball
RYAN LAWRENCE PATRICK	1941	M	Basketball
SADOWSKI EDWARD MARION	1939	M	Basketball
SAHM WALTER EDWARD JR.	1965	M	Basketball
SAHM WILLIAM S. JR.	1977	M	Basketball
SALINAS GILBERTO R.	1981	M	Basketball
SCHMELZER GREGORY PAUL	1974	M	Basketball
SCHNURR EDWARD JULIUS JR.	1962	M	Basketball
SCHUCKMAN MYRON JOSEPH	1976	M	Basketball
SCHUMACHER ALLAN FRANCIS	1932	M	Basketball
SEEBERG MARK SHAW	1971	M	Basketball
SHEEHAN WILLIAM F. SR.	1924	M	Basketball
SHEFFIELD LAWRENCE A.	1965	M	Basketball
SHUMATE JOHN H.	1974	M	Basketball
SILINSKI DONALD	1973	M	Basketball
SINGER CYRINES HOWARD	1947	M	Basketball
SINGLETON TIMOTHY EDWARD	1991	M	Basketball
SINNOTT THOMAS F. JR.	1971	M	Basketball
SKARICH SAMUEL JOHN	1964	M	Basketball
SKRZYCKI ROBERT EDWARD	1960	M	Basketball
SLEIGH ANDREW F. SR.	1927	M	Basketball
SLUBY THOMAS GRIFFIN	1984	M	Basketball
SMITH DONALD PAUL	1940	M	Basketball
SMITH EDWARD BERNARD	1930	M	Basketball
SMITH MAURICE FRANCIS	1921	M	Basketball
SMYTH JOHN PHILLIP REV.	1957	M	Basketball
SOBEK GEORGE EDWARD SR.	1942	M	Basketball
SPENCER BARRY STEVEN	1985	M	Basketball
STEINER THOMAS A. REV.	1899	M	Basketball
STEPHENS JOHN FRANCIS	1955	M	Basketball
STEVENS CHRISTOPHER L.	1974	M	Basketball
STRASSER DONALD J.	1952	M	Basketball
SULLIVAN JAMES EDWARD	1961	M	Basketball
SULLIVAN THOMAS E.	1957	M	Basketball
SULLIVAN WILLIAM JOSEPH	1954	M	Basketball
SWANAGAN HAROLD DARIUS	2002	M	Basketball
SWEET DAIMON LAWRENCE	1992	M	Basketball
TAYLOR WILLIAM PAUL	1995	M	Basketball
THEBAULT MARK JOHN	1988	M	Basketball
THOMAS CHARLES CALVIN	2002	M	Basketball
THOMAS CHRISTOPHER RYAN	2005	M	Basketball
TIMMERMANS THOMAS ANDRIES	2004	M	Basketball
TOWER KEITH RAYMOND	1992	M	Basketball
TOWNSEND MICHAEL LAVON	1974	M	Basketball
TOWNSEND WILLIE CORNELIUS	1974	M	Basketball
TRACY JOHN BRIAN	1968	M	Basketball
TRIPUCKA P. KELLY	1981	M	Basketball
TULLY JOHN DENNIS	1961	M	Basketball
VALES JOSEPH JOHN	1967	M	Basketball
VALES RAMON JOHN JR.	1961	M	Basketball
VARGA THOMAS JAMES JR.	1975	M	Basketball
VARNER WILLIAM J. JR.	1983	M	Basketball
VIGNALI ANTHONY LOUIS	1968	M	Basketball
VINCIGUERRA RALPH JOSEPH	1943	M	Basketball
VOCE GARY ANTHONY	1988	M	Basketball
VOEGELE JOSEPH THOMAS	1934	M	Basketball
WADE FRANCIS CHASE SR.	1936	M	Basketball
WALLJASPER DENNIS JOSEPH	1962	M	Basketball
WARD CHARLES J.	1926	M	Basketball
WATKINS BRIAN VINCENT	1995	M	Basketball
WEIMAN WILLIAM EDWARD	1956	M	Basketball
WHITE ADMORE VAUGHN	1997	M	Basketball
WHITMORE ROBERT LEE	1969	M	Basketball
WILCOX D. HUGHES	1952	M	Basketball
WILCOX STANLEY	1981	M	Basketball

NAME	YEAR	GENDER	SPORT
WILLIAMS DONALD EDGAR	1978	M	Basketball
WILLIAMS JASON JAMAL	1995	M	Basketball
WILLIAMS L. JAMES MR.	1958	M	Basketball
WILLIAMS TAVARES MONTGOMERE JR.	1993	M	Basketball
WILLS NICHOLAS JOSEPH	1998	M	Basketball
WITTENBERG CHARLES HENRY	1957	M	Basketball
WOLBECK KENNETH JAMES	1974	M	Basketball
WOLF CHARLES JOSEPH	1945	M	Basketball
WOOLRIDGE ORLANDO VERNADA	1981	M	Basketball
WUKOVITS THOMAS WILLIAM	1938	M	Basketball
WYCHE ANTONI TYJUAN	1999	M	Basketball
YOUNG MARCUS DION	1997	M	Basketball
ZIZNEWSKI JAY JAMES	1970	M	Basketball
ADAMS PAUL MICHAEL	1979	M	Cheerleader
BERGIN T. PATRICK MR. JR.	1979	M	Cheerleader
BERNAT JOHN JOSEPH	1961	M	Cheerleader
BINZ DAVID PATRICK	2005	M	Cheerleader
BORGMANN DOUGLAS PAUL	2003	M	Cheerleader
BOSBOUS MARK WALTER	2001	M	Cheerleader
BRODERICK L. G. MR.	1968	M	Cheerleader
BROUGHTON PAUL JAMES	1981	M	Cheerleader
BROWN MICHAEL ANTHONY	2001	M	Cheerleader
CAMPION DANIEL GEORGE	2005	M	Cheerleader
CARRICO HAROLD THOMAS	1977	M	Cheerleader
CHAMBERLIN KYLE EDWARD	2006	M	Cheerleader
CHISMIRE KEVIN JOSEPH DR.	1972	M	Cheerleader
CLARK JAMES BENEDICT	1933	M	Cheerleader
CLEMENTS DANIEL J. III	1970	M	Cheerleader
CLOUSE JAMES GERARD	1977	M	Cheerleader
CONLEY JOHN	N/A	M	Cheerleader
COREY MICHAEL JOHN	1975	M	Cheerleader
COSGROVE JOSEPH M.	1979	M	Cheerleader
CRAMER RICHARD J. II	1986	M	Cheerleader
CROUCH RICHARD LEE	1968	M	Cheerleader
D'ANGELO RONALD JOSEPH	1986	M	Cheerleader
DOWNARD ANDREW JOSEPH	2004	M	Cheerleader
EARLEY ANTHONY FRANCIS	1947	M	Cheerleader
ELLIS TRACY JOHN	1995	M	Cheerleader
ERTEL JASON RYAN	2003	M	Cheerleader
FIORE JAMES JOHN	1961	M	Cheerleader
FISCHER PETER ANTHONY	1964	M	Cheerleader
FOLEY THOMAS J. JR.	1935	M	Cheerleader
FREMER DANIEL TODD	2001	M	Cheerleader
GEE RYAN MURRAY	1998	M	Cheerleader
GHELARDI MICHAEL JOSEPH	1965	M	Cheerleader
GIESZELMANN JAMES BRIAN	2005	M	Cheerleader
GLOVER JAMES CARL	1995	M	Cheerleader
GOMEZ DON ANTHONY	1991	M	Cheerleader
GONZALES DOUGLAS MARION	1959	M	Cheerleader
HAWRYLUK MATTHEW JOHN	2000	M	Cheerleader
HEALY EDWARD MORELAND E.	1957	M	Cheerleader
HEFFERNAN PATRICK MICHAEL	1975	M	Cheerleader
HEROMAN FRED WILLIAM	1964	M	Cheerleader
HERRLE RICHARD ALLEN	1951	M	Cheerleader
HILLARD SAMUEL LAWRENCE	2003	M	Cheerleader
HOURIHAN EDWARD WILLIAM	1979	M	Cheerleader
HUEBNER CHADLEY RYAN DR.	1996	M	Cheerleader
INGRAM JAMES M. DR. III	1977	M	Cheerleader
JENISTA MICHAEL J.	2005	M	Cheerleader
KAHL THOMAS ALLAN	1965	M	Cheerleader
KEEGAN ROBERT JAMES	1956	M	Cheerleader
KEEGAN THOMAS JOHN	1960	M	Cheerleader
KENNEDY JOSEPH EDWARD	1932	M	Cheerleader
KIERL THOMAS PHILIP	2003	M	Cheerleader
KIZER RICHARD WILLIAM	1998	M	Cheerleader
KIZER ROBERT THOMAS	1997	M	Cheerleader
KOHLES GEOFFREY DAVID	1989	M	Cheerleader
LANKTREE C.J. MR.	2001	M	Cheerleader
LEICHT WILLIAM DAVID D.D.S.	1980	M	Cheerleader
LOTZE THOMAS H.	1950	M	Cheerleader
MACALUSO MICHAEL C.	2004	M	Cheerleader
MACDONELL JAMES RYAN	2005	M	Cheerleader
MASSA EDWARD CLEMENT	1933	M	Cheerleader
MATTINGLY EDWARD ALLEN	1971	M	Cheerleader
MATURI ROBERT KARL	1963	M	Cheerleader
MCDONNELL JESSOP MARK M.D.	1971	M	Cheerleader
MCGLINN JOHN FRANCIS JR.	1952	M	Cheerleader
MCGLINN TERRENCE JOSEPH SR.	1962	M	Cheerleader
MCGUIRE HUGH JOSEPH	1958	M	Cheerleader
MCLAUGHLIN GEORGE EDWARD JR.	1976	M	Cheerleader
MEDRICK EDWARD FRANCIS	2006	M	Cheerleader
MOORE NATHAN DANIEL	2001	M	Cheerleader
MOORE PAUL FRANCIS II	1966	M	Cheerleader
MOORE TYLER OWEN	1993	M	Cheerleader
MORAN TIMOTHY MATTHEW	1998	M	Cheerleader
MORRISON CHARLEY MR.	1974	M	Cheerleader
MUETHING STEPHEN EDWARD	1980	M	Cheerleader
MUGAVERO MICHAEL JAMES DR.	1995	M	Cheerleader
NIENABER J. WALTER	1937	M	Cheerleader
O'HARA DANIEL MOORE	1974	M	Cheerleader

NAME	YEAR	GENDER	SPORT
ISAACS JEROME PAGE	1956	M	Fencing
ISAACS JOHN HENRY DR. JR.	1971	M	Fencing
JACKSON CARL VICTOR	1999	M	Fencing
JACOBS JAMES FRANCIS	1952	M	Fencing
JANIS MICHAEL G. JR.	1985	M	Fencing
JANSEN GEORGE JAMES	1950	M	Fencing
JOAQUIN MANUEL J. JR.	1977	M	Fencing
JOCK PAUL F. II	1965	M	Fencing
JOE RONALD ALAN	1983	M	Fencing
JOHNSON DONALD WILLIAM	1986	M	Fencing
JOHNSON JAMES PAUL	1959	M	Fencing
JOHNSON JERRY MYERS	1960	M	Fencing
JOHNSSON PER ANDERS	1993	M	Fencing
JONES GERALD MICHAEL	1957	M	Fencing
JOYCE JACK ROY	1964	M	Fencing
KALIN GLENN ROSS	1971	M	Fencing
KANE STEVEN MICHAEL	2000	M	Fencing
KEARNS JOHN THOMAS	1958	M	Fencing
KEELER DAVID WILLIAM	1970	M	Fencing
KEHOE KEVIN O'NEILL	1936	M	Fencing
KELLEHER KEVIN CHARLES DR.	1976	M	Fencing
KENNEDY WILLIAM E. III	1964	M	Fencing
KENNEY DANIEL EUGENE	1962	M	Fencing
KEOUGH LAURENCE LEO II	1961	M	Fencing
KICA WILLIAM J.	1978	M	Fencing
KIRBY DAVID WALTER	1991	M	Fencing
KIRSCH MATTHEW BERNARD	1986	M	Fencing
KLEIN JOSEPH ALDRAN	1959	M	Fencing
KLIER JOHN DOYLE	1966	M	Fencing
KOESTER EDWARD CHARLES	1956	M	Fencing
KONZELMAN CHARLES M.	1982	M	Fencing
KORTH PATRICK JAMES	1967	M	Fencing
KOVACS Y. DAVID MR.	1988	M	Fencing
KOWALSKI JAMES FRANCIS	1989	M	Fencing
KROENER KENT MICHAEL	1989	M	Fencing
KRUG LUIS OSPINA	1979	M	Fencing
KURZ RICHARD MICHAEL JR.	1993	M	Fencing
LA VALLE LUKE PAUL III	1999	M	Fencing
LALOGGIA VITO PAUL	1981	M	Fencing
LANGFORD WALTER M. SR.	1930	M	Fencing
LAUCK JOHN ANTHONY	1973	M	Fencing
LAUERMAN JOHN H.	1959	M	Fencing
LAUGHLIN TERRY XAVIER	1960	M	Fencing
LAURENDEAU NORMAND MAURICE	1966	M	Fencing
LEARY PHILIP ADAM	1991	M	Fencing
LEE PHILLIP HOWARD	1997	M	Fencing
LEE THOMAS C. JR.	1959	M	Fencing
LEFEVRE EDOUARD CHARLES	1992	M	Fencing
LEISING JAMES WILLIAM	1942	M	Fencing
LENNERT B. DAVID MR.	1987	M	Fencing
LESSO WILLIAM GEORGE	1953	M	Fencing
LESTER WILLIAM KENNETH	1997	M	Fencing
LETSCHER DAVID MICHAEL	1992	M	Fencing
LONGEWAY THOMAS FRANCIS	1963	M	Fencing
LUBIN GERALD I. M.D.	1949	M	Fencing
LYONS CHRISTOPHER J.	1980	M	Fencing
LYONS JOHN THOMAS III	1970	M	Fencing
LYONS JOHN THOMAS IV	1998	M	Fencing
LYONS MICHAEL JAMES	1973	M	Fencing
MACAULAY MICHAEL GREGORY	2004	M	Fencing
MACDONALD COLIN FRANCIS D.M.D.	1950	M	Fencing
MADDALONE RAYMOND FRANK DR.	1970	M	Fencing
MADIGAN DAVID JUDE	1981	M	Fencing
MADIGAN JAMES EDWARD	1943	M	Fencing
MAGES PHILLIP ANTHONY	1997	M	Fencing
MAGGIO JORDAN SMITH	1995	M	Fencing
MAHONEY WILLIAM BERTRAND REV. OP	1938	M	Fencing
MALECZ RICHARD E. D.M.D.	1974	M	Fencing
MALFA JOHN DENNIS M.D.	1954	M	Fencing
MALISZEWSKI WILLIAM M.B. M.D.	1971	M	Fencing
MALONE JOSEPH ALFRED JR.	1966	M	Fencing
MANDOLINI ANTHONY MARIO	1954	M	Fencing
MARKEL MICHAEL LAWRENCE M.D.	1978	M	Fencing
MARKS RICHARD PAUL	1964	M	Fencing
MASSERER JOHANNES	2005	M	Fencing
MATRANGA MICHAEL THOMAS	1974	M	Fencing
MAUTONE STEVEN MICHAEL	2002	M	Fencing
MAZUR JOHN B. DR.	1969	M	Fencing
MCAULIFFE JOHN HERBERT JR.	1937	M	Fencing
MCBRIDE DAVID NEIL	1953	M	Fencing
MCBRIDE JOHN DAVID	1982	M	Fencing
MCCAHEY MICHAEL J.	1978	M	Fencing
MCCANDLESS PAUL LESLIE	1969	M	Fencing
MCCARTY SHAUN PATRICK	1983	M	Fencing
MCCONVILLE TERRENCE JAMES	1977	M	Fencing
MCCUE LEONARD JOSEPH	1962	M	Fencing
MCDONOUGH PATRICK JOHN	1970	M	Fencing
MCENEARNEY BURTON	1939	M	Fencing
MCGINN JOHN HUNT	1954	M	Fencing
MCGUIRE JOHN P.	1946	M	Fencing
MCGUIRE JOHN PATRICK DR.	1979	M	Fencing
MCNALLY THOMAS JOSEPH	2005	M	Fencing
MCNAMARA JOHN A. III	1986	M	Fencing
MCQUADE CHRISTOPHER MICHAEL	1997	M	Fencing
MCQUADE JOSEPH FRANCIS	1965	M	Fencing
MCQUADE MICHAEL D.	1965	M	Fencing
MCQUADE STEPHEN MICHAEL	1999	M	Fencing
MELTON HERBERT S. III	1971	M	Fencing
MELTON HERBERT S. JR.	1943	M	Fencing
MENDES ROBERT L.	1969	M	Fencing
MERGEN MATTHEW JAMES	1991	M	Fencing
MERRILL WILLIAM WOODROOF M.D.	1967	M	Fencing
MERTEN DEAN R.	1980	M	Fencing
METRAILER ANDREW MARK	1999	M	Fencing
MEYER GERALD FRANCIS	1958	M	Fencing
MILLER JOHN FRANCIS	2000	M	Fencing
MILLER LAWRENCE E.	1978	M	Fencing
MITALO BRIAN MICHAEL	1987	M	Fencing
MOCK PHILIP MONTAGUE	1977	M	Fencing
MOLINELLI MICHAEL JOSEPH	1982	M	Fencing
MONAHAN JOSEPH MICHAEL II	1995	M	Fencing
MONAHAN TIMOTHY FRANCIS	1999	M	Fencing
MOONEY JOHN PATRICK	1954	M	Fencing
MORTON CLAY ROBERT	2000	M	Fencing
MUCKENHIRN CARL FRANCIS	1982	M	Fencing
MULLENIX JAMES DAVID	1974	M	Fencing
MULLER-BERGH KLAUS	1959	M	Fencing
MULLIGAN DANIEL ANTHONY	1973	M	Fencing
MULLIGAN TIMOTHY GERARD	1977	M	Fencing
MULROONEY C. PATRICK REV. OP	1953	M	Fencing
MUOIO SALVATORE R.	1981	M	Fencing
MYRON JOSEPH BERCHMAN	1935	M	Fencing
NAHSER F. BYRON MR.	1962	M	Fencing
NANOVIC ROY MARTIN	1968	M	Fencing
NEE CHRISTOPHER CFA	1989	M	Fencing
NENOFF ROBERT JOHN	1968	M	Fencing
NERLINGER ANDREW SANDOR	2002	M	Fencing
NIGRO JOSEPH FRANCIS	1939	M	Fencing
NOWOSIELSKI LESZEK EUGENIUSZ	1991	M	Fencing
ORTIZ ALFREDO MANUEL	1947	M	Fencing
OTT WILLIAM JOHN M.D.	1966	M	Fencing
PACKO JOHN GEORGE III	1976	M	Fencing
PARISI DANIEL JOSEPH	1951	M	Fencing
PATEL RAKESH MAGAN	1995	M	Fencing
PATOUT RIVERS A. REV. III	1960	M	Fencing
PAUWELS JOSEPH HENRY	1972	M	Fencing
PECHINSKY GEOFFREY ALAN DR.	1993	M	Fencing
PECK LOUIS PROVOST	1950	M	Fencing
PEREZ JOHN DAVID	1986	M	Fencing
PERO JEFFREY TOWNE	1968	M	Fencing
PETRUNGARO CHARLES EUGENE	1960	M	Fencing
PIETRUSIAK WILLIAM JAMES JR.	1989	M	Fencing
PIKNA RAYMOND JOHN JR.	1976	M	Fencing
PIPER JEFFREY BROOKS	1993	M	Fencing
POWER CONOR CARUSO	1995	M	Fencing
PRENDERGAST BRENDAN MICHAEL	2004	M	Fencing
PRICE ARTHUR EARL M.D.	1957	M	Fencing
PROGAR MICHAEL JOSEPH	1975	M	Fencing
QUARONI ANDREA LORENZO	1985	M	Fencing
QUINN BRIAN J.	1987	M	Fencing
RADDE JAMES MORRIS REV. SJ	1960	M	Fencing
RAWLINGS STEVEN GILBERT	1989	M	Fencing
RAY BRIAN EDWARD	1993	M	Fencing
REARDON CHRISTOPHER WARREN	1988	M	Fencing
REARDON JAMES GARABAD	1971	M	Fencing
REARDON SEAN FITZPATRICK DR.	1986	M	Fencing
REICHENBACH THOMAS HENRY M.D.	1968	M	Fencing
REILLY JAMES WILLIAM	1988	M	Fencing
REUTER DAVID ANDREW	1986	M	Fencing
RICCI JOHN FREDERICK	1963	M	Fencing
RICE GEORGE FRANCIS	1963	M	Fencing
RIPPLE GREGORY PATRICK	1994	M	Fencing
RIVERA JUAN ERNESTO III	1973	M	Fencing
RIZZUTI ANTHONY ROBERT	2001	M	Fencing
RONAYNE JOHN F. JR.	1960	M	Fencing
RONEY DAVID TROMBLY	1944	M	Fencing
RONEY THOMAS JOSEPH	1950	M	Fencing
ROONEY PATRICK M.	1980	M	Fencing
ROSE WILLIAM BROWNING	1969	M	Fencing
ROSSI GEOFFREY ALLAN	1990	M	Fencing
ROVEDA JOSEPH SAMUEL	1984	M	Fencing
RUETER SCOTT ALAN	1981	M	Fencing
RUSSOMANO JAMES PHILIP JR.	1960	M	Fencing
RUTHERFORD SCOTT DAY	1983	M	Fencing
RYAN JOHN PATRICK	1957	M	Fencing
RYAN JOHN VINCENT M.D.	1955	M	Fencing
RYDER THOMAS KENNETH	1986	M	Fencing
SABOL MARK ANDREW	1968	M	Fencing
SALIMANDO STEVEN CHARLES	1979	M	Fencing
SALISIAN NEAL SAMUEL II	2002	M	Fencing
SAYIA ROBERT FORTUNE	1940	M	Fencing
SAZDANOFF MICHAEL LOUIS	1976	M	Fencing
SCALERA NICHOLAS HON	1951	M	Fencing
SCARLATA SALVATORE PAUL M.D.	1939	M	Fencing
SCHERMOLY MICHAEL DANIEL	1979	M	Fencing
SCHERPE CHRISTIAN	1986	M	Fencing
SCHERPEREEL JOHN ANDREW	1997	M	Fencing
SCHLOSSER ROBERT EDWARD	1950	M	Fencing
SCHNIERLE MICHAEL CHARLES	1969	M	Fencing
SCHUMACHER ALEXANDER MICHAEL	2006	M	Fencing
SCHUMACHER NICHOLAS ROBERT	2004	M	Fencing
SCHWARTZ DAVID LAWRENCE	1959	M	Fencing
SECO ROBERT ALAN	1937	M	Fencing
SEITZ ROY EDWARD DR.	1974	M	Fencing
SEYYID JUBBA	1992	M	Fencing
SHERIDAN THOMAS PATRICK	1968	M	Fencing
SHIPP THOMAS EDWARD	1962	M	Fencing
SIEK JEREMY GRAHAM	1997	M	Fencing
SIERRA JOSE P.	1981	M	Fencing
SILHA ELMER DONALD	1944	M	Fencing
SLEVIN EUGENE RICHARD	1944	M	Fencing
SMALLEY JOSEPH GABRIEL	1940	M	Fencing
SNOOKS RICHARD HORIGAN	1964	M	Fencing
SNOOKS RICHARD WILLIAM	1936	M	Fencing
SOBIERAJ MICHAL	2005	M	Fencing
SOLLITTO RONALD JOSEPH M.D.	1972	M	Fencing
SPAHN THOMAS JOSEPH	1973	M	Fencing
SPEJEWSKI EUGENE HENRY	1960	M	Fencing
SPITZER NORBERT JAMES	1960	M	Fencing
ST.CLAIR BRIAN FRANCIS	1986	M	Fencing
STABRAWA DAVID JACOB	1985	M	Fencing
STACHOWSKI RUSSELL EDWARD DR.	1981	M	Fencing
STONE BRIAN MICHAEL	1998	M	Fencing
STOUTERMIRE KEVIN EARL	1988	M	Fencing
STRASS JOHN JAMES	1978	M	Fencing
SULLIVAN JAMES THOMAS	1981	M	Fencing
SULLIVAN MICHAEL ERNEST	1979	M	Fencing
SWINEY MARK DONOVAN	1999	M	Fencing
SZELLE GABOR LAJOS	2003	M	Fencing
TALIAFERRO JAMES DONNELL	1993	M	Fencing
TATE FREDERICK J. JR.	1964	M	Fencing
TAYLOR J. TIMOTHY MR.	1972	M	Fencing
TEARNEY THOMAS WOODROW	1942	M	Fencing
TEJADA JOHN CARLOS	1998	M	Fencing
THOMPSON JAMES JOHN	1982	M	Fencing
TIETZ JOEL F.	1983	M	Fencing
TINDELL KEVIN ERSKIN	1982	M	Fencing
TODD DONALD GEORGE	1956	M	Fencing
TOWNSEND-PICO WILLIAM ARTURO M.D.	1986	M	Fencing
TRAYERS FREDERICK JOHN III	1991	M	Fencing
TRISKO MICHAEL OWEN	1992	M	Fencing
TSCHETTER JOHN HAROLD	1967	M	Fencing
TURGEON JOSEPH E. III	1977	M	Fencing
TYLER DAVID JR.	2001	M	Fencing
UBBING WILLIAM JOSEPH	1976	M	Fencing
VAGGO BJORNE	1978	M	Fencing
VALDISERRI RICHARD M.	1977	M	Fencing
VALDISERRI THOMAS M.	1981	M	Fencing
VALENTINO PAUL GENE JR.	1979	M	Fencing
VALERIO MICHAEL A. JR.	1981	M	Fencing
VANDERVELDEN MICHAEL THOMAS	1986	M	Fencing
VAUGHAN TIMOTHY JOSEPH	1988	M	Fencing
VEIT FRANCIS A. JR.	1942	M	Fencing
VENERUS JOSEPH CALISTO	1967	M	Fencing
VERMEERSCH DAVID RAYMOND	1980	M	Fencing
VIAMONTES GEORGE FREDERICK	2001	M	Fencing
VIAMONTES GEORGE&CLAUDIA DRS.	1973	M	Fencing
VINCENT JOHN THEODORE M.D.	1950	M	Fencing
VIVIANI JOSEPH J	2003	M	Fencing
VIZCARRONDO JULIO E. JR.	1956	M	Fencing
VOGT PAUL STUART JR.	1990	M	Fencing
VOZELLA JOHN JOSEPH JR.	N/A	M	Fencing
WAGNER JOHN RALPH JR.	1963	M	Fencing
WALKER KEVIN RICHARD DR. M.D.	1986	M	Fencing
WALSH JAMES JOSEPH	1952	M	Fencing
WALSH ROBERT EMMET JR.	1986	M	Fencing
WALTER ROBERT GEORGE CAPT.	1963	M	Fencing
WALTON FOREST ERIK	2004	M	Fencing
WARTGOW JEFFREY JEROME	1997	M	Fencing
WASSIL JOHN GEORGE DR. JR.	1960	M	Fencing
WATERS JAMES PETER JR.	1955	M	Fencing
WATTERS JOHN S. SR.	1944	M	Fencing
WAUGH RICHARD EMMET DR.	1973	M	Fencing
WESTRICK ROBERT CHARLES	1951	M	Fencing
WHEATON KELLY DANIEL	1982	M	Fencing
WHEATON KRISTAN J.	1980	M	Fencing
WHITE RICHARD LAWRENCE	1973	M	Fencing
WITUCKI RALPH E.	1949	M	Fencing
WOZNIAK GRZEGORZ WOJTEK	1994	M	Fencing
YAU WARREN WAI LUN	1972	M	Fencing

NAME	YEAR	GENDER	SPORT
COLLINS JOSEPH J.	1911	M	Football
COLLINS LEO THOMAS	1967	M	Football
COLOSIMO JAMES FRANCIS	1959	M	Football
COMPTON KENNETH DOUG	1984	M	Football
CONDENI DAVID A.	1981	M	Football
CONJAR LAWRENCE WAYNE	1967	M	Football
CONNOR GEORGE L.	1948	M	Football
CONWAY DENNIS LEE	1966	M	Football
COOK EDWARD JOSEPH	1955	M	Football
COOKE WILLIAM L. M.D.	1957	M	Football
COONEY JOHN M.	1987	M	Football
COOPER JOHN DELVICCHO	2000	M	Football
CORBISIERO JOHN VINCENT COL.	1948	M	Football
CORSARO DANIEL STEPHEN	1986	M	Football
COSTA DONALD JAMES	1959	M	Football
COSTA S. PAUL REV.	1965	M	Football
COTTER RICHARD ADRIAN	1951	M	Football
COTTER ROBERT F.	1971	M	Football
COTTON FORREST G.	1923	M	Football
COUREY MICHAEL J.	1981	M	Football
COUTRE LAWRENCE EDWARD	1950	M	Football
COVINGTON IVORY DONALD	1999	M	Football
COVINGTON JOHN SHAFT	1994	M	Football
COWHIG GERARD FINBAR	1947	M	Football
COWIN JEFFREY ALAN	1973	M	Football
CRABLE ROBERT E.	1982	M	Football
CREANEY R. MICHAEL	1973	M	Football
CREEVEY JOHN FRANCIS	1948	M	Football
CREEVEY THOMAS JOHN	1974	M	Football
CRIMMINS BERNARD ANTHONY	1942	M	Football
CRINITI FRANK JR.	1970	M	Football
CRIPPIN JEFFREY STEVEN DR.	1980	M	Football
CRONIN ARTHUR D.	1936	M	Football
CRONIN CARL MICHAEL	1931	M	Football
CRONIN RICHARD MARSHALL M.D.	1946	M	Football
CROTTY JAMES RICHARD	1960	M	Football
CROTTY MICHAEL FRANCIS	1972	M	Football
CROWE CLEM FREDERICK	1926	M	Football
CROWE EMMETT HOSTE	1939	M	Football
CROWLEY JAMES HAROLD	1925	M	Football
CROWTHER JOHN DAVID	2002	M	Football
CULLEN JOHN T.	1893	M	Football
CULVER ALVIN SAGER	1932	M	Football
CULVER RODNEY DWAYNE	1992	M	Football
CUNNINGHAM THOMAS JOHN	1957	M	Football
CURRY DEREK CHRISTOPHER	2005	M	Football
CURTIN JOHN BRENNAN	2003	M	Football
CUSACK PATRICK EDWARD	1986	M	Football
CUSHING THOMAS W.	1984	M	Football
CUSICK FRANK MICHAEL LT.	1945	M	Football
CZAJA MARK ANTHONY	1980	M	Football
CZAROBSKI ZIGGY PETER	1948	M	Football
DABIERO ANGELO RALPH	1962	M	Football
DAHL ROBERT ALLEN	1991	M	Football
DAHMAN RAYMOND J.	1928	M	Football
DAILER JAMES HERMAN	1950	M	Football
DAMPEER JOHN OSCAR III	1972	M	Football
DANBOM LAURENCE EDWIN	1937	M	Football
DANCEWICZ FRANCIS JOSEPH	1946	M	Football
DANSBY MELVIN JR.	1998	M	Football
DAVIS GREGORY LEON	1991	M	Football
DAVIS IRWIN VINCENT	1935	M	Football
DAVIS JACINTO SHAWN	1990	M	Football
DAVIS RAYMOND E.	1947	M	Football
DAVIS TRAVIS HORACE	1994	M	Football
DAWSON LAKE	1994	M	Football
DE ARRIETA JAMES ANDREW	1970	M	Football
DEBOLT CHAD MICHAEL	2003	M	Football
DECICCO NICHOLAS JOE	1978	M	Football
DEFRANCO JOSEPH FRANCIS	1940	M	Football
DEGREE EDWARD GEORGE	1923	M	Football
DEHUECK IAN DAVID	1985	M	Football
DEMANIGOLD MARC ALDEN	1992	M	Football
DEMMERLE PETER KIRK	1975	M	Football
DEMPSEY ANDREW PATRICK	2001	M	Football
DENARDO RONALD LEON	1958	M	Football
DENMAN ANTHONY RAY	2001	M	Football
DENNERY VINCENT PAUL JR.	1965	M	Football
DENNING DALE ALLEN	1972	M	Football
DENSON AUTRY LAMONT	1999	M	Football
DENVIR MICHAEL ROGER	1997	M	Football
DEPRIMIO DENNIS JOHN	1972	M	Football
DESIATO THOMAS JAMES	1981	M	Football
DETMER MARTIN J. JR.	1981	M	Football
DEVINE THOMAS ANDREW	1974	M	Football
DEVINE TIMOTHY LOUIS	1965	M	Football
DEVORE HUGH JOHN SR.	1934	M	Football
DEWAN DARRYLL ELIAS	1973	M	Football
DIBERNARDO RICK ANTHONY	1987	M	Football
DICARLO MICHAEL ANTHONY	1964	M	Football
DICKERSON SYDNEY J.	1885	M	Football
DICKMAN DANIEL DONAHOE	1968	M	Football
DICKSON GEORGE CHARLES	1950	M	Football
DIENHART JOSEPH STANLEY	1926	M	Football
DIERCKMAN BRIAN DOUGLAS	2002	M	Football
DIKE KENNETH H.	1978	M	Football
DIMINICK GARY JOHN	1974	M	Football
DINARDO GERARD PAUL	1975	M	Football
DINARDO LAWRENCE C.	1971	M	Football
DINGENS GREGORY GEORGE	1986	M	Football
DINGENS MATTHEW MARK	1988	M	Football
DIORIO DOUGLAS JAMES DR.	1990	M	Football
DOBBINS MARC BRADFORD	1990	M	Football
DOERGER THOMAS RICHARD	1986	M	Football
DOHERTY BRIAN BRUCE	1974	M	Football
DOHERTY KEVIN ROBERT	1976	M	Football
DOLAN PATRICK EDWIN	1958	M	Football
DOMIN THOMAS ALAN	1979	M	Football
DONAHUE JAMES MICHAEL DR.	1992	M	Football
DONOGHUE RICHARD LAURENCE	1931	M	Football
DORSEY ERIC HALL	1988	M	Football
DOUGHTY MICHAEL ZEBULON	1997	M	Football
DOVE ROBERT LEO	1943	M	Football
DOVER STEVEN CRAIG	1979	M	Football
DOWNS WILLIAM R.	1910	M	Football
DOYLE PATRICK T.	1961	M	Football
DRISCOLL JOHN ROGER	1978	M	Football
DRISCOLL JUSTIN LAWRENCE	1983	M	Football
DRISCOLL M. LEO	1978	M	Football
DRIVER TONY DANIELLE	2000	M	Football
DUBASAK PAUL JOHN	1958	M	Football
DUBENETZKY JOHN NICKOLAS	1977	M	Football
DUBOSE A. DEMETRIUS MR.	1993	M	Football
DUERSON DAVID RUSSELL	1983	M	Football
DUFF VONTEZ DOUGLAS	2003	M	Football
DUGAN MICHAEL JOSEPH	1959	M	Football
DUMAS RAYMOND LEE III	1989	M	Football
DUNCAN ROBERT FRANK JR.	1979	M	Football
DUNN CASEY RAYMOND	2005	M	Football
DUPUIS RICHARD EUGENE	1965	M	Football
DURANKO PETER NICHOLAS	1966	M	Football
DUSHNEY RONALD MICHAEL	1969	M	Football
DWAN ALLAN	1907	M	Football
DWYER JONATHAN RICHARD	1970	M	Football
DYKES DONALD DE JUAN	2001	M	Football
EARL GLENN E.	2004	M	Football
EARLEY J. FRED	1948	M	Football
EARLEY RICHARD PATRICK	1990	M	Football
EARLEY WILLIAM JOSEPH	1943	M	Football
EASON LAWRENCE ANTHONY	1988	M	Football
EASTMAN J. THOMAS JR.	1977	M	Football
EATON G. THOMAS	1971	M	Football
EBLI RAYMOND HENRY	1942	M	Football
ECKMAN MICHAEL JOSEPH	1972	M	Football
ECUYER ALLEN JOSEPH	1959	M	Football
EDDY NICHOLAS MATTHEW	1967	M	Football
EDISON WILLIE JARVIS JR.	1998	M	Football
EDMONDS WAYNE KING	1956	M	Football
EDWARDS EUGENE H.	1927	M	Football
EDWARDS MARC ALEXANDER	1997	M	Football
EICHENLAUB RAYMOND J.	1915	M	Football
EILERS PATRICK CHRISTOPHER	1989	M	Football
ELDER JOHN JOSEPH	1930	M	Football
ELLICK DWIGHT L.	2005	M	Football
ELLIS CLARENCE J. JR.	1972	M	Football
ELLIS RANDY KYLE D.D.S.	1983	M	Football
ELSER DONALD LEWIS	1936	M	Football
ELWARD ALLEN HENRY	1916	M	Football
ELY EUGENE JAMES	1938	M	Football
EMANUEL DENNIS GEORGE DR.	1938	M	Football
ENRIGHT REX EDWARD	1926	M	Football
EPSTEIN FRANK BERTELL	1953	M	Football
ETTEN NICHOLAS JOSEPH	1964	M	Football
ETTER WILLIAM F.	1972	M	Football
EURICK TERRY ALLEN	1978	M	Football
EVANS FREDERICK OWEN	1943	M	Football
EWALD MARK RICHARD	1977	M	Football
FAINE JEFFREY KALEI	2003	M	Football
FALLON JOHN J.	1949	M	Football
FANNING MICHAEL L.	1975	M	Football
FARMER JAMES C.	1984	M	Football
FARMER ROBERT E.	1997	M	Football
FARRELL BRENDAN PATRICK	2000	M	Football
FARRELL DANIEL PATRICK	1995	M	Football
FARRELL JOHN JUDE	1997	M	Football
FARRELL JOSEPH E. JR.	1964	M	Football
FARRELL JOSEPH EDWARD	1990	M	Football
FARRELL THOMAS A. SR.	1926	M	Football
FARREN JOHN EDWARD	1992	M	Football
FASANO ANGELO M.	1981	M	Football
FASANO ANTHONY JOSEPH	2006	M	Football
FAVORITE MICHAEL WILLIAM	1984	M	Football
FAY EDWARD J.	1949	M	Football
FAY WILLIAM C.	1940	M	Football
FAZIO JOSEPH STEVEN	1985	M	Football
FEDORENKO NICHOLAS JOHN	1976	M	Football
FEIGL CHARLES	1951	M	Football
FERGUSON VASQUERO DIAZ	1980	M	Football
FERRER RICHARD JOSEPH	2000	M	Football
FIBER EDWARD BERT	1973	M	Football
FIGARO CEDRIC NOAH	2000	M	Football
FILLEY PATRICK JOSEPH	1945	M	Football
FINE THOMAS WAYNE	1975	M	Football
FINNEGAN ROBERT SEAN	1985	M	Football
FINNERAN JOHN CLEMENT	1940	M	Football
FISCHER MARK FRANCIS	1983	M	Football
FISCHER RAYMOND CHARLES	1969	M	Football
FISCHER WILLIAM A.	1949	M	Football
FISHER ANTOINE MAURICE	2002	M	Football
FISHER PATRICK JAMES	1935	M	Football
FITZGERALD DAVID ROBERT	2006	M	Football
FITZGERALD EDWARD FRANCIS	1990	M	Football
FITZGERALD JAMES MICHAEL	1965	M	Football
FITZGERALD RICHARD P.	1956	M	Football
FITZPATRICK DANIEL JOSEPH	2005	M	Football
FLANAGAN CHRISTIE JOHN JR.	1928	M	Football
FLANAGAN JAMES HENRY REV.	1947	M	Football
FLANIGAN JAMES MICHAEL JR.	1994	M	Football
FLANNERY BRYAN EUGENE	1990	M	Football
FLEURIMA REGINALD BERNARD	1995	M	Football
FLINN NEIL WILLIAM	1923	M	Football
FLOOD DAVID MICHAEL	1953	M	Football
FLOOD JOHN CHRISTOPHER	1982	M	Football
FLOR OLIVER RONALD	1960	M	Football
FLYNN THOMAS VINCENT	1979	M	Football
FLYNN WILLIAM J.	1952	M	Football
FOGEL JOHN NICHOLAS M.D.	1938	M	Football
FOLEY JOHN AMOS	1990	M	Football
FOLEY TIMOTHY JOHN	1980	M	Football
FOOS BENJAMIN RICHARDSON	1996	M	Football
FORD JAMES HENRY JR.	1942	M	Football
FORD WILLIAM CHANDLER	1962	M	Football
FORYSTEK GARY F.	1980	M	Football
FOSTER HARVEY GOODSON	1939	M	Football
FOURNIER LOUIS JOHN	1968	M	Football
FOX HARRY FRANCIS JR.	1938	M	Football
FRAILEY DANIEL HENRY SR.	1979	M	Football
FRAMPTON JOHN P.	1949	M	Football
FRANCIS DWAYNE HARRINGTON II	2002	M	Football
FRANCISCO D'JUAN DANTE	1989	M	Football
FRANCISCO HIAWATHA NAHOMIA	1987	M	Football
FRANTZ MICHAEL JENNINGS	1973	M	Football
FRASCOGNA XAVIER MICHAEL	1996	M	Football
FRASOR RICHARD L.	1955	M	Football
FREDERICK JOHN FEDUS	1928	M	Football
FREDRICK CHARLES ANTHONY	1959	M	Football
FREEBERY JOSEPH JAMES	1969	M	Football
FREEMAN MARCUS LEON	2006	M	Football
FREEMAN THOMAS HENRY	1987	M	Football
FREISTROFFER THOMAS JOHN	1973	M	Football
FRERICKS ALFRED JERALD	1941	M	Football
FRERICKS THOMAS JOSEPH	1977	M	Football
FRIDAY JAMES ESLEY JR.	1999	M	Football
FROME CHRISTOPHER RYAN	2006	M	Football
FROMHART WALLACE LEO	1936	M	Football
FRY WILLIE JR.	1978	M	Football
FUNK ARTHUR STEPHAN	1906	M	Football
FURJANIC ANTHONY JOSEPH	1986	M	Football
FURLONG NICHOLAS RAYMOND	1970	M	Football
FURLONG THOMAS EDWARD DR.	1968	M	Football
GAGNON ROBERT JOHN	1983	M	Football
GALANIS JOHN LOUIS	1976	M	Football
GALARDO ARMANDO MICHAEL	1954	M	Football
GALLAGHER LAWRENCE FRANCIS	1951	M	Football
GALLAGHER THOMAS CHARLES	1941	M	Football
GALLAGHER WILLIAM	1972	M	Football
GALLOWAY THOMAS MICHAEL	1987	M	Football
GAMBONE JOHN ANTHONY	1974	M	Football
GANDER FIDEL JOHN	1952	M	Football
GANDY MICHAEL JOSEPH	2000	M	Football
GANEY MICHAEL J. JR.	1946	M	Football
GANN MICHAEL ALAN	1985	M	Football
GARDNER JOHN ADAMS	1971	M	Football
GARGIULO FRANK JOSEPH	1961	M	Football
GARNER TERRANCE JOHN	1973	M	Football
GASPARELLA JOSEPH RICHARD	1950	M	Football
GASSELING THOMAS WILLIAM	1971	M	Football
GASSER JOHN JOSEPH	1970	M	Football
GATEWOOD THOMAS	1972	M	Football
GATTI MICHAEL MAURICE	1990	M	Football

NAME	YEAR	GENDER	SPORT
GAUDREAU WILLIAM LUCIEN	1953	M	Football
GAUL FRANCIS E.	1949	M	Football
GAUL FRANCIS J. SR.	1936	M	Football
GAY WILLIAM T.	1951	M	Football
GAYDOS ROBERT MICHAEL	1958	M	Football
GEBERT ALBERT JOSEPH	1930	M	Football
GEERS MICHAEL A.	1978	M	Football
GEORGE DONALD H.	1954	M	Football
GERAGHTY JOHN ROBERT	1964	M	Football
GERAMI GERALD JAMES	1957	M	Football
GEREMIA FRANK JR.	1959	M	Football
GETHERALL JOSEPH ISAMU	2001	M	Football
GIBBONS THOMAS JOSEPH	1981	M	Football
GIBBS WILLIAM THOMAS	1997	M	Football
GIBSON HERBERT EMILE	1995	M	Football
GIBSON OLIVER DONNOVAN	1994	M	Football
GIBSON STEVEN J.	1980	M	Football
GILES ZACHARY RONALD	2005	M	Football
GILLIS RYAN EDWARD	2004	M	Football
GIVENS DAVID LAMAR	2002	M	Football
GLAAB JOHN PHILIP	1947	M	Football
GLADIEUX ROBERT JOSEPH	1969	M	Football
GLEASON MARC ALAN	1988	M	Football
GLUECKERT CHARLES J.	1925	M	Football
GMITTER DONALD ALAN	1967	M	Football
GOBERVILLE THOMAS JOHN M.D.	1964	M	Football
GODSEY GARY MICHAEL	2003	M	Football
GOEDDEKE GEORGE A.	1966	M	Football
GOHEEN JUSTIN PAUL	1995	M	Football
GOLIC GREGORY R.	1984	M	Football
GOLIC MICHAEL LOUIS	1985	M	Football
GOLIC ROBERT PERRY	1979	M	Football
GOMPERS WILLIAM GEORGE	1948	M	Football
GOODE TY MANDEL	1998	M	Football
GOODMAN RONNIE ANDREW	1975	M	Football
GOODSPEED JOEY A.	2000	M	Football
GOOLSBY MICHAEL RICHARD	2004	M	Football
GORDON DARRELL RODNEY	1988	M	Football
GORES THOMAS CAMBLIN	1970	M	Football
GORMAN THOMAS ANTHONY	1933	M	Football
GORMAN THOMAS GEORGE	1989	M	Football
GORMAN TIMOTHY JOHN JR.	1967	M	Football
GRADEL THEODORE FRANCIS	1987	M	Football
GRADY MICHAEL JAMES	2000	M	Football
GRAHAM KENT DOUGLAS	1988	M	Football
GRAHAM PETER LAWRENCE	1990	M	Football
GRAHAM TRACY DANIEL	1995	M	Football
GRAMKE JOSEPH EDWARD	1982	M	Football
GRANT DONALD CHESTER	1922	M	Football
GRANT RYAN BRETT	2005	M	Football
GRASMANIS PAUL RYAN	1996	M	Football
GRAU FRANCIS CHARLES	1962	M	Football
GRAY GERARD EDWARD JR.	1963	M	Football
GRAY IAN ANGLIN	1980	M	Football
GRAY RICHARD LLOYD	1984	M	Football
GREEN DAVID HUGH	1972	M	Football
GREEN MARK ANTHONY	1989	M	Football
GREEN MICHAEL SHAEMUS	1989	M	Football
GREENEY NORMAN J.	1933	M	Football
GRENDA EDWARD THOMAS	1971	M	Football
GRIEB JOHN TIMOTHY	1986	M	Football
GRIFFIN MICHAEL FRANCIS	1987	M	Football
GRIFFITH DANIEL ROBERT	1961	M	Football
GRIFFITH KEVIN E.	1982	M	Football
GRIGGS RAYMOND BERNIE	1992	M	Football
GRIMM DONN WESLEY	1991	M	Football
GRIMM PAUL JAMES	1998	M	Football
GRINDINGER DENNIS JOSEPH	1979	M	Football
GROBLE GEORGE WILLIAM	1957	M	Football
GROGAN PETER ANDREW	1982	M	Football
GROOM JEROME PAUL	1951	M	Football
GROOMS SCOTT ARDEN	1984	M	Football
GROTHAUS WALTER JOHN	1950	M	Football
GRUNHARD TIMOTHY GERARD	1990	M	Football
GUBANICH JOHN ALOYSIUS	1941	M	Football
GUERRERA JAMES PETER	1993	M	Football
GUGLIELMI RALPH VINCENT	1955	M	Football
GUILBEAUX BENNY CARLYLE	1999	M	Football
GULLICKSON THOMAS JOHN	1977	M	Football
GULYAS EDWARD TIBOR	1972	M	Football
GUSHURST FRED WM. SR.	1914	M	Football
GUTOWSKI DENNIS WAYNE	1973	M	Football
HACKETT WILLIAM FRANCIS	1992	M	Football
HAGERTY ROBERT F.	1967	M	Football
HAGGAR JOE MARION III	1973	M	Football
HAGOPIAN GARY	1972	M	Football
HAINES DAVID KRIS	1979	M	Football
HALEY DAVID FRANCIS	1968	M	Football
HALL JUSTIN MICHAEL	1993	M	Football
HALTER JORDAN WILLIAM	1993	M	Football
HALVORSON JASON JEFFREY	2003	M	Football
HAMBY JAMES HAROLD	1952	M	Football
HAMILTON BRIAN MITCHELL	1994	M	Football
HANKAMER GARY L.	1979	M	Football
HANKERD JOHN P.	1981	M	Football
HANLON ROBERT SELDON	1947	M	Football
HANOUSEK RICHARD JOSEPH	1927	M	Football
HANRATTY TERRENCE HUGH	1969	M	Football
HARDY KEVIN THOMAS	1968	M	Football
HARGRAVE ROBERT WEBB SR.	1942	M	Football
HARMON JOSEPH P. SR.	1925	M	Football
HARPER DEVERON ALFREDO	2000	M	Football
HARRIS BRANDON TYRONE	2006	M	Football
HARRIS GREGORY ALAN	1988	M	Football
HARRIS JAMES MARCUS	1933	M	Football
HARRISON RANDY LEE	1979	M	Football
HARRISON TYREO TREMAYNE	2002	M	Football
HARSHMAN DANIEL RYAN	1968	M	Football
HART KEVIN DAVID	1980	M	Football
HART LEON JOSEPH SR.	1950	M	Football
HARTMAN PETE WYLIE	1974	M	Football
HARTWIG STEVEN WAYNE	1980	M	Football
HARTZEL NICHOLAS JAMES SR.	1971	M	Football
HARVEY THADDEUS H.	1940	M	Football
HASBROOK MATTHEW THOMAS	2005	M	Football
HAUTMAN JAMES FRANCIS	1979	M	Football
HAYDUK GEORGE DAVID	1974	M	Football
HAYES JOHN WILLIAM	1941	M	Football
HAYWOOD MICHAEL ANTHONY	1986	M	Football
HEALY EDWARD DENNIS	1990	M	Football
HEAP JOSEPH LAWRENCE	1955	M	Football
HEARDEN THOMAS F.	1927	M	Football
HEATON J. MICHAEL	1968	M	Football
HEAVENS JEROME K.	1979	M	Football
HEBERT JOHNATHAN JASON	2001	M	Football
HEBERT L. CARL MR.	1958	M	Football
HECK ANDREW ROBERT	1989	M	Football
HECOMOVICH THOMAS JOSEPH	1962	M	Football
HEDMAN CHARLES RICHARD	2003	M	Football
HEENAN PATRICK DENNIS	1960	M	Football
HEFFERN SHAWN PATRICK	1986	M	Football
HEGGLAND KARL	1992	M	Football
HEIMKREITER STEVEN	1979	M	Football
HEIN JEFFREY CHARLES	1974	M	Football
HELDT MICHAEL JON	1991	M	Football
HELWIG JOHN FRANK	1951	M	Football
HEMPEL SCOTT MARTIN	1971	M	Football
HENDRICKS RICHARD JOSEPH M.D.	1956	M	Football
HENEGHAN CURTIS JOSEPH	1969	M	Football
HENNEGHAN WILLIAM MICHAEL	1961	M	Football
HENTRICH CRAIG ANTHONY	1993	M	Football
HICKMAN WILLIAM EDWARD	1959	M	Football
HIGGINS LUKE MARTIN	1947	M	Football
HIGGINS WILLIAM PATRICK	1951	M	Football
HILBERT STEVEN AUSTIN	1982	M	Football
HILDBOLD JOSEPH MATTHEW	2003	M	Football
HILDEBRAND KENT DAVID	1971	M	Football
HILL GREGORY ELLIS	1974	M	Football
HILLIARD CEDRIC DARNELL	2004	M	Football
HIMAN ERIK DILLON	1999	M	Football
HO REGINALD THOMAS M.D.	1989	M	Football
HOBERT CHESTER A. JR.	1959	M	Football
HOERSTER EWALD H.	1963	M	Football
HOFFMANN F. NORDHOFF MR.	1933	M	Football
HOGAN DONALD JOHN JR.	1965	M	Football
HOLDEN SEDRICK GERMAINE	1995	M	Football
HOLIDAY CARLYLE J.	2004	M	Football
HOLLISTER CHRISTOPHER VERN	1992	M	Football
HOLLOWAY JABARI JELANI	2001	M	Football
HOLLOWAY WALKER LEE III	1973	M	Football
HOLMES HUGH ALPHONSO	2001	M	Football
HOLOHAN PETER JOSEPH	1980	M	Football
HOLTZ LOUIS LEO JR.	1987	M	Football
HOLTZAPFEL MICHAEL JOSEPH	1969	M	Football
HOOTEN HERMAN MARCUS	1972	M	Football
HORANSKY THEODORE JOSEPH	1979	M	Football
HORNEY JOHN THADDEUS M.D.	1967	M	Football
HORNUNG PAUL V.	1957	M	Football
HOST PAUL ANTHONY	1933	M	Football
HOWARD ALLAN	1931	M	Football
HOWARD BOBBIE ALLEN JR.	1999	M	Football
HOWARD CHARLES PATRICK	1934	M	Football
HOWARD JOSEPH PERNELL	1985	M	Football
HOWARD TERRANCE ROCHELLE	2002	M	Football
HOWARD WALTER HENRY	1988	M	Football
HOYTE BRANDON D	2006	M	Football
HUARTE JOHN GREGORY	1965	M	Football
HUDAK EDWARD JAMES	1950	M	Football
HUFF ANDREW MICHAEL	1973	M	Football
HUFFMAN DAVID LAMBERT	1979	M	Football
HUFFMAN TIMOTHY PATRICK	1981	M	Football
HUFFORD LAWRENCE ROBERT DR.	1980	M	Football
HUGHES ERNEST LOYAL JR.	1978	M	Football
HUGHES ROBERT JAMES III	1994	M	Football
HUGHES THOMAS JAMES	1957	M	Football
HUMBERT JAMES RAYMOND	1972	M	Football
HUMENIK DAVID JAMES	1964	M	Football
HUNSINGER EDWARD THOMAS	1925	M	Football
HUNTER ALFONSE	1979	M	Football
HUNTER ANTHONY WAYNE	1984	M	Football
HUNTER ARTHUR JAMES	1954	M	Football
HUNTER BENJAMIN NATHAN	1999	M	Football
HUNTER JAVIN EDWARD	2002	M	Football
HURD DAVID BRUCE	1960	M	Football
HURD WILLIAM CHARLES M.D.	1969	M	Football
HURLBERT JAMES FRANCIS	1928	M	Football
HUSS BRIAN	N/A	M	Football
IRONS GRANT MICHAEL	2001	M	Football
ISMAIL RAGHIB RAMADAN	1994	M	Football
ISRAEL RONALD CLIFTON	2002	M	Football
IVAN KENNETH EUGENE	1966	M	Football
IZO GEORGE WILLIAM	1960	M	Football
JACKSON JARIOUS KAVAR	2000	M	Football
JACKSON MILTON F. JR.	1987	M	Football
JACKSON PRESTON FERNELL	2004	M	Football
JAMES MICHAEL BENJAMIN	1986	M	Football
JANDRIC DAVID ROBERT	1990	M	Football
JAROSZ JOSEPH ROBERT	1989	M	Football
JARRELL ADRIAN MAURICE	1993	M	Football
JASKWHICH CHARLES JOSEPH	1933	M	Football
JEFFERSON ALONZO JOHN-PENDER	1988	M	Football
JEFFERSON CLIFFORD EARL JR.	2002	M	Football
JENKINS JEFFREY ALAN II	2006	M	Football
JENKINS OMAR RASHEED	2004	M	Football
JEZIORSKI RONALD MARTIN DR.	1967	M	Football
JOCKISCH ROBERT ALLEN	1970	M	Football
JOHNSON ANTHONY SCOTT	1990	M	Football
JOHNSON CLINT LAMAR	1994	M	Football
JOHNSON FRANK ALBERT	1950	M	Football
JOHNSON JAMES MICHAEL II	2001	M	Football
JOHNSON LANCE HOUSTON	1993	M	Football
JOHNSON MALCOLM ALEXANDER	1998	M	Football
JOHNSON MATTHEW STEVEN DR.	1993	M	Football
JOHNSON MURRAY E. JR.	1950	M	Football
JOHNSON PETER JAMES	1979	M	Football
JOHNSON PHILLIP J.	1979	M	Football
JOHNSON ROBERT HENRY JR.	1973	M	Football
JOHNSON RONALD GLENN	1971	M	Football
JOHNSON JOSEPH I.	1986	M	Football
JOHNSTON FRANCIS ANTHONY	1954	M	Football
JOHNSTON MICHAEL GERARD	1983	M	Football
JONARDI RAYMOND C.	1951	M	Football
JONES ALBERT LEE II	1997	M	Football
JONES ANDRE FITZGERALD	1997	M	Football
JONES ANTWON TREMAINE	2000	M	Football
JONES ERIC LOUIS	1995	M	Football
JONES JAMES MICHAEL	2000	M	Football
JONES JULIUS ANDRE MAURICE	2003	M	Football
JORDAN JOHN WEAVER III	2001	M	Football
JOSEPH ROBERT	1954	M	Football
JOYNER BYRON VINCENT	1999	M	Football
JUAREZ JEREMY G	2002	M	Football
JURKOVIC MIRKO VJELKO	1995	M	Football
JUST JAMES ANTHONY	1959	M	Football
JUZWIK STEPHEN ROBERT	1942	M	Football
KACZENSKI RICK JUSTEN	1997	M	Football
KADISH MICHAEL SCOTT	1972	M	Football
KAFKA MICHAEL EDWARD	1977	M	Football
KANE JAMES JEFFREY	1961	M	Football
KANTOR JOSEPH	1964	M	Football
KAPISH GENE BERNARD	1956	M	Football
KAPISH ROBERT JOHN	1952	M	Football
KAPLAN CLARENCE PAUL	1931	M	Football
KASSIS THOMAS GEORGE	1931	M	Football
KEANE NOEL STEPHEN	1984	M	Football
KEGALY JOHN ANTHONY	1956	M	Football
KELL PAUL ERNEST	1939	M	Football
KELLEHER DANIEL SCOTT	1977	M	Football
KELLEHER JOHN CHARLES M.D.	1940	M	Football
KELLER RICHARD WILLIAM	1956	M	Football
KELLEY MICHAEL PETER	1984	M	Football
KELLY CHARLES EDWARD M.D.	1975	M	Football
KELLY GERALD THOMAS	1967	M	Football
KELLY JAMES EDWARD	1967	M	Football
KELLY JAMES HARRY	1964	M	Football
KELLY JOHN FRANCIS	1940	M	Football
KELLY KEVIN G.	1985	M	Football
KELLY PETER MULLEN	1941	M	Football
KELLY ROBERT JAMES	1953	M	Football
KELLY ROBERT JOSEPH	1947	M	Football

NAME	YEAR	GENDER	SPORT
KELLY TIMOTHY JAMES	1971	M	Football
KENNEALLY THOMAS FRANCIS	1930	M	Football
KENNEDY CHARLES JOSEPH	1970	M	Football
KEPPEL STEPHEN C.	1980	M	Football
KERR WILLIAM HOWARD	1940	M	Football
KIDD DONALD RAYMOND	1981	M	Football
KIEL BLAIR A.	1984	M	Football
KIERNAN MICHAEL RICHARD	1985	M	Football
KILBURG JEFF JAMES	1997	M	Football
KILEY ROGER JOSEPH HON. SR.	1923	M	Football
KILIANY DENNIS JAMES	1969	M	Football
KILLIAN CHARLES JOSEPH II	1989	M	Football
KINDER RANDOLPH SAMUEL III	1996	M	Football
KINEALY KEVIN PATRICK	1974	M	Football
KING JOSEPH JAMES	1959	M	Football
KING THOMAS H.	1918	M	Football
KISSNER LAWRENCE J.	1982	M	Football
KLEES VINCENT VESTAL	1977	M	Football
KLEINE WILLIAM WALTER	1986	M	Football
KLIMEK GERARD JOSEPH	1976	M	Football
KLOCKNER MICHAEL JOSEPH	2002	M	Football
KLUSAS TIMOTHY MARK	1995	M	Football
KNAPP LINDSAY HAINES	1992	M	Football
KNIGHT THOMAS BERNARD	1993	M	Football
KNOTT DANNY CHAVEZ	1978	M	Football
KOEGEL TIMOTHY J.	1982	M	Football
KOHANOWICH ALBERT JOHN	1953	M	Football
KOKEN MICHAEL RICHARD	1933	M	Football
KOLSKI STEPHEN JOSEPH SR.	1963	M	Football
KONDRLA MICHAEL J.	1971	M	Football
KONIECZNY RUDOLPH ANDREW	1968	M	Football
KOPCZAK FRANCIS GREGORY	1937	M	Football
KOPKA KEVIN MICHAEL	1999	M	Football
KORDAS JAMES MICHAEL	1995	M	Football
KORECK ROBERT LOUIS	1961	M	Football
KORNICK THOMAS LOUIS JR.	1981	M	Football
KORNMAN RUSSELL DREW	1976	M	Football
KOS GARY PATRICK	1971	M	Football
KOSKY EDWIN STEPHEN	1933	M	Football
KOSTELNIK THOMAS MARTIN	1965	M	Football
KOVALCIK GEORGE JOHN	1938	M	Football
KOVALESKI MICHAEL AARON	1987	M	Football
KOVATCH JOHN GEORGE	1942	M	Football
KOWALKOWSKI SCOTT THOMAS	1991	M	Football
KOWALSKI DAVID ROBERT	2004	M	Football
KRACH MICHAEL JAMES	1966	M	Football
KRAMER JEFFREY JORDAN	1995	M	Football
KRAMER PATRICK DANIEL	1983	M	Football
KRAUSE EDWARD W.	1934	M	Football
KRIMM JOHN JOSEPH JR.	1982	M	Football
KRUEGER MATTHEW JOHN	2004	M	Football
KRUEGER RYAN PATRICK	2002	M	Football
KRUG THOMAS WOLFGANG	1997	M	Football
KUCHTA FRANK W.	1958	M	Football
KUECHENBERG ROBERT JOHN	1969	M	Football
KUHARICH JOSEPH LAWRENCE	1938	M	Football
KULBITSKI VICTOR JOHN	1943	M	Football
KUNZ GEORGE JAMES	1969	M	Football
KUNZ JEFFREY TODD	1988	M	Football
KUNZ MATTHEW THOMAS	1998	M	Football
KURTH JOSEPH J.	1933	M	Football
KUTZAVITCH WILLIAM ANDREW	1963	M	Football
KUZMICZ MICHAEL ANTHONY	1968	M	Football
KVOCHAK CHRIS GERARD	1987	M	Football
LABORNE FRANK HENRY	1934	M	Football
LAFAYETTE LE-AIRIUS SYLVESTER	1999	M	Football
LAHEY JAMES HENRY	1938	M	Football
LAHEY MATTHEW DAVID	1993	M	Football
LAIBER JOSEPH JAMES	1942	M	Football
LALLI MICHAEL ROBERT	1993	M	Football
LALLY ROBERT JOHN	1950	M	Football
LAMANTIA PETER VINCENT	1967	M	Football
LAMONICA DARYLE PAT	1963	M	Football
LANAHAN JOHN FRANCIS	1943	M	Football
LANDOLFI CHARLES C.	1969	M	Football
LANDRI DEREK SCOTT	2006	M	Football
LANDRY JOHN WARREN	1951	M	Football
LANE GARRY DEAN	1974	M	Football
LANE GREGORY SEAN	1996	M	Football
LANEY THOMAS JOACHIM DR.	1975	M	Football
LANIGAN CRAIG PATRICK	1991	M	Football
LANZA CHARLES LOUIS II	1987	M	Football
LARKIN MICHAEL TODD	1985	M	Football
LATTNER JOHN JOSEPH	1954	M	Football
LAUCK CHARLES BERNARD	1969	M	Football
LAUERMAN JOSEPH ALBERT JR.	1957	M	Football
LAUTAR JOHN PAUL	1937	M	Football
LAUX COLE LEWIS	2005	M	Football
LAVIN JOHN MYRON	1968	M	Football
LAWRENCE DONALD JEROME	1959	M	Football
LAWRENCE STEVEN WESLEY	1989	M	Football
LAWSON THOMAS MICHAEL	1970	M	Football
LAYDEN FRANCIS LOUIS	1936	M	Football
LEAHY BERNARD PHILIP	1932	M	Football
LEAHY JAMES PATRICK	1969	M	Football
LEAHY RYAN TIMOTHY	1995	M	Football
LEARY TERRANCE C. DR.	1977	M	Football
LEBLANC MARK STEVEN	1983	M	Football
LECK CHRISTOPHER MICHAEL	2000	M	Football
LEE ALBERT BUSH	1941	M	Football
LEE JOHN PAUL COL.	1955	M	Football
LEGREE LANCE WILLIAMS	2001	M	Football
LEHMANN J. ROBERT	1964	M	Football
LEMEK RAYMOND EDWARD	1956	M	Football
LEON JOHN ANTHONY M.D.	1980	M	Football
LEONARD ANTHONY JOSEPH	1985	M	Football
LEONARD JAMES RAYMOND SR.	1934	M	Football
LEONARD ROBERT EMMETT III	1994	M	Football
LEOPOLD LEROY J.	1980	M	Football
LEPPIG GEORGE E.	1928	M	Football
LESKO ALEXANDER F.	1949	M	Football
LEVENS HERBERT DORSEY	1990	M	Football
LEVOIR MARK JACOB	2005	M	Football
LEVY DARCEY DARRELL	1998	M	Football
LEWALLEN BRIAN WILLIAM	1970	M	Football
LEWIS AUBREY CLEMMENS	1958	M	Football
LEZON TODD MICHAEL	1986	M	Football
LIGGIO THOMAS FRANCIS	1962	M	Football
LIKOVICH JOHN DOMINIC	1977	M	Football
LILLIS PAUL BERNARD	1942	M	Football
LIMA CHARLES J.	1958	M	Football
LIMONT J. PAUL	1945	M	Football
LIMONT MARK F.	1948	M	Football
LIND H. N. MICHAEL MR.	1962	M	Football
LINEHAN JOHN JOSEPH	1961	M	Football
LIPPINCOTT MARTIN JOSEPH	1989	M	Football
LISCH RUSSELL JOHN	1980	M	Football
LISICKI JOHN EDWARD	1931	M	Football
LIUM JOHN DENNIS	1967	M	Football
LIVINGSTONE ROBERT EDWARD	1948	M	Football
LOBOY ALAN M.	1966	M	Football
LOCKARD FRANK R.	1919	M	Football
LODISH E. MICHAEL D.O.	1960	M	Football
LONCARIC LOUIS THOMAS	1957	M	Football
LONERGAN FRANK J. HON.	1904	M	Football
LONG HAROLD DALE JR.	1966	M	Football
LONGHI EDWARD JOHN	1939	M	Football
LONGO THOMAS VICTOR	1966	M	Football
LOPIENSKI THOMAS JOSEPH	2003	M	Football
LOPIENSKI THOMAS VINCENT	1976	M	Football
LOULA JAMES RALPH	1962	M	Football
LOZANO RICHARD ANTHONY	1994	M	Football
LOZZI DENNIS C. JR.	1974	M	Football
LUECKE DANIEL F.	1961	M	Football
LUEKEN JEFFREY JAMES	1982	M	Football
LUJACK JOHN C.	1948	M	Football
LUKATS NICHOLAS PAUL	1934	M	Football
LYELL WILLIAM RALPH	1996	M	Football
LYGHT TODD WILLIAM	1991	M	Football
LYNCH EDWIN J.	1910	M	Football
LYNCH JAMES ROBERT	1967	M	Football
LYNCH RICHARD DENNIS	1958	M	Football
LYNCH TIMOTHY ROBERT	1999	M	Football
LYTLE DEAN LAMONT	1994	M	Football
MACAFEE KENNETH ADAMS DR. II	1978	M	Football
MACDONALD THOMAS LOUIS	1964	M	Football
MACDONALD THOMAS WESLEY	1995	M	Football
MACHTOLF DAVID JAMES	1985	M	Football
MACIAG RICHARD JOSEPH	1973	M	Football
MACK WILLIAM R. SR.	1961	M	Football
MADDOCK ROBERT CHARLES	1942	M	Football
MAGEE BRIAN ANTHONY	1996	M	Football
MAGGIOLI ACHILLE FRED	1947	M	Football
MAGLICIC KENNETH MICHAEL	1965	M	Football
MAGNOTTA MICHAEL ANGELO	1962	M	Football
MAHALIC DREW ALAN	1975	M	Football
MAHER WILLIAM RAYMOND	1924	M	Football
MAHONEY CHRISTOPHER JOHN	2002	M	Football
MAHONEY RICHARD	1932	M	Football
MAIDEN ALTON RAY	1997	M	Football
MALE CHARLES BERNARD	1980	M	Football
MALINAK DONALD ALLAN	1977	M	Football
MALONE MICHAEL PATRICK	1969	M	Football
MANN F. FRED MR.	1954	M	Football
MANNELLY JOSEPH BERNARD III	1992	M	Football
MANZO LOUIS VINCENT	1959	M	Football
MARIANI JOHN FRANCIS	1973	M	Football
MARRERO KEITH JOSEPH	1983	M	Football
MARSH ANDREW SCOTT	1994	M	Football
MARSHALL GEORGE L.	1991	M	Football
MARSHALL TIMOTHY J.	1984	M	Football
MARSHALL WALTER MICHAEL	1938	M	Football
MARSICO JOSEPH ANTHONY	1967	M	Football
MARTELL EUGENE JUDE	1956	M	Football
MARTIN DAVID KENNETH	1968	M	Football
MARTIN JAMES RICHARD	1950	M	Football
MARTIN JAMES RICHARD	1937	M	Football
MARTIN MICHAEL FRANCIS	1971	M	Football
MARTINOVICH ROBERT FRANCIS	1980	M	Football
MARTZ GEORGE AMES	1944	M	Football
MARX GREGORY ALLAN	1972	M	Football
MASCHMEIER THOMAS RAYMOND	1976	M	Football
MASINI MICHAEL ALINIO M.D.	1982	M	Football
MASSEY JAMES PATRICK	1972	M	Football
MASTRANGELO JOHN BATTISTA	1947	M	Football
MASZTAK DEAN MICHAEL	1982	M	Football
MATTERA VINCENT S.	1965	M	Football
MATTES BRIAN DAVID	2006	M	Football
MATZ PAUL ANTHONY	1955	M	Football
MAUNE NEIL JOHN	1984	M	Football
MAVRAIDES MENIL	1954	M	Football
MAXIM JOSEPH RALPH	1971	M	Football
MAXWELL J. SCOTT	1963	M	Football
MAXWELL JOSEPH W.	1927	M	Football
MAY PAUL ALBERT	1968	M	Football
MAYES DERRICK BINET	1996	M	Football
MAYL EUGENE A.	1924	M	Football
MAYS COREY LEMARD	2005	M	Football
MAZUR JOHN EDWARD	1952	M	Football
MAZZIOTTI ANTHONY JOSEPH	1936	M	Football
MCBRIDE MICHAEL DANIEL	1974	M	Football
MCBRIDE OSCAR BERNARD	1994	M	Football
MCBRIDE ROBERT JAMES	1944	M	Football
MCCABE JOHN PATRICK	1986	M	Football
MCCARTHY CHRISTOPHER PIERCE	1998	M	Football
MCCARTHY FRANCIS PAUL	1928	M	Football
MCCARTHY WILLIAM PATRICK	1938	M	Football
MCCARTY PATRICK FRANCIS	1938	M	Football
MCCONN ROBERT GEORGE JR.	1970	M	Football
MCCONNELL DANIEL THOMAS	1996	M	Football
MCCORMICK KEITH CLEMENT	1980	M	Football
MCCORMICK NEVIN FRANCIS	1938	M	Football
MCCOY MICHAEL PATRICK	1970	M	Football
MCCULLOUGH MICHAEL SEAN	1996	M	Football
MCDANIELS STEVE W.	1978	M	Football
MCDONALD DEVON LINTON	1992	M	Football
MCDONALD FRANCIS JOSEPH	1976	M	Football
MCDONNELL JOHN JOSEPH	1957	M	Football
MCDONNELL KEVIN PATRICK	1999	M	Football
MCDOUGAL KEVIN TRE'MON	1994	M	Football
MCGANN TERRENCE JOSEPH	1972	M	Football
MCGEE JOSEPH COY	1949	M	Football
MCGEHEE RALPH WALTER	1950	M	Football
MCGILL KARMEELEYAH	1993	M	Football
MCGILL MICHAEL RAY	1968	M	Football
MCGINLEY JOHN CHRISTOPHER	1958	M	Football
MCGINN DANIEL MICHAEL	1966	M	Football
MCGLINN MICHAEL GEORGE	1994	M	Football
MCGOLDRICK JAMES G. J.	1939	M	Football
MCGRAW PATRICK J.	1973	M	Football
MCGUFFEY DAVID MITCHELL	1986	M	Football
MCGUIRE MICHAEL JAMES	1975	M	Football
MCGUIRE WALTER EUGENE	1995	M	Football
MCGUNIGAL ANTHONY JAMES	1997	M	Football
MCGURK JAMES STANLEY	1947	M	Football
MCHALE JOHN JOSEPH JR.	1971	M	Football
MCHALE JOHN JOSEPH SR.	1943	M	Football
MCHUGH THOMAS FRANCIS	1954	M	Football
MCHUGH THOMAS J. JR.	1987	M	Football
MCINTYRE JOHN ALOYSIUS	1940	M	Football
MCKILLIP WILLIAM LEO	1951	M	Football
MCKINLEY THOMAS MICHAEL	1969	M	Football
MCKINNEY CHARLES JOSEPH	1929	M	Football
MCKNIGHT RHEMA L.	2006	M	Football
MCLANE MARK DENNIS SR.	1977	M	Football
MCLAUGHLIN JOHN RAYMOND III	1995	M	Football
MCLAUGHLIN PATRICK A.	1975	M	Football
MCMAHON JOSEPH PATRICK	1936	M	Football
MCMANMON ARTHUR T.	1931	M	Football
MCMANMON JOHN V.	1928	M	Football
MCMULLAN JOHN GERALD JR.	1956	M	Football
MCMULLAN JOHN M.	1926	M	Football
MCNAIR MICHAEL KEVIN	2002	M	Football
MCNALLY VINCENT A. SR.	1927	M	Football
MCNAMARA EDWARD GEORGE III	1990	M	Football
MCNAMARA REGIS CHARLES	1933	M	Football
MCNEW MATT LEE	2001	M	Football
MCSHANE KEVIN JAMES	1990	M	Football
MEADOWS DAVID GLEN	1984	M	Football
MEEKER ROBERT CHARLES	1966	M	Football

NAME	YEAR	GENDER	SPORT
MEHRE HARRY J.	1922	M	Football
MEKO JUSTIN ANDREW	1999	M	Football
MELINKOVICH GEORGE JOSEPH	1935	M	Football
MELLO JAMES ANTHONY	1948	M	Football
MENIE THOMAS DINO	1972	M	Football
MENSE JAMES JOSEPH	1956	M	Football
MERANDI JOHN MICHAEL	2000	M	Football
MERKLE ROBERT WOODS JR.	1968	M	Football
MERLITTI JAMES ANTHONY	1970	M	Football
MERRICK THOMAS FRANCIS	1983	M	Football
MERRITT THOMAS PAUL	1972	M	Football
MERRIWEATHER RONALD J.	1981	M	Football
MERTES ALBERT THOMAS	1909	M	Football
METER BERNARD JAMES	1947	M	Football
METER BRIAN LOCKHART	1995	M	Football
METZGER BERT LEO SR.	1931	M	Football
MEYER HOWARD HENRY	1979	M	Football
MEYER JOHN EDWIN	1964	M	Football
MICHALAK RICHARD N.	1987	M	Football
MICHUTA JOHN FRANCIS	1936	M	Football
MIESZKOWSKI EDWARD THOMAS	1946	M	Football
MIHALKO RYAN STEVEN	1991	M	Football
MIKACICH JAMES LAWRENCE	1962	M	Football
MILBAUER FRANK AUGUSTUS	1925	M	Football
MILLER ALVIN MAURICE	1988	M	Football
MILLER CREIGHTON EUGENE	1944	M	Football
MILLER DAVID ANDREW	2002	M	Football
MILLER DONALD CHARLES HON.	1925	M	Football
MILLER EDGAR EDWARD	1925	M	Football
MILLER FRED C.	1929	M	Football
MILLER MARTIN HARRY	1910	M	Football
MILLER MICHAEL ANDRE	1994	M	Football
MILLER STEPHEN C.	1936	M	Football
MILLER THOMAS SEEAY	1943	M	Football
MILLER WALTER R.	1920	M	Football
MILLHEAM CURTIS K.	1934	M	Football
MILLIGAN SEAN PATRICK	2004	M	Football
MILLNER WAYNE VERNAL	1936	M	Football
MILOTA JAMES FRANCIS	1957	M	Football
MINIK FRANK	1963	M	Football
MINNIX ROBERT JAMES	1972	M	Football
MINOR KORY DESHAUN	1999	M	Football
MIRER RICK FRANKLIN	1993	M	Football
MISETIC STEVE	1994	M	Football
MISHLER RONALD C.	1982	M	Football
MISKOWICZ LEWIS JOHN	1974	M	Football
MITCHELL DARIN WAYNE JR.	2005	M	Football
MITCHELL DAVID LEE	1980	M	Football
MITCHELL MARK NICHOLAS	2001	M	Football
MITCHELL MATTHEW NATHAN	2006	M	Football
MITOULAS BILL	1998	M	Football
MITTELHAUSER THOMAS PATRICK	1965	M	Football
MOLINARO JAMES ANTHONY	2004	M	Football
MONAHAN JOSEPH MICHAEL	1964	M	Football
MONAHAN MARK TIMOTHY DR.	1996	M	Football
MONAHAN THOMAS FRANCIS III	1987	M	Football
MONAHAN THOMAS FRANCIS JR.	1961	M	Football
MONAHAN WILLIAM PAUL	1900	M	Football
MONTANA JOSEPH C. JR.	1979	M	Football
MONTY TIMOTHY STEVEN	1969	M	Football
MOONEY ALAN BRENDAN SR.	1940	M	Football
MOONEY MARTIN EDWARD	2006	M	Football
MOORE ELTON DEAN	1977	M	Football
MOORE LARON ANTHONY	1996	M	Football
MORE ROBERT JOSEPH	1983	M	Football
MORGAN GERALD EUGENE JR.	2002	M	Football
MORIARTY GEORGE JOSEPH	1936	M	Football
MORIARTY KERRY STEPHEN	1977	M	Football
MORIARTY LARRY	1988	M	Football
MORIARTY TREVOR PATRICK	1992	M	Football
MORRIN DANIEL SR.	1974	M	Football
MORRIS RODNEY WAYNE	1983	M	Football
MORRISON PAUL EDWARD	1939	M	Football
MORRISON RICHARD JOSEPH JR.	1991	M	Football
MORRISSEY JOSEPH S.	1928	M	Football
MORRISSEY ROCKNE	1954	M	Football
MORRISSEY WILLIAM THOMAS	1976	M	Football
MORSE JAMES A. SR.	1957	M	Football
MORTON ROBERT JOSEPH	2006	M	Football
MOSCARDELLI CHRISTOPHER PAUL	1992	M	Football
MOSLEY EMMETT IV	1997	M	Football
MOSLEY JOHN ANTHONY	1984	M	Football
MOWL ROBERT HENNING	2001	M	Football
MOYNIHAN BRENDAN JAMES	1982	M	Football
MUDRON PATRICK FRANCIS	1971	M	Football
MUEHLBAUER MICHAEL JOHN	1960	M	Football
MUELLER BRYAN ALEXANDER	1999	M	Football
MUHLENKAMP CHRIS EDWARD	1980	M	Football
MULLINS LAURENCE A.	1931	M	Football
MULVENA BRYAN MICHAEL	2000	M	Football
MUNDEE FRED WILLIAM	1937	M	Football
MUNRO JAMES THOMAS	1957	M	Football
MURPHY DENNIS MICHAEL	1963	M	Football
MURPHY EMMETT FRANCIS	1933	M	Football
MURPHY JOHN JOSEPH	1982	M	Football
MURPHY JOHN PATRICK	1938	M	Football
MURPHY LOUIS CLARENCE	1933	M	Football
MURPHY TERRENCE THOMAS	1978	M	Football
MURPHY THOMAS E.	1984	M	Football
MURPHY THOMAS F.	1929	M	Football
MURPHY THOMAS FRANCIS	1953	M	Football
MURPHY TIMOTHY J. JR.	1924	M	Football
MURRAY JASON SETH	2002	M	Football
MURRAY JOHN BERNARD	1963	M	Football
MURRIN GEORGE P.	1926	M	Football
MUSURCA JAMES EDWIN	1973	M	Football
MUTSCHELLER JAMES FRANCIS	1952	M	Football
MYERS GARY ARTHUR	1959	M	Football
NAGURSKI BRONKO KANE	1959	M	Football
NALLY THOMAS PATRICK	2004	M	Football
NASH JOSEPH HENRY	1929	M	Football
NASH THOMAS JOHN	1970	M	Football
NAU JEREMY THOMAS	1995	M	Football
NAUGHTON MICHAEL D. J.	1974	M	Football
NAYLOR RICHARD DENNIS	1984	M	Football
NEBEL EDWARD JOSEPH DR. JR.	1960	M	Football
NEECE STEPHEN CRAIG	1975	M	Football
NEFF ROBERT HUDKINS	1943	M	Football
NEIDERT ROBERT ANDREW	1971	M	Football
NELSON ERIC NICHOLAS	2002	M	Football
NELSON RAKI DALAS	2002	M	Football
NEMETH STEVE JOSEPH	1946	M	Football
NICKS RONNIE GLENN	2000	M	Football
NICOLA NORMAN JOSEPH	1965	M	Football
NICOLAZZI ROBERT JOSEPH	1960	M	Football
NICULA GEORGE DANNY	1956	M	Football
NIEHAUS STEVE GERARD	1976	M	Football
NIGHTINGALE CHARLES GEORGE	1971	M	Football
NIGRO MARK ALLEN	1989	M	Football
NISSI PAUL FRANK	1961	M	Football
NOPPENBERGER JOHN A.	1925	M	Football
NORMAN MARK CALDWELL	1980	M	Football
NORMAN TODD MARTIN	1994	M	Football
NORRI ERIC JOHN JR.	1969	M	Football
NOSBUSCH KEVIN STUART	1975	M	Football
NOVAKOV ANTHONY JOSEPH	1976	M	Football
NOVAKOV DANIEL PATRICK	1972	M	Football
NOVAKOV DANIEL PATRICK JR.	2003	M	Football
NOZNESKY PETER HARRY	1957	M	Football
OBERST EUGENE G.	1924	M	Football
O'BOYLE HARRY W.	1927	M	Football
O'BRIEN COLEMAN CARROLL J.D.	1969	M	Football
O'BRIEN JOHN DENNIS	1941	M	Football
O'CONNELL EDWARD JOSEPH	2003	M	Football
O'CONNOR BRENDAN THOMAS	2001	M	Football
O'CONNOR DANIEL J.	1905	M	Football
O'CONNOR DANIEL PAUL	1969	M	Football
O'CONNOR PAUL ANTHONY DR. SR.	1931	M	Football
O'CONNOR PHILIP J.	1949	M	Football
O'CONNOR W. ZEKE MR.	1946	M	Football
O'CONNOR WILLIAM J. P.	1948	M	Football
O'CONNOR WILLIAM S.	1929	M	Football
O'DONNELL JOHN FRANCIS	1975	M	Football
ODYNIEC NORMAN ANTHONY M.D.	1959	M	Football
O'HARA CHARLES ROBERT REV.	1963	M	Football
O'HARA JAMES JOSEPH JR.	1983	M	Football
O'HARA MICHAEL PATRICK	2006	M	Football
O'HAREN DAVID MARK	1985	M	Football
O'LEARY DANIEL EDWARD JR.	2000	M	Football
O'LEARY JAMES	1912	M	Football
O'LEARY THOMAS MICHAEL	1968	M	Football
OLENICZAK BRIAN PAUL	2001	M	Football
OLIVER HARRY EDWARD JR.	1983	M	Football
OLOSKY MARTIN LOUIS	1964	M	Football
OLSON ROBERT LYLE	1970	M	Football
O'MALLEY JAMES JOHN	1973	M	Football
O'NEIL ROBERT MAIOLI	1953	M	Football
O'NEILL F. MICHAEL JR.	1992	M	Football
O'NEILL JEFF HENRY	1985	M	Football
O'NEILL JOSEPH I. JR.	1936	M	Football
O'NEILL TIMOTHY DENNIS	2002	M	Football
OPELA BRUNO PETER	1946	M	Football
O'PHELAN JOHN IRELAND	1904	M	Football
ORACKO STEPHEN FRANCIS	1950	M	Football
O'REILLY CHARLES WILLIAM	1938	M	Football
O'REILLY MARTIN GORDON JR.	1942	M	Football
O'REILLY MICHAEL J. O.D.	1971	M	Football
ORIARD MICHAEL VINCENT DR.	1970	M	Football
ORR JUSTIN PETER	1999	M	Football
ORSINI STEVEN P.	1978	M	Football
OSTERMAN ROBERT THOMAS	1941	M	Football
OSTROWSKI CHESTER CASMER	1952	M	Football
O'TOOLE DANIEL P.	1973	M	Football
OWENS JOHN DAY	2002	M	Football
PAGE ALAN CEDRIC	1967	M	Football
PAGLEY LOUIS ANTHONY	1980	M	Football
PALLADINO ROBERT FRANCIS	1947	M	Football
PALLAS PETE G.	1979	M	Football
PALMER WILLIAM JOHN LUKE	2005	M	Football
PALUMBO SAM FRANK	1955	M	Football
PALUMBO SCOTT IAN	1996	M	Football
PANELLI JOHN ROCCO	1949	M	Football
PAPA ROBERT CLEMENT	1966	M	Football
PARENTI CHRISTOPHER MATTHEW	1994	M	Football
PARISE THOMAS CHARLES	1976	M	Football
PARISIEN ARTHUR EMILE	1928	M	Football
PARKER MICHAEL JOSEPH	1974	M	Football
PASQUESI ANTHONY LEONARD	1955	M	Football
PATERNOSTRO VICTOR JOHN	1967	M	Football
PATERRA FRANCIS FALCO	1954	M	Football
PATTON ERIC OWEN	1972	M	Football
PATULSKI WALTER GEORGE	1972	M	Football
PAULY GREGORY LEE	2005	M	Football
PAWELSKI DONALD PAUL	1982	M	Football
PAYNE DAVID FOLSOM CHAMPE	1999	M	Football
PAYNE RANDOLPH ANTHONY	1976	M	Football
PEARCY VAN MARK	1985	M	Football
PEARSON P. DUDLEY	1920	M	Football
PEIFFER W. MICHAEL	1972	M	Football
PENDERGAST KEVIN FRANCIS	1994	M	Football
PENICK ERIC ANTHONY	1975	M	Football
PENMAN EUGENE JOHN	1965	M	Football
PENZA DONALD FRANCIS	1954	M	Football
PERGINE JOHN SAMUEL	1968	M	Football
PERKO JOHN FRANCIS	1949	M	Football
PERKOWSKI JOSEPH CARL	1961	M	Football
PERONA MICHAEL JAMES	1997	M	Football
PERRINO MICHAEL NICHOLAS	1986	M	Football
PERRY ARTHUR REYBURN	1952	M	Football
PETERS MARTIN JOSEPH	1936	M	Football
PETERSON ANTHONY WAYNE	1994	M	Football
PETITBON JOHN ELLIS	1952	M	Football
PETITGOUT LUCAS GEORGE	1998	M	Football
PETRUNGARO CHARLES EUGENE	1960	M	Football
PFEFFERLE RICHARD JOSEPH	1936	M	Football
PFEIFFER WILLIAM MARTIN	1964	M	Football
PHELAN VINCENT NEWELL	1988	M	Football
PHELPS ROBERT ALVIN III	1998	M	Football
PHILLIPS DENNIS JOSEPH	1963	M	Football
PHILLIPS TERRY MICHAEL	1972	M	Football
PICCIN ANTHONY P.	1985	M	Football
PIEPUL MILTON JOHN	1941	M	Football
PIERRE-ANTOINE CARL-PHILIPPE	2003	M	Football
PIETROSANTE NICHOLAS VINCENT	1959	M	Football
PIETRZAK ROBERT J.	1960	M	Football
PILNEY ANTON JAMES	1936	M	Football
PINKETT ALLEN JEROME	1986	M	Football
PIVARNIK JOSEPH JOHN	1934	M	Football
PIVEC DAVID	1963	M	Football
PLANTZ RONALD ANTHONY	1986	M	Football
POHLEN PATRICK JOSEPH	1976	M	Football
POJMAN HENRY FRANCIS	1937	M	Football
POLISKY JOHN	1928	M	Football
POLLARD WILLIAM REGINALD	1994	M	Football
POMARICO FRANK J.	1974	M	Football
POORMAN GEORGE RAYMOND	1992	M	Football
POSKON FRANK DUANE	1970	M	Football
POTEMPA GARY A. D.D.S.	1974	M	Football
POTTER THOMAS ANTHONY	1947	M	Football
POTTIOS MYRON	1961	M	Football
POWERS JOHN PAUL	1962	M	Football
POWERS-NEAL RASHON DARNELL	2005	M	Football
POWLUS RONALD LEE JR.	1997	M	Football
POZDERAC PHILIP M.	1981	M	Football
PRENDERGAST RICHARD C. D.D.S.	1958	M	Football
PRINZIVALLI DAVID EDWARD	1990	M	Football
PRINZIVALLI DOMENIC PHILIP	1988	M	Football
PRITCHETT WESLEY ANDREW	1989	M	Football
PROFETA MICHAEL VINCENT	2004	M	Football
PROKOP JOSEPH MICHAEL	1942	M	Football
PSZERACKI JOSEPH STANLEY	1976	M	Football
PUNTILLO ANTHONY MYERS DR.	1988	M	Football
PUNTILLO CHARLES C. D.D.S.	1959	M	Football
PUPLIS ANDREW JOSEPH	1938	M	Football
PURCELL RICHARD WADE	1990	M	Football
PUTZSTUCK JOHN	1981	M	Football
QUEHL STEPHEN RICHARD	1976	M	Football
QUINN CHARLES F. JR.	1934	M	Football
QUINN JAMES T.	1927	M	Football
QUINN STEPHEN TIMOTHY	1968	M	Football

NAME	YEAR	GENDER	SPORT
QUINN THOMAS HERMAN	1969	M	Football
QUIST DAVID ARTHUR	1996	M	Football
RACE ADRIAN JOSEPH REV.	1938	M	Football
RACHAL VINCENT PAUL	1979	M	Football
RAICH NICHOLAS S.	1956	M	Football
RANKIN G. PAUL	1972	M	Football
RANSAVAGE ANTHONY J.	1931	M	Football
RAO LUIGI KUO FENG	2001	M	Football
RARIDON SCOTT DAVID JR.	2006	M	Football
RASCHER NORBERT H. JR.	1963	M	Football
RASCHER NORBERT H. SR.	1934	M	Football
RASSAS GEORGE JAMES	1941	M	Football
RASSAS KEVIN W.	1968	M	Football
RASSAS NICHOLAS CHARLES	1965	M	Football
RATERMAN JOHN EDWARD DR.	1972	M	Football
RATIGAN BRIAN LEE DR.	1993	M	Football
RATKOWSKI RAYMOND JAMES	1961	M	Football
RATTERMAN GEORGE WILLIAM	1949	M	Football
RAUSCH PETER JOHN	1992	M	Football
RAY JOHN WILLIAM	1948	M	Football
RAYAM HARDY LAWRENCE	1980	M	Football
READY ROBERT EMMETT	1955	M	Football
REAGAN ROBERT P.	1924	M	Football
RECENDEZ JOSEPH EDWARD	2001	M	Football
REESE FRANK ALEXANDER	1925	M	Football
REEVE DAVID ALAN	1978	M	Football
REGAN MICHAEL J. JR.	1956	M	Football
REGNER THOMAS EUGENE	1967	M	Football
REHDER THOMAS BERNARD II	1987	M	Football
REID DONALD FRANCIS	1970	M	Football
REILLY JAMES CHRIS	1970	M	Football
REILLY TIMOTHY P.	1979	M	Football
RESTIC JOSEPH WILLIAM D.M.D.	1979	M	Football
REVELLE STANLEY CARROLL	2005	M	Football
REYNOLDS FRANK R. JR.	1959	M	Football
REYNOLDS PAUL RICHARD	1956	M	Football
REYNOLDS THOMAS JOHN	1969	M	Football
RHOADS THOMAS PATRICK	1967	M	Football
RICE JOHN NELSON	1983	M	Football
RICE KEVIN PHILIP	1999	M	Football
RICE TONY EUGENE	1990	M	Football
RICHARDSON MICHAEL ISAIAH	2006	M	Football
RICHERSON MICHAEL CONWAY	1985	M	Football
RIDDER TIMOTHY KEVIN	1999	M	Football
RIDGLEY TROY VAIL	1991	M	Football
RIFFLE CHARLES FRANCIS	1940	M	Football
RIGALI JOSEPH L.	1926	M	Football
RIGALI ROBERT JOHN	1954	M	Football
RILEY THOMAS PATRICK	1987	M	Football
RINI THOMAS MICHAEL	1960	M	Football
ROACH THOMAS GERARD	1934	M	Football
ROBB AARON TOM	1989	M	Football
ROBERTS CHARLES RAYMOND	1971	M	Football
ROBERTS RYAN LANIER	2002	M	Football
ROBIN CASEY JOHN	2001	M	Football
ROBINSON JOHN JOSEPH	1936	M	Football
ROBINSON MARVIN	1991	M	Football
ROBINSON TYRONE JESSE	1973	M	Football
ROBST PAUL KENNETH	1954	M	Football
RODAMER RONALD DIMITRIUS	2004	M	Football
RODDY MARTIN JOSEPH	1985	M	Football
RODDY STEPHEN JOHN	1989	M	Football
RODENKIRK DONALD FRANK	1977	M	Football
ROGERS JOHN B.	1932	M	Football
ROGERS PAUL CHRISTIAN	1997	M	Football
ROGGEMAN THOMAS JOHN II	1985	M	Football
ROHAN ANDREW JOSEPH JR.	1975	M	Football
ROHRS GEORGE HENRY	1933	M	Football
ROKICH PETER ALLEN	1988	M	Football
ROLLE RICHARD RAMON JR.	1996	M	Football
RONSTADT ROBERT CARILLO SR.	1941	M	Football
ROOLF JAMES M.	1973	M	Football
ROSENTHAL MICHAEL PAUL	1999	M	Football
ROSSUM ALLEN B.	1998	M	Football
ROVAI FREDERICK JOSEPH	1947	M	Football
ROY NORBERT WAYNE	1962	M	Football
ROYER RICHARD GEORGE	1959	M	Football
RUDDY TIMOTHY DANIEL	1994	M	Football
RUDNICK TIMOTHY JOHN	1974	M	Football
RUDZINSKI JOSEPH GERARD	1983	M	Football
RUETTIGER DANIEL EUGENE	1976	M	Football
RUETZ ESTATE OF JOSEPH H.	1938	M	Football
RUFO JOHN FRANCIS	1977	M	Football
RUGGIERO FRANCIS ALEX	1946	M	Football
RUSSELL MARVIN ARNELLE	1977	M	Football
RUSSELL WILLIAM W.	1949	M	Football
RUTKOWSKI EDWARD JOHN A.	1963	M	Football
RUTKOWSKI FRANCIS ANTHONY	1976	M	Football
RUZICKA JAMES LEE	1970	M	Football
RYAN F. LARRY MR.	1948	M	Football

NAME	YEAR	GENDER	SPORT
RYAN JAMES ALBERT	2003	M	Football
RYAN KENNETH CHARLES	1980	M	Football
RYAN PATRICK WALTER	2003	M	Football
RYAN TIMOTHY THOMAS	1992	M	Football
RYAN W. JAMES DR.	1967	M	Football
RYDZEWSKI FRANK X.	1918	M	Football
RYMKUS LOUIS JOSEPH	1943	M	Football
SABAL AL WALTER	1960	M	Football
SACK ALLEN LEONARD	1967	M	Football
SADDLER LESHANE O'BRIEN	1994	M	Football
SADOWSKI EDWARD MARION	1939	M	Football
SAGGAU ROBERT JOSEPH	1941	M	Football
SALMON LOUIS J.	1905	M	Football
SALSICH PETER WITHINGTON JR.	1959	M	Football
SALVADOR ANTHONY LEE	2006	M	Football
SALVINO ROBERT	1957	M	Football
SAMPLE JEREMY A.	1995	M	Football
SAMUEL ALPHONSO	1975	M	Football
SANDERS AJANI MAKALANI	2000	M	Football
SANDRI WINSTON LEWIS	1991	M	Football
SANSON JAMES ALLAN JR.	2000	M	Football
SANTUCCI DANIEL ALAN	2006	M	Football
SAPP GEROME DAREN	2003	M	Football
SAPP JASON TARRELL	2004	M	Football
SARB MATTHEW LEON	2002	M	Football
SARB PATRICK JOSEPH SR.	1976	M	Football
SASS JAMES MICHAEL	1988	M	Football
SATTERFIELD ROBERT MARK	1989	M	Football
SAUGET RICHARD ARNOLD SR.	1966	M	Football
SAVOLDI JOSEPH A.	1931	M	Football
SAWICZ PAUL JOSEPH	1974	M	Football
SCALES EDWARD CHARLES	1974	M	Football
SCANLON RAYMOND JOSEPH	1909	M	Football
SCANNELL ROBERT JAMES	1957	M	Football
SCANNELL TIMOTHY JOHN	1986	M	Football
SCAROLA RYAN PATRICK	2003	M	Football
SCARPITTO ROBERT FRANK	1961	M	Football
SCHAACK EDWARD MICHAEL	1893	M	Football
SCHAAF JAMES HOWARD	1959	M	Football
SCHAEFER DONALD THOMAS	1956	M	Football
SCHARER EDWARD E.	1927	M	Football
SCHICCATANO NATHAN LESTER	2006	M	Football
SCHIRALLI ANGELO PETER	1967	M	Football
SCHIRALLI ROCCO VICTOR	1935	M	Football
SCHIRO JOHN C. D.D.S.	1984	M	Football
SCHIVARELLI PETER JAMES	1971	M	Football
SCHLEZES KENNETH G.	1973	M	Football
SCHMIDT JOSHUA PATRICK	2005	M	Football
SCHMITT WILLIAM C.	1910	M	Football
SCHMITZ STEVE THOMAS	1978	M	Football
SCHNURR FREDRICK NELSON	1967	M	Football
SCHOEN THOMAS RALPH	1968	M	Football
SCHOLTZ ROBERT JOSEPH	1960	M	Football
SCHOMAS NATHAN CHRISTOPHER C.	2004	M	Football
SCHRADER JAMES LEE	1955	M	Football
SCHRAMM PAUL LAWRENCE	1957	M	Football
SCHRENKER PAUL E.	1936	M	Football
SCHROFFNER STEFAN PAUL	1995	M	Football
SCHULZ CLAY ISIDOR	1962	M	Football
SCHUMACHER LARRY CLARENCE	1970	M	Football
SCHUSTER DAVID ALFRED	1983	M	Football
SCHUSTER KENNETH ROBERT	1949	M	Football
SCHWARTZ MARCHMONT HOWARD	1932	M	Football
SCOTT ROBERT JACOB	2000	M	Football
SCOTT VINCENT JOSEPH SR.	1948	M	Football
SCRUGGS MARTIN ALEC	1992	M	Football
SCULLY JOHN FRANCIS JR.	1980	M	Football
SEAMAN NEIL JOSEPH	1959	M	Football
SEAMAN THOMAS JOSEPH	1953	M	Football
SEASLY MICHAEL ALAN	1987	M	Football
SEFCIK GEORGE P.	1962	M	Football
SEILER PAUL HERMAN	1967	M	Football
SELCER RICHARD JAMES	1959	M	Football
SETTA NICHOLAS	2004	M	Football
SEXTON JAMES EDWARD	1991	M	Football
SEYMOUR JAMES PATRICK	1969	M	Football
SHAKESPEARE WILLIAM V.	1936	M	Football
SHANNON BRIAN DAVID DR.	1991	M	Football
SHANNON DANIEL JAMES	1955	M	Football
SHARKEY EDWARD AURIN	1977	M	Football
SHAUGHNESSY FRANK J.	1906	M	Football
SHAW LAWRENCE T.	1922	M	Football
SHAY GEORGE DANIEL	1930	M	Football
SHEEKETSKI JOSEPH LAWRENCE	1933	M	Football
SHELLOGG ALEC REGIS	1939	M	Football
SHELTON MATTHEW LOUIS	2005	M	Football
SHERIDAN BENJAMIN MASON	1940	M	Football
SHERIDAN PHILIP F. JR.	1966	M	Football
SHERIDAN PHILIP F. SR.	1946	M	Football
SHERLOCK JAMES FRANCIS	1963	M	Football

NAME	YEAR	GENDER	SPORT
SHERRY WILLIAM J.	1921	M	Football
SHEY CHRISTOPHER FRANCIS	1990	M	Football
SHIELDS JACK M. MR.	1983	M	Football
SHINER MICHAEL ROSS	1984	M	Football
SHINGLER JOHN PATRICK	2000	M	Football
SHULSEN J. RICHARD	1959	M	Football
SICUSO PHILIP ANTHONY	1999	M	Football
SIEWE WILLIAM EDWARD	1981	M	Football
SIGNAIGO JOSEPH SALVATORE	1948	M	Football
SIGRIST TIMOTHY JOHN	1971	M	Football
SILVER NATHAN	1906	M	Football
SILVESTRO MICHAEL JOHN	1980	M	Football
SIMIEN ERIK PAUL	1990	M	Football
SIMMONS FLOYD WESTON	1948	M	Football
SIMON JOHN EDWARD JR.	1964	M	Football
SIMON TIMOTHY JAMES	1977	M	Football
SIMONICH EDWARD FRANCIS	1939	M	Football
SIPES SHERRILL F. JR.	1957	M	Football
SITKO EMIL MARTIN	1951	M	Football
SITKO STEVEN JOSEPH SR.	1940	M	Football
SKOGLUND LEONARD H. JR.	1938	M	Football
SKOGLUND ROBERT WALTER	1945	M	Football
SKRONSKI JOHN SIGMUND	1983	M	Football
SLAFKOSKY JOHN PAUL	1963	M	Football
SLAGER RICHARD RAMEY	1976	M	Football
SLETTVET THOMAS CHARLES	1969	M	Football
SLOVAK EMIL	1947	M	Football
SMAGALA STANLEY ADAM JR.	1994	M	Football
SMITH ANDREW MICHAEL DR.	1992	M	Football
SMITH ANTHONY DUANE	1992	M	Football
SMITH ANTHONY JOSEPH	1988	M	Football
SMITH CHRIS M.	1985	M	Football
SMITH DARNELL DUPREE	1997	M	Football
SMITH EUGENE DU BOIS	1977	M	Football
SMITH HUNTER DWIGHT	1999	M	Football
SMITH IRVIN MARTIN	1993	M	Football
SMITH JAMES ANTHONY	1966	M	Football
SMITH JOHN PHILIP	1929	M	Football
SMITH JUSTIN L.	2001	M	Football
SMITH KEVIN MARTIN	1984	M	Football
SMITH MAURICE FRANCIS	1921	M	Football
SMITH NICHOLAS JAY	1993	M	Football
SMITH RICHARD PAUL	1927	M	Football
SMITH RODNEY MARC	1992	M	Football
SMITH SCOTT	1973	M	Football
SMITH SHAWN ALI	1990	M	Football
SMITH SHERMAN M. JR.	1975	M	Football
SMITH W. LANCASTER MR. SR.	1950	M	Football
SMITH WILLIAM GEORGE	1933	M	Football
SMITHBERGER JAMES LAWRENCE	1968	M	Football
SNOW JACK THOMAS SR.	1965	M	Football
SNOW PAUL FRANCIS	1969	M	Football
SNOWDEN JAMES	1964	M	Football
SNYDER JAMES WILLIAM	1939	M	Football
SNYDER WILLIAM M. JR.	1962	M	Football
SOLARI FREDERICK C. JR.	1936	M	Football
SOLLMANN SCOTT ALBERT	1997	M	Football
SORENSEN DANIEL DUANE	1987	M	Football
SOUTHALL CORNELIUS CHRISTOPHER	1989	M	Football
SOUTNER JOHN PAUL JR.	1977	M	Football
SPANIEL FRANK JAMES	1950	M	Football
SPEARS KENNETH WAYNE	1992	M	Football
SPENCE MARVIN A.	1987	M	Football
SPENCER JAMEION LADELL	1999	M	Football
SPICKELMIER JONATHAN STEVEN	1998	M	Football
SPIELMAKER DAANE JEROME	1984	M	Football
SPRUELL BYRON ORAN	1987	M	Football
STAFFORD CHARLES CARNELL	1995	M	Football
STAMS FRANK MICHAEL	1989	M	Football
STANDRING JOHN JOSEPH JR.	1970	M	Football
STANGE AUGUSTAS HAROLD	1927	M	Football
STANITZEK FRANCIS JOSEPH	1957	M	Football
STARK CRAIG PHILIP	1971	M	Football
STEC GREGORY WALTER	1995	M	Football
STEENBERGE PATRICK WILLIAM	1973	M	Football
STENGER BRIAN FRANCIS	1969	M	Football
STEPANIAK RALPH MICHAEL	1972	M	Football
STEPHAN JOHN AUDLEY	1975	M	Football
STEPHENS SHANNON DELAWRENCE	1999	M	Football
STEPHENS W. CLAYTON MR.	1964	M	Football
STEVENSON DANIEL WHITNEY	2005	M	Football
STEVENSON HARRY JR.	1940	M	Football
STICKLES MONTY ANTHONY	1960	M	Football
STILLEY KENNETH LEONARD	1936	M	Football
STOCK JAMES P.	1976	M	Football
STOKES CLEMENT ODOM	2002	M	Football
STONE CHRISTOPHER L.	1983	M	Football
STONE DANIEL E.	1982	M	Football
STONE JAMES EDWARD JR.	1981	M	Football
STONEBREAKER MICHAEL DAVID	1990	M	Football

NAME	YEAR	GENDER	SPORT
STOVALL MAURICE AURILIUS	2006	M	Football
STREETER GEORGE LEON JR.	1989	M	Football
STROHMEYER GEORGE F.	1951	M	Football
STROUD CLIFFORD M.	1996	M	Football
STUDER DEAN PAUL	1957	M	Football
STUEBE DAVID C.	1962	M	Football
STUHLDREHER HARRY AUGUSTUS	1925	M	Football
SULLIVAN EDWARD ALLEN	1957	M	Football
SULLIVAN GEORGE A.	1948	M	Football
SULLIVAN LAWRENCE PATRICK	1943	M	Football
SULLIVAN PETER KENT	1969	M	Football
SULLIVAN THOMAS JOHN	1966	M	Football
SULLIVAN TIMOTHY JOHN	1974	M	Football
SUSKO LAWRENCE	1974	M	Football
SWATLAND RICHARD THOMAS	1967	M	Football
SWEARINGEN TIMOTHY M.	1969	M	Football
SWEENEY CHARLES A. SR.	1938	M	Football
SWEENEY JOHN FRANCIS M.D.	1983	M	Football
SWEENEY ROBERT JOSEPH	1975	M	Football
SWENDSEN FREDERICK LYMAN DR.	1972	M	Football
SWISTOWICZ MICHAEL PAUL	1950	M	Football
SWOBODA DAVID MICHAEL	1982	M	Football
SYLVESTER STEVEN P.	1975	M	Football
SZATKO GREG FRANCIS	1974	M	Football
SZOT DENIS EDWARD	1964	M	Football
SZYMANSKI FRANK STANLEY HON.	1947	M	Football
SZYMANSKI RICHARD FRANK	1955	M	Football
TAFELSKI MICHAEL DENNIS	1988	M	Football
TALAGA THOMAS TERRANCE	1966	M	Football
TALIAFERRO JOHN WILTON III	1995	M	Football
TANCZOS DANIEL EDWARD	1987	M	Football
TATUM KINNON RAY II	1997	M	Football
TAYLOR AARON MATTHEW	1994	M	Football
TAYLOR PERNELL	1987	M	Football
TAYLOR ROBERT HAROLD	1954	M	Football
TEASDALE JOHN PATRICK	2002	M	Football
TELFER ROBERT CHARLES	1965	M	Football
TERLEP GEORGE R.	1949	M	Football
TERRELL PATRICK CHRISTOPHER	1990	M	Football
THAYER THOMAS A.	1984	M	Football
THEISMANN JOSEPH ROBERT	1971	M	Football
THERNES MATTHEW JOHN	1936	M	Football
THESING JOSEPH ROGER	1940	M	Football
THOMANN RICHARD LOUIS	1972	M	Football
THOMAS JOHN FOSTER	1980	M	Football
THOMAS JOSEPH LEE	1999	M	Football
THOMAS JUSTIN TERRELL	2003	M	Football
THOMAS ROBERT R.	1974	M	Football
THOMPSON JEFFREY DEAN	2005	M	Football
THORNE MARCUS ALI	1996	M	Football
THORNTON PETER PAUL II	1966	M	Football
THUNEY MARK W.	N/A	M	Football
TIBBLE ADAM DAVID	2002	M	Football
TIMM DON PAUL	1957	M	Football
TOBIN GEORGE EDWARD	1948	M	Football
TOBIN JOHN EDWARD	1934	M	Football
TODOROVICH MARKO JOHN	1947	M	Football
TONEFF ROBERT	1952	M	Football
TONELLI MARIO GEORGE	1939	M	Football
TORAN STACEY J.	1984	M	Football
TOTH WILLIAM RONALD	1959	M	Football
TOWNSEND MICHAEL LAVON	1974	M	Football
TOWNSEND WILLIE CORNELIUS	1974	M	Football
TRAPP WILLIAM JOSEPH	1972	M	Football
TRAVER LESLIE JOHN	1962	M	Football
TRIBE MICHAEL TIMOTHY	2000	M	Football
TRIPP TIMOTHY ALAN	1982	M	Football
TRIPUCKA FRANCIS J.	1949	M	Football
TUCK EDWARD ANTHONY	1969	M	Football
TUCK JUSTIN LEE	2005	M	Football
TULL ROBERT FRANCIS	1978	M	Football
TWOMEY TIMOTHY ALOYSIUS	1930	M	Football
TYNER STUART DOUGLAS DR.	1993	M	Football
UNDERWOOD JOHN DREWERY	1985	M	Football
UNIACKE KEVIN ROBERT	1977	M	Football
UNIS JOSEPH ANTHONY	1980	M	Football
UNIS THOMAS C. JR.	1977	M	Football
URBAN GASPER G.	1948	M	Football
VAINISI JOHN ANTHONY	1950	M	Football
VAIRO DOMINIC M.	1935	M	Football
VAN HOOK-DRUCKER NOAH ASHTON	2000	M	Football
VAN HUFFEL ALAN FREDERICK	1968	M	Football
VAN SUMMERN ROBERT WILLIAM	1949	M	Football
VANDENBURGH THOMAS LEE	1980	M	Football
VANGEN WILLARD ROY	1949	M	Football
VARRICHIONE FRANK JOSEPH	1955	M	Football
VASYS ARUNAS BRUNO	1966	M	Football
VEHR NICHOLAS JOHN	1981	M	Football
VEJAR LAWRENCE MOSE	1934	M	Football
VERGARA GEORGE A.	1925	M	Football
VEZIE H. MANFRED	1931	M	Football
VINSON DAVID WILLIAMS M.D.	1978	M	Football
VIOLA EUGENE JOHN	1962	M	Football
VIRACOLA MICHAEL THOMAS	1984	M	Football
VIROK ERNIE	1945	M	Football
VISOVATTI MICHAEL FRANK	1988	M	Football
VLK GEORGE GALE	1931	M	Football
VOEDISCH JOHN T.	1928	M	Football
VOELKERS JOHN J.	1918	M	Football
VOGEL HAROLD R.	1963	M	Football
VOLLERS KURT FREDRICK	2002	M	Football
VONWYL HAROLD R. JR.	1986	M	Football
VUILLEMIN EDWARD A.	1969	M	Football
VUKELICH JASCINT PAUL	2001	M	Football
WACHTEL CHRISTOPHER ROBERT	1998	M	Football
WACKOWSKI JOHN PAUL	1986	M	Football
WADSWORTH MICHAEL ANDREW	1966	M	Football
WAGASY WILLIAM JASON	1996	M	Football
WAGNER JOHN RICHARD	1999	M	Football
WALLACE JOHN JAMES	1928	M	Football
WALLACE LEON EDWARD	2000	M	Football
WALLNER FREDERICK W. SR.	1951	M	Football
WALLS ROBERT THOMAS JR.	1976	M	Football
WALSH ADAM J. SR.	1925	M	Football
WALSH MAX THOMAS M.D.	1974	M	Football
WALSH MICHAEL P.	1984	M	Football
WALSH WILLIAM H.	1949	M	Football
WALTON SHANE SCOTT	2003	M	Football
WARD REGINALD EUGENE	1988	M	Football
WARD ROBERT NORMAN	1958	M	Football
WARNER JOHN ANDREW JR.	1943	M	Football
WASHINGTON ROBERT E. JR.	1974	M	Football
WATSON COURTNEY	2004	M	Football
WATTERS RICHARD J.	1990	M	Football
WAYBRIGHT DOUGLAS GILES	1950	M	Football
WAYMER DAVID B. JR.	1980	M	Football
WEAVER ANTHONY LEE	2003	M	Football
WEBB MICHAEL KERRY	1973	M	Football
WEBER ROBIN WILLIAM	1976	M	Football
WEBSTER MICHAEL CHARLES DR.	1966	M	Football
WEIDNER FREDERICK W.	1935	M	Football
WEILER JAMES EDWARD	1977	M	Football
WEINLE JEROME ALLEN	1984	M	Football
WEISSENHOFER RON ALLEN	1986	M	Football
WEITHMAN JAMES CARL	1953	M	Football
WELLS BRANDY ODELL	1988	M	Football
WENDELL MARTIN P.	1949	M	Football
WENGIERSKI TIMOTHY JOHN	1967	M	Football
WEST RODERICK KENNON	1990	M	Football
WESTON JEFFREY G.	1978	M	Football
WESTOVER MATTHEW R.	1983	M	Football
WETOSKA ROBERT STEPHEN	1959	M	Football
WHELAN BRIAN GREGORY	1982	M	Football
WHELAN JOHN DELAN	1953	M	Football
WHITE DONALD RICHARD	1960	M	Football
WHITE JAMES JOSEPH	1945	M	Football
WHITE STEPHEN ANTHONY	1985	M	Football
WHITESIDE WILLIAM ANTHONY JR.	1951	M	Football
WHITNEY RICHARD WAYNE III	2006	M	Football
WHITTINGTON MICHAEL SCOTT	1980	M	Football
WIGHTKIN WILLIAM JOHN	1950	M	Football
WILKE HENRY RUSSELL	1960	M	Football
WILKE ROBERT EDWARD	1937	M	Football
WILKE ROGER SR.	1962	M	Football
WILLERTZ STEPHEN JOHN	1985	M	Football
WILLIAMS BRADLEY JOHN	2000	M	Football
WILLIAMS GEORGE DUANE	1962	M	Football
WILLIAMS GEORGE ELMORE	1992	M	Football
WILLIAMS JOEL D.	1987	M	Football
WILLIAMS LAWRENCE R. II	1985	M	Football
WILLIAMS ROBERT ALLEN	1951	M	Football
WILLIAMS ROBERT WILLIAM M.D.	1959	M	Football
WILLIAMSON GREGORY S.	1982	M	Football
WILSON GEORGE ALLEN	1956	M	Football
WILSON MARCUS SCOTT	2005	M	Football
WILSON TROY ANTHONY	1987	M	Football
WINEGARDNER JAMES MICHAEL	1969	M	Football
WISNE ANDREW MICHAEL	2002	M	Football
WISNE GERALD EDWARD	1969	M	Football
WISNE JERRY EDWARD	1999	M	Football
WITCHGER JAMES D.	1971	M	Football
WITTY PETER NATHAN	1989	M	Football
WODECKI DARRYL JOSEPH	1991	M	Football
WOEBKENBERG HARRY B. III	1976	M	Football
WOLSKI WILLIAM FRANK	1966	M	Football
WOOD GREGORY M.	1963	M	Football
WOODEN SHAWN ANTHONY	1996	M	Football
WOODS ROBERT AUGUSTINE	2006	M	Football
WORDEN NEIL JAMES	1954	M	Football
WRAY C. ROBERT MR.	1952	M	Football
WRIGHT HARRY CHARLES	1943	M	Football
WRIGHT JAMES REID	1971	M	Football
WRIGHT THOMAS A.	1973	M	Football
WROBLEWSKI THOMAS JOSEPH	1980	M	Football
WUJCIAK ALAN ROBERT	1976	M	Football
WUNSCH HARRY F.	1934	M	Football
WYNN RENALDO LEVALLE	1996	M	Football
WYNNE ELMER B.	1928	M	Football
YODER JAMES CHARLES	1972	M	Football
YONAKOR JOHN JOSEPH	1948	M	Football
YOUNG BARRY JOEL	1984	M	Football
YOUNG BRYANT COLBY	1994	M	Football
YURA CHRISTOPHER JAMES	2003	M	Football
ZACKRISON KURT MATTHEW	1989	M	Football
ZAJESKI BENEDICT JAMES	1957	M	Football
ZALEJSKI ERNEST RAYMOND	1950	M	Football
ZAMBROSKI ANTHONY JOHN	1952	M	Football
ZANOT ROBERT JOSEPH	1976	M	Football
ZAPPALA ANTHONY JOSEPH	1977	M	Football
ZATAVESKI MARK JOSEPH	1995	M	Football
ZAVAGNIN MARK PETER	1983	M	Football
ZEIGLER CURTIS DUSTIN	1996	M	Football
ZEIGLER DUSTY	1995	M	Football
ZELENKA MICHAEL ROBERT	2001	M	Football
ZELLARS RAYMOND MARK	1995	M	Football
ZENNER ELMER JOHN	1937	M	Football
ZENNER JOHN JOSEPH	1967	M	Football
ZETTEK SCOTT C.	1981	M	Football
ZIEGLER EDWARD HAROLD	1970	M	Football
ZIELONY RICHARD ZBIGNIEW	1972	M	Football
ZIEMBA WALTER J.	1943	M	Football
ZIKAS MICHAEL S.	1972	M	Football
ZILLY JOHN LYNUS	1947	M	Football
ZIMMERMAN GEOFFREY LEE	1970	M	Football
ZLOCH CHARLES RICHARD	1971	M	Football
ZLOCH JAMES EDWARD	1974	M	Football
ZLOCH WILLIAM JOSEPH	1966	M	Football
ZONTINI LOUIS ROGERS	1940	M	Football
ZORICH CHRISTOPHER ROBERT	1991	M	Football
ZUBER TIMOTHY PATRICK	1972	M	Football
ZUROWSKI DAVID MATTHEW	1967	M	Football
ZWERS JOSEPH BERNARD	1937	M	Football
ANDERSON ADAM RAY	2001	M	Golf
ANTHONY JOHN JOSEPH	1986	M	Golf
ARQUILLA ARTHUR PAT JR.	1950	M	Golf
BALDERSTON THOMAS TALMAGE	2006	M	Golf
BALDWIN HARRY ALFRED	1937	M	Golf
BALDWIN MARK JOSEF	2006	M	Golf
BANKS JOHN LAWRENCE	1934	M	Golf
BATTAGLIA ROBERT JOSEPH	1971	M	Golf
BAUWENS J. ERIC M.D.	1980	M	Golf
BEAUPRE FRANCIS A.	1931	M	Golf
BEAUPRE RUSSELL JOSEPH	1931	M	Golf
BELMONTE ROBERT CAESAR	1977	M	Golf
BENNETT CHARLES R.	1939	M	Golf
BERLAND TERRANCE PAUL	1990	M	Golf
BESENFELDER JAMES J. SR.	1948	M	Golf
BEST MARTIN C.	1973	M	Golf
BETZ PAUL CHARLES	1974	M	Golf
BISCONTI PETER VINCENT JR.	1963	M	Golf
BONA CHRISTOPHER J.	1987	M	Golf
BRADLEY ARTHUR LOUIS	1931	M	Golf
BRANDS MICHAEL CLARK	1969	M	Golf
BREEN WILLIAM J.	1949	M	Golf
BURDA JEFFREY PAUL	1975	M	Golf
BURTON CHRISTOPHER FRENCH	1996	M	Golf
BYRD CHRISTOPHER H.	1973	M	Golf
CAMPBELL NORMAN PHILLIP	1988	M	Golf
CARROLL MARTIN JOSEPH JR.	1958	M	Golf
CASTLEMAN WILLIAM PRYOR JR.	1939	M	Golf
CHANEY MICHAEL PATRICK	1995	M	Golf
CLYNES JAMES J. HON. JR.	1945	M	Golf
COLE WILLIAM NOONAN	1935	M	Golf
COLNITIS STEVEN CHRISTOPHER	2005	M	Golf
CONLEY GEORGE T.	1948	M	Golf
CONNELL JEFFREY ALAN	2000	M	Golf
CONNELLY JOHN DAVID	N/A	M	Golf
CONNELLY RICHARD PATRICK	1988	M	Golf
CONROY DENIS SHANNON	1971	M	Golf
CONRY JOHN JOSEPH	1942	M	Golf
CORCORAN JOSEPH MICHAEL	1939	M	Golf
COSTELLO GEORGE KEARINS	1940	M	Golf
CRISANTI MICHAEL LAWRENCE	1992	M	Golf
CULVEYHOUSE JAMES KEVIN	1976	M	Golf
CVENGROS WILLIAM DAVID	1970	M	Golf
DANAHY J. PATRICK MR. SR.	1966	M	Golf
DAY WINFIELD S. JR.	1936	M	Golf
DAYTON CHRISTOPHER JOHN	1993	M	Golf
DELANEY JOHN PATRICK	1976	M	Golf
DENNEN JOSEPH MATTHEW	1993	M	Golf

NAME	YEAR	GENDER	SPORT	NAME	YEAR	GENDER	SPORT	NAME	YEAR	GENDER	SPORT
DEUTSCH ERIC JAMES	2006	M	Golf	MINNICH PAUL ALLAN	1954	M	Golf	ARENDT PATRICK JAMES	1992	M	Hockey
DIEMER DOUGLAS JAMES	1997	M	Golf	MOHAN PATRICK OWEN	1989	M	Golf	ARKELL THOMAS JESSE	1994	M	Hockey
DONOHOE BRIAN PATRICK	1997	M	Golf	MOLLER LAWRENCE F.	1931	M	Golf	AUGUSTINE JAMES LAURENCE	1976	M	Hockey
DONOHUE PHILIP ANDREW	1940	M	Golf	MONTEDONICO JOHN SCOTT	1935	M	Golf	BADALICH JEFFREY M.	1986	M	Hockey
DORE THOMAS PATRICK SR.	1949	M	Golf	MOORE WILLIAM AUSTIN HERBERT	1996	M	Golf	BAGNE TROY HERBERT	2000	M	Hockey
DOYLE MICHAEL A. JR.	1953	M	Golf	MOORHEAD WILLIAM C. JR.	1943	M	Golf	BALES CHRIS PHILLIP	1996	M	Hockey
DREW DAVID THOMAS	1973	M	Golf	MOORMAN DAVID JOHN	1984	M	Golf	BANKOSKE DAVID JOHN	1992	M	Hockey
DUNN JAMES WILLIAM	1971	M	Golf	MORESCO JOSEPH LEROY	1953	M	Golf	BANKOSKE ROBERT PAUL	1989	M	Hockey
EATON ROBERT LAWRENCE	1953	M	Golf	MOSHER ARTHUR JOSEPH	1946	M	Golf	BAUMGARTNER ROBERT VAN	1978	M	Hockey
EISENBEIS JOHN FRANCIS M.D.	1984	M	Golf	MRUS JAMES D.	1958	M	Golf	BELLOMY REX ROBERT	1983	M	Hockey
FARRELL CHARLES FRIEDRICHS	1998	M	Golf	MULFLUR W. JOSEPH MR. SR.	1956	M	Golf	BEMISS ROY WILLIAM	1989	M	Hockey
FEHLIG EUGENE ARTHUR	1943	M	Golf	MURPHY PRESTON VINCENT	1951	M	Golf	BENNING MARK	1983	M	Hockey
FEHLIG LOUIS CLEMENT	1937	M	Golf	MUSICK CHARLES R. JR.	1969	M	Golf	BERG ERIK VICTOR	1997	M	Hockey
FERLIC GAVIN FREDERICK	2004	M	Golf	NASH THOMAS DANIEL JR.	1942	M	Golf	BIANCHI STEVE	1983	M	Hockey
FERLMANN JAMES C. M.D.	1983	M	Golf	NEAD DENNIS MICHAEL	1959	M	Golf	BIECK MATTHEW GEORGE	1993	M	Hockey
FERREL ROBERT WILLIAM	1963	M	Golf	NIELD SAMUEL JOSEPH JR.	1941	M	Golf	BILTON ROBERT JOSEPH	1989	M	Hockey
FILIPIAK ROBERT C.	1956	M	Golf	NOLTA PAUL LAWRENCE	1991	M	Golf	BJORK KIRT FREDERICK	1983	M	Hockey
FISCHER WILLIAM EDWARD	1952	M	Golf	O'CONNELL CHRISTOPHER THOMAS	1995	M	Golf	BLACK STERLING DAVID	1993	M	Hockey
FISHER WILLIAM C.	1943	M	Golf	O'CONNELL MICHAEL ALAN JR.	1992	M	Golf	BLAINEY JAMES FREDERICK	1971	M	Hockey
FITZMAURICE SHAUN EARLE	1968	M	Golf	O'CONNELL MICHAEL THOMAS	1965	M	Golf	BONADIO ANTHONY MARSHALL	1984	M	Hockey
FITZPATRICK JOHN F.	1948	M	Golf	ODLAUG BRUCE GARLAND	1962	M	Golf	BONK JOSEPH ALEXANDER	1972	M	Hockey
FLANAGAN CHRISTIE STEPHEN	1960	M	Golf	O'DONOVAN JOHN FRANCIS III	1986	M	Golf	BONK MICHAEL ROBERT	1973	M	Hockey
FOLEY JOHN O'BRIEN	1955	M	Golf	O'MALLEY EDWARD ALBERT	1932	M	Golf	BOREGA NATHAN ALEKSANDER	2000	M	Hockey
FUHRER STEPHEN EDDY	1986	M	Golf	O'SHEA LEWIS JAMES	1931	M	Golf	BOSSY DAVID PATRICK	1977	M	Hockey
GARSIDE THOMAS ARTHUR M.D.	1958	M	Golf	O'TOOLE DANIEL P.	1973	M	Golf	BOURQUE ROGER A.	1977	M	Hockey
GENNETTE MICHAEL ROBERT	1979	M	Golf	PANGRAZE DAVID ROBERT	1984	M	Golf	BOWIE JOSEPH F.	1984	M	Hockey
GIORGIO DOUGLAS JOSEPH III	1989	M	Golf	PARK FELIX ROMAN JR.	1956	M	Golf	BRENNAN ROBERT JAMES	1929	M	Hockey
GORDON CHARLES PATRICK	1957	M	Golf	PATAK RAYMOND HENRY	1961	M	Golf	BRITTON BRUCE JOHN	1972	M	Hockey
GRACE JOSEPH MARKEY JR.	1958	M	Golf	PETERS CRAIG ALAN	1983	M	Golf	BROWN JAMES CARLTON JR.	1982	M	Hockey
GRACE THOMAS JAMES	1962	M	Golf	PIRRO JOHN JOSEPH JR.	1967	M	Golf	BROWNSCHIDLE JEFFREY PAUL	1981	M	Hockey
GREEN HERMAN WILLIAM	1936	M	Golf	PORTER PAUL P.	1948	M	Golf	BROWNSCHIDLE JOHN JOSEPH JR.	1977	M	Hockey
GSCHWIND A. EDWARD MR.	1954	M	Golf	POWERS JOHN RICHARD JR.	1953	M	Golf	BRUININKS BRETT DOUGLAS	1996	M	Hockey
GUSTAFSON SCOTT MICHAEL	2006	M	Golf	QUINN GARY JOSEPH	1973	M	Golf	BUMBACCO EDWARD MICHAEL	1974	M	Hockey
HAGEN WALTER CHAS. JR.	1940	M	Golf	QUINN JOHN J.	1949	M	Golf	BURKE BRIAN M.	1979	M	Hockey
HANLON MARK TIMOTHY	1986	M	Golf	RATAY STEVEN MICHAEL	2002	M	Golf	BYERS DANIEL ROGER	1978	M	Hockey
HANLON THOMAS F.	1949	M	Golf	REGNIER WILLIAM MAX	1966	M	Golf	BYERS TIMOTHY JOHN	1976	M	Hockey
HANSON COLE WILEY	1996	M	Golf	RICHERT DAVID WALTER	1979	M	Golf	CADDO TIMOTHY MARK	1989	M	Hockey
HARDIN BRADLEY ALLEN	1999	M	Golf	ROBERTS JOHN G.	1932	M	Golf	CAMERON SCOTT F.	1981	M	Hockey
HARRIGAN JOHN LOUIS	1943	M	Golf	ROLFS ROBERT THEODORE	1950	M	Golf	CAMPBELL JOHN J.	1972	M	Hockey
HEATON J. MICHAEL	1968	M	Golf	ROSE THOMAS JOSEPH M.D.	1960	M	Golf	CARLSON DANIEL PATRICK	2001	M	Hockey
HEPLER JOEL NEWTON	1997	M	Golf	RYAN THOMAS JAMES	1987	M	Golf	CARON DAVID ALBERT	1977	M	Hockey
HIGHDUCHECK ALBERT EDWARD	1962	M	Golf	SACHECK TIMOTHY JOHN	1981	M	Golf	CASTNER PAUL H.	1923	M	Hockey
HINIKER JAMES JOHN JR.	1965	M	Golf	SAURS TIMOTHY JOSEPH	1979	M	Golf	CATHCART CHRISTOPHER JOHN	1973	M	Hockey
HORAK ROBERT ALLEN	1982	M	Golf	SCHAFFLER PATRICK MARTIN	2001	M	Golf	CEY MORGAN LESTER	2005	M	Hockey
HUDAK PAUL ANTHONY	1951	M	Golf	SCHALLER WILLIAM JAMES	1940	M	Golf	CHAPMAN BRENT PAUL	1985	M	Hockey
HUFFMAN LON JOSEPH	1986	M	Golf	SCHLECK EVERHART JOHN	1948	M	Golf	CHIN MICHAEL	2003	M	Hockey
HUGGINS MATTHEW QUINTON	1998	M	Golf	SCHNURR EDWARD JULIUS JR.	1962	M	Golf	CHIPCHASE CHAD ANDREW	2001	M	Hockey
HUND FRANCIS XAVIER	1960	M	Golf	SCHREIBER GEORGE ARTHUR	1941	M	Golf	CLARK RYAN STEWART	2001	M	Hockey
KENNEDY JAMES GERALD JR.	1959	M	Golf	SCHUSTER PHILIP FRANCIS	1961	M	Golf	CLARKE PAUL M.	1977	M	Hockey
KENNEDY JAMES H.	1926	M	Golf	SCULLY DENNIS JAMES	1945	M	Golf	COE JEREMY PATRICK	1996	M	Hockey
KENNEDY ROBERT JOSEPH	1979	M	Golf	SCULLY THOMAS BERNARD M.D.	1983	M	Golf	COLLARD DANIEL C.	1982	M	Hockey
KENNEDY THOMAS JOSEPH	1947	M	Golf	SEIDEL RICHARD STEPHEN	1948	M	Golf	COLLIER GEOFFREY DENISON	1978	M	Hockey
KENNY JAMES PATRICK	1961	M	Golf	SHEEHAN THOMAS E.	1939	M	Golf	COLLINS MICHAEL JOSEPH M.D.	1971	M	Hockey
KENT ALEXANDER STEVEN	2001	M	Golf	SIEGLER CHRISTOPHER J.	1967	M	Golf	CONROY PATRICK A. JR.	1975	M	Hockey
KENT WILLIAM DANIEL	2000	M	Golf	SMITH JOSEPH VICTOR JR.	1967	M	Golf	COPELAND ROBERT RICH JR.	1992	M	Hockey
KISTNER MICHAEL CARL	1975	M	Golf	STAHL JAMES EDWARD JR.	1961	M	Golf	CORDES JAMES MARSHALL	1972	M	Hockey
KITCH C. TERRANCE	1963	M	Golf	STANIS BRADFORD JASON	1998	M	Golf	CORNELIUS SAM MCDONALD	2002	M	Hockey
KLAUER DANIEL GERARD	2006	M	Golf	STUHR GEORGE H.	1949	M	Golf	COTNOIR BENOIT	1999	M	Hockey
KLEFFMAN EDGAR K.	1948	M	Golf	SYRON E. LLOYD	1958	M	Golf	COX JOHN DAVID	1982	M	Hockey
KLEM TODD BERNARD	1994	M	Golf	TAYLOR WILLIAM JEFFREY	1931	M	Golf	CUNHA RICHARD J. JR.	1973	M	Hockey
KLETT THOMAS O'NEIL	1951	M	Golf	TENBROECK JAMES CHARLES	1964	M	Golf	CURRY MICHAEL JOSEPH	1992	M	Hockey
KLOSKA ROBERT LOUIS	1990	M	Golf	TERRY JAMES NICHOLS	1954	M	Golf	CURRY STEVEN O.	1974	M	Hockey
KNEE DAVID EDWARD	1980	M	Golf	TERRY ROBERT TRASK M.D.	1947	M	Golf	CUSEY TROY ANTHONY	1995	M	Hockey
KNEE RICHARD WILLIAM	1978	M	Golf	THORP MICHAEL ALAN	1967	M	Golf	DAIGLER E. DEAN MR.	1969	M	Hockey
KOPROWSKI PAUL ANDERTON	1976	M	Golf	TOTTEN JOSEPH CHESTER	1949	M	Golf	DAL GRANDE DAVIDE LUIGI	1996	M	Hockey
KUSEK PATRICK ALAN DR.	1991	M	Golf	VEECH THOMAS RENAUD	1952	M	Golf	DEASEY JOHN JOSEPH	1989	M	Hockey
LAFORTUNE JOSEPH A. JR.	1946	M	Golf	VEENEMAN WILLIAM H. JR.	1934	M	Golf	DELORENZI RAYMOND JOHN M.D.	1977	M	Hockey
LAFRANCE MICHAEL LEWIS	1973	M	Golf	VERNON TODD FABER	2000	M	Golf	DEVOE JOHN RYAN	1989	M	Hockey
LALLY TERRY EDWARD	1960	M	Golf	VOELKER CHARLES PAUL	1973	M	Golf	DEWERD THOMAS MICHAEL D.D.S.	1978	M	Hockey
LESLIE JOSEPH D.	1959	M	Golf	VOLLHABER CRAIG EDMUND	1962	M	Golf	DHADPHALE ANIKET PRAKASH	1999	M	Hockey
LEYES FRANK ALFRED	1985	M	Golf	VOSS P. MICHAEL MR.	1963	M	Golf	DOLDER RYAN THOMAS	2001	M	Hockey
LINBECK LEO EDWARD JR.	1956	M	Golf	WADDEN WILLIAM MARREN	1979	M	Golf	DOMAN MARK VICTOR	1983	M	Hockey
LUNDGREN JOHN PAUL D.D.S.	1980	M	Golf	WEBSTER GERALD WILLIAM	1959	M	Golf	DUNCAN GREGORY MCDOWELL	1986	M	Hockey
LUNKE BRANDON KRISTOFFER	2003	M	Golf	WEEKS BRYAN ELTON	1998	M	Golf	DUNLOP CONNOR PATRICK	2003	M	Hockey
MAILHES ALBIN ROLAND	1938	M	Golf	WHELAN EDWARD JAMES DR. III	1975	M	Golf	DUNPHY MICHAEL EMERSON	1974	M	Hockey
MALLOY PATRICK H. JR.	1936	M	Golf	WHITE MAURICE JOSEPH	1950	M	Golf	DUSBABEK JOSEPH DAVID	2000	M	Hockey
MARSHALL RYAN THOMAS	2005	M	Golf	WHITING RICHARD L.	1945	M	Golf	DWYER JOHN EDWARD	1999	M	Hockey
MARTINEZ CHARLES GLENNON	1970	M	Golf	WHITTEN WILLIAM CHRISTOPHER	2002	M	Golf	EATON MARK ANDREW	1998	M	Hockey
MARZOLF FRANCIS A. JR.	1952	M	Golf	WILKE JOHN MELVIN JR.	1944	M	Golf	EISLER MATTHEW J.	1998	M	Hockey
MATEY THOMAS WILLIAM	1953	M	Golf	WILKE ROBERT EDWARD	1937	M	Golf	ELY STEPHEN LAWRENCE DR.	1985	M	Hockey
MATT LEO SPALTI	1956	M	Golf	WILLIAMS DONALD EUGENE	1959	M	Golf	FAIRHOLM DONALD BLAIR	1978	M	Hockey
MCCABE EDWARD SCHUYLER M.D.	1938	M	Golf	WILSON ROBERT EDWARD	1970	M	Golf	FAIRHOLM TERRENCE ALLAN	1978	M	Hockey
MCCARTHY THOMAS JOHN	1981	M	Golf	WILSON WILLIAM LEROY SR.	1942	M	Golf	FARRELL THOMAS PATRICK	1979	M	Hockey
MCDONALD LAWRENCE GEORGE	1963	M	Golf	WISEMAN KEVIN CHRISTOPHER	2005	M	Golf	FITZGERALD THOMAS MARTIN	1989	M	Hockey
MCGUINNESS WILLIAM J.	1981	M	Golf	WOLF MILO EDWARD	1942	M	Golf	FOLEY PATRICK JAMES	1988	M	Hockey
MCGUIRE WILLIAM HAROLD	1957	M	Golf	ZESINGER CLARKE HENRY	1960	M	Golf	FRASER TYSON WILLIAM	2000	M	Hockey
MCLAUGHLIN CHARLES JOSEPH	1966	M	Golf	AMADO MATTHEW ALFREDO	2006	M	Hockey	FRIEDMANN JOHN GREGORY	1980	M	Hockey
MENTONE FRANCIS WILLIAM	1968	M	Golf	ANDRUSIAK LYLE TODD	1998	M	Hockey	GALVIN THOMAS RAYMOND	2004	M	Hockey
MERRA SABINO GERALD	1957	M	Golf	ANQUILLARE MARK VINCENT	1988	M	Hockey	GEAREN MICHAEL VINCENT	1971	M	Hockey
MILBOURN EUGENE FREDERIC	1939	M	Golf	ARCANGEL JUSTIN EDWARD	1994	M	Hockey	GHIA JOHN JOSEPH	1991	M	Hockey

NAME	YEAR	GENDER	SPORT
GILL AARON JOSEPH	2004	M	Hockey
GILL ANTHONY JAY	2006	M	Hockey
GIULIANI SCOTT RICHARD	1999	M	Hockey
GLOBKE ROBERT FREDERICK	2004	M	Hockey
GREEN WILLIAM ALAN	1973	M	Hockey
GREGOIRE ERIC ANDRE	1993	M	Hockey
GRUBER GARRYTT GRANT	1996	M	Hockey
GUAY BRUCE ANDRE M.D.	1990	M	Hockey
GUAY MARC ERIC DR.	1986	M	Hockey
GUISTI WILLIAM GEORGE	1976	M	Hockey
HAGKULL CRAIG STEPHEN	1999	M	Hockey
HAIKOLA BRUCE MATTHEW	1990	M	Hockey
HAMILTON CLARK IAN	1977	M	Hockey
HANZEL MATTHEW JAMES	1989	M	Hockey
HARBERTS TIMOTHY THOMAS	1997	M	Hockey
HASSELMAN JEFF JAMES	1995	M	Hockey
HAVERKAMP ALBERT EDWARD	1985	M	Hockey
HENNING BRETT EDWARD	2002	M	Hockey
HERBER ROBERT JOSEPH	1989	M	Hockey
HIGGINS JOHN BRADY	1983	M	Hockey
HOELZEL WILLIAM JAMES SR.	1989	M	Hockey
HOENE KEVIN ARTHUR	1972	M	Hockey
HOWE DAVID JOHN	1976	M	Hockey
HOWE RICHARD JAMES	1978	M	Hockey
HOWE ROBERT WILLIAM	1974	M	Hockey
HUMPHREYS KEVIN S.	1981	M	Hockey
INMAN DAVID STANLEY	2002	M	Hockey
ISRAELSON LARRY G.	1974	M	Hockey
JACKSON DONALD CLINTON	1978	M	Hockey
JANICKE CURTIS ALLAN	1993	M	Hockey
JOHNSON NEAL RICHARD	1999	M	Hockey
JOHNSON RAYMOND RICHARD	1977	M	Hockey
JURKOWSKI ANDREW ROSS	2000	M	Hockey
KARR FORREST LEE	1999	M	Hockey
KARSNIA ALLEN LEE	1977	M	Hockey
KEATING JOHN JEFFREY	1983	M	Hockey
KENNEDY RICHARD C. JR.	1987	M	Hockey
KIMENTO JEREMIAH WALTER	2002	M	Hockey
KOLQUIST KYLE DAVID	2001	M	Hockey
KOMADOSKI NEIL GRANT	2004	M	Hockey
KONESCO JASON TODD	1994	M	Hockey
KOPISCHKE JAY KEVIN	2001	M	Hockey
KRONHOLM MARK EDWARD	1974	M	Hockey
KUEHL TIMOTHY RICHARD	1990	M	Hockey
LAMPPA BRENT JEFF	1995	M	Hockey
LARSON LESLIE ALBIN JR.	1975	M	Hockey
LAURION DAVID JEROME	1982	M	Hockey
LEBDA BRETT STEVEN	2004	M	Hockey
LEHERR MICHAEL ROBERT	1990	M	Hockey
LING JAMES MICHAEL	1996	M	Hockey
LITCHARD TIMOTHY MANUEL	1994	M	Hockey
LOGAN JEFFREY STEPHEN	1982	M	Hockey
LONGAR MARK WILLIAM	1972	M	Hockey
LORENZ TERRY LORNE	1997	M	Hockey
LOTHROP BRENT LEE	1994	M	Hockey
LOUDER GREGORY BATES	1994	M	Hockey
LUCIA DAVID ERIC	1983	M	Hockey
LUCIA DONALD JAMES	1981	M	Hockey
LUKENDA TIMOTHY LOUIS	1987	M	Hockey
MADSON LANCE ROBERT	1990	M	Hockey
MARKOVITZ KEVIN LEE	1990	M	Hockey
MARUK JON DAVID	2002	M	Hockey
MARVIN DAN GIBSON	1993	M	Hockey
MATHIESON JOHN MARTIN III	2004	M	Hockey
MATUSHAK JAY STEPHEN	1996	M	Hockey
MCCARTHY BRIAN ROBERT	1997	M	Hockey
MCLEAN CORY WILLIAM	2005	M	Hockey
MCMAHON PATRICK MICHAEL	1972	M	Hockey
MCNAMARA ROBERT JOHN	1983	M	Hockey
MCNEILL MICHAEL FRANCIS	1988	M	Hockey
MEREDITH GREGORY P.	1980	M	Hockey
METZLER MICHAEL P.	1984	M	Hockey
MICHALEK THOMAS F.	1980	M	Hockey
MINISCALCO THOMAS LOUIS	1993	M	Hockey
MOHER G. LENNOX	1978	M	Hockey
MOLINA SEAN CONWAY	2000	M	Hockey
MONTGOMERY BRIAN JAMES	1989	M	Hockey
MOONEY THOMAS JOHN	1988	M	Hockey
MORIN JAMES IRVING	1972	M	Hockey
MORSHEAD JAMES NICHOLAS	1996	M	Hockey
MUSTY MICHAEL OWEN JR.	1992	M	Hockey
MYERS THOMAS PATRICK	1972	M	Hockey
NAGURSKI KEVIN KANE	1979	M	Hockey
NELSEN BENJAMIN SCOTT	1997	M	Hockey
NEMETH CAREY PATRICK	1995	M	Hockey
NICKODEMUS JOHN P.	1987	M	Hockey
NIELSEN EVAN COLE	2003	M	Hockey
NOBLE C. STEVE MR.	1998	M	Hockey
NOBLE JOHN FRANCIS	1973	M	Hockey
NORRI ERIC JOHN JR.	1969	M	Hockey
NOVITZKI PATRICK DAVID	1976	M	Hockey
NUGENT KEVIN JOHN	1978	M	Hockey
NYROP WILLIAM DONALD	1974	M	Hockey
O'BRIEN FRANK EDWARD III	1988	M	Hockey
O'BRIEN MICHAEL PATRICK	1993	M	Hockey
OLIVE MARK GREGORY	1976	M	Hockey
OLSON CHRISTOPHER DAVID	1991	M	Hockey
OLSON VICTOR CORDELL	1983	M	Hockey
O'NEIL PAUL CHRISTOPHER	1973	M	Hockey
OSIECKI MATTHEW THOMAS	1994	M	Hockey
O'SULLIVAN MARK ANTHONY	1989	M	Hockey
PARENT THOMAS ERIC DR.	1985	M	Hockey
PARSONS JOHN ADAM	1984	M	Hockey
PATRICK KEVIN MICHAEL	1992	M	Hockey
PATTEN LANCE WILLIAM	1988	M	Hockey
PERRY JEFFREY GEORGE	1983	M	Hockey
PETERSON JOHN CHARLES	1978	M	Hockey
PICCONATTO CARL ARGENTINO	1993	M	Hockey
PIRUS ALEX JOSEPH	1977	M	Hockey
POULIN DAVID JAMES	1982	M	Hockey
REGAN F. PAUL MR.	1973	M	Hockey
REGAN SEAN O.	1983	M	Hockey
REILLY TIMOTHY EDWARD	1985	M	Hockey
RICCI ROBERT ANTHONY	1985	M	Hockey
RIELY FRANK Z. JR.	1983	M	Hockey
ROSELLI JOHN THOMAS	1971	M	Hockey
ROSENTHAL J. GREGORY DR.	1980	M	Hockey
ROTHSTEIN WILLIAM PATRICK	1982	M	Hockey
RUSHIN JOHN EDWARD	1995	M	Hockey
SALEM PAUL	1983	M	Hockey
SALZMAN CHRISTOPHER WADE	1997	M	Hockey
SAWYER DANIEL ARTHUR	1993	M	Hockey
SCHAFER RICHARD ALLAN	1974	M	Hockey
SCHMIDT JOHN R.	1982	M	Hockey
SCHNEIDER STEVE L.	1979	M	Hockey
SEYFERTH SEAN FRITZ	2000	M	Hockey
SIMON BENJAMIN CLARKE	2000	M	Hockey
SLAGGERT ANDREW LEE	1989	M	Hockey
SMITH DEREK GEORGE	2005	M	Hockey
SMITH DONALD ALLAN	1974	M	Hockey
SMITH THOMAS RICHARD	1989	M	Hockey
SOBILO RICHARD	1988	M	Hockey
SODERLING STEPHEN BRUCE	1995	M	Hockey
STEINBORN MARK JOSEPH	1973	M	Hockey
TARDANI MICHAEL DAVID	1974	M	Hockey
THEBEAU ROBERT JOSEPH	1986	M	Hockey
THEEL JUSTIN ROSS	1998	M	Hockey
TIBERI JOHN JOSEPH	1986	M	Hockey
TOMASONI RICHARD CESTER	1972	M	Hockey
TRICK CHRISTOPHER THOMAS	2006	M	Hockey
TSCHUPP CHRISTOPHER ERIC	1992	M	Hockey
URICK BRIAN JOSEPH	1999	M	Hockey
VAN ARKEL MATTHEW GARRETT	2001	M	Hockey
VICKMAN SCOTT JOHN	1992	M	Hockey
WALDBILLIG DAVID KELLY DR.	1986	M	Hockey
WALLACE TIMOTHY TODD	2006	M	Hockey
WALSH BRIAN GERARD	1977	M	Hockey
WALSH MICHAEL CHRISTOPHER	2006	M	Hockey
WALSH RORY PATRICK	2006	M	Hockey
WANCHULAK BRADLEY WILLIAM	2005	M	Hockey
WELCH BRYAN MICHAEL	1997	M	Hockey
WELSCH JOHN ARMAND	1988	M	Hockey
WELTZIN THEODORE E. DR.	1980	M	Hockey
WHITMORE STEPHEN MORGAN	1986	M	Hockey
WIEGAND JACOB HENRY	2003	M	Hockey
WILLIAMS IAN MAXWELL	1974	M	Hockey
WITTLIFF PHILIP JAMES	1971	M	Hockey
WROBLEWSKI JOHN E.	2003	M	Hockey
ZADRA LOUIS JOHN	1992	M	Hockey
ZASOWSKI ANTHONY JAMES	2003	M	Hockey
ZURENKO JOSEPH RYAN	2005	M	Hockey
ADAMS MICHAEL EDWARD	2001	M	LaCrosse
AHMUTY WILLIAM RAYMOND	1994	M	LaCrosse
ANTOL NICHOLAS MARTIN	2003	M	LaCrosse
ASPLUNDH OWEN BOYD	2002	M	LaCrosse
BARNARD DAVID SCOTT	1991	M	LaCrosse
BELLON GREGORY PETER	1984	M	LaCrosse
BERGER DANIEL PETER	2004	M	LaCrosse
BERGKESSEL ERNEST JOHN	1973	M	LaCrosse
BESHLIAN MAURICE F. III	1981	M	LaCrosse
BIALOUS JOSEPH PAUL	1999	M	LaCrosse
BIALOUS TODD JOSEPH	1995	M	LaCrosse
BIDDISON DAVID O'MALLEY	1999	M	LaCrosse
BISHKO CRAIG JEFFREY	2005	M	LaCrosse
BISHKO STEVEN GREGORY	2001	M	LaCrosse
BLUM MICHAEL GERARD	2004	M	LaCrosse
BONDE WILLIAM JUDE	1982	M	LaCrosse
BRADY ARTHUR RYAN	1988	M	LaCrosse
BRENNAN MICHAEL SEAN	1989	M	LaCrosse
BURNS DANIEL JAMES	1985	M	LaCrosse
BURTIS JOHN BENEDICT	1988	M	LaCrosse
BURY CHRISTOPHER MATTHEW	1995	M	LaCrosse
BUTLER DANIEL P.	1998	M	LaCrosse
CADE ALEXANDER GLENN	1998	M	LaCrosse
CAHILL BRENDAN JAMES	1989	M	LaCrosse
CAMPION KEVIN MICHAEL	1981	M	LaCrosse
CAPANO JOHN EMMETT	1991	M	LaCrosse
CAPPELLI PAUL JAMES	2004	M	LaCrosse
CAREY DAVID RAYMOND JR.	1990	M	LaCrosse
CARILLO ROBERT GEORGE	1986	M	LaCrosse
CARROLL TOM	1993	M	LaCrosse
CASHEN DAVID VINCENT	1997	M	LaCrosse
CHARHUT DANIEL EDWARD	1981	M	LaCrosse
CLAGETT STEPHEN LANSDALE JR.	2004	M	LaCrosse
CLOUD STEPHEN MICHAEL	1985	M	LaCrosse
COCOMAN GLENN MICHAEL	1991	M	LaCrosse
COLLEY RANDALL SMITH	1994	M	LaCrosse
CORRIGAN TIMOTHY WILLIAM	1986	M	LaCrosse
CORSCADDEN SEAN PATRICK	1983	M	LaCrosse
COTTER TRACY PATRICK M.D.	1983	M	LaCrosse
CREANEY BRENNAN MICHAEL	2004	M	LaCrosse
CROSLAND EDWARD STEWART	2005	M	LaCrosse
CROSS RAMON VINCENT	1999	M	LaCrosse
CULLINAN KEVIN JAMES	1987	M	LaCrosse
DARCY PATRICK JOSEPH	2000	M	LaCrosse
DERISO WILLIAM JOSEPH	1997	M	LaCrosse
DRISCOLL DANIEL ANDERSON JR.	2006	M	LaCrosse
DUANE THOMAS GLYNN	1992	M	LaCrosse
DUFFY ROBERT K. JR.	1964	M	LaCrosse
DUGAN KEVIN JOSEPH	2001	M	LaCrosse
DURGIN ROBERT ELLSWORTH	1981	M	LaCrosse
DUSSEAU CHRISTOPHER JOHN	1999	M	LaCrosse
ERICKSON BRIAN ANTON	1996	M	LaCrosse
FALLON CHRISTOPHER C. III	2002	M	LaCrosse
FALLON JAMES C.	1987	M	LaCrosse
FARINO MARK WILLIAM	1982	M	LaCrosse
FATTI COLIN MICHAEL	2005	M	LaCrosse
FIAMINGO STEVEN MICHAEL	2000	M	LaCrosse
FINN PATRICK MICHAEL	1995	M	LaCrosse
FINNERAN THOMAS PATRICK	1966	M	LaCrosse
FLANDINA JOHN ALBERT	2002	M	LaCrosse
FRANKLIN JOSEPH JAMES JR.	1986	M	LaCrosse
FRIES MICHAEL JOHN	2003	M	LaCrosse
FRIGON KYLE	2003	M	LaCrosse
GALLAGHER WILLIAM ANDREW	1995	M	LaCrosse
GALLI LAURENCE CHRISTOPHER	1999	M	LaCrosse
GAYHARDT DONALD F. JR.	1986	M	LaCrosse
GILFILLAN BRIAN JAMES	1996	M	LaCrosse
GILLIN PETER JOSEPH	1992	M	LaCrosse
GIORDANO BRIAN THOMAS	2005	M	LaCrosse
GLADUE JOSEPH	1981	M	LaCrosse
GLATZEL THOMAS PATRICK	2001	M	LaCrosse
GLAZIER JEFFREY LAWRENCE	1990	M	LaCrosse
GLENDAY GREGORY SCOTT	1996	M	LaCrosse
GROTE THOMAS JOSEPH	1986	M	LaCrosse
GULDE JEFFREY CLEMENT	1988	M	LaCrosse
HAGERTY JOHN MICHAEL	2005	M	LaCrosse
HART JOSEPH FRANCIS	1985	M	LaCrosse
HARVEY JONATHAN PIKE	2002	M	LaCrosse
HAYES BURKE F. JR.	1998	M	LaCrosse
HEXAMER MARK FRANCIS	1994	M	LaCrosse
HICKS DWAYNE MERRON	1985	M	LaCrosse
HIGGINS KEVIN PATRICK	2000	M	LaCrosse
HOEY STEPHEN EDWARD	1981	M	LaCrosse
HOGAN WILLIAM JOSEPH	1998	M	LaCrosse
HOWELL EVERETTE KIRK	2001	M	LaCrosse
HOWELL MATTHEW CRAMER	2004	M	LaCrosse
HUBSCHMANN BRIAN MICHAEL	2006	M	LaCrosse
IORIO MICHAEL ANTHONY	1995	M	LaCrosse
JACKSON BRETT M.	1980	M	LaCrosse
JANK PATRICK MICHAEL	1982	M	LaCrosse
JEWELL RYAN PHILLIP	1995	M	LaCrosse
KARWECK MATTHEW KANE	2006	M	LaCrosse
KEARNEY TIMOTHY RONALD	1997	M	LaCrosse
KEENAN JAMES EDWARD	1998	M	LaCrosse
KIDDER DAVID MICHAEL	1989	M	LaCrosse
KNOTT OWEN MICHAEL	2000	M	LaCrosse
KRUMMENACHER TYLER RANDALL	2005	M	LaCrosse
LA NOUE ROBERT JAMES R	1999	M	LaCrosse
LAFFEY THOMAS PAUL	1970	M	LaCrosse
LAMB EDWARD JAMES JR.	1993	M	LaCrosse
LANAHAN THOMAS SEAN	1988	M	LaCrosse
LEISEN MATTHEW JOHN	2002	M	LaCrosse
LEVESQUE GERALD E. JR.	1984	M	LaCrosse
LEWIS DAVID ANTHONY	1982	M	LaCrosse
LINEHAN STEPHEN	1982	M	LaCrosse
LIVINGSTON MICHAEL	1991	M	LaCrosse
LONSDALE CHARLES ANDREWS	1993	M	LaCrosse
LUNDBLAD CARL ROY JR.	1981	M	LaCrosse
LYNCH MICHAEL J.	1982	M	LaCrosse

NAME	YEAR	GENDER	SPORT
LYNN ROBERT PATRICK III	1990	M	LaCrosse
LYNYAK KEVIN SCOTT	1995	M	LaCrosse
MAHONEY KEVIN TIMOTHY	1996	M	LaCrosse
MALAKOFF MATTHEW SHANE	2005	M	LaCrosse
MANLEY STEVEN KEITH	1994	M	LaCrosse
MANNELLO LOUIS JAMES JR.	1986	M	LaCrosse
MARONEY MICHAEL THOMAS	1996	M	LaCrosse
MASTERSON CHRISTOPHER JAMES	2004	M	LaCrosse
MATARAZZO FRANK ANDREW	2005	M	LaCrosse
MATTHEWS ROBERT TAYLOR	2005	M	LaCrosse
MAYGLOTHLING BRIAN WILLIAM	1993	M	LaCrosse
MCANANEY EDWARD GEORGE III	1991	M	LaCrosse
MCCANN AARON THOMAS	2001	M	LaCrosse
MCDONALD RANDAL SEAN	1988	M	LaCrosse
MCHUGH BRIAN JOSEPH	1990	M	LaCrosse
MCKEON BRIAN PATRICK	1985	M	LaCrosse
MCLACHLAN JOHN STANLEY	1987	M	LaCrosse
MCMANUS MARTIN JAMES	1983	M	LaCrosse
MCNICHOLAS JOHN TERRENCE	1988	M	LaCrosse
MCQUILLAN MATTHEW S.	1988	M	LaCrosse
MEEHAN SEAN MICHAEL	1999	M	LaCrosse
MICHELS TIMOTHY KEVIN	1981	M	LaCrosse
MILONE RICHARD DOMINICK JR.	1987	M	LaCrosse
MORRISON JAMES ALFRED	2005	M	LaCrosse
MOUCH THOMAS NORMAN DR.	1977	M	LaCrosse
MULFLUR JOHN WALTER	2004	M	LaCrosse
MULFORD OWEN BARRY	2004	M	LaCrosse
MURPHY JOHN FRANCIS	1981	M	LaCrosse
MURPHY KEVIN ARTHUR	1994	M	LaCrosse
MURRAY DOUGLAS JOSEPH	1992	M	LaCrosse
MUSA SCOTT ANTHONY	1992	M	LaCrosse
NEFF CHARLES THOMAS	1981	M	LaCrosse
NELSON CHRISTOPHER JOHN	1992	M	LaCrosse
OAKEY STEDMAN DAVIS	2000	M	LaCrosse
O'BRIEN FRANK EDWARD III	1988	M	LaCrosse
O'BRIEN THOMAS MICHAEL	1993	M	LaCrosse
O'CONNOR KEVIN JAMES	1989	M	LaCrosse
OLMSTEAD JOHN FRANCIS M.D.	1989	M	LaCrosse
ONDERDONK CHRISTOPHER ANDREW	1995	M	LaCrosse
O'NEILL DAVID MARTIN	1987	M	LaCrosse
OWEN G. BRADLEY DOUGLAS	1999	M	LaCrosse
PACE DANIEL GRAHAM	1983	M	LaCrosse
PARENDO KEITH LAWRENCE	2000	M	LaCrosse
PARENT CHRISTOPHER MICHAEL	1993	M	LaCrosse
PASQUALE MARC ALEXANDER	1995	M	LaCrosse
PATRICK KEVIN MICHAEL	1992	M	LaCrosse
PEARSALL STEVEN WRIGHT	1984	M	LaCrosse
PERRIELLO VITO ANTHONY	1993	M	LaCrosse
PETCOFF NICHOLAS JAMES	2004	M	LaCrosse
PETERS DREW ALEXANDER	2006	M	LaCrosse
PETT CONNOR BENTLEY	1998	M	LaCrosse
PETT JASON TANIS	1995	M	LaCrosse
PFEFFER MICHAEL PHILLIP	2001	M	LaCrosse
PHILLIPS EDWARD J.	1987	M	LaCrosse
POLETTI PATRICK EDWARD	1985	M	LaCrosse
QUIGLEY KEVIN JAMES	1981	M	LaCrosse
QUIGLEY MICHAEL EAMONN	1990	M	LaCrosse
QUIGLEY SEAN WHALEN	2005	M	LaCrosse
QUINN MICHAEL JAMES	1984	M	LaCrosse
RASSAS TODD NICHOLAS	1998	M	LaCrosse
REID-SUBER ANTHONY JERMAINE	1997	M	LaCrosse
REILLY GARRETT ANTHONY JR.	1994	M	LaCrosse
RETTINO ANTHONY A. JR.	1986	M	LaCrosse
RICE MICHAEL TIMOTHY	1986	M	LaCrosse
RICHEZ CHRISTOPHER RAYMOND	2005	M	LaCrosse
RIZZIERI MARK THOMAS	1989	M	LaCrosse
ROONEY KEVIN JOSEPH	1985	M	LaCrosse
ROWLEY CHRISTOPHER FRANCIS M.D.	1991	M	LaCrosse
RUBANO DAVID JONATHAN	2000	M	LaCrosse
RYAN DEVIN PATRICK	2002	M	LaCrosse
RYAN MATTHEW JOSEPH	2006	M	LaCrosse
SALAMON JEFFREY MICHAEL	1990	M	LaCrosse
SAMMON WILLIAM JOSEPH	1978	M	LaCrosse
SANGER WARREN JOHN	1989	M	LaCrosse
SANTORIELLO ANDREW PETER	2001	M	LaCrosse
SARGENT ADAM MICHAEL	1999	M	LaCrosse
SAVAGE BENJAMIN JAMES	1999	M	LaCrosse
SCHIRF BRIAN EDWARD DR.	1992	M	LaCrosse
SCHULTHEIS BRANDON JOHN	2006	M	LaCrosse
SCOLLAN ANDREW JOSEPH	1996	M	LaCrosse
SEAMAN MICHAEL JOHN	1998	M	LaCrosse
SENGER PETER DANA	1993	M	LaCrosse
SENNETT MICHAEL PATRICK	1991	M	LaCrosse
SEPETA STEPHEN MARK	1999	M	LaCrosse
SFORZO CHRISTOPHER ROBERT DR.	1994	M	LaCrosse
SHAY JEFFREY FRANCIS	1988	M	LaCrosse
SHAY JUSTIN SCOTT	1985	M	LaCrosse
SHIELDS JAMES T.	1987	M	LaCrosse
SIMON ERIC MICHAEL	2003	M	LaCrosse
SIMPSON ROBERT PAUL	1985	M	LaCrosse
SMITH KEVIN E.	1984	M	LaCrosse
SNYDER PETER HAMILTON	1995	M	LaCrosse
SNYDER ROBERT JOSEPH	1994	M	LaCrosse
SOUCH JOHN JOSEPH	2003	M	LaCrosse
SPENCER DOUGLAS JAMES	1989	M	LaCrosse
STACK WALTER JOSEPH	1987	M	LaCrosse
STERANKA MARK	1986	M	LaCrosse
STEVENS MICHAEL ERIC	1990	M	LaCrosse
STEWART ROBERT JOHN	1981	M	LaCrosse
STOHLMAN EDWIN LAWRENCE IV	1998	M	LaCrosse
SULLIVAN MICHAEL CHARLES	1992	M	LaCrosse
SUTTON WILLIAM KENNEDY	1994	M	LaCrosse
TAYLOR STEPHEN WARD	1999	M	LaCrosse
TITTERTON JOHN PATRICK	1991	M	LaCrosse
TOBIN ROBERT JEREMY	1993	M	LaCrosse
TREMANTE JAMES III	1996	M	LaCrosse
TROCCHI ROBERT JUDE	1985	M	LaCrosse
ULRICH DAVID JOHN	2001	M	LaCrosse
ULRICH TODD HAMILTON	2001	M	LaCrosse
WALSH JOHN THOMAS	1985	M	LaCrosse
WALSH PATRICK CHARLES JR.	2006	M	LaCrosse
WEBSTER EDWIN HANSON III	1999	M	LaCrosse
WELLS TRAVIS CLIFTON	2003	M	LaCrosse
WICKEL RICHARD JOHN	1982	M	LaCrosse
WILLIAMSON ROBERT MICHAEL	1993	M	LaCrosse
WILSON JOHN JOSEPH	1985	M	LaCrosse
WRIGHT ANTHONY JUDE	2002	M	LaCrosse
YANICKY KENNETH JOHN	2000	M	LaCrosse
YOUNG CHRISTOPHER JOHN	2001	M	LaCrosse
ZOCCOLA WILLIAM LOUIS	1981	M	LaCrosse
ABLIAN JONATHAN PAUL	1994	M	Manager
ABOWD STEPHEN VINCENT	1984	M	Manager
ADAMS JOHN EDMUND	1986	M	Manager
AJHAR JEFFREY MICHAEL	1993	M	Manager
ALBERTINI MICHAEL ANDREW	1996	M	Manager
ALLEN MARTIN JOSEPH JR.	1958	M	Manager
ALLISON RICHARD KYLE	1981	M	Manager
AMATO NICHOLAS JOSEPH	1944	M	Manager
ANDROSKI CHRISTOPHER MICHAEL	1995	M	Manager
ANDROSKI MICHAEL ALAN	1971	M	Manager
ARNDT PETER ANGUS	1979	M	Manager
ARNN ROY ELMORE D.V.M.	1969	M	Manager
AUGUSTYNIEWICZ FRANK JOSEPH	1992	M	Manager
BACSIK CHRISTOPHER MICHAEL	2001	M	Manager
BACSIK JOHN ANDREW	2004	M	Manager
BAKER RYAN KENDALL	1999	M	Manager
BAKER TERRY ALLYN	1994	M	Manager
BALFE ROBERT CRAMER	1931	M	Manager
BALL EDWARD VINCENT	1952	M	Manager
BALL MICHAEL DAVID	2003	M	Manager
BANNAN JOHN JOSEPH	1991	M	Manager
BARD TIMOTHY BASIL	1966	M	Manager
BARKER KENNETH ALLEN	1988	M	Manager
BARKER PAUL FRANCIS	1937	M	Manager
BARKO RANDALL SCOTT	1973	M	Manager
BARONE JOSEPH JAMES JR.	1994	M	Manager
BARR JAMES MILTON	1958	M	Manager
BARRETT BRADFORD J. DR.	1984	M	Manager
BARTOLINI BRIAN JOSEPH	1989	M	Manager
BARWICK JOHN L.	1984	M	Manager
BASARA DENNIS EDWARD	1977	M	Manager
BAUER JOHN LOUIS JR.	1942	M	Manager
BAUMGARTEN MICHAEL PAUL	1984	M	Manager
BECCHETTI CHARLES L.	1947	M	Manager
BELDEN BRIAN DAVID	2000	M	Manager
BERES GERALD THOMAS	2006	M	Manager
BERMINGHAM JOHN C.	1942	M	Manager
BESTON WILLIAM JOHN	1989	M	Manager
BIASOTTI CHRISTOPHER JAMES	2001	M	Manager
BIEBL RICHARD TOBIAS	2003	M	Manager
BITTNER MATTHEW CLAYTON	1998	M	Manager
BLACKWELL JOHN KENNETH	2004	M	Manager
BLAINE DUANE ANTHONY	1980	M	Manager
BOCKRATH GARY EDWARD	1974	M	Manager
BOEHK ERIC MICHAEL	1997	M	Manager
BOLAND MICHAEL JOSEPH	1997	M	Manager
BOLZ ROBERT CHARLES	1939	M	Manager
BOND THOMAS DECHANT	1938	M	Manager
BOOI DOUGLAS EUGENE	2001	M	Manager
BORGES JOSEPH W. DEACON	1952	M	Manager
BOSS WILLIAM E. JR.	1944	M	Manager
BOUFFARD DONALD EDWARD JR.	1966	M	Manager
BOWER JOHN ELLIOTT JR.	1956	M	Manager
BOWLING JOHN RAYMOND JR.	1961	M	Manager
BRALEY C. PATRICK MR.	1995	M	Manager
BRIGHAM PHILIP LOUIS	1983	M	Manager
BROCCOLETTI PETER PAUL	1964	M	Manager
BROCKMAN BERNARD N. JR.	1941	M	Manager
BROCKMOLE JAMES ROBERT DR.	1999	M	Manager
BROWN WILLIAM C.	1949	M	Manager
BRUTON MICHAEL GERARD	1982	M	Manager
BUCHANAN JAMES LAWRENCE	1971	M	Manager
BUCK DANIEL MICHAEL	1977	M	Manager
BUHRFIEND RICHARD MALACHY	1959	M	Manager
BULLARD JOEL	1950	M	Manager
BURGDORF KEVIN DOLAN	2003	M	Manager
BURKE JAMES BYRON	1936	M	Manager
BURKE LEO FRANCIS II	1970	M	Manager
BURNS EDWARD KILROE	1943	M	Manager
BUSBY MICHAEL DOUGLAS	1969	M	Manager
BUSICK C. MICHAEL	1973	M	Manager
BUTTLER JOHN ARTHUR	1967	M	Manager
BYRNE MARK	1990	M	Manager
BYRNE PETER MICHAEL	1999	M	Manager
CAEMMERER JOHN D.	1949	M	Manager
CAFFARELLI RICHARD MICHAEL JR.	1989	M	Manager
CAIN SEAN PATRICK	1983	M	Manager
CANNY JAMES P. JR.	1957	M	Manager
CAPUTO MICHAEL JOHN	1991	M	Manager
CAREY CORNELIUS J. JR.	1930	M	Manager
CAREY CSC JOSEPH H. REV.	1962	M	Manager
CAREY JOSEPH E.	1975	M	Manager
CAREY JOSEPH EDWARD JR.	1977	M	Manager
CARONE JOHN PATRICK CPA	1985	M	Manager
CARR MICHAEL J.	1942	M	Manager
CASSIDY GLENN JOSEPH	1994	M	Manager
CASSIDY JOHN E. JR.	1948	M	Manager
CAULFIELD JUSTIN JEROME	1995	M	Manager
CAVALIER JOHN CAMILLE	1961	M	Manager
CHAIN MARK M.	1978	M	Manager
CHARDOS KENNETH STEPHEN	1996	M	Manager
CHELF JONATHAN HILTON	2006	M	Manager
CHIARAVALLOTI MICHAEL JOSEPH	1996	M	Manager
CHOJECKI LAWRENCE FRANCIS	1973	M	Manager
CHRISTMAN WILLIAM	1996	M	Manager
CIERZNIAK JOHN FRANCIS	1986	M	Manager
CLELAND FRANCIS LYLE JR.	1955	M	Manager
CLEMENS PHILIP M.	1953	M	Manager
COARY SEAN PATRICK	2002	M	Manager
COGGINS JAMES ALOYSIUS	1983	M	Manager
COLABRARO RICHARD JOSEPH	2002	M	Manager
COLBURN TRAVIS PATRICK	2002	M	Manager
COLLINS JAMES JOSEPH	1997	M	Manager
COLLINS JASON ROBERT	2000	M	Manager
COLLODEL DOUGLAS JOSEPH	1980	M	Manager
CONDON TIMOTHY J. JR.	1986	M	Manager
CONDON WILLIAM PATRICK	1939	M	Manager
CONTE JONATHAN ALBERT	2003	M	Manager
COOLEY DANIEL SHERMAN	2000	M	Manager
COPPOLELLA JOHN JOSEPH	2000	M	Manager
CORR STEPHEN ANTHONY	1989	M	Manager
COSTELLO LEO JOSEPH	1948	M	Manager
COTTER KEITH JOHN	1974	M	Manager
COX MICHAEL JOSEPH	1994	M	Manager
CRAWFORD DAVID FRANCIS	1995	M	Manager
CREAGAN JAMES JOSEPH	2002	M	Manager
CRONIN DANIEL RICHARD	1974	M	Manager
CRONIN JOSEPH E.	1979	M	Manager
CROUCH STEPHEN HUGH DR.	1988	M	Manager
CUNNINGHAM THOMAS JOSEPH	1985	M	Manager
CURTO FREDERICK JAMES	1951	M	Manager
DAIGNEAULT RAYMOND MANUEL	1986	M	Manager
DAKOSKE EMORY A.	1953	M	Manager
DALTON STEVEN MICHAEL	1995	M	Manager
DANIELS WILLIAM F.	1949	M	Manager
DANIK DREW LAWRENCE	1975	M	Manager
DANKOSKI PAUL CHRISTOPHER	1990	M	Manager
DANT JOHN WALLACE JR.	1962	M	Manager
DAVIS BYRON SCOTT	1997	M	Manager
DAY REGINALD E.M JR.	1970	M	Manager
DELLAPIETRA RICHARD EUGENE	1991	M	Manager
DELLAPINA JEFFREY WILLIAM	1984	M	Manager
DELVECCHIO LEONARD FREDERICK	1996	M	Manager
DEMARIA JAMIE EDWARD DR.	1995	M	Manager
DEMETRIO GEORGE TYNAN SR.	1935	M	Manager
DEMETRIO MICHAEL KELLY	1976	M	Manager
DEMPSEY DAVID PHILIP	1976	M	Manager
DENIS GEORGE A. III	1982	M	Manager
DEVLIN KENNETH FRANCIS	1996	M	Manager
DI IORIO WILLIAM ROBERT	1998	M	Manager
DIAMANTOPOULOS PAUL K.	2001	M	Manager
DIECKELMAN DAVID HENRY	1975	M	Manager
DIECKELMAN ROBERT JOSEPH	1974	M	Manager
DIECKELMAN THOMAS MARK	1984	M	Manager
DIGGINS KEVIN THOMAS	1985	M	Manager
DLUGOLECKI JOHN BOLES	1975	M	Manager
DOERR JASON EDWARD	1988	M	Manager
DONAHUE JOHN L.	1967	M	Manager
DONNELLY JOHN PATRICK	1939	M	Manager
DOOLEY FRANCO ANDREW	1991	M	Manager

NAME	YEAR	GENDER	SPORT
DOYLE ADRIAN FRANCIS	1959	M	Manager
DOYLE WILLIAM EVERETT	1952	M	Manager
DRATHS JOHN WILLIAM	1980	M	Manager
DRAY JOSEPH F. JR.	1939	M	Manager
DREZNES JOHN JOSEPH	1970	M	Manager
DRUGAN DYLAN ANWAR	2006	M	Manager
D'SOUZA CARLISLE JAMES ELIAS	2004	M	Manager
DUBA CHRISTOPHER JOHN	1994	M	Manager
DUFFY THOMAS LEO	1944	M	Manager
DUMICH MARK PETER	2006	M	Manager
DUNCAN RAYMOND T.	1952	M	Manager
DURBIN HUGH AUGUSTINE	1952	M	Manager
DUVE CHRISTOPHER JOHN	2005	M	Manager
DWYER MARK HARLAN	1973	M	Manager
EARLS THOMAS JOSEPH	1948	M	Manager
EARLY JOHN DANIEL	1990	M	Manager
EBBEN BRAD PATRICK	1992	M	Manager
EBBERWEIN CHRISTOPHER ANTHONY DR.	1993	M	Manager
EL-ETR DONALD AHMED	1987	M	Manager
ELZEN THOMAS MICHAEL	1963	M	Manager
ERKINS ROBERT ALTER	1945	M	Manager
ETLING THOMAS CLIFFORD	1980	M	Manager
EUVINO STEPHEN JOSEPH	1976	M	Manager
EXLEY MARK KING	1975	M	Manager
FADUSKI BRENT MICHAEL	1997	M	Manager
FAHEY WILLIAM THOMAS	1970	M	Manager
FARAH ANDREW ESBER	1982	M	Manager
FARRELL MATTHEW EVAN	2002	M	Manager
FAVAZZO JOSEPH ANGELO	1993	M	Manager
FEDOR BRUCE GEORGE	1957	M	Manager
FEELEY MICHAEL EDWARD	1999	M	Manager
FEENEY JUSTIN ANTHONY	2004	M	Manager
FENTON BRYAN PATRICK	1987	M	Manager
FERRELLO LOUIS CAMPI	1973	M	Manager
FILAR JAMES MARION JR.	1984	M	Manager
FINK SHELDON ROBERT	1994	M	Manager
FINKELMEIER JEFFREY RENNER	1996	M	Manager
FINNEGAN FRANK R. JR.	1960	M	Manager
FINNEGAN JOHN DRURY	1950	M	Manager
FINNERTY MICHAEL	1968	M	Manager
FIORINA TERRY JOHN	1969	M	Manager
FISHER BRIAN THOMAS DR.	1995	M	Manager
FISHER DONALD WILLIAM SR.	1938	M	Manager
FISHER EDWARD JAMES	1934	M	Manager
FITZGERALD EDWARD W. JR.	1963	M	Manager
FLAHERTY MICHAEL JOSEPH JR.	1987	M	Manager
FLAHERTY WILLIAM F. JR.	1947	M	Manager
FLANAGAN KEVIN FRANCIS	1974	M	Manager
FLIGG JONATHON ANDREW	1993	M	Manager
FLYNN J. TERRENCE DR.	1961	M	Manager
FLYNN JAMES FRANCIS	2003	M	Manager
FLYNN PATRICK TIMOTHY	1987	M	Manager
FLYNN WILLIAM F. JR.	1959	M	Manager
FOX FRANK MILTON	1958	M	Manager
FRALEIGH JAMES PATRICK	1988	M	Manager
FRENCH JONATHAN LEE	2000	M	Manager
FRENZEL ALLAN JOSEPH	1969	M	Manager
FRERICKS JEFFREY MATTHEW	1996	M	Manager
FRERICKS JOSEPH THOMAS	1999	M	Manager
FRONING ANDREW JOHN	1972	M	Manager
FULLMER EDWARD FRANCIS	1984	M	Manager
GABBIANELLI RICHARD ANGELO	1978	M	Manager
GAGLIARDI JOHN THOMAS	1961	M	Manager
GALLAGHER JAMES G.	1987	M	Manager
GALVAN ANTHONY RAUL	1999	M	Manager
GANNON MICHAEL PATRICK	1988	M	Manager
GANSEN BRETT DAVID	2002	M	Manager
GAST FREDERICK C. JR.	1969	M	Manager
GEARY CORNELIUS E.	1940	M	Manager
GENNUSO PETER MURPHY	2002	M	Manager
GERMAINE ROBERT THOMAS	2000	M	Manager
GESS MARK ALAN	1986	M	Manager
GIBBON PHILIP JOSEPH	1991	M	Manager
GILMAN BRADLEY MARK	1998	M	Manager
GILSINGER MATTHEW JOSEPH	2004	M	Manager
GIMBER DOUGLAS ALAN	1960	M	Manager
GIORDINO ANDREW JOSEPH	1965	M	Manager
GIOVACCO JOHN WILLIAM JR.	1996	M	Manager
GOODRICH ZACHARY JAMES	2005	M	Manager
GORMAN JOSEPH R. MR.	1939	M	Manager
GOTTSACKER RICHARD JAMES	1947	M	Manager
GOZDECKI THOMAS S. JR.	1958	M	Manager
GRAHAM EDWARD JOHN	1953	M	Manager
GRAIF JOHN HENNESSEY	1946	M	Manager
GRAMS AUGUST M.	1928	M	Manager
GRAMS JOHN ALBERT	1933	M	Manager
GREEN MICHAEL SHAEMUS	1989	M	Manager
GROLLER RAYMOND RICHARD	1965	M	Manager
GRUZS JOSEPH LIAM	2005	M	Manager
GRYLEWICZ BENEDICT E. JR.	1954	M	Manager
GUARNIERI ALBERT STEPHEN	1951	M	Manager
GULDE JEFFREY CLEMENT	1988	M	Manager
GURDAK MICHAEL P.	1984	M	Manager
GWADZ ROBERT WALTER	1962	M	Manager
HACKETT THOMAS LEWIS	1977	M	Manager
HADLEY DAVID ELINUS	1976	M	Manager
HAFFEY KENNETH MARK	1978	M	Manager
HAFNER LOUIS ALBERT	1950	M	Manager
HAGGARD KEVIN MICHAEL	1997	M	Manager
HALE CRAIG MARSHALL	1983	M	Manager
HALPIN DANIEL DELACEY	1931	M	Manager
HAMMELL BRIAN EDWARD	2003	M	Manager
HAMMER DANIEL WILLIAM	1954	M	Manager
HANLEY JOHN JOSEPH	1934	M	Manager
HARKINS SCOTT PATRICK	1989	M	Manager
HAROUSE DAVID KYLE	1986	M	Manager
HARRIS WALLACE WILLIAM JR.	1987	M	Manager
HART JOSEPH FREDERICK	1940	M	Manager
HART MARK JOSEPH	1995	M	Manager
HART WALTER MARK	1986	M	Manager
HARTLE STEVEN DAVID	1988	M	Manager
HARVEY MICHAEL JAMES	1985	M	Manager
HAWES WILLIAM RICHARD	1941	M	Manager
HAYES THOMAS DAVID	1975	M	Manager
HE YI	2001	M	Manager
HEADY MATTHEW WILLIAM	1997	M	Manager
HEIDRICH STEVEN JOHN	1982	M	Manager
HEILMANN TIMOTHY MICHAEL DR.	1979	M	Manager
HEISNER JAMES EDWARD III	2006	M	Manager
HELLAND MICHAEL CHRISTIAN	1992	M	Manager
HENDRICKS WILLIAM DONALD	1974	M	Manager
HERBERT SIMON JAMES	1991	M	Manager
HESSION WILLARD GEORGE	1989	M	Manager
HESTER BERNARD FRANCIS	1953	M	Manager
HIGNEY ANDREW JAMES	1989	M	Manager
HILZ MARK DAVID	1970	M	Manager
HODAPP STEVEN MATTHEW	1999	M	Manager
HOFFMAN DAVID JOHN	2001	M	Manager
HOFFMAN J. SEAN	1989	M	Manager
HOFFMAN JOHN JAMES JR.	1980	M	Manager
HOGAN DYLAN JOHN	1993	M	Manager
HOGAN RICHARD PAUL	1970	M	Manager
HOLLAND EDWARD WORTHINGTON	2003	M	Manager
HOLLOWAY PHILLIP REAGIN JR.	1992	M	Manager
HOOVER LUCAS AARON	2006	M	Manager
HORMUTH MICHAEL PATRICK	2001	M	Manager
HORN THOMAS JEFFERY	2005	M	Manager
HOUK DAVID WILLIAM	1965	M	Manager
HUESER MICHAEL THOMAS	2001	M	Manager
HUFFMAN MARK ROBERT	1975	M	Manager
HUGHES JOHN MINER	1931	M	Manager
HULL ROBERT JOSEPH JR.	1977	M	Manager
HURLEY DENIS O'HERREN	1975	M	Manager
HUSSEY JOHN JOSEPH	1940	M	Manager
HUURMAN WALTER W. M.D.	1958	M	Manager
HYDUK SHANNON CORY	2003	M	Manager
IGOE JOHN DANIEL	1928	M	Manager
JACOBS JOHN J.	1949	M	Manager
JANCHAR MATTHEW AARON	1993	M	Manager
JARNOT JOHN WALTER	1954	M	Manager
JENNINGS EMMIT MARTIN M.D.	1944	M	Manager
JOHNS CHRISTOPHER P.	1982	M	Manager
JOHNSON MATTHEW CUMMINGS	1986	M	Manager
JORDAN JOHN CRAIG	1967	M	Manager
JUNKER GEORGE EDWARD II	1980	M	Manager
KABAT DAVID LEE	1968	M	Manager
KEALY J. KIERNAN MR. JR.	1961	M	Manager
KEANE ROBERT JOSEPH	1989	M	Manager
KEARNEY SEAN ROBERT	1979	M	Manager
KEATING DENNIS PATRICK	1975	M	Manager
KEATING MICHAEL ANTHONY	1975	M	Manager
KEATING RAYMOND BENEDICT	1935	M	Manager
KEATING WILLIAM ARTHUR	1943	M	Manager
KEENAN MICHAEL J.	1984	M	Manager
KEGOWICZ ANTHONY WILLIAM	1932	M	Manager
KELLER CHARLES JOSEPH	1954	M	Manager
KELLEY RICHARD E.	1934	M	Manager
KELLEY ROBERT KRAMER SR.	1934	M	Manager
KELLY EDWARD FRANCIS	1955	M	Manager
KELLY JOSEPH PATRICK	1961	M	Manager
KENNARD GEORGE A. JR.	1948	M	Manager
KENNAUGH MICHAEL A.	1987	M	Manager
KENNEDY EDWARD THOMAS	1960	M	Manager
KENNEDY KEVIN ANTHONY	1970	M	Manager
KENNELLY MICHAEL JOSEPH	1985	M	Manager
KENNEY JOHN FRANCIS	1933	M	Manager
KEOUGH GEORGE CAREY M.D.	1988	M	Manager
KERLS MATTHEW WOODSMALL	2004	M	Manager
KERWIN PETER JAMES	1984	M	Manager
KESSING ROBERT L.	1949	M	Manager
KEY ROBERT FARISH	1976	M	Manager
KFOURY EDWARD JAMES	1960	M	Manager
KHOREY DAVID EUGENE	1981	M	Manager
KILLILEA WILLIAM BURNELL	1960	M	Manager
KIRCHMIER EDWARD JUDE	1988	M	Manager
KIRKPATRICK JESSE LEE	2004	M	Manager
KIRLEY PHILIP HARRISON	1935	M	Manager
KLEPPEL KENNETH JUDE	2001	M	Manager
KLISH WILLIAM JOHN JR.	1999	M	Manager
KLUCZYK RICHARD CHRISTOPHER	1982	M	Manager
KNAPKE ANDREW LEE	1997	M	Manager
KNIGHT TIMOTHY WADE	1966	M	Manager
KNOTT MATTHEW MITCHELL	1992	M	Manager
KOLASINSKI JOHN THOMAS	1979	M	Manager
KOLUCH BRIAN PETER	1995	M	Manager
KORALEWSKI JASON ROBERT	2005	M	Manager
KOURY GREGORY KENT M.D.	1983	M	Manager
KOZICKI JEFFREY JOSEPH	1988	M	Manager
KRAMER J. ALAN	1967	M	Manager
KRASOVEC DAVID J.	1980	M	Manager
KRAUS JOHN PAUL	1983	M	Manager
KRUG JOSEPH ALPHONSE	1983	M	Manager
KRUSZEWSKI DAVID MICHAEL D.O.	1983	M	Manager
KUBERSKI ESTATE OF REV.LEONARD	1964	M	Manager
KUHARICH MICHAEL PATRICK	1999	M	Manager
KULICK THOMAS A.	1964	M	Manager
KUSS JOHN ARTHUR	1992	M	Manager
KVATSAK ROBERT JULIUS	1939	M	Manager
LACROIX LUCIEN JOHN	1939	M	Manager
LALUZERNE LAWRENCE ROBERT	1982	M	Manager
LAMADRID LORENZO WILLIAM	1993	M	Manager
LAMARCHE MATTHEW JAMES DR.	1997	M	Manager
LAMB TERRENCE PATRICK	1970	M	Manager
LANDRY ROBERT EDWARD JR.	1986	M	Manager
LANGHEIM MARK ANTHONY	1983	M	Manager
LARKIN RICHARD LEO	1985	M	Manager
LAVERY HARRY DAVID	1944	M	Manager
LAWLESS JOHN NOEL JR.	1977	M	Manager
LEAHY JOHN HENRY HON.	1959	M	Manager
LEARY JOSEPH M. M.D.	1984	M	Manager
LEININGER GREGORY ALAN	1990	M	Manager
LENK PETER ANDREW	1973	M	Manager
LEONARD THOMAS JOHN	1981	M	Manager
LEWIS CLYDE AUGUSTINE	1934	M	Manager
LINDGREN JOHN A. III	1967	M	Manager
LINDGREN ROBERT DONALD JR.	1973	M	Manager
LOGAN TIMOTHY DAVID	1996	M	Manager
LONG THOMAS JAMES	1980	M	Manager
LOVELL LUKE RICHARD	1990	M	Manager
LUECK DONALD CHRIST	1950	M	Manager
LUNDEN FRANCIS GERARD	1957	M	Manager
MACDONALD JAMES JOSEPH	1972	M	Manager
MACDONALD MICHAEL PAUL	N/A	M	Manager
MADDEN DARYL PAUL	1979	M	Manager
MADDEN EDWARD V.	1949	M	Manager
MAGEE TERENCE JOSEPH	1969	M	Manager
MAGUIRE JOHN EDWARD	1958	M	Manager
MAGUIRE ROBERT BARRIE	1960	M	Manager
MAHER BRIAN JAMES	1993	M	Manager
MAHER EDWARD JOSEPH	1940	M	Manager
MAHONEY ROBERT JOSEPH	1951	M	Manager
MALLORY ROBERT JAMES	2002	M	Manager
MANKEY EDWIN LAWR. JR.	1967	M	Manager
MANNELLO LOUIS JAMES JR.	1986	M	Manager
MANNING ROBERT ANDRES	1936	M	Manager
MARK STEPHEN PHILIP	1990	M	Manager
MARQUIS ANTHONY JAMES	2005	M	Manager
MARTIN BRUCE WILLIAM	1978	M	Manager
MARTIN JESSE ALAN	1998	M	Manager
MARTIN W. DONALD	1933	M	Manager
MARTINY RICHARD JOHN	1966	M	Manager
MATARAZZI MARK VICTOR	1972	M	Manager
MATARAZZI WILLIAM HENRY	1975	M	Manager
MATHER PATRICK EDMUND	1981	M	Manager
MATTES JAMES LEROY	1974	M	Manager
MCAWARD KEVIN JEREMY	1995	M	Manager
MCCABE THOMAS J. JR.	1982	M	Manager
MCCANN DAVID THOMAS	1979	M	Manager
MCCARTHY JAMES RYAN	1968	M	Manager
MCCARTHY JOHN STEPHEN	1965	M	Manager
MCCARTHY PATRICK STUDER	1998	M	Manager
MCCARTHY PAUL JOSEPH JR.	1965	M	Manager
MCCARTHY THOMAS JOSEPH	1986	M	Manager
MCCARTY WILLIAM H.	1949	M	Manager
MCCLOSKEY BRENDAN JAMES	1999	M	Manager
MCCLURE DENNIS DELON	1984	M	Manager
MCCONVILLE JAMES BRADLEY DR.	1969	M	Manager
MCCULLOCH PATRICK O'ROURKE	1998	M	Manager
MCCUTCHAN ROBERT DENNIS JR.	1961	M	Manager
MCDERMOTT KEVIN PATRICK	1973	M	Manager

NAME	YEAR	GENDER	SPORT
MCDERMOTT WILLIAM T. JR.	1985	M	Manager
MCDONOUGH MICHAEL PATRICK	1974	M	Manager
MCFADDEN JAMES JOSEPH	1965	M	Manager
MCFADDEN JOHN EDWARD	1963	M	Manager
MCFADDEN JOHN WALTER JR.	1958	M	Manager
MCFADDEN PATRICK MATTHEW	1971	M	Manager
MCGILLICUDDY MICHAEL JAMES JR.	1997	M	Manager
MCGOLDRICK ROBERT LAWRENCE	1956	M	Manager
MCGRAW JAMES J. JR.	1971	M	Manager
MCHUGH JAMES WILLIAM	1937	M	Manager
MCKEAN JOSEPH EDWARD	1932	M	Manager
MCKINNEY KENNETH PATRICK	1993	M	Manager
MCLAUGHLIN THOMAS E. III	1973	M	Manager
MCMAHON PATRICK J.	1962	M	Manager
MCMORROW BRIAN CHARLES	1981	M	Manager
MCNALLY MICHAEL PHILIP	1997	M	Manager
MCNULTY MARK P.	1984	M	Manager
MCPEAK HARRY DELANEY	1967	M	Manager
MCSWEENEY EUGENE TERRENCE	1968	M	Manager
MEDLAND NATHANIEL KYRAN	2000	M	Manager
MEISKEY STEPHEN JAY	1978	M	Manager
MELLON JAMES ANDREW	1982	M	Manager
MERCADO KEVIN JOSEPH	1991	M	Manager
MEYERS RONALD PHILLIP	1965	M	Manager
MICHALAK CHRISTOPHER JOHN	1985	M	Manager
MICHAUD ROBERT HENRY	1950	M	Manager
MILLENBACH ROBERT GEORGE	1953	M	Manager
MOFFITT BRIAN EDWARD	1988	M	Manager
MOLIDOR JAMES FRANCIS	1946	M	Manager
MONAGHAN ARTHUR RAYMOND	1993	M	Manager
MONG JAMES JOSEPH	1966	M	Manager
MOODY ANDREW JOHN	2003	M	Manager
MOORE JOHN MICHAEL	2004	M	Manager
MORALES JAIME ANTONIO	2001	M	Manager
MORAN J. KEVIN MR.	1967	M	Manager
MORIN ERIC JOHN	2005	M	Manager
MORRISON THOMAS ANTHONY	1942	M	Manager
MORRISSEY WILLIAM THOMAS	1976	M	Manager
MUDD CHRISTOPHER DOLAN	2001	M	Manager
MUELLER ERIC GERARD	2005	M	Manager
MULAC ADAM JOSEPH O.D.	1990	M	Manager
MULHERN JAMES WOODROW	1938	M	Manager
MULLIS RICHARD ALLEN	1985	M	Manager
MURPHY GREGORY MICHAEL	1996	M	Manager
MURPHY JAMES STEPHEN M.D.	1966	M	Manager
MURPHY JOHN TIMOTHY JR.	1957	M	Manager
MURPHY KEVIN MICHAEL	2001	M	Manager
MURPHY MARK JAMES	1986	M	Manager
MURPHY MICHAEL JOSEPH	2002	M	Manager
MURRAY DANIEL PATRICK	1996	M	Manager
MURRAY JAMES CARROLL	1943	M	Manager
MUSCARELLA CHRIS JAMES	1974	M	Manager
NAVARRE MARK JOHN	1976	M	Manager
NECAS EMMETT JOHN	1941	M	Manager
NELSON ANDREW ROWAN	1998	M	Manager
NESSELHUF C. RYAN MR.	1995	M	Manager
NEVALA THOMAS JOSEPH	1990	M	Manager
NICOLOSI RAPHAEL JEROME	1994	M	Manager
NIGRO JOSEPH AUGUSTINE	1936	M	Manager
NOLAN PATRICK MARTIN	1986	M	Manager
NOTTO LAWRENCE F. III	1984	M	Manager
NYTES STEVEN THOMAS	1990	M	Manager
OAKES RAYMOND WILLIAM	1935	M	Manager
O'BRIEN JOHN JOSEPH JR.	1987	M	Manager
O'CONNELL JOHN JOSEPH	1939	M	Manager
O'CONNELL JOSEPH CLEOPHAS	1940	M	Manager
O'CONNOR RAYMOND FRANCIS	1951	M	Manager
O'DONNELL MATTHEW B. COL. JR.	1951	M	Manager
O'GORMAN KEVIN M.	1987	M	Manager
OGREN THOMAS JOHN	1978	M	Manager
O'KEEFFE ANDREW ELLIS	1933	M	Manager
OLSON MICHAEL JEROME DR.	1968	M	Manager
OLSZEWSKI JOHN CHRISTOPHER	1999	M	Manager
O'REILLY PETER LINDSAY	1994	M	Manager
O'ROURKE MATTHEW MARTIN	2006	M	Manager
O'ROURKE RICHARD NASON	1955	M	Manager
OSEAN BRENDAN CHRISTOPHER	1998	M	Manager
OWENS CHARLES V. JR.	1948	M	Manager
PACILIO ANTHONY VINCENT	1960	M	Manager
PADANILAM JOSEPH GEORGE	1988	M	Manager
PADLEY ALBERT F. III	1975	M	Manager
PALKOVICS JOHN JAMES	1974	M	Manager
PALMER JOHN WILLIAM	2005	M	Manager
PALMER JOSEPH CHRISTIAN	1999	M	Manager
PARIETTI RYAN JAMES	2006	M	Manager
PARISO THOMAS EDWARD	2002	M	Manager
PATRICK SHAWN JOSEPH	1989	M	Manager
PAULUS ALAN GERARD	1978	M	Manager
PECK WILLIAM TOWNSEND II	2006	M	Manager
PELOQUIN DAVID O.	2003	M	Manager
PEPE CHRISTOPHER PATRICK	2004	M	Manager
PEPLINSKI RICHARD JEROME JR.	1963	M	Manager
PETZ JOHN RICHARD	1998	M	Manager
PEZZO JAMES MICHAEL	1974	M	Manager
PEZZO WILLIAM JOSEPH	1972	M	Manager
PHILLIPS MICHAEL JAMES	1977	M	Manager
PILAWSKI EUGENE MICHAEL	1989	M	Manager
PINI JOHN LEWIS	1964	M	Manager
PONICKI PAUL EDWARD	1964	M	Manager
PORCARI JAMES ANTHONY JR.	1955	M	Manager
POWER JAMES WILLIAM	1932	M	Manager
POWERS TODD JOSEPH	1992	M	Manager
PRESTON DAVID BENSON	2006	M	Manager
PRIGAL TODD STEVEN	1980	M	Manager
PRINGLE T'AUGUSTUS	1991	M	Manager
PUETZ JOHN CHARLES	1988	M	Manager
PUETZ JOSEPH MATTHEW	1987	M	Manager
QUENAN PATRICK W.	1990	M	Manager
QUENAN TIMOTHY JOHN	1993	M	Manager
QUINN JOHN JOSEPH	1930	M	Manager
QUINN THOMAS P. JR.	1984	M	Manager
RADEMAKER THEODORE C.	1946	M	Manager
RAFFERTY PAUL EDWARD	1960	M	Manager
RANK HUGH DUKE	1954	M	Manager
RAUSCHER ERNEST WARREN	1945	M	Manager
RAYMOND ROBERT JENNINGS	1951	M	Manager
REAM JOSEPH A.	1958	M	Manager
REARDON KEVIN JOSEPH	1969	M	Manager
REEVES ADAM PENNINGTON	2004	M	Manager
REILLY TIMOTHY JAMES	1985	M	Manager
RESCINITI S. EDMUND JR.	1956	M	Manager
REYNOLDS HUGH EDWARD JR.	1950	M	Manager
RHATICAN JAMES PATRICK	1992	M	Manager
RIGALI JAMES FRANCIS	1983	M	Manager
RILEY ROBERT JUDGE	1962	M	Manager
RITTERBUSCH CHRISTOPHER JAMES	1990	M	Manager
ROBBINS DAVID A.	1987	M	Manager
ROBERTS THERON BERNARD	1985	M	Manager
ROBINSON DAVID ANDREW	1985	M	Manager
ROBINSON DOUGLAS SEAN	1992	M	Manager
ROCK JONATHAN MICHAEL	1994	M	Manager
ROCK TIMOTHY RONALD	1991	M	Manager
RODDY TIMOTHY E. JR.	1969	M	Manager
RODGERS EDWARD JAMES	1946	M	Manager
RODOCK JOHN N.	1978	M	Manager
RODRIGUEZ FRANCISCO BERNARDO IV	1991	M	Manager
RODRIGUEZ JORGE	1995	M	Manager
ROSS DONALD K.	1953	M	Manager
ROSS JOHN JOSEPH	1932	M	Manager
RUSSO STACY THOMAS	1980	M	Manager
RUSSO WILLIAM BRIAN DR.	1968	M	Manager
RYAN JOHN JESS	1926	M	Manager
RYAN JOHN JOSEPH	1973	M	Manager
RYAN JOHN MICHAEL HON.	1941	M	Manager
RYAN JOHN PHILLIP JR.	1961	M	Manager
RYCZAK PAUL STANLEY	1975	M	Manager
SALMON JOHN KEVIN	1994	M	Manager
SANTONI PEDRO MIGUEL DR.	1978	M	Manager
SANTOS JOSEPH A.	1957	M	Manager
SAUNDERS JOHN F.	1931	M	Manager
SAYOUR PETER E.	1960	M	Manager
SCANLON MICHAEL LONERGAN	1982	M	Manager
SCAZZERO JAMES DOMINICK	1990	M	Manager
SCHEIDLER JOSEPH ANTHONY	1980	M	Manager
SCHIEWE ROBERT GEORGE	1991	M	Manager
SCHMID JAMES ALPHONSE	1944	M	Manager
SCHMITT DEREK WILLIAM	2004	M	Manager
SCHULTZ MICHAEL WANG	2004	M	Manager
SCHWARTZ ALBERT JOHN SR.	1937	M	Manager
SCOTT ANTHONY M.	1983	M	Manager
SCROOPE HENRY JOHN IV	1997	M	Manager
SEAMAN DAVID EDWARD	1963	M	Manager
SEAMON MICHAEL DAVID	1992	M	Manager
SEIM EDWARD STACEY	1954	M	Manager
SELLICK JAY ANTHONY	1987	M	Manager
SENKIER CHARLES DAVID	2005	M	Manager
SHANNON THOMAS PATRICK	1969	M	Manager
SHEEDY DANIEL CRYSDALE	1939	M	Manager
SHEEHAN TIMOTHY JOHN	2005	M	Manager
SHERIDAN PHILIP JAMES	1992	M	Manager
SHERIFF WILLIAM S. IV	1987	M	Manager
SHERIN KEITH SEAN	1981	M	Manager
SHINNERS BURTON MICHAEL DR.	1933	M	Manager
SIMKO JEFFREY PAUL	2002	M	Manager
SKATTUM THOMAS JOHN	1997	M	Manager
SKURKA MICHAEL PAUL	1981	M	Manager
SLATTERY JAMES FRANCIS SR.	1950	M	Manager
SMITH DANIEL OWEN	1989	M	Manager
SMITH DONALD ANTHONY	1980	M	Manager
SMITH EDWARD ALBERT SR.	1993	M	Manager
SMITH JOHN ROBERT	1982	M	Manager
SMITH JOHNNIE III	1982	M	Manager
SMITH KELLY	1997	M	Manager
SMITH RUSSELL E.	1960	M	Manager
SOBANSKI ROBERT GERARD	1978	M	Manager
SOLAN STEPHEN JR.	1976	M	Manager
SOLDATO DANIEL CARMEN	2002	M	Manager
SOMMERS GREGORY RAYMOND	1984	M	Manager
SONGER THOMAS JOSEPH	1983	M	Manager
SOUTER JOHN ROBERT JR.	1988	M	Manager
SPANGENBERG CHARLES EDWARD	1932	M	Manager
SPRINGMAN SCOTT FRANCIS	1999	M	Manager
SQUIRES EDWARD COYLE	1970	M	Manager
SRSIC RAYMOND PETER M.D.	1948	M	Manager
STAELGRAEVE MARK BERNARD	1990	M	Manager
STANIECKI WILLIAM A.	1981	M	Manager
STEWART PETER W. BUEL DR.	1942	M	Manager
STILLWAGON WOODROW AUGUST	1936	M	Manager
STOELLER JOHN ALAN	1953	M	Manager
STORIN MATTHEW V.	1964	M	Manager
STUKAS ROBERT PAUL	1955	M	Manager
STUMP JOHN PHILIP JR.	1955	M	Manager
SULLIVAN BRENDAN JOSEPH	2001	M	Manager
SULLIVAN EDWARD FRANCIS	1952	M	Manager
SULLIVAN JAMES PETER JR.	1987	M	Manager
SULLIVAN JOHN FRANCIS	1967	M	Manager
SULLIVAN MICHAEL GERARD	1994	M	Manager
SULLIVAN WILLIAM JAMES	1965	M	Manager
SWEENEY JOSEPH MICHAEL	1974	M	Manager
SWIFT JAMES P.	1924	M	Manager
SWINEHART JAMES ROBERT	1979	M	Manager
SYLVESTER ANTHONY JOSEPH	2006	M	Manager
TALARICO ANTHONY P.	1990	M	Manager
TARGGART ALAN WAYNE	1985	M	Manager
TAYLOR DANE EDWARD	1979	M	Manager
TAYLOR ROBERT GENE	1989	M	Manager
THEBAULT MARK JOHN	1988	M	Manager
THOMAS RICHARD KEITH D.D.S.	1982	M	Manager
THOMPSON THOMAS WM. JR.	1935	M	Manager
THURSTON MICHAEL ANTHONY	1988	M	Manager
TIERNEY BRIAN SCOTT	1993	M	Manager
TIERNEY EDWARD WILLIAM D.P.M.	1990	M	Manager
TILL MARK ANDREW M.D.	1979	M	Manager
TIMM DON PAUL DR. II	1987	M	Manager
TODDY JOSEPH MICHAEL	1979	M	Manager
TOLLE CHRISTOPHER MICHAEL	1991	M	Manager
TOTARO ANTHONY JOSEPH	1981	M	Manager
TRACY PATRICK WILLIAM	1971	M	Manager
TSOMBANIDIS JOSEPH ANTHONY	1995	M	Manager
URIAH JAMES JOHN	1976	M	Manager
VANHUFFEL ALBERT	1939	M	Manager
VANHUFFEL HAROLD EMIL JR.	1956	M	Manager
VANIC MICHAEL JOHN CPA	1981	M	Manager
VANOVERWALLE J. JERALD	1962	M	Manager
VARALLO NICK FRANK JR.	1963	M	Manager
VASQUEZ ROMEO JAVIER JR.	1991	M	Manager
VECCHIONE THOMAS RAY M.D.	1963	M	Manager
VELASQUEZ ARTHUR R.	1987	M	Manager
VETO DONALD ROY	1981	M	Manager
WACLAWIK JAMES JOHN	1981	M	Manager
WALSH BRENDAN MICHAEL	2000	M	Manager
WALSH BRIAN JAMES	1987	M	Manager
WALSH EDWARD FRANCIS	1942	M	Manager
WALSH JAMES LEE	1966	M	Manager
WALSH THOMAS JEROME	1935	M	Manager
WALTERS DAVID EDWARD	1994	M	Manager
WALZ NICHOLAS EDWARD	1963	M	Manager
WARBURTON WALTER KENNETH	1940	M	Manager
WARCHOL MATTHEW DAVID	2005	M	Manager
WARMENHOVEN PETER FRANCIS JR.	1978	M	Manager
WATKINS J. LOUIS JR.	1949	M	Manager
WEBER CARL WITTRY	1935	M	Manager
WEBER GREGORY JOHN	2002	M	Manager
WEGLARZ DOUGLAS ANDREW	1989	M	Manager
WEINER ADAM THOMAS	2004	M	Manager
WEISS CHARLES F.	1932	M	Manager
WELBORN CHRISTOPHER JAMES	1989	M	Manager
WERTZ WILLIAM WHITE LT.	1996	M	Manager
WHITE MICHAEL VINCENT	1985	M	Manager
WIGGINS JOHN LAWSON	1943	M	Manager
WILKIN SIDNEY CLARENCE	1956	M	Manager
WILKS SHAWN MICHAEL	1991	M	Manager
WILLACKER JOHN FRANCIS	1963	M	Manager
WILSON ANDREW FREDERIC	1939	M	Manager
WIRRY ANTHONY WILLIAM	1933	M	Manager
WITTY PETER NATHAN	1989	M	Manager
WOLF CHRISTOPHER MICHAEL	1995	M	Manager
WOLNITZEK MARCUS STEPHEN	2000	M	Manager
WOOD RICHARD ALLEN II	1994	M	Manager
WOULFE JOHN VINCENT JR.	1957	M	Manager

NAME	YEAR	GENDER	SPORT
CHESTNUT PAUL COTTER	1960	M	Swimming
CHILES ROBERT LOUIS	1968	M	Swimming
CLARK JOHN FRANCIS JR.	1963	M	Swimming
CLARK PATRICK THOMAS	1961	M	Swimming
COFFEY JOHN JOSEPH	1986	M	Swimming
COFFEY STEPHEN JAMES	1987	M	Swimming
COHEN MICHAEL GEORGE	1968	M	Swimming
COLBERT DAVID MICHAEL	1972	M	Swimming
CONSIDINE JAMES PATRICK	1983	M	Swimming
COOLEY COLIN STEPHEN	1993	M	Swimming
COONEY JAMES FRANCIS JR.	1971	M	Swimming
CORNICK GREGORY ALLEN	1993	M	Swimming
COUGHLAN BRIAN PATRICK	2004	M	Swimming
COX JOHN DAVID	1970	M	Swimming
COX JOHN EDWARD	1932	M	Swimming
CRONIN WILLIAM F. JR.	1961	M	Swimming
CULHANE RORY MICHAEL	1965	M	Swimming
DAILEY RYAN WILLIAM	1999	M	Swimming
DALTON MATTHEW PAUL	1980	M	Swimming
DAVIS MICHAEL QUINN	1969	M	Swimming
DAVIS PATRICK MICHAEL	2006	M	Swimming
DEBRUYNE DALE THOMAS	1979	M	Swimming
DEFRANK TROY JASON	2004	M	Swimming
DEMPSEY TERRENCE W. DR.	1987	M	Swimming
DERMOTT JOSHUA LEE	2004	M	Swimming
DEVLIN PAUL JOHN JR.	1965	M	Swimming
DILLENBURGER PHILIP WILLIAM	1962	M	Swimming
DILUIA EDWARD ANTHONY	1978	M	Swimming
DINGER FRANK SADLIER	1961	M	Swimming
DIVER JOSEPH WILLIAM	1968	M	Swimming
DIXON STEPHEN CHARLES	1968	M	Swimming
DOERFLER GREGORY EDWARD D.D.S.	1969	M	Swimming
DOHERTY DAVID M.	1996	M	Swimming
DONOVAN MICHAEL BARRY	1999	M	Swimming
DORAN JAMES BRIAN	1994	M	Swimming
DOWD JAMES EDWARD JR.	1988	M	Swimming
DOYLE MICHAEL THOMAS	1999	M	Swimming
DRUCKER P. MICHAEL MR.	1965	M	Swimming
DRURY ELLIOTT CHARLES	2002	M	Swimming
DUGAN PATRICK JOSEPH	1992	M	Swimming
DURKIN THOMAS JAMES JR.	2003	M	Swimming
EBEL ROBERT ALLAN	1977	M	Swimming
EGAN EDWARD JOSEPH JR.	1965	M	Swimming
FAHEY FRANK JOSEPH JR.	1972	M	Swimming
FARMER NICHOLAS ALLEN	1990	M	Swimming
FELLRATH ROBERT ANDREW	1996	M	Swimming
FERRARIS ROBERT PAUL D.M.D.	1974	M	Swimming
FERRELL M. CRAIG M.D.	1971	M	Swimming
FETTER ROBERT JOSEPH	2000	M	Swimming
FINK ROBERT PAUL	1981	M	Swimming
FISCHER JAMES NIELSON	1974	M	Swimming
FITZMORRIS STEVEN JOSEPH M.D.	1978	M	Swimming
FITZPATRICK JASON STEVENS	2003	M	Swimming
FITZPATRICK JOHN RAYMOND III	2000	M	Swimming
FITZSIMONS EDWARD JOSEPH	1978	M	Swimming
FITZSIMONS JOHN P.	1984	M	Swimming
FLANAGAN KEVIN ANDREW	1994	M	Swimming
FLANAGAN MICHAEL MCCABE	2003	M	Swimming
FLYNN DANIEL JOSEPH	1984	M	Swimming
FLYNN ROBERT EDWARD	1996	M	Swimming
FONSECA ANTONIO EDMUND	2000	M	Swimming
FOSTER MARK LAWRENCE	1976	M	Swimming
FREE DOUGLAS MICHAEL	1973	M	Swimming
FREY JOHN JOSEPH DR. III	1966	M	Swimming
FROMAN JOHN LOUIS	1989	M	Swimming
FUGATE CHRISTOPHER KEITH	1999	M	Swimming
GARCIA W. ROCKE	1965	M	Swimming
GARRITY JAMES ALOYSIUS	1959	M	Swimming
GEHRKE WILLIAM JOHN	1967	M	Swimming
GIBBONS JOHN FRANCIS	1982	M	Swimming
GIBBONS MATTHEW RICHARD	1995	M	Swimming
GODFREY JOHN ANDREW DR.	1993	M	Swimming
GODFREY PAUL TIMOTHY	1991	M	Swimming
GRACE JEFFREY MARTIN	1988	M	Swimming
GRAHAM EDWARD A. JR.	1974	M	Swimming
GREEN CHRISTOPHER N.	1987	M	Swimming
GREEN WILLIAM HERBERT	1984	M	Swimming
GRENDA TYLER ROSS	2006	M	Swimming
GREVER JAMES WAGNER	1962	M	Swimming
GRUNEWALD MATTHEW CHARLES	2001	M	Swimming
GUARNIER BRYAN JOHN	2006	M	Swimming
HARDING ALPHONSE H. DR. III	1984	M	Swimming
HARDING BLAISE DREW	1986	M	Swimming
HARTZELL ROLAND MCDONALD	1988	M	Swimming
HASKE ANTHONY JAMES SR.	1961	M	Swimming
HAUSWIRTH JEFFREY LAMONT	1983	M	Swimming
HEDDEN MATTHEW EDWARD	2001	M	Swimming
HEFFERNAN PATRICK MYLES	2006	M	Swimming
HESSE PAUL ROBERT	1977	M	Swimming
HESSLER MARK GERHARD	2004	M	Swimming
HILGER MICHAEL BRIEN	1982	M	Swimming
HIRSCHFELD ADAM BENEDICT	1989	M	Swimming
HOCK THOMAS PAUL	1969	M	Swimming
HOFWEBER JAMES EDWARD	1968	M	Swimming
HORAK DAVID JAMES	2002	M	Swimming
HORENKAMP THOMAS HENRY	1996	M	Swimming
HUDSON JOHN CLEMENT	2003	M	Swimming
HUESMAN HERBERT DAVID	2001	M	Swimming
HUGHES JAMES HOWARD	1963	M	Swimming
HUNT E. BRETT MR.	1991	M	Swimming
HUSSON ROBERT JOSEPH	1967	M	Swimming
HYDE MATTHEW WILLETS	2003	M	Swimming
HYER SEAN PATRICK	1994	M	Swimming
JACKOBOICE WILLIAM WHEATON	1990	M	Swimming
JACOB TIMOTHY DOUGLAS M.D.	1984	M	Swimming
JENSEN MARK A.	1987	M	Swimming
JESSUP SCOTT ALAN	1977	M	Swimming
JORDAN EUGENE FUSZ	1960	M	Swimming
JUSZLI GREGORY MICHAEL	2001	M	Swimming
KANE JAMES GERARD	1975	M	Swimming
KATIS RICHARD MATHEW	1959	M	Swimming
KEELEY JAMES MICHAEL JR.	1995	M	Swimming
KEENAN JAMES TRACEY III	1973	M	Swimming
KENNEDY MICHAEL P.	1985	M	Swimming
KENNETT THOMAS WADE	1965	M	Swimming
KILEY ANDREW ROBERT	1995	M	Swimming
KING MICHAEL JOSEPH	1967	M	Swimming
KINSELLA PETER WILLIAM JR.	1978	M	Swimming
KLIMEK GERARD JOSEPH	1976	M	Swimming
KLINE TRAVIS LAWYER	2003	M	Swimming
KOMORA JOHN P.	1981	M	Swimming
KOROWICKI KEVIN	1981	M	Swimming
KOSELKA JOHN JOSEPH	1988	M	Swimming
KOSS MICHAEL JAMES	2002	M	Swimming
KRAKOWSKI FRANK JOSEPH	2005	M	Swimming
KRATUS EUGENE ALBERT	1973	M	Swimming
KRISTL TIMOTHY O.	1965	M	Swimming
KRUTSCH THOMAS KIRK	1981	M	Swimming
KUNA VINCENT AMORY	1999	M	Swimming
LADOUCEUR WILLIAM J. JR.	1969	M	Swimming
LAFRATTA LAURENCE ANTHONY	1974	M	Swimming
LAMBERT ROBERT MICHAEL	1997	M	Swimming
LAPLATNEY D. PATRICK MR.	1981	M	Swimming
LATHROP GEORGE RYAN DR.	1996	M	Swimming
LECCESE SALVADOR FRANCIS	1964	M	Swimming
LECHNER BRENDAN PATRICK	2000	M	Swimming
LEDRICK DAVID JAMES DR.	1989	M	Swimming
LESLIE JAMES PETER	2000	M	Swimming
LICHTENFELS J. REID MR.	1970	M	Swimming
LIEB ROBERT ANTHONY	1963	M	Swimming
LONDRIGAN THOMAS FOSTER SR.	1959	M	Swimming
LOWNEY MARK JEROME	1990	M	Swimming
LUBKER JOHN RYAN	2000	M	Swimming
LUND R. CHRISTOPHER MR.	1961	M	Swimming
LUTKUS JAMES GRIFFIN	2006	M	Swimming
MACLEOD JOHN A.	1963	M	Swimming
MAERTZ TYLER STEVENS	2000	M	Swimming
MAGGIO ANDREW JAMES	2003	M	Swimming
MAHANEY MICHAEL WILLIAM	1961	M	Swimming
MAKIELSKI DANIEL JOSEPH	1975	M	Swimming
MARSHALL ROY TARTARET III	1968	M	Swimming
MAUS TODD LAWRENCE	1989	M	Swimming
MAY EDWIN GEORGE DR. JR.	1959	M	Swimming
MAY JOHN JOSEPH M.D.	1969	M	Swimming
MCALLISTER PATRICK THOMAS	1983	M	Swimming
MCCARTHY WILLIAM SHANE	1995	M	Swimming
MCCORRY BRIAN JOHN	1976	M	Swimming
MCDERMOTT JOHN JAMES JR.	1966	M	Swimming
MCDIVITT PATRICK WILLIAM	1982	M	Swimming
MCDONOUGH E. MICHAEL	1972	M	Swimming
MCGOWAN PAUL JOHN	1983	M	Swimming
MCGRAW CSC SEAN DAVID CSC	1992	M	Swimming
MCGUIRE FRANCIS XAVIER	1980	M	Swimming
MCLAUGHLIN RODERICK ROBERT	1981	M	Swimming
MCMANUS PATRICK REILLY	1988	M	Swimming
MEAGHER JAMES LOUIS III	1975	M	Swimming
MEANY JOSEPH M.	1961	M	Swimming
MESSAGLIA MICHAEL JOSEPH	1990	M	Swimming
MILLER CLAY CRESSWELL	2003	M	Swimming
MILLER JOSEPH FLORIAN	2003	M	Swimming
MILLIGAN JOSHUA OWEN	1998	M	Swimming
MIRO ROGELIO G.	1989	M	Swimming
MOISAN DAVID MICHAEL	2005	M	Swimming
MURPHY RICHARD ANTHONY	1997	M	Swimming
NAGLE RICHARD CLARK M.D.	1959	M	Swimming
NAJARIAN BRIAN CHRISTOPHER	1998	M	Swimming
NATHE DAVID MONTGOMERY	1995	M	Swimming
NEIDHOEFER CHARLES CHRISTIAN	1989	M	Swimming
NEWMAN DAVID ANDREW	1987	M	Swimming
NIEHAUS BERNARD F.	1987	M	Swimming
NOLAN JOHN E. JR.	1979	M	Swimming
NOONAN THOMAS JOSEPH	1979	M	Swimming
O'BERRY PATRICK COULTER	2006	M	Swimming
OBRINGER MATTHEW MICHAEL	2004	M	Swimming
O'CONNOR JOSEPH J.	1974	M	Swimming
ODDO THOMAS CHARLES REV. CSC	1965	M	Swimming
PAGE JEFFREY BRADFORD	1999	M	Swimming
PAPE GERALD FRANCIS	1961	M	Swimming
PAYNE CHRISTOPHER A.	1975	M	Swimming
PENN THOMAS JOSEPH III	1990	M	Swimming
PETERSON KARL IVAR	1992	M	Swimming
PETRILLO DENNIS CHRISTOPHER	1989	M	Swimming
PETRO ANDREW JOSEPH	1978	M	Swimming
PIERCE JONATHAN DAVID	2002	M	Swimming
PISZKIN F. ANDREW	1981	M	Swimming
PITTMAN ANDREW WALTER	2005	M	Swimming
PRESTON RUSSELL STANTON	2002	M	Swimming
RAHILL DANIEL F.	1979	M	Swimming
RAMIS GUILLERMO J.	1966	M	Swimming
RAND ROGER SCOTT	1992	M	Swimming
RANDOLPH TIMOTHY KYLE	2006	M	Swimming
RANIERI GREGORY CARL	1969	M	Swimming
REILLY ROBERT EMMETT JR.	1977	M	Swimming
REMMERS JAMES HENRY	1963	M	Swimming
RENTZ JOSEPH HARRY	1992	M	Swimming
RICHARDSON WESLEY JEROME	1999	M	Swimming
RIDGEWAY JOSEPH A. DR. IV	1985	M	Swimming
RINI BRIAN IGNATIUS	1991	M	Swimming
ROSE MATTHEW DEREK FRANCO	1997	M	Swimming
ROTH THOMAS LEE DR.	1969	M	Swimming
ROYER HARRISON RONALD	1998	M	Swimming
SAMADDAR KRIS KUMAR	1995	M	Swimming
SAMADDAR ROBIN KUMAR	1995	M	Swimming
SAYLOR JOSHUA RAYMOND	1997	M	Swimming
SCHATZ THOMAS GERARD DR.	1970	M	Swimming
SCHIRALLI NICHOLAS JOHN HON.	1970	M	Swimming
SCHMITZ WILLIAM JAMES	1989	M	Swimming
SCHROEDER RYAN DOUGLAS	1996	M	Swimming
SCHUCK FRANCIS MICHAEL	1966	M	Swimming
SCOTT KEVIN CHRISTOPHER	1995	M	Swimming
SCOTT WILLIAM A. DR.	1978	M	Swimming
SCOTT-BROWNE JAMES PATRICK	2003	M	Swimming
SEVERYN GARY MICHAEL	1983	M	Swimming
SEVERYN JAMES A.	1978	M	Swimming
SHADLEY FREDERIC XAVIER	1978	M	Swimming
SHAW ALAN EDMUND	1995	M	Swimming
SHEPARDSON MICHAEL THOMAS	1982	M	Swimming
SHERK JOHN JOSEPH	1973	M	Swimming
SHOMBERGER STEPHEN JOHN	2006	M	Swimming
SHORT BRIAN PATRICK	1972	M	Swimming
SIEGLER CHRISTOPHER J.	1967	M	Swimming
SKORNEY BRIAN PETER	2002	M	Swimming
SMITH CHARLES GEORGE JR.	1992	M	Swimming
SPOHN VINCENT MARTIN	1970	M	Swimming
STARK R. KEITH	1966	M	Swimming
STAUBLIN MARK ANTHONY	1984	M	Swimming
STEFANI RAYMOND T.	1962	M	Swimming
STOLTZ JOHN ROBERT	1966	M	Swimming
STOLZ DARRYL SLADE	1998	M	Swimming
STRACK EDWARD RAYMOND	1974	M	Swimming
STRACK RICHARD CRAIG	1967	M	Swimming
SZILIER DANIEL ROBERT	2001	M	Swimming
SZNEWAJS TIMOTHY RYAN	1996	M	Swimming
TEDDY FRANKLIN DWAYNE	2004	M	Swimming
TEMPLE LAWRENCE ROBERT	1963	M	Swimming
THOMAN DAVID SCOTT DR.	1990	M	Swimming
THOMPSON ROBERT EARL	1975	M	Swimming
UMHOFER DONALD GEORGE	1966	M	Swimming
VASU WILLIAM V. JR.	1963	M	Swimming
VEOME EDMOND ALLEN JR.	1990	M	Swimming
VERLIN RYAN PATRICK	2001	M	Swimming
VOGEL BRIAN MATTHEW	1989	M	Swimming
WALCZAK CHARLES THOMAS	1995	M	Swimming
WALLACH ANDREW S. III	1976	M	Swimming
WALSH CHRISTOPHER WILLIAM	1987	M	Swimming
WEBER THOMAS JOHN	1962	M	Swimming
WEST THOMAS M.	1965	M	Swimming
WHOWELL STEELE GORDON	1999	M	Swimming
WHOWELL THOMAS GORDON	1993	M	Swimming
WILCOX MARK DEAN	1973	M	Swimming
WISE RANDOLPH ENGLISH	1963	M	Swimming
WITCHGER DAVID JOSEPH	1962	M	Swimming
WITCHGER EUGENE WOLF	1961	M	Swimming
WOLF DEAN WILLIAM	2005	M	Swimming
WOLZ MICHAEL STEFAN	1975	M	Swimming
WOODS JOHN JAMES DR. JR.	1965	M	Swimming
WYMORE LUCAS RYAN	2004	M	Swimming
XIE TONG	2003	M	Swimming
YOHON RICHARD KEITH	1985	M	Swimming
ZELL RICHARD ALLAN M.D.	1990	M	Swimming

NAME	YEAR	GENDER	SPORT
ZMICK CLIFFORD ANTHONY D.D.S.	1972	M	Swimming
ZUMBACH SCOTT KEVIN	1999	M	Swimming
ALLARE JOHN PAUL	1972	M	Tennis
ANGYAL KENNETH JOHN	1954	M	Tennis
ANTHONY PAUL VINCENT	1993	M	Tennis
ARNOLD WILLIAM PATRICK	1938	M	Tennis
BAIOCCHI RALPH FRANCIS	1949	M	Tennis
BASS JAMES CRENNAN JR.	2005	M	Tennis
BEIRNE EOIN PATRICK	1994	M	Tennis
BEMIS JAMES JOSEPH	1963	M	Tennis
BENDER RAYMOND THOMAS	1961	M	Tennis
BIITTNER EUGENE CONWAY	1950	M	Tennis
BIITTNER GEORGE T.	1943	M	Tennis
BORDA JOSEPH L.	1933	M	Tennis
BOWLER HAROLD HENRY	1940	M	Tennis
BROWN C. MAXWELL DR. JR.	1959	M	Tennis
BROWN ELBERT S. JR.	1972	M	Tennis
BROWN J. MICHAEL MR. JR.	1992	M	Tennis
BROWN STANTON JOSEPH M.D.	1963	M	Tennis
BROWN WILLIAM LLOYD	1967	M	Tennis
BRUNO ANTHONY JOSEPH	1978	M	Tennis
BUCHANAN PATRICK DENNIS	2006	M	Tennis
BUCHART EDWARD EIGD JR.	1935	M	Tennis
BURNS HENRY L. SR.	1929	M	Tennis
CABELLO HECTOR MANUEL	1959	M	Tennis
CAHILL RICHARD ANTHONY	1989	M	Tennis
CAMPANARO A. BRYAN MR.	1960	M	Tennis
CANALE DANIEL D.	1942	M	Tennis
CANNON GEORGE W. JR.	1936	M	Tennis
CAPARO EDWARD PAUL	1945	M	Tennis
CARRICO JOHN LEONARD	1975	M	Tennis
CARRIEDO CARLOS RAUL	1969	M	Tennis
CARRIEDO RUBEN ANTHONY DR.	1965	M	Tennis
CENTLIVRE HERMAN G.	1925	M	Tennis
CHIMERAKIS NICHOLAS JAMES	2005	M	Tennis
CHINN VINCENT MING	1966	M	Tennis
CHMURA ANDREW JOHN	1996	M	Tennis
CHREIST LOUIS RUBEN JR.	1933	M	Tennis
CIANCI JOHN M.	1929	M	Tennis
CLANCY JOHN JR.	1965	M	Tennis
CLARKE WALTER JAMES	1955	M	Tennis
COLEMAN CHARLES STEVENS II	1993	M	Tennis
CRAM JACOB J.	2003	M	Tennis
DAGGS PAUL DAVID	1988	M	Tennis
DALY MATTHEW JAMES	2001	M	Tennis
D'AMICO BRENT NICHOLAS	2005	M	Tennis
DAVID ROBERT WALKER	1950	M	Tennis
DAVIDSON ALAN RICHARD	1964	M	Tennis
DEWALD MAURICE JUDE	1962	M	Tennis
DILUCIA DAVID EDWARD	1992	M	Tennis
DOLHARE WALTER ERNESTO	1990	M	Tennis
DOUGHERTY CHARLES MICHAEL	1926	M	Tennis
DZIURA HORST GERHARD	1996	M	Tennis
EARLEY ANTHONY F. JR.	1971	M	Tennis
ECKERT THEODORE MARK	1994	M	Tennis
ENLOE ERIC LEE	1998	M	Tennis
ERD HARRY STEPHEN JR.	1946	M	Tennis
EVERT GERALD J.	1948	M	Tennis
EVERT JAMES A.	1948	M	Tennis
FALLON WILLIAM HUME	1937	M	Tennis
FALVEY JAMES GERARD	1982	M	Tennis
FARRELL BRIAN PATRICK	2003	M	Tennis
FAUGHT JAMES JOSEPH	1971	M	Tennis
FINNEY GERARD JOSEPH	1954	M	Tennis
FITZGERALD ROBERT WILLIAM	1965	M	Tennis
FORSYTH WILLARD LINCOLN	1993	M	Tennis
FOUNTAIN RICHARD WILLIAM DR.	1947	M	Tennis
FREDERICKS NORMAN JOHN SR.	1935	M	Tennis
FREEMAN VIJAY ANTON	1998	M	Tennis
GAGLIARDI JOHN THOMAS	1961	M	Tennis
GALLAGHER CHARLES GEORGE	1954	M	Tennis
GARVEY JOSEPH ROCHE	1941	M	Tennis
GARZA SERGIO HECTOR	1959	M	Tennis
GIBBONS MICHAEL REDMOND	1985	M	Tennis
GOETZ JAMES PETER DR. SR.	1965	M	Tennis
GONZALEZ ANTHONY F.	1925	M	Tennis
GRAHAM PETER GILLINGHAM	2005	M	Tennis
GREGORY WHITNEY IRWIN JR.	1940	M	Tennis
GRIER THOMAS ANDREW	1987	M	Tennis
GRIFFIN JAMES DRISCOLL	1945	M	Tennis
GRIFFIN TED JAMES	1929	M	Tennis
GUILFOILE THOMAS JOHN	1957	M	Tennis
HADDOCK LUIS JAVIER	2004	M	Tennis
HAINLINE BRIAN WILLIAM M.D.	1978	M	Tennis
HARRIS BRIAN CHRISTOPHER	1996	M	Tennis
HARRIS CARLTON M. JR.	1980	M	Tennis
HARTMAN RICHARD A.	1948	M	Tennis
HARTZELL THOMAS C. JR.	1982	M	Tennis
HECKLER NORMAN BERNARD	1941	M	Tennis
HEINBECKER PETER PAPIN M.D.	1960	M	Tennis
HEINBECKER WILLIAM PAPIN	1961	M	Tennis
HENNESSY JAMES CARLYLE	1951	M	Tennis
HIDAKA PAUL SACHIO	2004	M	Tennis
HOENE HERBERT BERNARD	1951	M	Tennis
HOFFMAN RAYMOND J. JR.	1944	M	Tennis
HONERKAMP FRANK WILLIAM JR.	1967	M	Tennis
HOPWOOD HERBERT G.	1981	M	Tennis
HORAN MARTIN JOSEPH	1979	M	Tennis
HORSLEY MATTHEW LEE	2000	M	Tennis
HOYER MARK HENRY M.D.	1981	M	Tennis
HURLEY DENIS O'HERREN	1975	M	Tennis
IDZIK PAUL THOMAS	1983	M	Tennis
INCHAUSTE JUAN CARLOS	1977	M	Tennis
INCHAUSTE RONALD A.	1976	M	Tennis
JORDAN CHRISTIAN ALEXANDER	1996	M	Tennis
JOYCE J. LYLE DR.	1944	M	Tennis
JOYCE JOHN LAWTON SR.	1941	M	Tennis
KALBAS BRIAN JOSEPH	1989	M	Tennis
KALBAS TIMOTHY JOSEPH	1991	M	Tennis
KANE J. CHRISTOPHER	1975	M	Tennis
KATTHAIN RAUL CUANHTEMOC	1965	M	Tennis
KENDALL ROBERT DANIEL	1931	M	Tennis
KENNEDY DONALD JOSEPH	1954	M	Tennis
KILRAIN EDWIN T. JR.	1938	M	Tennis
KILWAY JAMES BERNARD DR. II	1990	M	Tennis
KOVAL ROBERT ALAN	1979	M	Tennis
KUHLMAN DAVID CHRISTOPHER	1992	M	Tennis
LAFLIN ANDREW PATRICK	2002	M	Tennis
LANGENKAMP ERIC JOSEPH	2006	M	Tennis
LANGFORD WALTER M. SR.	1930	M	Tennis
LESAGE BERNARD EDWARD	1971	M	Tennis
LEWIS JOSEPH BERNARD	1939	M	Tennis
LOPEZ SEPRANO ALLAN ARTHUR	1994	M	Tennis
LUKATS NICHOLAS PAUL	1934	M	Tennis
LUTZ EDMUND J. JR.	1924	M	Tennis
LYONS PHILIP EDWIN	1948	M	Tennis
MAGNANO MARCO JOSEPH	1996	M	Tennis
MALHAME JAMES MARSHALL	2002	M	Tennis
MARTIN PHILIP P. JR.	1945	M	Tennis
MASSICOTTE JEAN PAUL	1951	M	Tennis
MCGUIRE HARRY ALOYSIUS	1925	M	Tennis
MCMAHON MARK EDWARD	1983	M	Tennis
MCNULTY JOSEPH MARTIN	1937	M	Tennis
MEADE RICHARD EUGENE	1933	M	Tennis
MEADE THOMAS EDMUND	1932	M	Tennis
MENCIAS RONALD GENE	1997	M	Tennis
MEYER CARL F.	1932	M	Tennis
MILLER TRENT KIMBALL	2000	M	Tennis
MURPHY THOMAS EDWARD DR. JR.	1968	M	Tennis
MURRAY GREGORY STANTON	1971	M	Tennis
NAGEL FRANCIS A.	1949	M	Tennis
NAJARIAN PAUL JOHN	1985	M	Tennis
NELLIGAN JOSEPH W. JR.	1986	M	Tennis
NIGRO DENNIS MICHAEL M.D.	1969	M	Tennis
NOONAN TIMOTHY DOLAN	1984	M	Tennis
NORTH THOMAS MILTON	1994	M	Tennis
NOVATNY JOHN A.	1985	M	Tennis
OBERT DAVID MICHAEL	1985	M	Tennis
O'BRIEN BARTHOLOMEW F.	1949	M	Tennis
O'BRIEN JOHN JOSEPH	1997	M	Tennis
O'BRIEN MATTHEW MARK	1931	M	Tennis
O'BRIEN MICHAEL JULIUS	1931	M	Tennis
O'BRIEN SEAN PETER M.D.	1988	M	Tennis
ODLAND PAUL THOMAS	1991	M	Tennis
O'DONNELL MICHAEL LAWRENCE	1976	M	Tennis
O'HANLON JOHN ROCCA	1934	M	Tennis
O'MALLEY ROBERT F. DEACON JR.	1970	M	Tennis
OVERDEVEST MARK CLINTON	2001	M	Tennis
OVERHOLSER THOMAS EDWARD	1952	M	Tennis
PATTERSON BRIAN ROBERT	1999	M	Tennis
PIETROWSKI JAKUB FILIP	1998	M	Tennis
PRATT DOUGLAS JOSEPH	1986	M	Tennis
PRATT THOMAS GREGORY	1985	M	Tennis
PRATT WILLIAM MICHAEL	1982	M	Tennis
PUN JASON	1996	M	Tennis
QUINN JAMES EDWARD	1947	M	Tennis
RAJU ASHOK VADREVU	2001	M	Tennis
RALPH DONALD EDWARD DR.	1961	M	Tennis
RATTERMAN GEORGE WILLIAM	1949	M	Tennis
REALE WILLIAM ANTHONY	1955	M	Tennis
REAUME WILLIAM STERLING	1931	M	Tennis
REEVES RICHARD GEORGE	1934	M	Tennis
REID GREGORY FRANCIS	1972	M	Tennis
REIDY MAURICE TIMOTHY	1955	M	Tennis
REILLY MARK GERARD	1974	M	Tennis
REILLY MICHAEL TIMOTHY M.D.	1972	M	Tennis
REILLY PAUL CHRISTOPHER	1976	M	Tennis
REITER DAVID SCOT	1989	M	Tennis
REPPENHAGEN FRANCIS ALBERT	1939	M	Tennis
RICH JAMES C. M.D.	1957	M	Tennis
RICHARDS DEAN J.	1957	M	Tennis
RIESER GARY RAYMOND D.D.S.	1967	M	Tennis
RIGEL FRANCIS JACOB DR.	1932	M	Tennis
ROBISON THOMAS JOHN DR.	1982	M	Tennis
RODGERS CHARLES FAY	1939	M	Tennis
RODGERS JAMES F.	1949	M	Tennis
ROSAS RONALD RUDY	1993	M	Tennis
ROSSELLO PEDRO JUAN	1966	M	Tennis
ROTHSCHILD DANIEL JOHN	1998	M	Tennis
SACHIRE RYAN ROY	2000	M	Tennis
SAENZ JAIME IGNACIO	1954	M	Tennis
SAMSON CHARLES H. JR.	1947	M	Tennis
SANGUINETTI JOHN HENRY III	1974	M	Tennis
SCHAEFER JOSEPH JOHN JR.	1944	M	Tennis
SCHEFTER ROBERT PAUL DR. JR.	1973	M	Tennis
SCHMIDT MARK ALEXANDER	1993	M	Tennis
SCHOENBERG RONALD RUDOLF HON.	1959	M	Tennis
SCOTT MATTHEW KYLE	2004	M	Tennis
SEWARD EDWARD JAMES MGR.	1934	M	Tennis
SHIELDS PATRICK JOHN	1986	M	Tennis
SILK JOHN DAVID	1992	M	Tennis
SIMME RYAN PATTERSON	1997	M	Tennis
SIMON J. FREDERICK JR.	1939	M	Tennis
SIMONE STEPHEN JOSEPH	1986	M	Tennis
SINGH JASJIT	1968	M	Tennis
SLAGER RICHARD RAMEY	1976	M	Tennis
SMITH HARRY EARL	1957	M	Tennis
SMITH MCCASEY REDMAN	2002	M	Tennis
SMITH RAYMOND JOSEPH	1953	M	Tennis
SOBKOWIAK ROGER T.	1964	M	Tennis
SOLLAN NEAL ANTHONY	1965	M	Tennis
SPROUSE MICHAEL CHRISTIAN	1996	M	Tennis
STALEY FREDERICK SETON	1933	M	Tennis
STEHLIK RANDALL RAY	1977	M	Tennis
STEPHENS CHARLES OLIVER M.D.	1959	M	Tennis
STEVENSON DEE COOPER	1960	M	Tennis
TABORGA PAULO JAVIER	2002	M	Tennis
TALARICO AARON SCOTT	2002	M	Tennis
TAVARES CARLOS	1927	M	Tennis
TONTI A. PATRICK	1951	M	Tennis
TROUP JOHN ELMSLEY JR.	1943	M	Tennis
TRUEBLOOD MARK CHRISTOPHER	1979	M	Tennis
TUITE MATTHEW FRAN JR.	1953	M	Tennis
VAN DYKE DUANE JOHN	1958	M	Tennis
VANONCINI CHARLES JOHN	1958	M	Tennis
VOSBURG BRUCE DAVID	1965	M	Tennis
WALDRON JAMES ALBERT	1937	M	Tennis
WALLACE MICHAEL WAYNE	1990	M	Tennis
WALSH BRANDON EYRE	1974	M	Tennis
WALSH DANIEL JOSEPH	1988	M	Tennis
WARFORD ANDREW HELD	1999	M	Tennis
WELCH AL	N/A	M	Tennis
WELDON FRANCIS JOSEPH	1935	M	Tennis
WENGER RYAN TERRENCE	1991	M	Tennis
WESTPHAL THOMAS JORDAN	1980	M	Tennis
WHEATON DAVID MICHAEL	1976	M	Tennis
WHELAN JAMES F. JR.	1962	M	Tennis
WHITING TIMOTHY RICHARD	1970	M	Tennis
WHITMYER STEPHEN J.	1983	M	Tennis
WILSON TODD WILLIAM	1994	M	Tennis
WITHERS PETER CRAIG JR.	1976	M	Tennis
WOJTALIK CHRISTOPHER RAYMOND	1993	M	Tennis
WOLF JOHN MARTIN	1940	M	Tennis
ZABRISKIE LEON FRANCIS	1930	M	Tennis
ZURCHER J. ANDREW MR.	1993	M	Tennis
ABBOTT JOSEPH ALOYISIUS	1930	M	Track
ABERNETHY JOHN A.	1933	M	Track
ALBER DAVID LEIGH	2004	M	Track
ALEXANDER JOHN FRANCIS	1954	M	Track
ALLARD BERNARD JAMES	1956	M	Track
ALLMENDINGER WILLIAM ANTHONY	1978	M	Track
ALMAGUER BENJAMIN G.	1952	M	Track
ALT ANTHONY JAMES	N/A	M	Track
ALTHOFF MATTHEW KENDRIC	1997	M	Track
AMBRICO VINCENT JOHN	1970	M	Track
AMBRICO VINCENT JOHN	2006	M	Track
AMITIE DANIEL DEAN	1994	M	Track
ANDERSON JEFFREY MARTIN D.D.S.	1979	M	Track
ANDRASSY ALEXANDER JOHN	2006	M	Track
ANDRULONIS NATHAN DAVID	2002	M	Track
ANTOINE RICHARD MCLAURENCE	1995	M	Track
ARAGON CHARLES LEO M.D.	1981	M	Track
ARCE ANTONIO JOSE	1999	M	Track
AUTRY JOEL ALLISON	1987	M	Track
BACHMAN CHARLES WILLIAM	1917	M	Track
BAILIE ROY CONKLIN JR.	1931	M	Track
BAKER JAMES EDWARD	1955	M	Track
BALISTRIERI JOSEPH PHILIP	1962	M	Track
BARBER MARK DANIEL	2004	M	Track
BARR WILLIAM R.	1926	M	Track

NAME	YEAR	GENDER	SPORT
HOGAN MICHAEL CHARLES	1976	M	Track
HOGUE ROLLY RAYMOND	1944	M	Track
HOJNACKI JEFFREY ALAN	1997	M	Track
HOLDENER CHRISTOPHER LEE	2004	M	Track
HOLINKA BRIAN DAVID	2000	M	Track
HOLLERAN PATRICK ANTHONY	1972	M	Track
HOOVER ROBERT NOLAN DR.	1964	M	Track
HORGAN DANIEL JAMES	1978	M	Track
HOUSLEY MICHAEL KEVIN	1975	M	Track
HOWARD KENNETH JOHN	1968	M	Track
HOWREY EUGENE E.	1932	M	Track
HOYT JOHN ALOYSIUS JR.	1933	M	Track
HUNTER JACK RANDOLPH	1950	M	Track
HUNTER OLIVER HENRY III	1943	M	Track
HURD RYAN KENNETH	2005	M	Track
HURD WILLIAM CHARLES M.D.	1969	M	Track
HURT JAMES VINCENT	1976	M	Track
HYDE RONALD HILLARY M.D.	1982	M	Track
IRBY ADRIAN NORRIS	1999	M	Track
ISMAIL RAGHIB RAMADAN	1994	M	Track
JOHNSON CLINT LAMAR	1994	M	Track
JOHNSON GERALD BUCHANAN	1950	M	Track
JOHNSON RYAN DEAN	2005	M	Track
JOHNSTON DENNIS GEORGE	1961	M	Track
JOHNSTON RALPH EDWARD	1930	M	Track
JOHNSTON TODD LORING	1996	M	Track
JONES AUSTIN GERARD JR.	1944	M	Track
JONES FRED ALLAN JR.	1947	M	Track
JORDAN CHARLES BUTLER SR.	1937	M	Track
JUBA EDWARD J. II	1984	M	Track
JUDGE CHARLES E.	1927	M	Track
JUSTICE LAMARR EDWARD	1995	M	Track
KALASUNAS MICHAEL PAUL	1969	M	Track
KANIA JAN THOMAS	1983	M	Track
KARDOK TIMOTHY M.	1979	M	Track
KASPER THOMAS CYRIL	1921	M	Track
KAUFFMAN F. MICHAEL	1957	M	Track
KAZIMI A. J. MR.	1980	M	Track
KEACH LEROY J. SR.	1908	M	Track
KEANE JOHN PATRICK	2003	M	Track
KEARNS MICHAEL C. II	1957	M	Track
KEARNS PATRICK JOSEPH	1992	M	Track
KEEGAN KEVIN JOHN	1992	M	Track
KEEGAN WILLIAM HOWARD	1957	M	Track
KEENAN LAURENCE PAUL	1948	M	Track
KELLY EDWARD WALTER	1964	M	Track
KELLY JAMES VINCENT	1950	M	Track
KELLY THOMAS D.	1929	M	Track
KELLY WILLIAM JOSEPH	1944	M	Track
KELLY WILLIAM P. II	1942	M	Track
KENNEDY DAVID MICHAEL	1963	M	Track
KENNY BRIAN JAMES	1968	M	Track
KENNY KEVIN JOSEPH	1980	M	Track
KENNY PATRICK J. REV. SJ	1949	M	Track
KENNY PATRICK RICHARD DR.	1997	M	Track
KERR MICHAEL JOHN	2001	M	Track
KERRIGAN ELIE ETHAN LIAM	1989	M	Track
KERWIN BRIAN JAMES	2004	M	Track
KILBURG WILLIAM JUDE	1955	M	Track
KINDER RANDOLPH SAMUEL III	1996	M	Track
KING EDWARD CASHIN	1934	M	Track
KIRKLAND FRANK MONROE	1917	M	Track
KITTELL C. JAMES	1951	M	Track
KNUTH NATHAN DUANE	1994	M	Track
KOBER TIMOTHY PAUL	2000	M	Track
KOHANOWICH ALBERT JOHN	1953	M	Track
KRAAS JONATHAN RICHARD	1997	M	Track
KRAMER F. RICHARD	1951	M	Track
KRAUS THOMAS GREGORY	1990	M	Track
KRAUSE EDWARD W.	1934	M	Track
KRIDER WILLIAM ANTHONY	1925	M	Track
KUBICKI BRIAN MICHAEL	1994	M	Track
KUHN J. REGIS	1932	M	Track
KUZAN JOHN DAVID	1981	M	Track
LAFRAMBOISE PAUL HUBERT SR.	1934	M	Track
LAHEY JOHN P.	1928	M	Track
LANG GEORG.	1980	M	Track
LANGDON JOHN H.	1984	M	Track
LANGEVINE RICHARD TROY	1997	M	Track
LANGTON HAROLD FRANCIS	1938	M	Track
LAVELLE EDWARD PATRICK	1993	M	Track
LAVERY MARK ANDREW	1990	M	Track
LAVERY MARK ROBERT	1991	M	Track
LAWRENCE ROBERT HOWARD	1940	M	Track
LAYDEN ELMER FRANK	1925	M	Track
LAYDEN FRANCIS LOUIS	1936	M	Track
LEAHY WILLIAM JOSEPH	1968	M	Track
LEHNER JAMES TIMOTHY M.D.	1970	M	Track
LEKANDER GARY MICHAEL M.D.	1986	M	Track
LENNON THOMAS JOSEPH	2002	M	Track
LEONARD WILLIAM G. JR.	1949	M	Track
LEONAS THEODORE JOSEPH	1940	M	Track
LEPRY LOUIS ANTHONY	1951	M	Track
LEVICKI JOHN JOSEPH	1937	M	Track
LEWIS AUBREY CLEMMENS	1958	M	Track
LEWIS PAUL JOSEPH	2000	M	Track
LIEB THOMAS JOHN	1923	M	Track
LILLY CHRISTOPHER ALLEN	1994	M	Track
LINEHAN JOHN FRANCIS	1956	M	Track
LINK H. CARL	1935	M	Track
LLOYD RICHARD K.	1927	M	Track
LUCAS LOUIS ANTHONY	1963	M	Track
LUCEY CHRISTOPHER WILLIAM	1988	M	Track
LUDECKE CARL RUDOLPH	1963	M	Track
LUNDERGAN C. DONALD MR.	1945	M	Track
LUNNEY STEPHEN JAMES	1988	M	Track
LYNCH JAMES HENRY JR.	1965	M	Track
LYNCH WILLIAM K.	1980	M	Track
LYONS JOHN CHARLES	1950	M	Track
LYTLE DEAN LAMONT	1994	M	Track
MAC DEVITT JAMES C.	1935	M	Track
MACAULEY TIMOTHY S.	1981	M	Track
MACBETH FREDERICK W. JR.	1933	M	Track
MACK JOHN EDWARD	1940	M	Track
MACKEN THOMAS RICHARD	1991	M	Track
MACKEY JEFF DAVID	1995	M	Track
MADIGAN MICHAEL CHARLES	2003	M	Track
MAGILL JOHN MICHAEL	1986	M	Track
MAHONEY PETER JOSEPH IV	1967	M	Track
MAHONEY WILLIAM P. HON. JR.	1939	M	Track
MALEC DENNIS JOSEPH	1956	M	Track
MALONEY ANTHONY J. JR.	1943	M	Track
MALONEY PAUL THOMAS	1993	M	Track
MANEY MICHAEL H.	1981	M	Track
MANNING MICHAEL THOMAS	2005	M	Track
MANSOUR MICHAEL PATRICK	2002	M	Track
MANVILLE KEITH ROLLIN	1966	M	Track
MARKEZICH RONALD LEE JR.	1989	M	Track
MARTIN FRANCIS PAUL M.D.	1945	M	Track
MARTIN JOHN JOSEPH	1940	M	Track
MARTISUS DEREK MICHAEL	1996	M	Track
MARTUSCELLO PAUL JOHN	1977	M	Track
MASLOSKI JESSE COLE	2000	M	Track
MASTERSON FRANK XAVIER	1927	M	Track
MATSUMOTO JEFF ROBB	1994	M	Track
MATT MARSHALL WALTER	1980	M	Track
MATTEO CHRISTOPHER JOHN	1988	M	Track
MATTEO GEORGE WILLIAM JR.	1978	M	Track
MATTEO GREGORY JAMES	1991	M	Track
MAXFIELD R. CRAIG MR.	1987	M	Track
MAXWELL RYAN JOSEPH	1999	M	Track
MAYER FRANK G.	1927	M	Track
MBAGWU GODWIN OKECHUKWU	2004	M	Track
MCAULIFFE BRIAN F.	1981	M	Track
MCAULIFFE KEVIN ROBERT	1972	M	Track
MCCANN MICHAEL JAMES	1970	M	Track
MCCARTHY FRANCIS FINNEY	1946	M	Track
MCCLAIN-DUER TREVOR RICHARD	2005	M	Track
MCCLOUGHAN JOHN WILLIAM	1982	M	Track
MCCORMICK WILLIAM H.	1932	M	Track
MCCULLOUGH ERNEST J.	1949	M	Track
MCDAVID ROBERT FINLEY JR.	1949	M	Track
MCDONALD CHESTER P.	1927	M	Track
MCDONALD ROBERT LOUIS	1930	M	Track
MCDONOUGH JUSTIN KILDERRY	1954	M	Track
MCFARLANE LEO PAUL	1936	M	Track
MCGAULEY EDWARD JOSEPH	1928	M	Track
MCGRATH JOSEPH JAMES	1936	M	Track
MCGUIRE J. CHRISTOPHER MR.	1989	M	Track
MCKENNA JOHN FRANCIS	1937	M	Track
MCMANNON MICHAEL C.	1972	M	Track
MCMANUS SEAN PATRICK	2001	M	Track
MCNAMEE DAVID LOYOLA D.D.S.	1965	M	Track
MCNELIS JOHN THOMAS	1986	M	Track
MCQUAID BRIAN CHARLES	1996	M	Track
MCSWEENEY EDWARD LOUIS	1928	M	Track
MCTERNAN LEO MICHAEL	1927	M	Track
MCWILLIAMS MICHAEL JAY	1994	M	Track
MEAGHER GEORGE BEYER M.D.	1936	M	Track
MELORO JAMES ROBERT	1995	M	Track
MERCER GENE VICTOR	1972	M	Track
MESCALL THOMAS JOSEPH II	1996	M	Track
METRAILER FRANK M. MR.	1929	M	Track
MEYER MICHAEL JOSEPH	1978	M	Track
MICHNO JOHN C.	1957	M	Track
MICK THOMAS MARCUS	1988	M	Track
MIHALKO RYAN STEVEN	1991	M	Track
MILLER CREIGHTON EUGENE	1944	M	Track
MILLER JAMES JR.	1950	M	Track
MINEBURG RYAN ANDREW	2005	M	Track
MIRANDA JAY SEGUNDO	1980	M	Track
MISHKA PHILLIP JON	2000	M	Track
MOBLEY TODD ALLEN	2005	M	Track
MOES LEON JOSEPH.	1926	M	Track
MOHAR JOHN RICHARD	1952	M	Track
MONAHAN CHRISTOPHER F.	1961	M	Track
MONJEAU RICHARD L.	1961	M	Track
MONNELLY EDWARD PATRICK M.D.	1958	M	Track
MONTABON FRANK LLOYD	1991	M	Track
MONTAGUE JOHN MICHAEL	1923	M	Track
MOORE TIMOTHY JOHN	2006	M	Track
MORANDO MICHAEL JOSEPH	1959	M	Track
MORETTI GREGORY SCOTT	1995	M	Track
MORGAN DONALD WILLIAM	1939	M	Track
MORGAN PETER JOSEPH JR.	1929	M	Track
MORRIS ROY ARLEN	1956	M	Track
MORRISON ERIC JAMES	2005	M	Track
MORTENSEN WALTER A. JR.	1932	M	Track
MOYAR JAMES R.	1984	M	Track
MUENCH RICHARD ARTHUR JR.	1988	M	Track
MULLALEY PATRICK KEVIN	1972	M	Track
MULROONEY JOHN JOSEPH	1963	M	Track
MULROONEY NEIL PATRICK DR.	1992	M	Track
MULVEY RICHARD WALTHER	1988	M	Track
MURPHY CHARLES HAYES	1943	M	Track
MURPHY FRANCIS AMBROSE	1933	M	Track
MURPHY G. DAVID	1945	M	Track
MURPHY JAMES E.	1949	M	Track
MURPHY JOHN ALOYSIUS	1951	M	Track
MURPHY JOHN ALOYSIUS	1948	M	Track
MURPHY JOHN LEONARD	1923	M	Track
MURPHY VINCENT BENEDICT	1935	M	Track
MUSCATO VALENTINE PETER	1951	M	Track
MUSIAL RICHARD STANLEY	1962	M	Track
NEWQUIST HARVEY PAUL	1954	M	Track
NICHOLS JOHN BERNARD	1933	M	Track
NICHOLSON WILLIAM ROBERT	1943	M	Track
NOBLES ROBERT EUGENE	1987	M	Track
NOLAND MICHAEL C.	1982	M	Track
NOONAN WILLIAM J.	1918	M	Track
NOVAK MARC THOMAS	1980	M	Track
NULTY JOSEPH A.	1927	M	Track
NURUDEEN SELIM TILEWA	2005	M	Track
OBERGFALL RUDOLPH C.	1934	M	Track
OBERST EUGENE G.	1924	M	Track
O'BRIEN DANIEL JOSEPH	1964	M	Track
O'BRIEN JAMES MATTHEW	1978	M	Track
O'BRIEN KEITH TERRENCE	1997	M	Track
O'BRIEN KEVIN JOHN	1969	M	Track
O'BRIEN MATTHEW JAMES	2001	M	Track
O'CONNOR JERRY JOSEPH	1964	M	Track
O'CONNOR JOHN JOSEPH	1953	M	Track
O'CONNOR MICHAEL JOHN	1990	M	Track
O'DONNELL SEAN MICHAEL	2006	M	Track
O'FLAHERTY SHANE THOMAS	1989	M	Track
O'HARE RUSSELL JAMES	1924	M	Track
O'KEEFFE RICHARD JOSEPH	1956	M	Track
OLBRYS JOSEPH BOLESLAUS	1941	M	Track
O'NEIL WILLIAM EDWARD	1946	M	Track
O'NEILL TERRENCE JAMES	1913	M	Track
O'REILLY THOMAS JOSEPH	1940	M	Track
O'ROURKE J. KEITH	1942	M	Track
O'ROURKE THOMAS JAMES	1990	M	Track
PAINTER JOHN O.	1947	M	Track
PANTEA VICTOR JOHN	1974	M	Track
PARSONS JAMES LINCOLN	1937	M	Track
PATTERSON JAMES H. III	1985	M	Track
PAYTON DANNY LAMAR	1998	M	Track
PEARCY VAN MARK	1985	M	Track
PEPPARD BRIAN PATRICK	1992	M	Track
PESTRICHELLA ALEXANDER A.	1956	M	Track
PILLA JAMES ANTHONY	1998	M	Track
PITCAVAGE JAMES GEDDES M.D.	1955	M	Track
POKIGO FRANK JOHN JR.	1975	M	Track
POLSELLI ELIO REMO	1972	M	Track
POREDEN GEORGE THOMAS	1933	M	Track
PORTER ALBERT PATRICK	1957	M	Track
POSTEL RYAN JOSEPH	2005	M	Track
POWELL EDWARD JOHN	1953	M	Track
PROSCHE RICHARD EARL	1947	M	Track
PROVOST STEPHEN BISHOP	1949	M	Track
PUMA JEFFREY ANDREW	1998	M	Track
PURCELL ROBERT PUTNAM	1946	M	Track
QUADERER JOSEPH ERNEST	1970	M	Track
QUIGLEY JOSEPH JAMES	1932	M	Track
QUIGLEY JOSEPH JOHN	1969	M	Track
QUIGLEY THOMAS JOSEPH	1929	M	Track
QUINN COLIN PATRICK	2004	M	Track
RADEMAKER THEODORE CHAS SR.	1919	M	Track
RADKEWICH NICHOLAS EDWARD	1993	M	Track

NAME	YEAR	GENDER	SPORT
WHITTEN CARROLL J.	1981	M	Trainers
WUNDER STEPHEN JOSEPH JR.	2004	M	Trainers
YAWMAN DANIEL MCGLYNN DR.	1993	M	Trainers
YORK GEOFFREY SCOTT	1990	M	Trainers
MCLAUGHLIN THOMAS EDWARD IV	2002	M	Video Technician
SMITH TYLER EDWARD	2006	M	Video Technician
WELTLER ADAM PETER	2003	M	Video Technician
ABRAMS GREGORY LEE	1970	M	Wrestling
AGOSTINO FRANK JAMES	1992	M	Wrestling
AGOSTINO JOSEPH FRANK	1984	M	Wrestling
AGOSTINO PETER JOHN	1983	M	Wrestling
AMES WILLIAM DAVID	1963	M	Wrestling
ANDERS MARSHALL E.	1967	M	Wrestling
ANDREETTI JOSEPH PETER	1985	M	Wrestling
ARMSTRONG JOHN MURPHY	1958	M	Wrestling
BARRY JOHN E. JR.	1964	M	Wrestling
BATY PHILIP JOHN DR.	1985	M	Wrestling
BENNETT ROBERT	1973	M	Wrestling
BENTIVENGA SCOTT C.	1985	M	Wrestling
BIASETTI SCOTT A. DR.	1987	M	Wrestling
BOWERS JAMES E.	1967	M	Wrestling
BOYD JAMIE LEE	1993	M	Wrestling
BOYD PATRICK KERRY	1989	M	Wrestling
BOYER DAVID LEE	1976	M	Wrestling
BRANNAN ARTHUR DANIEL	1979	M	Wrestling
BROWN MATTHEW GEORGE	1985	M	Wrestling
BRUENING FREDERICK LEO M.D.	1976	M	Wrestling
BRUNETTE JAMES ROBERT	1961	M	Wrestling
BUBOLO DEAN CHARLES	1989	M	Wrestling
CADMAN KYLE THOMAS	1993	M	Wrestling
CAFFARELLI RICHARD MICHAEL JR.	1989	M	Wrestling
CAHILL PETER JAMES	1992	M	Wrestling
CAIN JAMES MICHAEL	1976	M	Wrestling
CARBONE DOMINICK D.	1959	M	Wrestling
CARLIN DAVID ANTHONY	1989	M	Wrestling
CARNESALE JOHN LAWRENCE	1985	M	Wrestling
CARNESALE LOUIS VINCENT	1985	M	Wrestling
CARRIGAN DANIEL PATRICK	1988	M	Wrestling
CARROLL M. SCOTT M.D.	1963	M	Wrestling
CHURNETSKI JOHN LAWRENCE	1962	M	Wrestling
CIACCIO THOMAS GABRIEL D.D.S.	1971	M	Wrestling
CROWLEY TERENCE DR.	1957	M	Wrestling
CROWN ERIC CHARLES	1986	M	Wrestling
CURCIO PETER	1979	M	Wrestling
DAHLHAUSER KARL JOSEPH	1984	M	Wrestling
DANIK DREW LAWRENCE	1975	M	Wrestling
DAY CHARLES JOSEPH	1958	M	Wrestling
DIKE KENNETH H.	1978	M	Wrestling
DILLON SEAN FRANCIS	1989	M	Wrestling
DISABATO DAVID ANTHONY	1980	M	Wrestling
DISABATO LUKE PETER	1986	M	Wrestling
DOWD JOHN GERARD	1976	M	Wrestling
DREGER ROBERT MARTIN JR.	1978	M	Wrestling
DUELL MICHAEL WILLIAM	1970	M	Wrestling
DURSO JEROME B.	1990	M	Wrestling
EIBEN MICHAEL ROBERT	1965	M	Wrestling
ENGLER CURTIS JOHN	1993	M	Wrestling
ERARD BRIAN EDWARD	1982	M	Wrestling
FAVO CHRISTOPHER M.	1980	M	Wrestling
FINLAY EDWARD EMILE	1959	M	Wrestling
FISHER MARK ROLLAND	1985	M	Wrestling
FLEMING GREGORY ANDREW	1987	M	Wrestling
FOX MICHAEL EDWARD	1995	M	Wrestling
GEDNEY GEORGE III	1979	M	Wrestling
GENESER CHRISTOPHER MARTIN	1990	M	Wrestling
GERARDI MARK ALAN	1991	M	Wrestling
GIBBONS J. BRIAN MR.	1964	M	Wrestling
GILLOON RICHARD JAMES	1974	M	Wrestling
GIRON KEITH SAMUEL	1970	M	Wrestling
GLOGAS GLENN ALAN	1986	M	Wrestling
GOLIC ROBERT PERRY	1979	M	Wrestling
GOODRICH ALBERT ADRIEN	1964	M	Wrestling
GORSKI JAMES OTTO	1968	M	Wrestling
GOWENS MARCUS ANTHONY	1992	M	Wrestling
HANSEN JAMES RUSSELL JR.	1970	M	Wrestling
HASBROOK WILLIAM ANDREW	1970	M	Wrestling
HEFFERNAN DANIEL PAUL D.D.S.	1977	M	Wrestling
HEINTZELMAN DONALD LOUIS	1985	M	Wrestling
HELMER DAVID HILDING	1987	M	Wrestling
HERRMANN JEFFREY JOHN	1985	M	Wrestling
HIGGINS MICHAEL WILLIAM	1969	M	Wrestling
HILDINGER CARL JAY	1987	M	Wrestling
IACOPONI DAVID ANTHONY	1992	M	Wrestling
IGLAR JOHN DALE	1982	M	Wrestling
IMHOFF JOHN HARVEY JR.	1972	M	Wrestling
JAMIESON EDWIN WILLIAM	1995	M	Wrestling
JOLIN PATRICK VINCENT	1984	M	Wrestling
KANE JAMES JEFFREY	1961	M	Wrestling
KARAS SPERO GUS DR.	1989	M	Wrestling
KEMP MICHAEL JUDSON	1975	M	Wrestling

NAME	YEAR	GENDER	SPORT
KESZEI VINCENT ANDREW M.D.	1979	M	Wrestling
KLEINKNECHT KENNETH CHARLES	1970	M	Wrestling
KRUG JOHN WILLIAM	1986	M	Wrestling
LAHEY DENNIS WILLIAM	1965	M	Wrestling
LANDFRIED PATRICK LEE	1978	M	Wrestling
LARSEN MELVIN L.	1958	M	Wrestling
LAYTON JOHN TODD	1991	M	Wrestling
LOCKSMITH GUY GOODWINE	1985	M	Wrestling
LOESCH CARL ANDREW	1990	M	Wrestling
LOGSDON GEORGE LUNDY JR.	1990	M	Wrestling
MAAS JOHN MICHAEL	1970	M	Wrestling
MARTIN RICHARD JOSEPH	1963	M	Wrestling
MCFADDEN E. J. MCGUINNESS	1960	M	Wrestling
MCKILLEN PATRICK J. JR.	1978	M	Wrestling
MEADE PETER CHARLES	1974	M	Wrestling
MEHL M. STEELE MR.	1981	M	Wrestling
MILLS MICHAEL R.	1983	M	Wrestling
MOORE WILLIAM GERARD	1979	M	Wrestling
MORELLI FRED MICHAEL JR.	1963	M	Wrestling
MORK THOMAS JEFFREY LTC. M.D.	1968	M	Wrestling
MORRIS JEFFREY ALBAN	1982	M	Wrestling
MORRISSEY TIMOTHY HUGHES DR.	1968	M	Wrestling
MOYLAN STEPHEN CRAIG	1975	M	Wrestling
MURPHY BRIAN JAMES	1995	M	Wrestling
O'CONNOR PAUL ANTHONY DR. JR.	1959	M	Wrestling
PADDEN MICHAEL PATRICK	1978	M	Wrestling
PASSARO THOMAS JOSEPH	1970	M	Wrestling
PIETRANGELI NEIL JON	1967	M	Wrestling
PIVONKA ROBERT C. M.D.	1958	M	Wrestling
PRINZIVALLI DOMENIC PHILIP	1988	M	Wrestling
PSZERACKI JOSEPH STANLEY	1976	M	Wrestling
RADENBAUGH ANDREW JEROME	1991	M	Wrestling
RAFFERTY PAUL EDWARD	1960	M	Wrestling
RANKIN JAMES LOWRY	1959	M	Wrestling
REIDY JAMES WILLIAMS	1992	M	Wrestling
ROCEK ALBERT CHARLES	1974	M	Wrestling
RODGERS DAVID W.	1982	M	Wrestling
ROMANO DANIEL MICHAEL	1978	M	Wrestling
ROOD CURTIS JAMES	1983	M	Wrestling
ROZMAN MICHAEL LOUIS	1978	M	Wrestling
SACHSEL GERARD RICHARD	1960	M	Wrestling
SALVINO ROBERT	1957	M	Wrestling
SALVINO THOMAS JOHN	1992	M	Wrestling
SAPP RICHARD STEPHEN DR.	1960	M	Wrestling
SCHICKEL WILLIAM JOHN	1967	M	Wrestling
SCHMITT MICHAEL FRANK	1984	M	Wrestling
SEMERAD LARRY STEPHEN	1973	M	Wrestling
SHEEHY JOHN JOSEPH	1988	M	Wrestling
SHEEHY MICHAEL MATTHEW	1992	M	Wrestling
SHEETS MICHAEL DAVID	1990	M	Wrestling
SKINNER JERRY DOUGLAS	1983	M	Wrestling
SMITH DAVID JOHN	1990	M	Wrestling
SOEHNLEN EMIL ANDREW	1993	M	Wrestling
SOLLAN NEAL ANTHONY	1965	M	Wrestling
STAMM MATTHEW JAMES	1985	M	Wrestling
STAVELY-O'CARROLL KEVIN F. DR.	1986	M	Wrestling
TICUS GARY LAWRENCE	1968	M	Wrestling
TOMAZIC TODD WILLIAM	1991	M	Wrestling
TORRES JOHN DAVID	1980	M	Wrestling
TOWER MICHAEL J.	1981	M	Wrestling
WEAVER CHARLES DEWAYNE	1993	M	Wrestling
WELSH DAVID JOSEPH DR.	1980	M	Wrestling
WILDA MICHAEL G.	1980	M	Wrestling
WILLEMS CLETUS ROBERT JR.	1967	M	Wrestling
WISNIEWSKI RONALD LEE JR.	1988	M	Wrestling
WITHERS PETER CRAIG JR.	1976	M	Wrestling
WROBLEWSKI THOMAS JOSEPH	1980	M	Wrestling
ZANETTI VICTOR B.	1980	M	Wrestling

CURRENT-STUDENT MONOGRAM WINNERS

WOMEN'S BASKETBALL
CHAREL ALLEN
MELISSA D'AMICO
CRYSTAL ERWIN
TULYAH GAINES
BREONA GRAY
LINDSAY SCHRADER
CHANDRICA SMITH
AMANDA TSIPIS

WOMEN'S CROSS COUNTRY
KATIE DERUSSO
RAMSEY KAVAN
SUNNY OLDING

WOMEN'S FENCING
MELANIE BAUTISTA
RACHEL COTA
KIM MONTOYA
ADRIENNE NOTT
AMY ORLANDO
EMILIE PROT
VALERIE PROVIDENZA
ASHLEY SERRETTE
MADELEINE STEPHAN
ANGELA VINCENT
MARIEL ZAGUNIS

WOMEN'S GOLF
LISA MAUNO
NORIKO NAKAZAKI

WOMEN'S LACROSSE
ALICIA BILLINGS
SHANNON BURKE
JILLIAN BYERS
MARY CARPENTER
HEATHER FERGUSON
MEAGHAN FITZPATRICK
KRISTIN HOPSON
CAITLIN MCKINNEY
MEGHAN MURPHY
KATHERINE ORR
BECKY RANCK
JANE STOECKERT

ROWING
MEGHAN BOYLE
BRITTANY BURNHAM
SHANNON CASSEL
ALYSSA CLOSE
CASEY FAIRBANKS
EILEEN FROEHLKE
ELLI GREYBAR
JESSICA GUZIK
SARAH KATE HAFNER
KAITLIN JACKSON
ANKA JEDRY
SARAH KEITHLEY
BETSY MADISON
ALLISON MARSH
LINDSAY MCQUAID
CHRISTINA PADAYHAG
LAURA PEARSON
AMANDA POLK
MARY QUINN
MARIA ROMANO
KENDRA SHORT
JULIE SOBOLEWSKI
ASHLEY ST. PIERRE
CHRISTINE TREZZA

WOMEN'S SOCCER
BRITTANY BOCK
JENNIFER BUCZKOWSKI
AMANDA CINALLI
CAROLINE DEW
CLAIRE GALLERANO
KERRI HANKS
MOLLY IAROCCI
KERRY INGLIS
ASHLEY JONES
LAUREN KARAS
BETH KOLOUP
JILL KRIVACEK
KIM LORENZEN
REBECCA MENDOZA
SUSASN PINNICK
LIZZIE REED
ANNE SCHEFTER
CHRISTIE SHANER
NICOLE WESTFALL

SOFTBALL
BRITTNEY BARGAR
STEPHANIE BROWN
ERIN GLASCO
BRITTANY GLYNN
GESSICA HUFFNAGLE
CARISA JAQUISH
LINDA KOHAN
KATIE LAING
STEPHANIE MOLA
BETH NORTHWAY
MEAGAN RUTHRAUFF
SARAH SMITH

WOMEN'S SWIMMING
KRISTINA ARCHER
ANN BARTON
KELLY BATTLE
MORGAN BULLOCK
NATALIE BURKE
KATIE CARROLL
KAYLA GRAHAM
REBECCA GROVE
KATIE GUIDA
LUCY HIRT
KATIE HOPKINS
CLAIRE HUTCHINSON
TARA HYER
CAROLINE JOHNSON
ELLEN JOHNSON
MEGHAN LINNELLI
JULIA QUINN
CHRISTA RIGGINS
GEORGIA STEENBERGE
JESSICA STEPHENS
ABBY STRANG
ANNE SWEENEY
CASEY WAGNER

WOMEN'S TENNIS
BROOK BUCK
KATIE POTTS
KELCY TEFFT
CATRINA THOMPSON
CHRISTIAN THOMPSON

WOMEN'S TRACK AND FIELD
LAUREN BISCARDI
JACQELINE CARTER
BRIENNE DAVIS
KATIE DERUSSO
MARYANN ERIGHA
CASSIE GULLICKSON
ALYISSA HASAN
AMANDA KOHLMEIER
DOMENIQUE MANNING
KATE MATTOON
OKECHI OGBUOKIRI
SUNNI OLDING
JULIANNE OPET
ELIZABETH PHILIPP
MARY SAXER
BRIANNE SCHMIDT
ANNA WEBER
NICOLE YERGLER

VOLLEYBALL
MADISON CLARK
MALLORIE CROAL
ELLEN HEINTZMAN
DANIELLE HERNDON
MEGAN MCGUIRE
ANNIE MOKRIS
ADRIANNA STASIUK
JUSTINE STREMICK
ASHLEY TARUTIS

BASEBALL
JEREMY BARNES
ROSS BREZOVSKY
DANIEL DRESSMAN
MIKE DURY
SAM ELAM
SEAN GASTON
BRETT GRAFFY
DAVID GRUENER
WADE KORPI
BRETT LILLEY
JEFF MANSHIP
EDDY MENDIOLA
DAVID PHELPS
JEFF SAMARDZIJA
EVAN SHARPLEY
CHRIS SORIANO
JESS STEWART
KYLE WEILAND
JOEY WILLIAMSON

MEN'S BASKETBALL
RYAN AYERS
RUSSELL CARTER
COLLIN FALLS
ZACH HILLESLAND
ROB KURZ
KYLE MCALARNEY
KIERAN PILLER
LUKE ZELLER

MEN'S CROSS COUNTRY
BRETT ADAMS
KURT BENNINGER
TODD PTACEK
PATRICK SMYTH

MEN'S FENCING
AARON ADJEMIAN
FRANK BANTEMPO
RYAN BRADLEY
PATRICK GETTINGS
PATRICK GHATTAS
ALEX GRIGORENKO
TOM HORTON
GREG HOWARD
JAKUB JEDEKOWIAK
KAROL KOSTKA
MARK KUBIK
JESSE LAEUCHLI
DIEGO QUINONEZ
MATT STEARNS
BILL THANHOUSER

FOOTBALL
VICTOR ABIAMIRI
CHASE ANASTASIO
NICK BORSETI
JOE BROCKINGTON
JUSTIN BROWN
DAVID BRUTON
JOHN CARLSON
MAURICE CRUM, JR.
CASEY CULLEN
LEO FERRINE
MARCUS FREEMAN
CHRIS FROME
DAVID GRIMES
RYAN HARRIS
RAY HERRING
JJ JANSEN
TERRAIL LAMBERT
DEREK LANDRI
TREVOR LAWS
BRIAN MATTES
RHEMA MCKNIGHT
BOB MORTON
CHINEDUM NDUKWE
BRADY QUINN
STEVE QUINN
MIKE RICHARDSON
JEFF SAMARDZIJA
DAN SANTUCCI
ASAPH SCHWAPP
JOHN SULLIVAN
RONALD TALLEY
MITCHELL THOMAS
TRAVIS THOMAS
DARIUS WALKER
AMBROSE WOODEN
TOM ZBIKOWSKI

MEN'S GOLF
COLE ISBAN
MIKE KING
JOSH SANDMAN

HOCKEY
NOAH BABIN
MICHAEL BARTLETT
DAVID BROWN
ERIK CONDRA
CHRISTIAN HANSON
TAYLOR JINDRA
WES O'NEILL
JASON PAIGE
JORDAN PEARCE
EVAN RANKIN
GARRETT REGAN
TOM SAWATSKE
JOSH SCIBA
BROCK SHEAHAN
MARK VAN GUILDER
DAN VENARD

MEN'S LACROSSE
PETER CHRISTMAN
TAYLOR CLAGETT
RYAN CUNN
SEAN DOUGHERTY
JOHN GREANEY
BRANNON HALVORSEN
RYAN HOFF
JOSEPH KEMP
WILLIAM LIVA
REGIS MCDERMOTT
MICHAEL PODGAJNY
LUCIUS POLK
JOEY RALLO
DUNCAN SWEZEY
ROSS ZIMMERMAN

MEN'S SOCCER
ANDREW BENTON
MATT BESLER
CHRIS CAHILL
GREG DALBY
CHINEDU DIKE
JOSEPH LAPIRA
KURT MARTIN
JUSTIN MCGEENEY
RYAN MILLER
NATHAN NORMAN
JACK TRAYNOR
ALEX YOSHINAGA

MEN'S SWIMMING
JUSTIN BARBER
WILLIAM BAUMAN
THEODORE BROWN
MICHAEL BULFIN
ALAN CARTER
DAVID CAVADINI
LOUIS CAVADINI
SCOTT COYLER
STEVEN CROWE
NICHOLAS FANSLAU
DEAN FERNANDEZ
BRIAN FREEMAN
BRYAN GUARNIER
JACE HOPPER
CHRISTOPHER KANE
TIMOTHY KEGELMAN
DANIEL LUTKUS
ANDREW MACKAY
GRAHAM PARKER
DANIEL RAVE
ROBERT SEERY
MITCHELL SHERMAN
SAMUEL STONER
ERIC SWENSON
JAY VANDEN BERG
CHRISTOPHER ZECHES

MEN'S TENNIS
IRACKLI AKHVLEDIANI
STEPHEN BASS
BRETT HELGESON
RYAN KECKLEY
BARRY KING
SANTIAGO MONTOYA
SHEEVA PARBHU
ANDREW ROTH

ATHLETIC TRAINERS
ERIC INGULSUD
DANIEL L'JEUREUX
KATHERINE MUENZER
JANE PEACOCK
KYLE WINKING

CHEERLEADERS
KATY MARVIN
GABRIELLA OBREGON

Celebrate the Sports Heroes of Notre Dame and College Football in These Other Releases from Sports Publishing!

Digger Phelps's Tales from the Notre Dame Hardwood
by Digger Phelps with Tim Bourret
- 5.5 x 8.25 hardcover
- 200 pages
- photos throughout
- $19.95

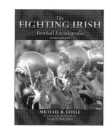

The Fighting Irish Football Encyclopedia: Third Edition
by Michael R. Steele
- 8.5 x 11 hardcover
- 530 pages
- 200+ photos throughout
- $39.95

Gerry Faust's Tales from the Notre Dame Sideline
by Gerry Faust, John Heisler, and John Heisler
- 5.5 x 8.25 hardcover
- 200 pages
- photos throughout
- $19.95

The Golden Dream
by Gerry Faust with Steve Love
- 6 x 9 softcover
- 361 pages
- eight-page photo insert
- $14.95

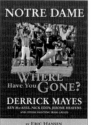

Notre Dame: Where Have You Gone?
by Eric Hansen
- 6 x 9 hardcover
- 192 pages
- photos throughout
- $19.95

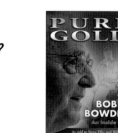

Pure Gold: Bobby Bowden — An Inside Look
by Steve Ellis and Bill Vilona
- 6 x 9 hardcover
- 192 pages
- photos throughout
- $24.95
- 2006 release!

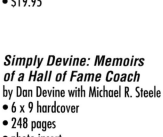

Simply Devine: Memoirs of a Hall of Fame Coach
by Dan Devine with Michael R. Steele
- 6 x 9 hardcover
- 248 pages
- photo insert
- $22.95

Don Nehlen's Tales from the West Virginia Sideline
by Don Nehlen with Shelly Poe
- 5.5 x 8.25 hardcover
- 192 pages
- photos throughout
- $19.95
- 2006 release!

Knute Rockne: A Portrait of a Notre Dame Legend
by Michael R. Steele
- 8.5 x 11 hardcover
- 145 pages
- 100+ photos throughout
- $24.95

Tiller: Not Your Average Joe
by Joe Tiller with Tom Kubat
- 6 x 9 hardcover
- 250 pages
- photo insert
- $24.95
- 2006 release!